TYPO3
Enterprise Content Management

Leaders of the TYPO3 community guide you through this powerful, enterprise-level, open source content management system

Werner Altmann
René Fritz
Daniel Hinderink

BIRMINGHAM - MUMBAI

TYPO3: Enterprise Content Management

First edition: July 2005

Published by Packt Publishing Ltd.
32 Lincoln Road
Olton
Birmingham, B27 6PA, UK.

ISBN 1-904811-41-8

www.packtpub.com

Cover Design by www.visionwt.com

Translation from the German language edition of:
TYPO3 - Enterprise Content Management
by Wernver Altmann - René Fritz - Daniel Hinderink
© 2004 Open Source Press, Munich, Germany.

Credits

Authors
Werner Altmann
René Fritz
Daniel Hinderink

Commissioning Editor
Louay Fatoohi

Technical Editor
Ashutosh Pande

Layout
Ashutosh Pande
Niranjan Jahagirdar

Proofreader
Chris Smith

Translator
Steve Tomlin

Cover Designer
Helen Wood

About the Authors

Werner Altmann is the author of the original German handbook for editors, and a member of the TYPO3 documentation team. As the technical project manager, he is in charge of planning and implementing major TYPO3-based projects.

René Fritz has created parts of the TYPO3 core and has programmed various extensions to the system, including the digital asset management system. He was also among the first TYPO3 users. He works as a freelance technical consultant and developer, and continues to be part of the core developer team for TYPO3. He is also an active member of the TYPO3 Association.

Daniel Hinderink is a managing partner with a consulting company specializing in web-technology-based information systems for medium to large companies. He has been associated with the TYPO3 project for a long time, and has provided strategic advice and practical work in research and planning, as well as marketing. He is also an active member and currently the vice-chairman of the TYPO3 Association.

Table of Contents

Foreword by Kasper Skårhøj

There is a picture of a child standing on the shelf next to me here in my office. It was in my grandmother's possession until she moved to an old people's home. The boy in the image holds an object in his hand while looking at the camera, interrupted from his investigations by the photographer. I don't have kids yet myself; the boy is me as a three-year old.

The picture fascinates me because it helps me to understand myself and God's design of our creative souls. It rips me out of TypoScript, PHP variables, and for...each loops for a moment and puts a smile on my face. The picture captures the essence of my personality, which has always been curious and creative—from building playhouses on my uncle's farm, shooting VHS-movies as a teenager, wiring up a house automation system to, well, accidentally programming a "little" CMS tool which I needed in the early days of the passion we all share, the modern Internet.

Opening the Playground

Creativity defines a lot of who I am. TYPO3 has been the output valve of this energy. It is the "Very best of" album from my life until now, even with all the quirks it has. I love TYPO3 because I know it is an authentic expression of my creative pulse. But how did it ever come this far?

Let's turn back the clock to 1997 when I began to study at the Technical University of Denmark. I think after 5 minutes at the introduction course I had spotted another restless soul in the class for whom Taylor polynomials had no significance for the greater meaning in life. We teamed up; I created my own little company (Curby Soft Multimedia) and college was where I slept the extra hours I missed at night. Back then I was extremely inspired by David Siegel's visions for web design (www.killersites.com). In fact, my "creativity valve" pointed in the visual direction back then; my teammate handled the Linux-stuff, I just juggled around with the colors.

The Binary Brainwash

The CMS mantra of "separating content from code" was not the brilliant idea of any one individual, but what happened to all of us at that time; everyone realized that customers needed a CMS tool to maintain their websites. In late 1997 we began the first prototypes of what some years later became TYPO3. Unfortunately, my teammate didn't deliver the technical work and my proactive gene autoresponded by closing down Photoshop and starting up Homesite, a web browser pointed at www.php.net and the installation of a RedHat 6.2 server; one week later, I had the minimum knowledge required to make lookups in MySQL and present the content in an HTML page. And I hated it.

At the time in 1998 I met another guy with a lot more marketing experience than myself. He wanted to commercialize the early version of TYPO3. So we set up the "superfish.com" company together, hired employees, and even managed to team up with Saatchi & Saatchi in Copenhagen. But I had one condition; that I would be relieved from my role as the programmer behind the CMS as fast as possible! It was "Too much work and no fun makes Jack a dull boy" for me and my inside was a desert. I was crying out for colors, poetry, and visual universes to explore. I hated programming; it dried me out and I had accepted it only as a temporary necessity.

Maybe this should scare me, but guess what; now the pain of programming is gone! Slowly I was swallowed by PHP until the influence of booleans and arrays made me forget my visual gold age; the "re-coding" of a designer into a programmer was successfully complete. But even now, the spring of creativity couldn't be suppressed. Rather than being expressed in visual terms it permeated the making of TYPO3; programming is an art! Programming contains love and passion for beauty just as much as photography or oil painting does.

Goodbye World, Hello GPL

When I realized that running a company like Superfish was not my cup of tea, nothing mattered more than my creation, TYPO3. I left the company with the rights to the code, my partner kept the rest. I felt I had passed some kind of "Point of no Return" and all I wanted was to finish my work. For what purpose? That question wasn't even asked at the time. I agreed with myself to do just enough freelance work to live and put the rest of my time into finishing TYPO3 over the next six months (it's funny to look back at the repeatedly naive time-estimates I have made in the past— and still do :-).

During my short flirtation with the commercial production of TYPO3, I realized that commercial pressures tend to corrupt the quality of the product; ready or not, it has to go on the shelf to generate income. That was one thing I couldn't accept as an artist; I believed in quality, and compromise in this area was no option to me. On the other hand, with no company behind I could probably sell my CMS solution to only a handful of local companies. Compared to the perspectives of sharing TYPO3 with a whole world and thereby helping thousands of people, the latter would far outweigh the joy of making a bit of money locally in Denmark—even if I never saw a single Euro coming back.

So I chose the GPL way.

Living Waters

Giving away TYPO3 for free also has a strong root in my faith in Jesus. I have been raised in a Christian family and always believed in God. But passionate faith can't be inherited and my most recent "conversion" happened after having worked 16 hours a day for a long time. I think many of you reading this book know the situation and how passion can drive you into intense work. It can be fun and rewarding. But in the long run it dries you out inside, and eventually you ask yourself, "What is the point; what am I living for?" This is where some people burn out and get depressed. For me it triggered the logical question; if I really believe in the Bible, why not open it and read about what a balanced life should be like?

This had a dramatic effect on my life. I began to take my faith seriously and re-align my actions with my beliefs. I met my wife, Rie. And I discovered my identity and some personal gifts, so I could understand my "mission" in life. I also thought about how to live in a Christian way in the modern world. I read "feed the hungry" and found that a useful tool like TYPO3 would be just that. I read "love your neighbor" and found that sharing TYPO3 as the best I had would be an act of love. I read "seek and you shall find" and thought that TYPO3 could be just such a reward for those who dare to search for alternatives. I read "you got it for nothing, give it for nothing" and thought that TYPO3 was possible through a talent I could only attribute to God, so what would be lost by giving it away?

Reasons to Believe

Mixing TYPO3 with Jesus must seem strange to most of you. Why would an apparently intelligent guy believe in something fuzzy like God? But in fact I think programmers have nothing but good reasons to conclude that some kind of higher intelligence must exist. Every day I spend hours writing characters carefully combined into a computer program. I know that a single misplaced byte will make TYPO3 fail to run. I also know that sometimes I need to make an internal redesign that does not add new functionality to TYPO3, but merely opens the possibility of further development. And who would believe me if I claimed to have created TYPO3 by repeatedly combining random bytes and trying to execute them until something useful came out—even if doing this a trillion times? TYPO3 required conscious, intelligent design! I have to admit that the complexity of life points to something outside the universe itself. It doesn't put a name tag on who is behind it all, but there are good reasons for believing in a mastermind.

I declare that I am not a perfectionist. Perfection is not obtainable for humans, it is an ideal. And although the ideal of perfection is our beacon of light, we have to settle for less. What is obtainable is completeness. Completing what you have started is what gives the first step you took a meaning.

TYPO3 is my baby, it takes enormous amounts of my time and often it consumes most of my awareness. When people ask me about TYPO3 and my own working life, I ask them to think about how it was preparing for exams or writing a large thesis at university. I believe that captures the intensity of how my life has been for the last four years, while TYPO3 has been a public project.

It has been a privilege, fun, and challenging all along, but it has also worn me out. The most precise way to describe this state is to compare me with a fragile ecosystem. Even small changes in the environment can have great impacts on stability. Luckily, I have developed an equally good understanding of my inner self and daily I try to walk the roads that motivate, rather than those which lead to despair. I have learned to focus on single issues, and suppress the view from the top of the mountain, which can be overwhelming. I have had to trust myself to be right many times, when it would have been fair to have doubts. And I have learned to strive for perfection but settle for something complete, and sometimes less. It's a strategy of survival, and without it the wave you are surfing will swallow you.

Growing a Community

It's easy for me to remember for how long I have been married to Rie; I just think about when TYPO3 was first released to the public—that was also in August 2000 :-). Anyhow, the launch of TYPO3 to the public was supposed to be the end of the line but it became a whole new beginning! At the time, I was exhausted after developing for a year on my own with no external response. I remember how lonely I felt.

Publishing TYPO3 under GPL changed all this and the growing community became a solid source of power that changed the whole perspective of the project; suddenly my work mattered to someone! This was a fulfilment of my personal "prophecy" that giving TYPO3 away for free would be much more valuable than selling licenses to local customers in Denmark. In addition, the new situation greatly compensated for the loneliness in the office, since I now had virtual colleagues all around the globe!

As an Open Source project, a small community quickly grew up around TYPO3, including René Fritz (co-author of this book) as one of the very first personalities on the scene. People contributed by setting up mailing lists, archives, providing support to others, creating small plugins, offering help to port TYPO3 to Windows, and most significantly, translating TYPO3 into their native languages.

In April 2001, Rie and I conceived the idea of arranging a snowboard tour for the community, and the next winter, we did it! 25 people showed up and suddenly e-mail addresses had faces. The first snowboard tour was an amazing event and Jan-Hendrik Heuing would still quote me for saying "I'm starting to believe in it" back then. The year after we were 50 people snowboarding on the slopes of Splügen, the next year we were more than 80 gathered in Kitzbühel. More than anything else, the annual snowboard event has become the identity of the TYPO3 community.

Life in the Bazaar

The community of TYPO3 has grown at an exponential rate ever since. From being a small village where everyone knew each other on the mailing lists, it is now a big city with all that entails. The manpower to help is far greater but the risk of getting impersonal is equally high. I often receive e-mails from people asking me support questions. I have to delete them flatly. Even answering back that they should use the mailing list can become stressful to me and it really breaks my heart, because on the other hand I hold the ideal to be personal to everyone. But today I have to trust that the community will take good care of the newbie asking for guidance, while I optimize my time for general development, which helps thousands, rather than a single person.

The growth of the community also holds great developmental potential. Centered on code contributions via the Extension Repository, it is directly possible for anyone to contribute quality code to the system in a safe way, which protects the integrity of everyone's work, as well as their motivation for contributing.

My greatest vision for TYPO3 is extensions. I strongly believe they are the perfect vehicle for bringing broad innovation to the project and offering maximum freedom for every developer to demonstrate his or her personal love for the art and beauty of coding web applications. This is the democracy of our community and everyone has equal chances.

The challenge we face, as I see it, is to maintain the friendly atmosphere for which we have traditionally been known. We also have to maintain an effective framework for contributions from the growing number of code authors and apply more quality assurance to contributions of all kinds. In another field, we have realized the need to enforce the GPL license, as TYPO3 has become a popular software that obviously would be nice to re-brand and sell as one's own work. And finally, we have to fight the prejudiced minds that think Open Source has nothing to offer, since there is no fee to pay.

Credits

So many people truly deserve to be mentioned here. Unfortunately, any attempt to list some names would exclude others equally merited. It is like inviting people to your wedding; it's not hard to invite your best friend, but it is hard to find the criteria to decide whom you will exclude, since there is not room for everyone.

However, it will be safe to mention my wife, Rie. She is my best friend; she loves me and challenges me. She prays for me and we share faith in God. She has followed TYPO3 all the way and supported every bit of it, often with personal sacrifice when I was stressed out and mentally absent. She has accepted that she is second choice at times, and we all owe her big time for that.

I want to mention Christian Jul Jensen (Denmark) who has been my good friend and mental support through the years, and also my right hand in professional matters. Christian has been my personal proxy for a while, taking the load from my shoulders as times changed and TYPO3 needed more of my dedication, rather than me helping old customers. His help has been priceless.

Daniel Hinderink is another cornerstone in the history of TYPO3. Daniel is professional and very skilled. In addition to this, he has been a showcase of proactivity to me. Daniel has taken the initiative and become the solution to problems, rather than a part of them. As the coordinator of marketing efforts for TYPO3, he carries a lot of the responsibility for the marketing success TYPO3 has had. But his initiatives have borne even more fruit in areas such as initiating innovation, team building, and project organization. I am impressed and thankful!

Now the list of names would explode if I wanted to thank everyone who has contributed to TYPO3 with code, support or has otherwise been active in the community. Money is good but sharing your talents in the community is worth even more! Thank you so much everyone. I hope you can recognize the value of sharing the best you have got with the world, as my experience described in this preface has been, and I encourage you hang on in there!

I have received an increasing amount of money donations during the time TYPO3 has been public. To everyone who has sent money I also want to say thanks from my heart. You have enabled me to spend more and more time on TYPO3 rather than doing irrelevant freelance work. Your donations prove how many small streams make one large flood that eventually can power an Open Source project into stable and continual development. I encourage you to stay true to your promises of financial support so we can employ more people developing TYPO3 in the future!

I also want to mention Dassault Systemes web department in Paris for their generosity and the inspiring friendship we have shared during my times in Paris. Through their belief in TYPO3, they have supported the development in countless ways.

Finally, I want to say "Hello" to all my future friends in the community! TYPO3 and the snowboard tours are a social pit-stop for me. These relations somehow make the hours behind the screen less lonely and in some cases spark real-world friendships like the one I have been so lucky to establish with Robert Lemke from Luneburg.

Three Men in Blue Overalls

To me the third snowboard tour in 2004 was a fantastic experience. I saw old friends again, I got my own snowboard this time, and I met many new and inspiring people. And finally it demonstrated the powerful initiative of the "self-ignited fireworks" that has popped up in the community. The men in the mirror finally jumped into their blue overalls and began work.

Even though the history and status of TYPO3 is more than I could ever ask for, I always joked about the day when there would be a book about TYPO3 on the shelves in my local bookstore. Three talented community members have now made this dream come true. They asked for a book and found the answer to its creation in their own mirror reflections. I am thrilled about the outcome and thankful for your contribution to the big picture of completeness we are striving for.

Enjoy the book and welcome to the TYPO3 corner of cyberspace!

— Kasper

Authors' Introduction

TYPO3 is an extremely successful Open Source Content Management System, with a reputation for being very powerful but also complex. With this book we have tried to draw an overall picture of TYPO3, providing an insight into how it can be used by users, administrators, and developers.

In view of the numerous references and a number of tutorials, the question was raised as to what this book can achieve. The flood of questions in mailing lists has apparently not been dammed by the existing documentation. After considerable observation of the problems and typical questions, we decided to write a book that attempts to illustrate the principles of TYPO3 and demonstrate its practical application through examples. This book should not be seen as a replacement for the references and tutorials on TYPO3.org; it should rather be a connecting link for developing a coherent picture of TYPO3 for beginners, users, and developers, allowing them to navigate on their own through the flood of information.

The TYPO3 project attempts to divide all layers of documentation and communication into three groups, to simplify navigation. This book will do the same:

1. Editing: Provides the means of the system for production and describes methods for their effective use.
2. Administration: Involves the organizational tasks that are necessary to implement content management using TYPO3.
3. Development: Describes the creation of a website and its graphical interface using templates, as well as programming your own applications in the TYPO3 framework.

For *decision makers* who are not yet familiar with the topic of Content Management, and in particular with Enterprise Content Management, we provide an Introduction at the beginning of this book; during the course of the book we regularly return to relevant issues, in terms of the various task areas in the company process.

Chapter 1 and Chapter 2 primarily deal with the theoretical basis of content management. With this background, the advantages of TYPO3 become clear, and from this we can form the basis for decisions on its strategic use. In addition, these introductory chapters take readers who have no previous knowledge on an excursion through the subject, presenting the most important terms and concepts. This is followed by installation and configuration of TYPO3 in detail.

In Chapter 3 we demonstrate the system using practical situations of content production. A complex tool must prove its value in a particular way, through the user-friendliness of its interface. After presenting the TYPO3 options and their functions, the section closes with a practical example on working effectively with TYPO3.

Chapter 4 deals with the administration of the system, and then with adjustments to conditions and processes that are defined by producers in their work with the system. In doing so, we show, using examples, how the means available intertwine, and how they are used in practice.

Chapter 5 describes the production of websites using TYPO3. Starting with the installation, we discuss the programming of templates with TypoScript and see the different methods available.

In Chapter 6 and 7 we introduce the extension interface of TYPO3, the Extension System, describing the basics and ways to develop your own functional extensions in the TYPO3 framework. Here we can observe, from a developer perspective, the integration with core functions and the different parts of the TYPO3 architecture that can be extended.

The entire text is annotated with footnotes and so-called "softlinks". The footnotes are aimed at encouraging further reading in areas not directly involved with technical aspects of TYPO3. The softlinks connect the book to TYPO3.org and other resources.

By entering the number code on the TYPO3.org website (`http://www.typo3.org/book/`) you will be taken to the corresponding topic in the online documentation, or to sources going into more detail. In this way, technical references and documentation are included, which are as up-to-date as possible, but the reader is also introduced to the thematic structural online resources, providing him or her with a sense of orientation in an ever-growing profusion of information.

About This Book

What You Need for Using This Book

You will require TYPO3 installed on a web server that has PHP4 and MySQL installed. Some extras you may need are ImageMagick, GDLib/Freetype, zlib, and a PHP accelerator, such as Zend.

Conventions

In this book you will find a number of styles of text that distinguish between different kinds of information. Here are some examples of these styles, and an explanation of their meaning.

There are three styles for code listings. Code words within text are shown as follows: "If we want to change the background color to a nice gray, we can go into the `plone_styles` layer and customize `base_properties`."

If we have a block of code, it will be set as follows:

```
$result = $this->query($query);
$row = $this->fetch_array($result);

$result = $GLOBALS['TYPO3_DB']->sql_query($query);
$row = $GLOBALS['TYPO3_DB']->sql_fetch_assoc($result);
```

When we wish to draw your attention to a particular part of a code block, the relevant lines or part will be made bold:

```
<body>
    <div id="rootline">rootline</div>
    <div id="header">
    <div id="logo"}>logo</div>
    <div id="headerimagetext">headerimagetext</div>
</div>
```

New terms and *important words* are introduced in an italic-type font. Words that you see on the screen—in menus or dialog boxes, for example—appear in the text as follows: "Clicking the **Next** button moves you to the next screen".

Any command-line input and output is written as follows:

```
mysql> create table books (name char(100), author char(50));
Query OK, 0 rows affected (0.03 sec)
```

Reader Feedback

Feedback from our readers is always welcome. Let us know what you think about this book, what you liked or may have disliked. Reader feedback is important for us to develop titles that you really get the most out of.

To send us general feedback, simply drop an e-mail to feedback@packtpub.com, making sure to mention the book title in the subject of your message.

If there is a book that you need and would like to see us publish, please send us a note in the **SUGGEST A TITLE** form on www.packtpub.com or e-mail title@packtpub.com.

If there is a topic that you have expertise in and you are interested in either writing or contributing to a book, see our author guide on www.packtpub.com/authors.

Customer Support

Now that you are the proud owner of a Packt book, we have a number of things to help you to get the most from your purchase.

Downloading the Example Code for the Book

Visit http://www.packtpub.com/support, and select this book from the list of titles to download any example code or extra resources for this book. The code files available for download will then be displayed.

> The downloadable files contain instructions on how to use them.

Errata

Although we have taken every care to ensure the accuracy of our contents, mistakes do happen. If you find a mistake in one of our books—maybe a mistake in text or code—we would be grateful if you would report this to us. By doing this you can save other readers from frustration, and also help to improve subsequent versions of this book.

If you find any errata, report them by visiting http://www.packtpub.com/support/, selecting your book, clicking on the **Submit Errata** link, and entering the details of your errata. Once your errata have been verified, your submission will be accepted and the errata added to the list of existing errata. The existing errata can be viewed by selecting your title from http://www.packtpub.com/support/.

Questions

You can contact us at questions@packtpub.com if you are having a problem with some aspect of the book, and we will do our best to address it.

1

Introduction

This book is based on the original German version, which has seen several updates for various sections. This is mostly because of changes to the TYPO3 core in the last two versions (3.7.0 and 3.8.0). A certain amount of other differences stem either from errors that have been corrected in the English version, or from structural changes due to the circumstances in the UK and US markets.

The authors would like to thank all German readers for the many helpful comments and hints and of course the considerable success that the book has been.

More thanks are in order for the community that supports us, starting top-down with Kasper Skårhøj, the members of the TYPO3 association, and all the people in user groups, mailing lists, and supporting consultancies.

1.1 History

Kasper Skårhøj, born in 1976, had already been working since the end of 1997 for the Copenhagen start-up company "Superfish" on one of the very first content management systems. Two years of development, a trip to the Seybold trade fair in San Francisco, a number of practical projects, and several meetings (with Internet-Guru David Siegel) later, he realized that "Superfish" was not really the right or ideal environment to continue developing TYPO3.

On the one hand this was because "Superfish" was moving in a new direction in the type of services that it provided, but more important was a reason that is all too familiar to many software developers: the pressure of deadlines to get new versions ready for the next trade fair, and the general tendency to give more importance to the visible parts and neglect the invisible ones, which in the long-term are more important as far as quality is concerned.

The consequences that Kasper drew from this situation are by no means the standard ones: while most Open Source developers of the first generation grew up in a university environment – Linus Torvalds being a prime example – Kasper decided to give up the security of a flourishing company, in which he also had a partnership, to work full-time on his vision of a content management system. A year later, having done nothing except work on the implementation of this vision, version 1.5 appeared. That was in July 2000.

The development of TYPO3 remained a one-man show until July 2002, with the crucial advantage that quality and consistency remained on a very high level.

One disadvantage lay in the fact that further development and a number of features had, in this respect, to pass through "the eye of Kasper's needle". After a number of discussions on the mailing list, followed by a phase of frantic work, Kasper published a new version in 2002, version 3.5b1, which, with its new Extension Manager, immediately transformed TYPO3 into a modular system. Since then the community has continuously published new extensions, allowing the range of functions for TYPO3 to increase rapidly.

Softlink **314624**   As a consequence, project groups have been formed which are working on all areas of TYPO3. At the core of the project, Kasper Skårhøj is still responsible for releases, and works personally on solving quite a number of problems.

It should not be forgotten that his commitment essentially depends on whether it is economically viable for him to concentrate on these topics. This is why contributions and consultation work on large commercial projects are crucial for the TYPO3 project so that it can continue to be able to afford its most important specialists.

1.2 What is a CMS?

Content management systems have become the standard for creating and deploying mission-critical content on the World Wide Web and intranets. Software systems with this scope are usually referred to as Web Content Management Systems (WCMS), or Content Management Systems (CMS) in short. When aiming for an integrated end-to-end approach on content, reaching from document management to web but also print output, such systems are named Enterprise Content Management Systems.

1.2.1 Separation of Content from Layout

An important basic principle is the division of content and layout. In practice this means that the definition of layout is stored independently of the actual content, be it text, images of other formats. This principle has many advantages when it comes to changing the layout, or protecting the layout from eager content authors. While the content can be edited by authors, without any influence on the details of display, the layout definition can be edited independently, thus effectively enabling design changes across even very large websites.

1.2.2 Content Lifecycle Functionality

Content Management Systems support the Content Lifecycle depicted below through all it's stages, from creation of contents with Editors to organizing content snippets (assets) to actual deployment when published and finally archiving content elements.

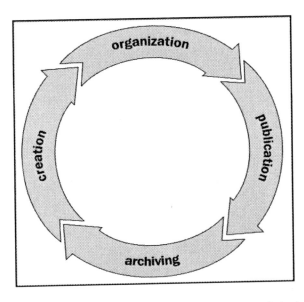

Figure 1.1:

Content life cycle

Activities in the creation phase have the acquisition and design of information as their goal. After planning, relevant information is written, structured where applicable, and made available as components. This phase also includes editing and didactic refinements added by authors.

3

The organization or preparation stage involves administration and storage of content in a scheme suitable for information products and sources, as well as making available and assigning user permissions.

Publication refers to distribution and presentation, that is, the output as an information commodity. This can be implemented as a website, a printed product or in another output format.

The archiving stores the content in a manner which best serves the purposes of research, statistical evaluation, and ultimately re-use.

1.2.3 Modularity

TYPO3 is one of the systems that have modularized the functionality in several layers. From storage to deployment, these layers describe classes of modules. The storage level contains an API for connecting TYPO3 to different Databases or enables storage in XML-files via so-called handlers using the database abstraction layer. On the other end TYPO3 established an API for extending the core software, aptly named the "extension" system. These extensions connect to TYPO3 through the TYPO3 extension manager, which also serves as an IDE.

Extensions can add functionality to all levels and interfaces of the software, without changing the core and thus ensuring easy updates and a stable code base. All serious vendors of content management software have adopted this modular approach, and so have Open Source systems like TYPO3, albeit pursuing different technical concepts considering the individual API.

1.2.4 Target Group

In a relatively short time, TYPO3 has expanded very quickly, very far. In terms of numbers, the strongest user group is small and medium-sized companies, of course, because TYPO3 is often still too powerful for private use, and it is also difficult to learn.

Softlink **027059** Companies that can buy entry into the TYPO3 world through the services of suitably qualified specialists can, however, appreciate the advantages of Open Source software in general, and TYPO3 in particular. The reasons most mentioned include the license (GPL), quality, the extensive documentation, the rapidly growing community and the many references from renowned companies and organizations. A selection of these is published on TYPO3.com, under the soft link shown here.

Among the approx. 122,000 installations that have logged in to the TYPO3 Extension Repository between July 2002 and the beginning of 2005, there is a large number of well-known names and famous brands who have put their faith in TYPO3, proving the validity of Open Source enterprise systems by using them in intranets and other critical areas.

1.2.5 TYPO3 References

The list of reference entries at TYPO3.org represents a cross-section of all the TYPO3-based projects entered there.

Softlink **589606**

Among the agents providing services, there are a number of leading names from Germany and the rest of Europe, but also many small and medium-sized companies that see an opportunity to compete on a technical level with larger providers, offering attractive prices and project turnaround times.

The GPL: GNU General Public License

The GNU General Public License is the most widely used Open Source license. Its seemingly simple content, however, continues to cause contradiction in different countries, and with different legal systems. One legal opinion follows the next, and because the software is handed over free of charge, issues are raised concerning consumer protection, warranty regulations and the interests of programmers, which can be of significance, depending on the field of application and how critical the use of the software is to a company. So it is advisable to find out about the contents of the GPL, and its legal consequences, in the country where it is to be used. Where appropriate, claims of warranty towards an agency or a technical service provider who takes over or works on the implementation, must be regulated.

The extensions take on a special role, and as long as they cannot be operated as an independent application, they are also subject to the GPL. A function that is deeply anchored in the TYPO3 framework, that is normally set up as an extension, and that is not just a wrapper or script around an existing program, will equally be subject to the conditions of the GPL, and is Open Source.

This means that the author is not obliged to publish, but also cannot prevent publication once it has been passed on, perhaps to a customer. Neither can the author restrict modifications or further modification by others, once they have come into possession of the code.

As far as economic interests are concerned, problems may arise in terms of utilization for some producers who are used to thinking in terms of commercially viable products.

But one should bear in mind that TYPO3 has been provided as a basis for such developments, in just the same way, license-free and cost-free.

De facto, the community in our case reacts in two different ways:

Many extensions are not published; of the registered extension keys that are necessary for exchange via TYPO3.org, only about a fifth are published extensions. This does not include many unregistered extensions, but does include many unfinished extensions, and ones too specialized to justify publication.

It is certainly very unlikely that customers will themselves publish extensions that they have obtained from an agency.

Many TYPO3 specialists use several different projects to create and further develop an extension, until their investment in time and knowledge has been returned, and only then publish their work when it may also create promotional value.

1.3 The TYPO3 Community

The TYPO3 community is a rapidly growing and increasingly international community of TYPO3 enthusiasts and users.

The core of the community is represented by mailing lists – above all, the main english mailing list, which can also be subscribed to via newsgroup. Consult TYPO3.org for details on the mailing lists.

The community ensures, as in most Open Source projects, that support is available, offering quick and practical help, even for more technically complicated problems, as long as the standard "rules of etiquette" and precise formulation of questions are observed. It is important to read the archive, FAQs, and beginners' help documents, so that you don't clog up the lists with questions that have already been answered many times, something which can annoy experienced users. Please remember that the help you are getting is voluntary and unpaid, and that you have no automatic rights to it.

Softlink **139514** Anyone who needs higher availability, training material, or who has more complex questions should get in touch with one of the many service providers who can be found under TYPO3.com in the "Consultancies" area. The companies listed here represent a cross-section of the entries in TYPO3.org, which have been selected according to criteria of competence demonstrated in their projects.

Softlink **314623**

Anybody who has already built up relevant TYPO3 know-how will perhaps want to be useful in further developing documentation, or contribute to the project in some other way. The project comes alive from such contributions at all levels, so that help and feedback are very welcome, and are discussed at length. If you want to do this, it is important to get a general impression beforehand of what topics have already been discussed, and with what results. For this purpose we recommend that you visit the archives of the mailing lists on TYPO3.org in the field of Documentation/Mailing-Lists/. Depending on the subject, you may need to look in the Developer lists, the Marketing list, or another mailing list.

Then you should make sure that a project with a similar, or overriding, objective does not already exist.

Under TYPO3.org, in the Development/Projects area, you can find a list of all current projects and work areas, with the corresponding contact partners.

Softlink **424461**

A special feature of TYPO3 and the community is that many of the participants have already met up, most of them in the context of the annual meeting, the TYPO3! Snowboard Tour, which attracts more and more participants each year.

Apart from the discussions, work-intensive evenings and many questions which are answered, as well as projects launched here, the focus is also on getting to know the people behind the mail addresses, and not least on enjoying winter sports together. So whoever wants to combine intensive know-how with leisure time will hardly find a better opportunity than at this event.

Due to the extensive use of TYPO3 in organisations and the very large community the first international conference was a question of time. It will take place in September 2005 in Karlsruhe/Germany and has been named TyCON3. For more Information, visit the following website: http://tycon3.typo3.org

1.4 The TYPO3 Association

In November 2004 a group of people from the TYPO3 community including Kasper Skårhøj and other long-term contributors prepared and founded a non-profit organisation called the TYPO3 Association. The main goal is to support core development on a more steady basis and improve the transparency and efficiency of various aspects of the TYPO3 project.

1.4.1 Goals and Objectives

- Organisation of events for the purpose of information and education of its members;

- Communication with its members and the general public, to spread and further knowledge and proficiency for the usage of the TYPO3 software, especially by virtue of it's project website;

- Education and certification to ensure quality of service;

- Fostering development of TYPO3;

- Supporting the adaption of international software standards within TYPO3;

- Representation of the members;

- Public Relations and activities helping to spread knowledge and usage of the TYPO3 software.

1.4.2 Membership and Application

The TYPO3 Association has two types of members:

Active Members

Active members are people that have consistently worked for TYPO3 and are willing and able to attend general assemblies, where they have the exclusive right to vote and decide on the Associations future. Active members are appointed on a basis of merit and need to be recommended by two existing active members, or a fifth of the general assembly.

Supporting Members

Softlink **394945** Supporting Membership is open to everyone, but requires formal application. The Association provides an online application form and payment method of membership fees at http://association.typo3.org. Members are either people or companies and are required to endorse the goals and objectives of the Association through their actions.

All Members will be entitled to exclusively advertise their membership and thus support for TYPO3 following admission to membership.

Bodies and Practical Work

The Association consists of the following bodies:

Board

 The board is the executive body taking care of daily administrative work and legal matters and accounting.

General Assembly

The GA is the highest authority and elects the board, controls their work and generally decides on all matters of importance in its annual meeting. It is open to all members, but only active members have the right to vote.

Committees

Committees are the groups that do the actual work when it comes to discussing the usage of funds, community communication, education, events, and so forth. Legally they are appointed by the board and the GA and make recommendations, which are then executed by the board.

2

Installation

In this chapter we will introduce variations and the recommended fields of application for various installation types, and describe the necessary steps to implement them. With the many thousands of installations of TYPO3 already made, you would think that the installation hurdles are not actually set too high. However, the authors of this book can also tell a tale about "the first time" and of some of the problems that might throw the beginner off course.

Finally you will find an overview of some resources available to you that are rich in content, to find answers to any problems you may have.

2.1 Criteria for System and Package Selection

TYPO3 requires just a database and a web server that is PHP-capable; on this basis, details such as the hardware used, the operating system, the database system, and the web server can be selected using various criteria, the most important of which we will explain here.

A basic decision you need to make concerns the operating system. TYPO3 can run on most UNIX-based variants, and on Windows systems. There is no difference in the scope of the two versions in terms of core functionality, although a number of extensions do require UNIX programs. Please consult the documentation for the relevant extension, so that such restrictions can be considered. [1]

One technical advantage of using UNIX systems is that updates are

---

[1] *Indexed Search*, for example, a powerful search engine in the TYPO3 framework, requires UNIX software to index documents. Various services of the DAM also need this, as do the PDF converter extensions.

considerably faster, which is made possible by so-called "symbolic links".[2]

The dissemination of knowledge through the community is also important. The trend, certainly in terms of numbers, is dominated by the use of Linux systems, and to this extent support and operating system-dependent new development for extensions are much more widespread for this system. So if there are no compelling counter-arguments—such as a predefined Windows-based infrastructure, or your own (lack of) knowledge—the Linux variation makes the better choice, from a TYPO3 point of view.

In the following sections you will find further information on hardware and software selection in terms of the web server, the database system, other useful software, and finally the package selection of TYPO3 itself.

2.1.1 Hardware

As PHP-based software, TYPO3 at the minimum requires hardware equipment capable of running a web server. Even though this may still be possible with old 286 and 32 MB RAM machines, these cannot provide a useful platform for operating a TYPO3 system. The system should have 512 MB RAM or more in order to provide a solution with adequate performance.

If you want to use your own server, consider the following factors when *sizing* your hardware:

Type of Usage

The decisive factor is how the information provided on your website is to be used: will the website be mainly, or completely, static? Do you want to operate a portal and do you need dynamic content generation on the web server? Are you planning an application to be made available to normal visitors to your site, such as a shop, eCards, or forums? The following basic rule applies: More functions operated on the web server translate to increased hardware requirements and expense in separating the live system from the production system.

Expected Capacity

A number of parameters can be expressed in numbers:

- How many users will use the system at the same time?

---

[2] This can now be remedied by the use of Junction, an additional software package, see soft link 394 945.

- How fast (in seconds) should the server deliver a page?

- How many pages per hour do you intend delivering?

- How many *page impressions* do you expect per month?

- How much data *traffic*, in MB or GB, do you expect per month?

If you do not know the appropriate values, you will find it difficult to make a well-based decision. If you have any doubts, try to make contact with operators of similar services to collect relevant information. We shall look at three very typical scenarios:

1. Small to Medium Performance Requirements

These include sites that do not economically justify the costs of having their own server, expect no more than five to 10 users in parallel in the back end and 50 in the front end, a page delivery of up to 1.5 seconds, no more than 100 pages per hour, and less than 100,000 page impressions per month. In all, you expect data traffic of less than 5 GB per month. If your profile matches this in certain critical points, you should look around for a good and cheap hosting provider, who might even provide preinstalled TYPO3.

If you decide on a solution without preinstalled TYPO3, clarify beforehand whether the necessary requirements for installation are fulfilled:

- At least 100 MB free memory space

- MySQL database

- PHP from version 4.3.x with GDLib and Freetype

- ImageMagick

- Access via SSH

A few notes of warning at this point: for a long time now, miraculous abilities are no longer needed to hire out web space. Through cheap offers for dedicated servers, in principle anybody who has a few Euros and a month to spare can set up store as a reseller and hosting provider. Knowledge and ability are not mandatory requirements, and this can sometimes have dramatic consequences.

The hosting business is subject to the same economic constraints as any other business, and low-level prices are almost certainly linked to one or more of the following:

1. Poor knowledge of the material, since someone with experience in this business knows that server downtime can cancel out the earnings of months

2. Low personal costs, since the commodity itself is purchased from one of the mass providers (with correspondingly little room for maneuver for your contract partner)

3. Size of provider—due to its large size, it is worth employing experts

Of course, it is perfectly legitimate to search for as cheap an offer as possible. Just take into account the fact that at such low prices you cannot expect an optimal service and protection of values, with respect to installation and content in your CMS.

To proceed carefully, and at least have a basic level of security (and a supplier who is in liquidity and from whom you can seek compensation), you should pay a fair price, probably not below 25 Euro per month. It is here that you may be able to benefit from smaller providers, who can offer an individual service and be a reliable partner with whom you can trust your work.

Irrespective of the price class in which your project is located, a situation without an automatic backup must never occur—make this one of the fundamental criteria on which to base your decision.

2. Medium to Large-Sized Requirements and Intranet

It is a good idea to have your own web server if your CMS application justifies the expense for operating and setting it up. In doing this, the price for renting such a server and/or for co-location or housing will constitute the least of the costs to be expected.

Most studies yielded a ratio of 35% to 65% in the distribution of costs between purchase or rent on the one hand, and maintenance and other running costs on the other.

In the intranet, you have no choice but to run your own server. The key question here is that of sizing. A sound calculation, which also takes into account growth through scaling (two servers are not just 10 percent more work than one server), is very advisable so that you can arrive at a balanced decision.

The generally accepted formula of calculating overall costs during the life-cycle of an investment commodity, the so-called *total cost of ownership*, is (for this example) calculated as follows:

The TCO "Iceberg"

visible costs

+ capital expenditure
+ HW/SW purchase price
+ installation
+ implementation

invisible costs

+ system adoption
+ support
+ administration
+ training
+ maintenance
+ degree of non-usage

_____

= total cost of ownership

This calculation model has become very refined indeed [3], but for demonstration purposes and a rough assessment of the actual costs of an operation, the above list is normally sufficient.

If your calculation indicates making a decision in favor of your own server, the following technical points should be clarified: performance capability of the hardware, its ability to be updated, availability of replacement parts, backup strategy, and security (access restrictions, etc.).

3. Heavy-Duty Operation

In heavy-duty operation, above one million page impressions per month, the standard solution is to combine a number of servers into a *cluster*. The reason for this lies not only in the spread of the load, but also in its fault tolerance. Depending on the purpose it is used for, the maximum load the server has to cope with can be exceeded even with a small amount of traffic. Also, the task conditions of the application may not allow—for example in a management information system—any downtime. And yet web servers and database servers can also be operated separately and separately scaled, depending on the load to which they are subjected. Scenarios exist both with 10 Apache web servers, each with its own hardware and one MySQL server, as well as ones with 3 Apache servers and 5 MySQL servers.

Whatever the case, special solutions are required here which require

---

[3] Cf. Bensberg/Dewanto: "TCO VOFI for eLearning Platforms", http://www.campus-source.de/org/opensource/docs/bensbergVor.doc.pdf

precise planning and implementation, as well as continual maintenance.

2.1.2 Web Server

Softlink **504537** In theory, TYPO3 can be operated with Apache, IIS, or any other web server that can run PHP. The most common combination, according to numbers of installations, is Apache and PHP. Each particular version and installation type of PHP has, to some extent, an influence on TYPO3, which will be described in the "Server Compatibility" section on TYPO3.org.

2.1.3 Database

The standard database for TYPO3 is MySQL, for a long time the only option. Because the database abstraction that has now been introduced uses MySQL-compatible SQL instead of a meta language, this combination still provides the highest performance, since database queries do not have to be transformed. In addition, many existing extensions use their own database queries, so checks need to be made in individual cases to see whether an extension is fully functional without having to make modifications to other databases.

The decision to choose another RDBM system instead of MySQL should be considered very carefully; ultimately the costs of installation and updates will for the time being be greater than for the standard setup.

An interesting variation on the use of other databases is to combine different systems, so that specific data is kept on your own database system, and this store is made available for use in a specific application in the TYPO3 framework. In this way data can be integrated directly from other database systems, and the disadvantages of replication or synchronization of data stores avoided. The database abstraction is not in the least restricted to RDBM systems—flat files such as XML data can also be addressed via SQL queries.

Softlink **613803** Below we shall only cover the standard situation with MySQL, as more information for other scenarios is not yet available now. However, the documentation of the *Database Abstraction Layer* system (DBAL) does provide a number of hints (see soft link).

2.1.4 Other Software

Two software packages are necessary to be able to use the image-processing functions of TYPO3. These functions are entirely optional; TYPO3 still works without graphical processing and without these packages. The first package is *GDLibrary*, a PHPextension, which itself can be extended by *Freetype* with functions for representing typefaces. GDLibrary is already included in the standard PHP installation; it will not be discussed separately here.

The second software package, used predominantly in the scaling and generation of image file previews, is *ImageMagick*. With TYPO3, using an older version of ImageMagick (Version 4.2.9) is recommended, as it has a number of advantages over later versions. [4]

Softlink **353034**

TYPO3 can be used with current versions of ImageMagick if the disadvantages in functions for masking, sharpening, and softening of images do not affect your website.

The recommended version 4.2.9 is available for download on the TYPO3.org website under the soft link shown here. Current ImageMagick versions can either be installed with the packet manager of your Linux distribution or downloaded from the ImageMagick homepage. [5]

Softlink **436028**

Alternatively you could use *GraphicsMagick*, an offshoot of the ImageMagick project, which pledges to maintain a more strict line to the API development. [6]

---

[4] A corresponding question sent to the development team of ImageMagick, asking why objective disimprovements had been introduced in some areas, yielded no satisfactory response. The e-mail communication, explaining individual disadvantages, can be found under the soft link shown above.

[5] http://www.imagemagick.com/

[6] http://www.graphicsmagick.org/: In particular the changing story of the ImageMagick API has stopped many developers from basing their development on this software. TYPO3 went along with this capricious behavior of recent years, and the configuration options reflect the changes made in the list of exceptions for individual ImageMagick versions.

2.1.5 TYPO3 Package Selection

TYPO3 exists in various different packages, depending on the use to which it will be put. The main distinction is initially between the two different operating systems:

All UNIX packages can be found as so-called "tarballs" [7] and have the file ending .tar.gz. Windows packages can be found as zip archives, and have the .zip file extension.

There is no difference between the actual files contained in each version. The difference between the two versions lies in the fact that the tar.gz-distribution may be smaller, because it does not have double folders, since these are represented by symbolic links instead. In the zip-distribution these folders exist twice, as shown in the screen shot.

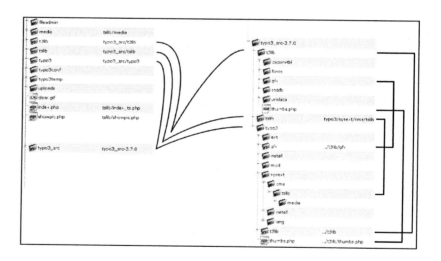

Figure 2.1:

left: *symbolic links with their relations to the original files in the src directory*

right: *relations of symbolic links to the original directories within the src directory*

The double use of directories (using symbolic links) is essentially due to historical factors. You must bear in mind that symbolic links cannot be set up via an FTP access. If your access to the web server is limited to FTP, choose a zip-distribution.

Softlink **394945**   For some time now it has also been possible, through utility software such as *Junction*, to set up links in the file system (similar to symbolic links) in NTFS-formatted partitions of Windows.

---

[7] Tarball is the name given to archives generated with the tar program (and usually compressed with gzip as well). Symbolic links are supported with this file format.

The TYPO3 version is always the most up-to-date one for all packages; they differ only in the examples they contain. Generally all tar.gz-packages do *not* contain the actual core system, which needs to be downloaded additionally as `typo3_src` followed by the version number. All zip-distributions include the system core.

In essence, the TYPO3 project offers the following different packages for download:

QuickStart

This is the installation for beginners and includes the beginner's tutorial. You should choose this package if you want to make use of the tutorial, since it includes material and defaults for the examples. You can also find the tutorial in the German version under the soft link shown here.

Softlink **995697**

Test Site

The Test Site contains a number of examples of TypoScript templates, menu variations, and extensions such as Shop, address lists, and news. For tests, and to get to know the system on your own by means of examples, this rather old package can be used—as far as the examples are concerned.

Dummy

The Dummy package differs from the Quickstart and Test Site only in its empty database and the absence of example material. It is the standard package for experienced developers who are starting a new project with a clean slate.

The included database dump contains an administrator account, which can be called after installation with the user name `admin` and the password `password`.

TYPO3 Source

The TYPO3 source is a tarball that contains all the directories needed for running the base system. Zip-distributions already contain this source package by default.

With the help of symbolic links, a number of TYPO3 installations (websites) can be operated using a single source. Corresponding extensions can be stored in the global extension directory `typo3/ext/` or in the corresponding `typo3conf/ext/` directory valid for that instance.

2.2 Installing a Test and Training Installation

Softlink **056013**

TYPO3.org provides a whole range of complete packages for various systems. We shall now take a close look at the two classical distributions, the WAMP (Windows Apache MySQL PHP) Installer for Windows by Ingmar Schlecht and the Quickstart package for Linux. There are other packages and installation guides for BigApache, Mac OS X, Debian, Gentoo, Mandrake, and others. A look at the download page and at the documentation matrix at TYPO3.org may also help you to find new ideas for the purpose of your installation.

2.2.1 The WAMP Windows Installer

You will find the WAMP installer under the installer packages on the download page of TYPO3.org. It is very simple to use:

1. Load the installer onto your computer.

2. Open the file by double-clicking on it.

3. After a short time you will see a dialog asking you to accept the GPL. The GPL is a comparatively short license, which you should now read if you want to know about your rights. If you do not agree, this is the temporary end of your TYPO3 career: there is no other license agreement for TYPO3 apart from this one, and you must adhere to its conditions if you do not want to lose the right to use it.

4. Then a message appears that the installer will write all the files to C:\apache. Accept this only if you do not have such a directory, or if you want to delete the data saved there, since all data stored at this location will be irretrievably lost.

5. The installation is now finished.

You will now find a new **TYPO3** entry in your start menu with these options:

- *Start Apache*: Starts the Apache web server

- *Start MySQL*: Starts the MySQL database server

- *Stop MySQL*: Ends the MySQL database server

- *TYPO3 start servers before*: Calls up the TYPO3 front end in a window of your default browser under `http://localhost`

- *TYPO3 (Alternative URL)*: Calls up TYPO3 under
  `http://127.0.0.1`

If you now start Apache and MySQL and call up the TYPO3 start page, you will find all the information you need on the front end and back end. The WAMP installer has already carried out the other steps of the installation, and TYPO3 is now ready for tests, and for your own programming attempts.

2.2.2 Linux (et al.) Quick Install

If you already have a web server available that supports MySQL and PHP, you will reach your destination very quickly under Linux and other comparable *NIX-flavours, like BSD, OS X, etc.

Softlink **056012**

If you have SSH access to the web server, you should log in there and download the Quickinstall archive from TYPO3.org, using `curl` or `wget`. The addresses are mentioned on the download page of TYPO3.org.

If you only have FTP access on your web server, use the zip-distribution. Transfer all the files onto the web server in the directory from which your website will be provided (typical directory names are `.../htdocs/`, `.../html/`, or `.../www/`).

You must now change some permissions so that certain parts of TYPO3 can be edited. If you do not have any access via SSH, you need another way of changing permissions. Many web servers have graphical tools to edit files, such as `Cpanel`, `Confixx`, or `Webmin`. If in doubt, ask your administrator or provider.

The permissions of the following files must be changed as shown below:

```
chmod 777 typo3/temp/
chmod 777 typo3/ext/
chmod 777 typo3temp/
chmod 777 typo3conf/
chmod 777 typo3conf/ext/
chmod 777 uploads/
chmod 777 fileadmin/
```

Beware: by making all the files world-writeable, security of your system could be compromised by other users with access to your server. You can consult section 2.3.1 for more information on how to set up a safe environment.

You can call up TYPO3 from `http://www.yourdomain.de/index.php` on your web server.

If you do not have a file called `index.html` in the directory of your web server, you can omit `index.php`. Otherwise we recommend that you rename the file `index.html`, perhaps to `index_alt.html`. You can delete it of course, providing you no longer need it.

Before the Installation Tool is called up in the so-called "1-2-3 mode", you will see a warning, which asks you to change the Installation Tool password immediately.

Now enter a user name and password for the MySQL database and send off the form. Then you either create a new database or select an existing one. Please remember that all data contained in it will be deleted!

Import the file `quickinstall.sql` into the database. You can now log in to the back end with the user name `admin` and the password `password`, under `http://www.yourdomain.de/typo3`. You can log in to the Installation Tool with the password `joh316`.[8] Please make sure you change the Installation Tool password on your first log in!

The basic installation for test purposes is now finished.

2.3 Installation for Productive Use

The installation for productive use is distinguished mainly by selecting the package that only contains the source, without the example data, and takes up a minimum amount of space. In addition, the Installation Tool contains considerably more options than are available in the simplified mode. Not only is it essential to know this to be able to configure the system optimally, the options also provide a number of insights into the structure of TYPO3.

2.3.1 LAMP Installation

As the most widely used operating system for web servers, UNIX/Linux is also a very good choice for using TYPO3. Especially when performing updates, the Linux platform has a clear advantage; there are a number of supporting software packages that are only available under Linux, and that are required for certain additional modules of TYPO3. So it really is worth taking a look at the online documentation for an extension before downloading and installing it. Below, we will assume a standard installation with MySQL.

---

[8] For the curious: Kasper Skårhøj refers here to the following verse of John the Evangelist: "For God so loved the world that he gave his only begotten Son, that whosoever believeth in him should not perish but have everlasting life".

Depending on the Linux distribution, there may be differences in the installation of Apache/PHP and MySQL. For image scaling and processing, ImageMagick is required. Alternatively you could use GraphicsMagick, an offshoot of ImageMagick. Please consult the documentation of your system or the relevant package manager. Whatever the case, you should ensure that PHP has at least 16 MB of memory available (this is set in the `php.ini` file) and also allows uploads of sufficient size (configured in `php.ini` and Apache).

For the installation of TYPO3 you first require an empty MySQL database with user name and password, as well as one of the above described packages from TYPO3.org.

There you can download the source and the so-called dummy distribution, which contains symbolic links and a configuration directory, and which will save you a bit of typing work on the command line.

The best way is to open the download page for the desired package in the browser. At the same time, open a command line application (*bash, term, putty*) and make a connection via SSH to the web server:

```
user@linux:~> ssh user@domain.de
```

Change to the directory of your web server, which lies one level above the website directory:

```
user@domain:~> cd /srv/www
```

Download the current version of the dummy and the source package. The correct address and the name of the file can be found on the packages page at TYPO3.org (see soft link):

Softlink **056011**

```
user@domain:/srv/www> wget
> http://typo3.sunsite.dk/unix-
archives/3.6.2/dummy/dummy-3.7.0.tar.gz
```

and

```
user@domain:/srv/www>wget
> http://typo3.sunsite.dk/unix-
archives/3.7.0/typo3_src/typo3_src-3.7.0.tar.gz
```

Here, `srv/www/` stands for the directory in which the directory of the website (in our example, `htdocs/`) will be located. If necessary, consult the configuration file for your web server to find out the correct path.

After downloading to the `/srv/www/` directory, unpack the archive with the commands:

```
user@domain/srv/www> tar xzf typo3_src-3.7.0.tar.gz
```

and

```
user@domain{/srv/www> tar xzf dummy-3.7.0.tar.gz
```

Now move the files in the dummy-3.7.0 directory, with the command

```
user@domain/srv/www> mv dummy-3.7.0/* htdocs/
```

to the htdocs directory, or the directory from which your website should be issued.

You can now delete the archive and the empty folder:

```
user@domain/srv/www> rm -r dummy-3.7.0
user@domain/srv/www> rm dummy-3.7.0-3.tar.gz
```

After this, if you call your htdocs directory with

```
user@domain/srv/www> ls -al htdocs/
```

it should appear as follows:

```
total 648
drwxr-xr-x 21   user group    714 11 Mar 22:13  .
drwxr-xr-x 6    user group    204 11 Mar 22:00  ..
-rw------- 1    user group    621 24 Jul 2003  Changelog
-rw------- 1    user group   4815 24 Jul 2003  INSTALL.txt
-rw------- 1    user group    608 24 Jul 2003  PACKAGE.txt
-rw------- 1    user group   8087 24 Jul 2003  README.txt
-rw-r----- 1    user group    134 27 Sep 2003  _.htaccess
-rw-r----- 1    user group     46  7 Sep 1999  clear.gif
drwxr-x--- 4    user group    136 12 Dec 2003  fileadmin
lrwxr-xr-x 1    user group     18 11 Mar 22:05  index.php
                                    -> tslib/index_ts.php
lrwxr-xr-x 1    user group     12 11 Mar 22:05  media ->
                                             tslib/media/
lrwxr-xr-x 1    user group     17 11 Mar 22:05
                            showpic.php -> tslib/showpic.php
lrwxr-xr-x 1    user group     16 11 Mar 22:05  t3lib ->
                                          typo3_src/t3lib/
lrwxr-xr-x 1    user group     16 11 Mar 22:05  tslib ->
                                          typo3_src/tslib/
lrwxr-xr-x 1    user group     16 11 Mar 22:05  typo3 ->
                                          typo3_src/typo3/
lrwxr-xr-x 1    user group     18 11 Mar 22:05  typo3_src
                                    -> ../typo3_src-3.7.0
drwxr-x--- 6    user group    204 16 Feb 2003  typo3conf
drwxr-x--- 2    user group     68 12 Dec 2002  typo3temp
drwxr-x--- 7    user group    238 12 Dec 2002  uploads
```

Run the following commands one after another to make the directories writable for the web server:

```
chmod 777 typo3/temp
chmod 777 typo3/ext
chmod 777 typo3temp
chmod 777 typo3conf
chmod 777 typo3conf/ext
chmod 777 uploads
chmod 777 fileadmin
```

Assigning 777 permissions is not without risk, however, since this gives access to all users of the system. It would be better to set the permissions to 770, if the user can be set to the name of the webmaster, and if the group can be set to the group name under which the web server is running. But this depends on the administrative options and the permissions on the web server available to you; 777 functions in all cases.

Now release the security lock in the Installation Tool by opening the following file in an editor (in our example, vi, available on most Linux platforms):

```
user@domain/srv/www> vi typo3/install/index.php
```

At the beginning, change the following line:

```
die("In the main source distribution of TYPO3, the
install script is disabled by a die() function
call.<BR>Open the file typo3/install/index.php
and remove/out-comment the line that outputs this
message!");}
```

If you are using vi (or vim), enter dd followed by zz. You have now deleted the line, saved the file and exited vi. Alternatively you can comment out the line by entering //, if you want to reactivate the lock later for reasons of security. To do this, enter i to reach insert mode. After entering // at the beginning of the line, exit the insert mode by pressing *Esc*, and then :wq!, to save your changes and close the editor.

In the browser you can now call the Installation tool, by entering http://www.yourdomain.de/typo3/install/.

2.3.2 WAMP Installation

The Windows installation of TYPO3 requires a running WAMP system with an installed Apache web server with the current PHP and MySQL distributions. You can find installers for Windows at http://www.php.net/ or http://www.bigapache.org/.

After installing Apache, MySQL and PHP, you should install ImageMagick. *Softlink* **892286**

This is also Open Source software; under the soft link shown here you will find a corresponding version of ImageMagick, optimized for use with TYPO3. You need Windows binaries (also called executables) for the installation if you do not want to compile the software yourself.

Install ImageMagick on your computer and then you can continue with the TYPO3 installation.

For this, download the dummy package in the zip distribution from the download page of TYPO3.org to your computer. Unpack the zip archive in the directory from which Apache will publish the website. Normally this is the following directory:

```
C:\Programs\apache\htdocs\
```

In the next step the user permissions for the web server must be set, so that the user under which Apache is running can read and edit all the necessary areas . You must be able to edit the following directories:

```
typo3\temp\
typo3\ext\
typo3temp\
typo3conf\
typo3conf\ext\
uploads\
fileadmin\
```

In the file `typo3\install\index.php` the line

```
die("In the main source distribution of TYPO3, the
install script is disabled by a die() function
call.<BR>Open the file typo3/install/index.php
and remove/out-comment the line that outputs this
message!");}
```

must be deleted or comment out by placing `//` at the beginning of the line.

Let's move on to the Installation Tool.

2.3.3 WIIS Installation

The Windows Internet Information Server installation consists of seven steps:

1. *System preparation*: To prepare the system, you should set up a separate partition for the web server, so that the permissions you have to set do not influence the permissions on your system partition, which could otherwise potentially jeopardize your system.

2. *MySQL installation*: Load a current MySQL version from

`http://www.mysql.com/` to your Windows server, unpack the installation file, and follow the instructions. When the installation is complete you will see a graphical interface with the program `WinMySQLadmin`, with which you can set up users and databases. Create an empty database and a user for this database.

3. *ImageMagick installation (optional)*: The ImageMagick software is also Open Source; and under the soft link shown here you will find a version optimized for use with TYPO3. You need Windows binaries, also called executables, if you don't want to compile the software yourself.

Softlink **892286**

4. *PHP installation*: After the PHP installation you should check a number of settings in the file `php.ini` and adjust them where necessary. The `php.ini` file contains the PHP configuration parameters. The most important setting for the operation of TYPO3 is:

```
memory_limit=8M
```

This should be increased to at least 16M (16 MB). The Installation Tool checks a number of other parameters, but in general these have been correctly set in the default configuration.

5. *IIS configuration*: The IIS configuration contains no special features in terms of TYPO3; the settings can either be taken over automatically by the PHP installer or carried out manually, as described in the installation guide for PHP. For reasons of performance, it is generally highly recommended that you operate PHP in ISAPI mode.

6. *Unpack TYPO3*: The selected zip package is unpacked in the target directory, usually `F:\inetpub\wwwroot\`, although the drive name may vary, of course.

7. *Assign NTFS permissions*: Finally, permissions must be given to both users under whom IIS is operated. These users are called `IUSR` and `IWAM`, to which their server name is added. The user `IUSR_MACHINENAME` needs read permissions for the entire file system, in order to carry out the PHP functions `file_exists()`, `is_file()`, etc., and not just for the directories in which TYPO3 is installed. This user must also be assigned read and execute permission for the program `cmd.exe` in order to run ImageMagick, where appropriate, and must also have read permission for the file `php.ini`. In the web server directory the following permissions must be assigned to the user `IUSR_MACHI-NENAME`:

TYPO3	Permission
web server directory (normally: `Drive:\inetpub\wwwroot`)	Read
`fileadmin\`	Edit (with subdirectories)
`typo3temp\`	Edit (with subdirectories)
`uploads\`	Edit (with subdirectories)
`typo3ext\`	Edit (with subdirectories)
`typo3conf\`	Edit (with subdirectories)
`C:\PHP\uploadtemp\`	Edit
ImageMagick	Read and Execute
`C:\Windows\system32\cmd.exe`	Read and Execute

2.4 The Installation Tool

The Installation Tool is essentially a graphical interface for editing TYPO3 system settings saved in the file `localconf.php`, in the directory `typo3conf/`. This file, as well as the entire `localconf` directory must therefore also be writable for the web server.

Let's try to understand the functioning of the configuration system. At run time, TYPO3 generates cache files in the `typo3conf` directory, on whose configuration parameters TYPO3 operates. So if configuration data is modified, these cache files must be deleted for the changes to take effect. Normally this is done automatically, but if the sources are replaced, especially when downgrading the version, TYPO3 may not become active by itself, so the cache files have to be deleted manually. These files have names such as `temp_CACHED_ps2268_ext_localconf.php`.

By adding `/typo3/install/` on to the name of your domain, you call up the Installation Tool: `http://www.yourdomain.de/typo3/install/`.

To be able to use the Installation Tool, a locking function must be removed from the script `typo3/install/index.php`. This has already been described in the section on the LAMP and WAMP installations.

The default password for the Installation Tool is `joh316` and should be changed immediately after the first login. After this, the installation can be started, by entering various information. You need to enter the following:

1. User name and password as well as host name and, if appropriate, the name of an already created database that

TYPO3 should use.

2. The path to the directory where ImageMagick is installed on your system. With the command

```
user@linux:~> locate identify
```

you can quickly find this out on most Linux distributions.

The Installation Tool is divided into the following areas, where the first three have to be edited to some extent when it is installed. The other views are for system maintenance.

2.4.1 Basic Configuration

The tab for basic configuration checks the permissions of the directories that need to be writable for TYPO3, and also checks the PHP configuration in the php.ini file. Any problems that might prevent the installation from being performed are shown here, with corresponding warnings.

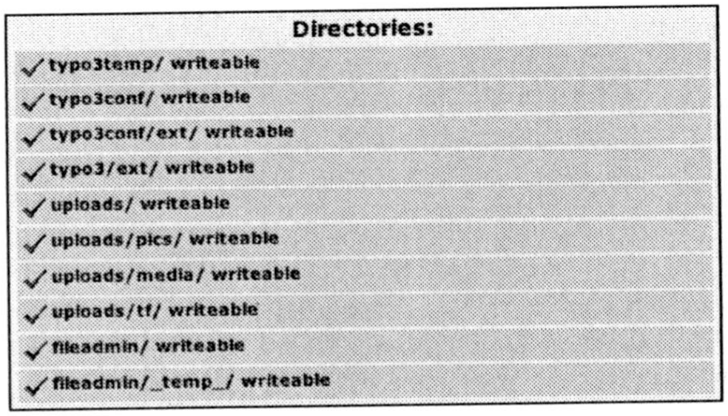

Directories:
- ✓ typo3temp/ writeable
- ✓ typo3conf/ writeable
- ✓ typo3conf/ext/ writeable
- ✓ typo3/ext/ writeable
- ✓ uploads/ writeable
- ✓ uploads/pics/ writeable
- ✓ uploads/media/ writeable
- ✓ uploads/tf/ writeable
- ✓ fileadmin/ writeable
- ✓ fileadmin/_temp_/ writeable

Figure 2.2:

All directories required by TYPO3 were identifed as being correctly configured

Here you must also specify the access data for your database. After entering the user name, password, and host name (usually "localhost", if MySQL is installed on your server), the form must be submitted once with the **update configuration** command in order to select a database or, if your user has the appropriate permissions (create), to create a new database.

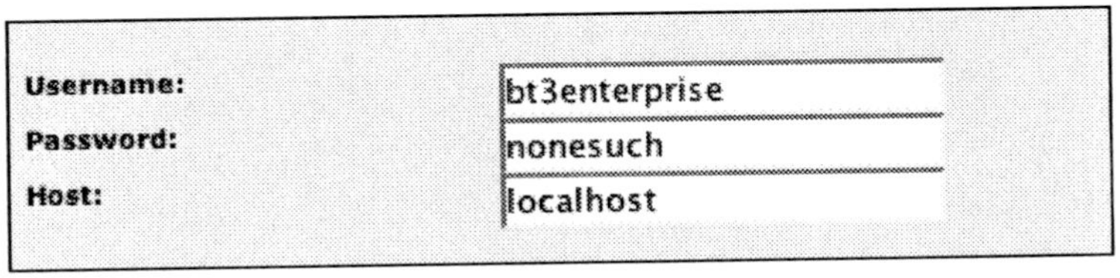

Username:	bt3enterprise
Password:	nonesuch
Host:	localhost

Figure 2.3:

Access data for the database

Next we will discuss the settings for generating images. If you have installed ImageMagick, you should specify the path to your installation here. TYPO3 searches automatically in the default directory for ImageMagick and also determines independently whether you have compiled the GDLib with Freetype into PHP. With current Freetype versions, the text in the test picture might extend beyond the edges. If this problem persists, we will fix it at a later stage (see section 2.4.4).

Figure 2.4:

Output of the Freetype test at the correct resolution

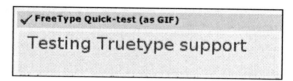

If you submit the form, the Installation Tool will write the corresponding values to the `localconf.php` file.

2.4.2 Database Analyzer

The script for database analysis enables you to both edit and update an existing database as well as to fill it for the first time with a database definition and standard contents. A basic database definition is included in the dummy package. The corresponding SQL file is in the "localconf" directory, `typo3conf/`, and is displayed automatically in the Installation Tool.

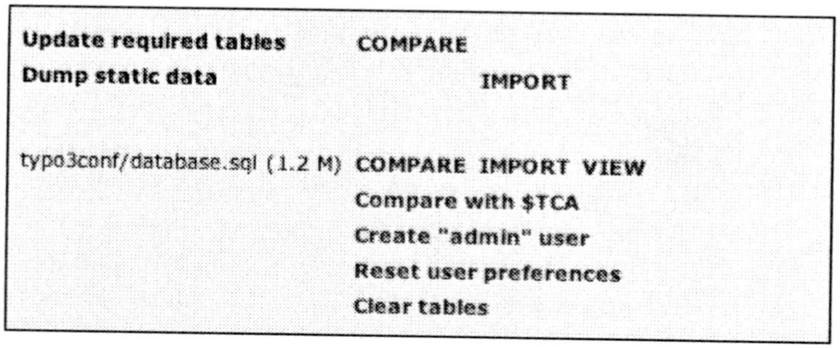

Figure 2.5:

Display of the default SQL file with the basic database contents and the database definition

With the **Import** option, the database is imported. After clicking on this option, you will receive a security query, where you should select the option to read in all data, and submit the form with **Write to database**.

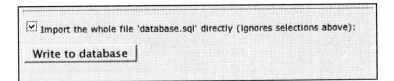

Figure 2.6:

Importing the database

Depending on the performance provided by your web server, this process-ing may take a while. In the next step you will see a list of all database tables, with the warning that they already exist. If this is not the case, and a number of tables are displayed as not yet existing, then the import process has failed, and you should try it again. Initialization of the database is now finished. An administrator account is then set up with the user name `admin` and with the password `password`.

Import SQL dump:

i) Select tables to import

This is an overview of the CREATE TABLE definitions in the SQL file. Select which tables you want to dump to the database. Any table you choose dump to the database is dropped from the database first, so you'll loose all data in existing tables.

be_groups		◈ Table exists!
be_sessions		◈ Table exists!
be_users	Rows: 1	◈ Table exists!
cache_hash		◈ Table exists!
pages		◈ Table exists!
sys_be_shortcuts		◈ Table exists!
sys_filemounts		◈ Table exists!
sys_history		◈ Table exists!
sys_lockedrecords		◈ Table exists!
sys_log		◈ Table exists!
cache_pages		◈ Table exists!
cache_pagesection		◈ Table exists!
cache_typo3temp_log		◈ Table exists!
cache_md5params		◈ Table exists!
fe_groups		◈ Table exists!
fe_session_data		◈ Table exists!
fe_sessions		◈ Table exists!
fe_users		◈ Table exists!
pages_language_overlay		◈ Table exists!
static_template	Rows: 61	◈ Table exists!
sys_domain		◈ Table exists!
sys_language		◈ Table exists!
sys_template		◈ Table exists!
tt_content		◈ Table exists!
static_tsconfig_help	Rows: 203	◈ Table exists!
sys_tabledescr	Rows: 249	◈ Table exists!
sys_tabledescr_dk	Rows: 7	◈ Table exists!
sys_tabledescr_local		◈ Table exists!
sys_note		◈ Table exists!
sys_notepad		◈ Table exists!

Figure 2.7:

Message of the Database Analyzer after successful import of the SQL file (attention: your display may contain different tables!)

An alternative method that does not need the `database.sql` file from the dummy package can be used to initialize the database—select the **COMPARE** option. A list of all required database tables is shown. These have been pre-selected. Press the confirm button in the form to create the database tables. Then select the **Create "admin" user** function and set up an administrator account.

2.4.3 Image Processing

This script is a collection of test outputs to test the function of ImageMagick and the GDLib and Freetype. It has no influence on the configuration of your system, and is therefore not discussed further here.

2.4.4 All Configuration

The **All Configuration** script contains entry fields with short explanations on all configuration options of TYPO3, which are named in the `TYPO3_CONF_VARS` array. In general, only a few entries are important. If the text in the previously introduced Freetype test extends beyond the edges, adjust the resolution for Freetype and increase it from 72 to 96 dpi.

Enter this value in the field `[GFX] [TTFdpi]`; you will find it as the final part of section `[GFX]`, before the `[SYS]` section.

Further entries are not normally necessary here.

2.4.5 typo3temp/

Here you are shown a statistical overview of the files stored in the `typo3temp` directory, and you can also delete them from here. This is an important function for maintaining the installation. The directory is used by TYPO3 to store image files shown in the front end. The images are freshly generated each time the page cache is deleted, while the old ones remain in this folder. For large websites with large amounts of image material, many MBs can quickly accumulate here. If the images are deleted from this directory, although the files are still referenced from the pages, the image is newly generated, as long as you emptied the page cache after deleting the files. You can also take a look in the back end of your TYPO3 installation, in the **Tools | Check DB** module under **Missing Relations**, to see how many files without a database relation are located in this directory.

versions 5+. The `tslib_cObj` class by default uses the PNG format, because generating is faster and puts lesser load on the CPU. But since some IM versions above 5 do not correctly support the PNG format, this can be suppressed here.

Example: `[im_mask_temp_ext_gif] = 0`

[im_mask_temp_ext_noloss]

String. While images are being masked, the temporary files should be stored in a loss-free format, of course. ImageMagick's own format, named `miff`, is ideal for this. Unfortunately version 5.4.9 is not in a position to generate its own file format, so that this function became necessary. If problems occur with masked files, TIF, PNG, or JPG can be used instead.

Example: `[im_mask_temp_ext_noloss] = miff`

[im_noScaleUp]

Boolean value (0,1). If enabled, images are not enlarged.

Example: `[im_noScaleUp] = 0`

[im_combine_filename]

String. More recent IM versions have renamed the `combine` command to `composite`; the proper name can be given here.

Example: `[im_combine_filename] = combine`

[im_noFramePrepended]

Boolean value (0,1). Some image formats such as GIF or TIF allow several images to be saved in one file. ImageMagick provides an option to work only with the first image, which in general increases working speed. Unfortunately, some IM versions contain an error that causes the IM to simply ignore these images. In such a case, this option must be enabled.

Example: `[im_noFramePrepended] = 0`

[enable_typo3temp_db_tracking]

Boolean value (0,1). Here it is specified whether all files in `typo3temp/` are recorded in a database table. This prevents files from being doubly rendered, since the relation between the temporarily rendered output file and the source file is noted here. In addition, in the **Tools | Database check** module in the back end and in the Installation Tool, you can find out how many old files there are in the `temp/` directory.

Example: `[enable_typo3temp_db_tracking] = 0`

[TTFLocaleConv]

String. Up to version 3.6.0 you could specify here, using the recode designations, in what encoding TrueType functions were generated. Since version 3.6.0, the output has always been in UTF-8.

Example: `[TTFLocaleConv] =`

[TTFdpi]

Integer. This important option is for setting the resolution in dpi (dots per inch) in which the existing Freetype system on your server works. Since version 2 this has been 96 instead of 72 dpi; this causes fonts to be displayed too large if the value is not changed to 96 dpi for a more recent version.

Example: `[TTFdpi] = 96`

2.5.2 [SYS]:$TYPO3_CONF_VARS["SYS"]

This section describes configuration options involving system behavior in the back end and front end.

[textfile_ext]

You can specify here, via file extensions, which file types may be edited in the back end.

Example: `[textfile_ext] =`
`txt,html,htm,css,inc,php,php3,tmpl,js,sql`

[contentTable]

With this option you can specify what the page content table should be called. The default value is `tt_content`.

Example: `[contentTable] = tt_content`

[sitename]

This is the name of the installation and is shown at the top of the page tree next to the globe. The name can also be set directly in the **Basic Configuration** view of the Installation Tool.

Example: `[sitename] = BT3 Enterprise`

[ddmmyy]

Format of the date display—corresponds to the notation of the PHP function, `date()`.

Example: `[ddmmyy] = d.m.y`

[notificationPrefix]

This option allows a header to be set for messages from the system to the administrator.

Example: `[notificationPrefix]` = Miracles may happen...

2.5.5 [FE]: $TYPO3_CONF_VARS["FE"]

Configuration parameters in the following section referred to the front end, that is, the websites published by TYPO3.

[png_to_gif]

Boolean value (0,1). The value `1` enables the conversion of all PNG files generated in the front end to GIF files. This leaves behind a large number of temporary files in the `typo3temp/` directory.

Example: `[png_to_gif]` = 0

[tidy]

Boolean value (0,1). If `1` is set, the HTML code is cleaned and optimized with the `tidy` program. This option is recommended, especially during development periods, so that the HTML code generated can be more easily read. But remember that `tidy`, depending on the options, cleans or repairs defective HTML code. This option should be switched off on live systems, to prevent unnecessary load on the server. `tidy` can be obtained here: `http://www.w3.org/People/Raggett/tidy/`

Example: `[tidy]` = 0

[tidy_option]

Options: `[all, cached, output]`. `all` causes `tidy` to clean up all content before it is saved in the cache. `cached` causes content only to be cleaned before it is saved to the cache. `output` cleans HTML code only if it is requested from the cache.

Example: `[tidy_option]` = cached

[tidy_path]

Here the command `tidy` is specified, including the path and all necessary options, where appropriate. Apart from the default setting, other parameters can be defined in accordance with the documentation of `tidy`. To generate XHTML through `tidy`, for example, the expression `--output-xhtml true` should be added.

Example: `[tidy_path]` = tidy -i --quiet true --
tidy-mark true -wrap 0

[logfile_dir]

Path. In the directory given here, TYPO3 writes log files in the notation of a web server for evaluation by statistical programs. The directory must be writable for the web server. The directory name must be concluded with a slash. More information can be found in Chapter 4.12.2.

Example: `[logfile_dir]` = /srv/www/logs/

[logfile_write]

The log files can be written using various methods. Without further settings, TYPO3 uses the UNIX command `echo`. Entering `fputs` causes TYPO3 to use the PHP function of the same name, which also works in `safe_mode` mode.

Example: `[logfile_write]` = fputs

[publish_dir]

Path to a directory in which TYPO3 should statically publish HTML pages. The directory must be writable for the web server. The pages can then be published from the Admin Panel in the `publish` area.

Example: `[publish_dir]` = /srv/www/htdocs/publish/

[addAllowedPaths]

Path, comma-separated list: other directories can be specified in which resources are stored for use in TypoScript. Paths must be specified relative to the web directory. The default is specified with a leading slash; without a slash, every directory is accepted that begins with the same expression.

Example: `[addAllowedPaths]` = b2b/, /b2c/

[allowedTempPaths]

Path, comma-separated list: additional paths where temporary images may be located for use by `imgResource` in TypoScript.

Example: `[allowedTempPaths]` = b2btemp/

[debug]

Boolean value (0,1). If enabled with 1, debug information is shown in the front end. This can also be set in TypoScript.

Example: `[debug]` = 1

[simulateStaticDocuments]

Boolean value (0,1). Display of simulated static URL addresses is switched on by default with this entry, but needs to be enabled separately in TypoScript.

Example: `[simulateStaticDocuments] = 1`

[noPHPscriptInclude]

Boolean value (0,1). If enabled, PHP scripts are only called by TypoScript if they are located in the directory `media/scripts/`.

Example: `[noPHPscriptInclude] = 0`

[compressionLevel]

This value defines the compression of HTML pages in the front end through the `zlib` function in PHP. `1` is the lowest compression rate, and `9` the highest. Compression helps to spare bandwidth, but also puts more load on the server, the higher the compression rate. If you enter `TRUE`, the compression rate is automatically adjusted to the system load.

Example: `[compressionLevel] = 0`

[compressionDebugInfo]

Boolean value (0,1). If enabled, the size of the compressed and uncompressed versions of a page are shown at the bottom of the page. This should only be used for test purposes, as the pages for static evaluation are compressed twice.

Example: `[compressionDebugInfo] = 0`

[pageNotFound_handling]

String. With this option you can configure how TYPO3 should react to queries for unavailable pages. The default behavior is to display the next page. With `TRUE` or `1`, an error message is displayed. Alternatively an HTML page can be specified, which will be displayed.

Example: `[pageNotFound_handling] =`
`http://www.brunching.com/gone.html`

[pageNotFound_handling_statheader]

String. If the option `[pageNotFound_handling]` is enabled, the string set here is always sent as the header.

Example: `[pageNotFound_handling_statheader] =`
`Status: 404 Not Found`

[userFuncClassPrefix]

This prefix must be the first part of each function or of the name of a class that is called from TypoScript, e.g. in the `stdWrap` function.

Example: `[userFuncClassPrefix] = user_`

[addRootLineFields]

Comma-separated list. A list of additional database fields in the `pages` table; should be used for Rootline queries.

Example: `[addRootLineFields] =`

[checkFeUserPid]

Boolean value (0,1). If enabled, login forms in the front end must specify the page ID (pid) of the front end user under which these are stored. If this is disabled, with `0`, the `eval` configuration of `uniqueInPid` in the `$TCA` for the `fe_users.username` field should be changed to `unique`. The entry then looks like this:

```
$TCA['fe_users']['columns']['username']['config']
        ['eval'] =   'nospace,lower,required,unique';
```

The storage location no longer has to be specified in the TypoScript page on which the login form is located; all FE users are globally valid for the TYPO3 instance.

Example: `[checkFeUserPid] = 1`

[defaultUserTSconfig]

String. TSConfig entries can be predefined here for all front end users and groups.

Example: `[defaultUserTSconfig] =`

[defaultTypoScript_constants]

String. Option to predefine TypoScript for constants systemwide.

Example: `[defaultTypoScript_constants] =`

[defaultTypoScript_editorcfg]

String. Option, to define the TypoScript `editorcfg` configuration systemwide. Is used by the CSS Styler (extension key: `tstemplate_cssanalyzer`).

Example: `[defaultTypoScript_editorcfg] =`

[dontSetCookie]

Boolean value (0,1). If enabled, the system does not set any cookies in the front end, which also causes logins to be switched off.

Example: `[dontSetCookie] = 0`

[get_url_id_token]

String. In the front end, users can log in without a cookie if the TypoScript option `config.ftu` is enabled. In this case the user session is managed via a `GET` parameter, the name of which is specified here. In principle this type of session administration is not recommended, as it is more error-prone than the cookie variant.

Example: `[get_url_id_token] = SESSID`

[content_doctypes]

String. Page types (type number of the field `pages.doctype`) that are to be recognized by the system as pages or SysFolders are defined here as a comma-separated list.

Example: `[content_doctypes] = 1,2,5,7`

[enable_mount_pids]

Boolean value (0,1). With this option the function of Mountpages can be switched off globally (`0`).

Example: `[enable_mount_pids] = 1`

[pageOverlayFields]

String. The specified fields are used in database queries for multi-language websites. This option is relevant for extensions that add their own fields to the `pages` table.

Example: `[pageOverlayFields] = title,subtitle, nav_title,media,keywords,description,abstr...`

2.5.6 Other Options

[MODS: $TYPO3_CONF_VARS["MODS"]]

Used to contain options for configuring modules, but was replaced by the extension system.

[USER: $TYPO3_CONF_VARS["USER"]]

Used to contain options for configuring parameters for your own scripts, but was replaced by the extension system.

[SC_OPTIONS: $TYPO3_CONF_VARS["SC_OPTIONS"]]

This section is used to make available your own configuration options for any scripts at all (in general, BE modules) in TYPO3.

[EXTCONF: $TYPO3_CONF_VARS["EXTCONF"]]

Here you can add configuration options for your own extensions. During the installation in the EM, these should be displayed using the file `ext_conf_template.txt`.

Example: `$TYPO3_CONF_VARS['EXTCONF']`
`['my_extension_key']['my_option'] = 'my_value';`

2.6 Separation of Production Server/Live Server

In cases where increased performance capacity is required and also for security reasons, it can be useful or even necessary to share the processing of pages and other contents, as well as their presentation across several different servers.

A simple possibility would be the publication of the website as static HTML pages, without a database or TYPO3 on the live system. But in the standard scenario, the website itself contains these dynamic elements generated from a database, which make TYPO3 necessary on the live system. The essential problem in such a scenario therefore lies in the synchronization of database content between different systems, where several different servers might be involved, perhaps to spread the load.

Depending on the database used, some very different synchronization mechanisms are available for this purpose. Please consult the documentation of your database vendor.

With direct synchronization, you cannot make any further decisions in the publication: what is live on the production system is automatically placed online. Alternatively the synchronization can be performed manually, depending on the RDBMS used, in case a further release step is necessary.

For the TYPO3 installation delivering the site and offering no editing functions, it is advisable to disable the back end logins of regular users altogether by setting the following parameter in the **All Configuration** tab of the Install Tool: `$TYPO3_CONF_VARS['BE']['adminOnly']='1';`

2.6.1 Static Pages

A second and simpler variation is to publish static pages, already mentioned briefly in section 2.4.4. The following entry in the Installation Tool and configuration in the Admin Panel of the front end causes all webpages to be saved in a predefined directory of the server.

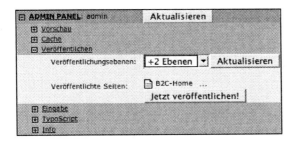

Figure 2.8:

Selecting the page levels to be published, in the Admin Panel of the front end

Apart from the TYPO3-like systems for generating static pages, there are many other software solutions for all standard platforms. An example is `HTTrack`, available under both Linux and Windows, and which can be obtained without charge as an Open Source tool at `http://www.httrack.com/`.

2.7 Backup

You can use various methods to create backups. Most companies have proper backup strategies, and the safest way is to include the relevant directories of the web server in these backup routines, not forgetting the directory where the database files are stored.

If it is just a matter of creating backups from TYPO3 alone, there are various extensions available to perform this task. However, a relatively inexperienced administrator can easily set up an automatic backup system at the operating system level, which is normally a better solution, because the backups do not have to be manually started each time.

With an entry in the crontab system (UNIX), this script can be called up regularly: in the example below, this is done every 24 hours, at 1 o'clock in the morning.

After this, the backup files should be copied automatically onto a physically separate system. A script such as the following one could perform this conveniently and automatically via `rsync`. To do this, an SSH key is necessary to enable the data to be transmitted in encrypted form.

Here is an example script (with thanks to Harald Oest from `http://www.ixsys.de/`):

```sh
#!/bin/sh
# script rsync_backup.sh
# backup of web server document root via rsync to
# backup server
# additionally do a dump of typo3-db

# ip or fqhn of backup server
SERVER="my_backup_server"
# user account at backup server
USER="my_username"
# ssh-key (without passphrase!) used for login
SSHKEY="/root/.ssh/backup_server_key"
# destination dir at backup server
DSTDIR="/typo3_bkp"
# name of local typo3 database
DB="typo3_db"
# user account to access typo3 database
DB_USER="typo3_db_user"
# password to access typo3 database
DB_PASS="typo3_db_password"

# these directories will be rsynced with backup server
DIRS="/srv/www"

# do a mysql-dump and store result in source dir
/usr/bin/mysqldump --password=$DB_PASS -u $DB_USER $DB
            > \ /srv/www/typo3db_bkp.sql

# rsync all requested dirs
for DIR in $DIRS; do
logger "rsync backup $DIR to $SERVER"
rsync --rsh="ssh -i $SSHKEY"
                        -a $DIR $USER@$SERVER:$DSTDIR
done;

# get actual size of backup
ACT_SIZE=`ssh -i $SSHKEY $USER@$SERVER
                        "du -sh $DSTDIR"

logger "total backup size: $ACT_SIZE"
```

You can generate an SSH key without a password query as follows:

```
linux:~# ssh-keygen -t rsa
Generating public/private rsa key pair.
Enter file in which to save the key (/root/.ssh/
                    id_rsa): /root/.ssh/backup_server_key
Enter passphrase (empty for no passphrase): [Enter]
Enter same passphrase again: [Enter]
Your identification has been saved in /root/.ssh/
                    backup_server_key.
Your public key has been saved in /root/.ssh/
                    backup_server_key.pub.
The key fingerprint is:
8b:1f:f9:c9:54:65:bc:f5:d6:ce:79:0d:e4:1d:56:2f
                    root@local_box
```

The key pair has now been created, and the private key is already in its correct location (/root/.ssh/backup_server_key). The public key now needs to be sent to the backup server:

```
linux:~# scp /root/.ssh/backup_server_key.pub \
> user@my_backup_server:/home/.ssh
```

Now make a connection to my_backup_server and activate the SSH key:

```
root:my_backup_server:~# cat  /home/.ssh/
                    backup_server_key.pub >> \

> /home/.ssh/authorized_keys
```

In order to clear up after this:

```
root:my_backup_server:~# rm  /home/.ssh/
                    backup_server_key.pub
```

And the same on the local computer:

```
linux:~# rm /root/.ssh/backup_server_key.pub
```

You can now make a connection to the backup server without a password:

```
linux:~# ssh -i /root/.ssh/backup_server_key
                    user@my_backup_server
```

Here is an example of an appropriate crontab entry, which calls up the rsync backup at 1 a.m. in the morning:

```
# call backup script every night at 01.00
0 1 * * * root test -x /root/bin/rsync_backup.sh && \
/root/bin/rsync_backup.sh
```

2.8 Updates

TYPO3 updates are particularly enjoyable for the administrator, since they rarely last more than a few minutes. The reason for this lies in the often mentioned symbolic links, which summarize the actual TYPO3 version in a single directory; all the other files are either version-independent, and remain where they are, or are also symbolic links.

However the first step in every update is to make a backup of the entire installation, or at least of the database. With the command

```
linux:/srv/www># mysqldump -u user -p databasename
                                            backup.tgz
```

you can create a backup file, after entering the password of the database user in MySQL. In emergencies, you can unpack this backup with the command

```
linux:/srv/www># tar xzf backup.tgz
```

and then, with the command

```
linux:/srv/www># mysql -u user -p databasename <
backup.sql
```

write it back to the database.

Back to the update: to use the new version instead of the old one, you must delete the old symbolic link. For example, with

```
linux:/srv/www># {rm typo3_src}
```

your site is now offline!

With the command

```
linux:/srv/www># {ln -s ../typo3-src-3.8 typo3_src}
```

a new symbolic link is set to the new source that was previously placed on the server (see section 2.3.1).

Under Windows and generally with zip-distributions, if you are not using Junction, all the TYPO3 directories (typo3, t3lib, tslib) have to be replaced manually.

So if the symbolic link that points to the TYPO3 version is replaced, the update on the file level is already complete.

Please remember that after an update (or a downgrade) of TYPO3, you should first call up the Database Analyzer of the Installation Tool. With the **COMPARE** function, necessary changes to the database are identified and displayed. These are new database fields as well as changes in the field definition of existing fields. Select **Implement All Changes** and carry out the update. The **COMPARE** function can also remove database tables that are no longer required from uninstalled extensions. It goes without saying that you should know what you are doing when carrying out this function, and of course: back up, back up, back up! The tables and fields to be removed are first renamed and then provided with the prefix `zzz_`. They can be reactivated by removing this prefix, for example with `phpMyAdmin`.

It is recommended, for obvious reasons, not to carry out the update on heavily visited sites. Instead you can duplicate the database and the file system, adjust the access data to the new database in the copy, and carry out emergency test scenarios. This helps you switch over in a few seconds, by changing the web server or swapping directories.

2.9 Help with Problems

The TYPO3 community maintains various contact points regarding installation problems. These can be wide-ranging due to the various possible combinations of web server, database, and PHP distributions used. Two mailing lists exist for installation questions, one each for Linux and Windows operating systems, which can also be used by nntp-client (newsgroups). In addition, there is an online archive you really should browse through to make sure that a question has not already been answered. Bear in mind that all those providing help are volunteers: as someone seeking help, you should try not to distract them with unnecessary or repeat questions. If you have discovered a bug not yet described anywhere, you can register it at `http://bugs.typo3.org/`.

3

TYPO3 for Editors

In 1999 Tim Berners-Lee, father of the World Wide Web, exclaimed: "From the point of view of users, the biggest change I want to see is to make everyone capable of writing web pages and making links just as easily as people can create e-mail messages today." [1]

One of the main reasons that content management systems have made a breakthrough is that they have put this demand of hypertext authors into practice. However, this has varying degrees of success in terms of user-friendliness—especially for enterprise content management systems. Forrester Research, a market research company, diagnosed in a study in 2001 that there is an urgent need for improvement in usability among the systems reviewed in the study. [2]

Usability can be achieved and measured in concrete steps. Here are some common requirements:

- The user interface must be appropriate, intuitive, and simple to use.

- It should follow consistent logic and have a uniform structure.

- It should be possible to customize it, according to the different tasks of each user and/or group.

- Each function of the application should support the user with context-sensitive help functions, a user manual, and examples for beginners.

- It should be possible to revoke individual working steps in a work session at the push of a button (the "Undo" function). An editing history helps to recreate previous working states of the record.

[1] http://www.time.com/time/community/transcripts/1999/092999berners-lee.html

[2] http://www.forrester.com/ER/Research/Report/Summary/0,1338,14981,00.html

- In addition, wizards are important, helping users to perform specific work steps.

In general, the following applies: too little functionality blocks the workflow—and too much functionality does the same. For this reason it must be possible to extend or reduce functions: the system must provide users with exactly those functions they require for their work. In addition, the technical requirements for using the CMS on the user side must be as low as possible, in order to be able to keep installation work to a minimum.

All this (and more) can be managed by TYPO3. In the course of its six years of development, the user interface has been optimized in terms of user-friendliness, thanks to the experiences of users (there are now some 122,000 installations in operation) who use it in their daily work.

3.1 The Role of the Editor

The task of the editor is to create new content and assets, to prepare this content for the appropriate media, and to integrate it into the corresponding application, for example, a web site. For this purpose, the administrator, in the context of user permissions, puts the user into a kind of "sandpit", from within which he or she has (restricted) access to the system and its functionality. So the user's view of the back end, workspace, and of the resources allocated to him or her are limited (see Chapter 4). In contrast to an editor in the press department, for example, who "works in" new articles into the system (this is the jargon in CMS circles), an editor-in-chief uses an expanded view, because of his or her (system-internal) group and individual permissions.

Softlink **509060** Depending on the size of the content life cycle and complexity of working procedures, the editor merely processes parts of the content on its way to publication. This means that the editor works within a so-called *workflow*, together with other editors.

Below, we will introduce the user interface in which the content is edited, and a tasks module—a communication center for those involved in a project. We will then go on to explain how pages can be created and content added. The focus here is not on the explanation of all the entry fields (context-sensitive help exists for this purpose, as well as the extensive "Manual for Editors", see soft link), but on the general representation of pages and content types, and practical use. Individual aspects, such as handling the *Rich Text Editor*, will be treated separately. Finally, routines and utilities are presented that can simplify the daily work with TYPO3 for editors, and make it more efficient.

3.2 Logging in to the System

TYPO3 is a web-based content management system. It is installed in the intranet on an internal company server, or on the web/extranet on a publicly-accessible server. To access the system, editors need nothing more than a browser and the correct Internet address, in order to create and update page contents, irrespective of time and place.

TYPO3 makes a distinction between two different areas: the *back end* or administration area for managing pages and data, and the *front end*, the actual web site as the normal visitor views it. The editor logged in can use both modes in TYPO3 to edit content. While the back end provides a complete work environment with many functions, the front end can be operated in a very simple and intuitive manner. The primary editing options are all very similar; the operating elements and ways of functioning introduced here can to some extent be also found in the front end.

3.2.1 The Correct Browser Settings

TYPO3 works with current browsers (Netscape Navigator 6.x, 7.x, Mozilla Firefox, Internet Explorer 5.x, 6.x, etc.), some of which have a slightly different display and functionality. These differences in display are not significant, apart from the fact that the Rich Text Editor is only available in Internet Explorer, since it also requires Microsoft ActiveX. There are several alternatives for Mozilla, which have to be installed as extensions on the system.

Softlink **352869**

The browser must accept cookies, and JavaScript must be activated. Settings for the browser cache should be adjusted so that when a page is called, a fresh version is requested from the server each time.

3.2.2 Login

In order to log in to the system, you just need to enter the corresponding URL (web address) in the browser, adding `/typo3` (e.g. `http://www.your-domain.com/typo3`). There you will find the login window, shown in the following figure. Enter your user name and password here. Passwords for back-end users are transmitted in encrypted form by TYPO3 and saved securely in the database system.

Figure 3.1

Login with username
and password

3.3 User Interface and Module

Softlink **502403**

Back end is the name given to the user interface of TYPO3 where the editor works. The administration of pages and content through so-called front-end editing will be discussed separately (section 3.8). Once the editor has logged in, he or she will be in his or her workspace. Remember: the appearance of the user interface may change drastically from one editor to another, depending on settings made by the administrator.

So you are either taken to a help page, with a short description of all the elements in the module bar, or to the module **User | Task center**.

After clicking on one of the navigation options on the left of the page in the **Web** area you will see the structure of the back end:

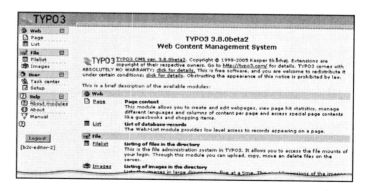

Figure 3.2

The module **Help |
About Modules** after
the login

The user interface of TYPO3 is generally divided into three areas: the *Module Bar* on the left-hand side, the *Navigation Area* with the page tree in the middle, and the *Details View* on the right-hand side.

3.3.1 Areas of the User Interface

If several different editors are working on the same system, the **User |
Task center** module (the TYPO3-internal communication and administration center) usually has preselected settings when it is called up for the first time. Here you can see the typical division of the user-interface into three parts.

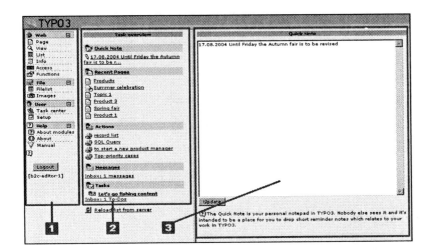

Figure 3.3

The three areas of the desktop in terms of the Tasks module: module bar [1], navigation area [2], details view [3]

Module Bar

The *module bar* is what the top navigation layer in the back end of TYPO3 is called. Here you can find a list of modules that are available for a particular editor.

The main module (**Web, File, Document,...**) contains various submodules (e.g. **Page, View, List**, etc.), where actual editing functions can be found.

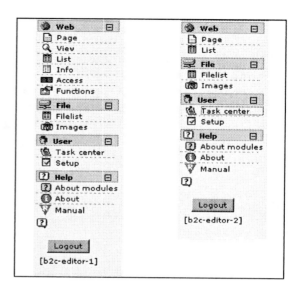

Figure 3.4

*Different back-end
congurations: two
users with different
permissions and
editing options*

Navigation Area

Depending on the module, navigation is done through the *navigation area*. In the main **Web** module you can see the *page tree* [1], where all the pages that the editor may see are displayed.

Access to the file system for the main **File** module is obtained through the *directory tree*.

Exactly as in Windows Explorer and other file managers, the levels of the directory structure are expanded and collapsed with the "+" and "-" icons. If you click on the title, a Details View of the selected element will open on the right.

If you click on an icon in the page tree, a context-sensitive menu opens for quick access to the most important work functions. For Windows browsers, this menu opens directly in the page tree, for other browsers, the functions appear in the top bar.

Bear in mind the following rules of thumb:

Click on icon=
> Call file functions (copy elements, cut, etc.)

Click on title=
> View/Edit contents

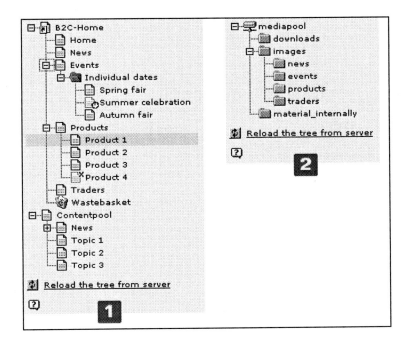

Figure 3.5

Page tree [1] and directory tree for the file system [2]

Details View

The actual workspace is represented in the so-called *Details View* (third column). Depending on the modules selected, various information and records may appear here. In the main **Web** and **File** modules, a context-sensitive menu is also available (remember: click on the icon), which simplifies your work.

3.3.2 Main Modules and Submodules—An Overview

Web

The **Web** module area is the one used most by the editor. Pages and content are stored, managed, and edited here. Individual sub-modules often allow you to achieve the same results using different ways.

Softlink **762976**

Pages

New pages and content are created and edited using the **Page** module, .

The individual options are:

Quick Edit

> The contents are opened directly in editing mode. Using another foldout menu or the graphical navigation in the footer bar, you can switch between the elements to be edited.

Columns

> Displays the content of a page, according to how it is placed in the columns of the page, and according to the sequence of text.

Languages

> Represents the contents of a page, sorted by language. Since multi-language applications can be implemented within a single page tree with TYPO3, administering several language versions is no great problem.

Page Information

> Provides an overview of basic data for the selected page; you can see, for example, what type the page is stored as in the cache, whether it is to be published on a time-controlled basis, whether only certain front-end user groups have access to it, or what meta-information is contained in the page for search engines.

View

The **View** module shows a page just as the visitor will get to see it later. It also includes small pencil icons that can be used to edit the page in View mode. In this mode you can view pages that have not yet gone online.

List

The List View gives direct access to pages and contents. More experienced users in particular prefer working with this. By activating **Extended View** and the so-called **clipboard** using the checkboxes at the foot of the Details View, together with various sort functions, it is possible to edit records together, in a target-oriented manner. You can find more information on the use of this function in section 3.10. The Localization View gives you an overview of the current state of the translation of the contents.

Info

In the **Info** module, important information on the current page is summarized. Depending on his or her access permissions, it provides the editor with different views of the database contents:

Pagetree Overview

Includes basic settings (e.g. time-controlled publishing or access permissions for front-end user groups), cache, and age, as well as an overview of the types of records contained in the pages that may be processed by the editor. If you operate this view over several layers of the page tree, then the fields listed in each case for entire groups of pages can be edited with one mouse click, using the pencil icon.

Localization Overview

The translation overview allows you to enter several page levels to inspect the state of the translations. At the same time new translation headers can be added to alternative page languages, and you can edit these and the translation of the content.

Log

This logs all changes made to the records for each editor; the view can be adjusted in the navigation bar in terms of the number of levels to be displayed and the time period for the modifications. In the **Details** column the history of individual records can be displayed and opened for editing with the **- > His** link.

Page TSConfig

Page TSConfig is not of much significance to the editor, and should be deactivated by the administrator; the view shows the page-specific and user-specific TypoScript details, which are important for administrators and programmers (the rule also applies here: what has been determined in one page is also valid for all the pages beneath it).

Hit Statistics

Hit Statistics are useful for the daily evaluation of user accesses. Provided that the `Simple hit statistics` extension is installed on your system, the administrator can quickly find a good summary of individual page impressions for the web site.

Access

If the module is released for the editor, he or she can have editing permissions displayed for individual pages, via the **User Overview** module.

Only if the editor is the "owner" of the respective page, that is, if he or she has created it, can the editor, using the pencil icon, transfer permissions to, or remove them from, a group of which he or she is a member, or transfer the ownership of the page entirely to a different group member. The **Permissions** module lists owner, group permissions, and permissions for everybody. Also, here the editor may only change permissions of the pages of which he or she is the owner.

Functions

The **Functions** module contains some practical help functions that can simplify the creation and administration of pages and contents. A prerequisite here, of course, is that the respective extension is installed and has been released for the editor. The various **Wizards** it contains allow entire page structures to be quickly created and sorted. The **Import** mode allows the import of entire page structures from a TYPO3 page tree. The **Text tools** allow specific text searches and the replacement of text passages in content elements.

In section 3.10.6 we will take a closer look at the use of this function in practical situations.

File

TYPO3 manages all resources, such as HTML templates, images, or documents, that are required to create a web site, on its file system in the `fileadmin/` directory. The editor is granted access to the branches of the file system required, according to his tasks. In addition to this, the administrator can more precisely determine the type of access: for example, whether the editor is allowed to upload, copy, move, delete, rename, edit, or create new files, or even recursively delete files.

Filelist

The **Filelist** submodule allows the editor to access the above-mentioned resources. The contents of the selected folder are displayed via the List View. You can also navigate here via the folder icons of the directory tree.

To make files accessible, they can be uploaded directly from the editor's local computer or network to the respective directory in TYPO3, via the context-sensitive menu. Here the same rules of thumb apply as mentioned earlier:

Click on icon =

>   Call file functions (copy element, cut, etc.)

Click on title =

>   View/Edit contents

3.4.4 Messages

In the **Messages** area, the editor will find a simple messaging system for internal project communication. The editor can use this to send and receive internal messages to individual members or to entire groups. New messages are displayed in the **User | Task center** module and stored in the Inbox folder [1]. Mail inboxes can be moved to an archive or deleted [2]. For a user who is sent a message to notice this before he next logs in, the sender can send a message directly to the e-mail address of the user. This assumes, of course, that the web server also has a mail server. Received messages [3] can be answered using the original message [4].

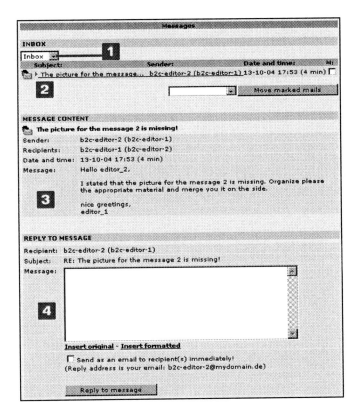

Figure 3.9

You have mail: mailbox folder [1], moving or deleting emails folder [2], message content [3], reply to messages [4]

3.4.5 Tasks

The **Tasks** function area contains the workflows for the editors, defined by the administrator. [3]. In the navigation bar the To-Do entries for the editors

---

[3] How workflows are created is described in section 4.9.

are displayed. Depending on permissions within a workflow, the editor may be authorized to start new tasks. An author can only carry out one processing step and make a status change, or cause the record to be released.

The Details View (3rd column) in the header shows incoming To-Do entries [1], outgoing To-Do entries [2]—as long as permissions for this exist—and the corresponding selected entries [3]. The status log [4] notes all the instances through which the record has passed until now, with the option of opening the record for editing. If the editor has completed his editing, or certain points are still unresolved, he or she adds a new status, with a comment, and sends the workflow on for further processing [5]. Only task managers are authorized to start a new workflow [6].

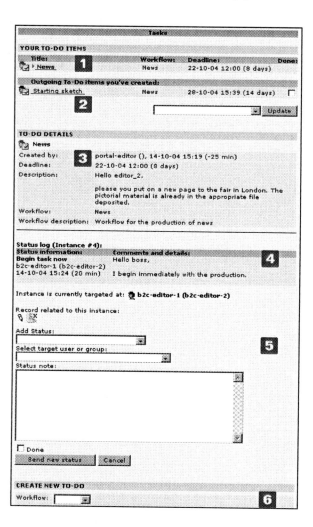

Figure 3.10

Editing a record by means of a workow via the **Task Center** *function area*

3.5 Pages as Containers for Contents

3.5.1 Site Structure, Page Tree, and Contents

Before we present the main tasks performed by the editor (creating pages and content), we would like to say a few words in advance about the basic concept of TYPO3. This is aimed primarily not at an understanding of the technical background but (a) at handling hierarchies safely when creating site structures, which are mirrored in the front end in the shape of menus, and (b) at an understanding of how content for individual pages behaves.

To illustrate this, we have chosen an example of a small application from the classical B2C-environment. This already contains different pages of various types (see the following figure). In the course of this book we will modify this example application. We would like to encourage you to set it up for practice purposes. In section 5.9 we will use a variation of this as a basis for the further development and configuration of front-end outputs. The page tree of the web site consists of individual pages, such as "Home", "Imprint", and "Contact", and the main areas "News", "Events", and "Products".

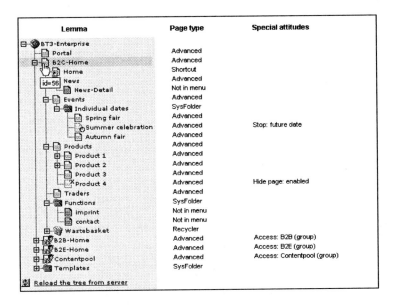

Figure 3.11

Page tree of the example web site

A page itself does not have content saved within it! It merely serves as a frame or container for those elements that are assigned to it.

The editor in TYPO3 hardly has to worry about technical issues. The only things that matter are at what points, in what sequence, and of which type he or she should create new pages and subpages in the hierarchy of the page tree, and how to move these around, if necessary. Handling is taken over by TYPO3 internally.

Each page has a unique identification number (ID). It appears if you move the mouse over a page icon, and it is also shown in the editing form of the page title. In the preceding figure you can see ID 56 for the page "B2C Home".

The editor does not need to know the IDs, even if they play a crucial role in the background. Internal TYPO3 links use IDs for reference. This has the advantage that the links remain, even if a page is moved about, since the IDs are never changed.

The site structure is shown in the page tree. This ordering principle should be very familiar to PC users. The tree stands on its head, so to speak: the globe (right at the top of the page tree) forms the roots (also called *root* or *Rootline*). Pages can be added to any point of the tree, which form branches. Individual pages, or even whole branches of the tree, can be moved. This structure also matches the navigation structure of the web site, because the menus are created from it.

What can also be seen from the various icons in the page tree are the different page types. TYPO3 already provides a number of preconfigured page types, which differ in their behavior and functionality. Certain settings are also made clear by the icons, such as hidden pages, access permissions, and time restrictions. Below we will explain the individual page types and additional functionalities in more detail.

3.5.2 Creating and Editing New Pages

Softlink **195486**

Creating new pages with TYPO3 is very simple: in the **Web** module area, select the **Page** or **List** submodule. The navigation area now shows the page tree with all those areas to which you have access. To create a new page, call the context-sensitive menu by clicking with the left mouse button on the icon for the page to which the new page should refer. Select the action **New**. In the Details view, pages or content can now be created in various ways, depending on the extensions installed and their permissions in the system. Depending on where you want to create the new page, select **Page (inside)** (page is created one level further down) or **Page (after)** (page is created on the same level). If you prefer to create the page via the **Wizard**, you can simply define the position by clicking on a positioning arrow.

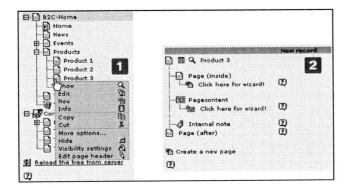

Figure 3.12

Context menu for the "Product 3" icon [1] and Detail view [2]

After defining the position, you are taken to the create page form. The basic structure of this Details view is always the same for pages and content elements: the header and footer contain icons for saving (floppy disk), saving and viewing (floppy disk with magnifying glass), saving and closing (floppy disk with X), undoing changes (X) or deleting the data record (trashcan with yellow warning triangle). If the data record has already been edited, editing steps can be undone using the **undo** button (wavy blue arrow). With two selection lists, you can either switch between two opened data records or initiate actions such as "Save Document" or "Clear Page Cache" [1].

Specifying the page type and entering the compulsory details (marked by a yellow warning triangle if the corresponding field has not been completed) is done through the form fields. These are organized by subject, in blocks. All page types have the blocks **Type** [2], **Pagetitle** [3], **Localization settings** [4] and **General options** [5] in common.

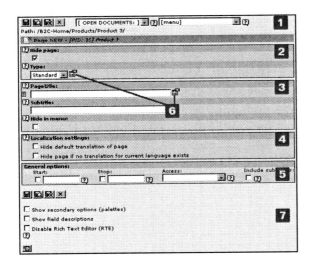

Figure 3.13

Figure 3.13 Details view with input form when creating a new page (type: Standard). Not visible here for the editor: the fields TSconf and General Record Storage page

Type

TYPO3 provides a series of predefined page types, simplifying daily work. They differ in terms of their functionality and their appearance in the front end. The most important ones for the editor are **Standard** and **Advanced**. The form block also contains the **Hide page** marker, with which a page can be switched online (visible) or offline (hidden). If a page is "hidden" (that is, not visible in the front end), this is marked by a faded page icon with a red cross.

Pagetitle

The **Pagetitle** is the only compulsory field when creating new pages. Within the advanced options (page type: **Advanced**), you can assign a so-called *Alias* to the page, and you can then call the page using the URL http://www.your-domain.com.

As a rule, pages are "cached"—they are generated entirely by TYPO3 and the result is stored in the database. Why is this done? It costs time and server capacity to generate a page. An already created page can be served much quicker. In order that the cached pages are still up to date, they are freshly generated every 24 hours. But this cache interval can be set individually by the administrator for each page or area. The editor can, however—assuming he or she has the appropriate permissions—overwrite the cache interval, or even specify that the page should not be cached at all (**No cache**).

This may be necessary for pages with content that changes by the minute, or by the second (e.g. stock market prices or in a forum).

Localization Settings

Here you can determine whether the respective page is translated into the default language in general, or if it remains off-line only if no translation is present.

General Options

Here you can define the behavior of a page for a time-controlled publication or for a page with restricted user rights. **Start** specifies the time at which the page will automatically be switched online (made visible), **Stop** is the time at which it will become invisible.

Date fields use the format "day-month-year", that is, "23-01-2004", for example. A tip: if you enter d and move with the tab key to the next field, the current date is entered automatically in the correct format. If you want the page, for example, to be published automatically in 14 days, simply enter d+14. With the **Access** fold-down menu, a page can be displayed in the front end exclusively for certain groups, and you can also specify whether a page should be visible or invisible after logging in to the front end. With the **Include subpages** marker, you can apply the above mentioned settings (Start, Stop, Access) to all sub pages of the page selected.

All form input fields contain context-sensitive help in the question mark icon. The **Form with a hand** icon [6] allows optional entry fields (**More options**) to be shown in the gray horizontal bar at the top (not shown in the picture). In the page footer [7] you can alter the Details View via checkboxes or restrict the functionality for all text context elements on this page. You can obtain a short description by clicking on **Show field descriptions**. Clicking on **Show secondary options (palettes)** displays the optional entry fields directly in the Details View. In this way you can decide if you want to have the form clear, or prefer to have all the options permanently displayed. Via the **Disable Rich Text Editor (RTE)** checkbox, the RTE can be activated or deactivated for all page elements that use it as an option.

3.5.2 Different Page Types

The page types define in the first instance what part of a page is visible in the front end and is displayed in the menus, or whether it is just serving as an invisible data storage for the back end. You can see what a page is used for from the icon in the page tree.

Standard

The **Standard** type is usually sufficient; it provides a simple selection of the most important information on a page, as already shown above. When changing to a different page type with more or different options, and switching back again, the extra entries outside the options of the **Standard** type are not lost. So if you have made entries in fields that are only available for the **Advanced** type, and you change this type to the **Standard** type, all the entries will still be available if you change back to the extended mode. From a technical point of view the page types are just different input dialogs for different sections of the same database table (Pages).

Advanced

The **Advanced** page type provides considerable advantages: meta-information can be specified here, and files and plugins can be integrated. You can also give the page a title different from the navigation title, so that the page can appear in the navigation of the web site with a different name than in your back end.

Meta-fields like **Abstract, Keywords,** and **Description** are important for external search engines and for the internal TYPO3 search function. Correspondingly informative titles are recommended when naming pages.

A number of extensions must be integrated directly into the page via **Contains plugin** for them to function. If **Files** are to be integrated from the file system or from your local network via the Element Browser, it depends on the configuration of the template whether and how they are displayed.

Figure 3.14

Integrating files from the file system via the Element Browser [1] or "Browse" [2]

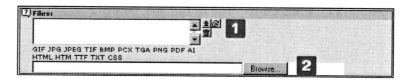

Depending on the task, you can search through pages or directories of the file system with the Element Browser, for example to integrate records, place links, or integrate files directly (e.g. images, video, sound, print). Individual files are integrated by clicking on the title, or are grouped together using the "+" sign. You can also create new folders or upload files from the local workplace to the server, from the page or content editor.

Figure 3.15

Element Browser accessing the file system: directory tree [1], individual selection of files via the title or multiple selection via "+" [2], file upload to the file system [3]

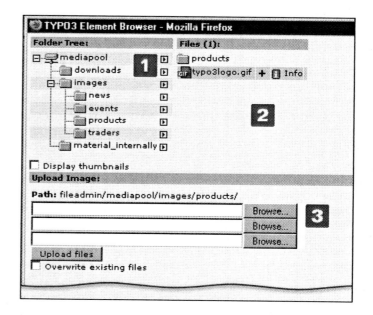

The assistant then translates your entries automatically into the already mentioned form syntax.

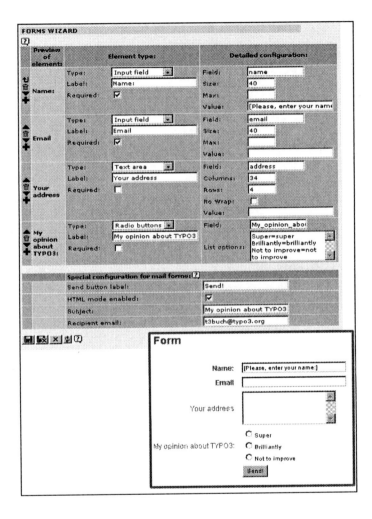

Figure 3.35

Form assistant and output in the front end

Search

A simple but powerful search function is already included in the basic TYPO3 installation. Using this, the front-end user can search through the site for contents, headings, and keywords. The corresponding form is created via the **Search** content type. If the search result is to be displayed on a separate page, and not on the same page as the form, a **Send to page** must be specified—this should be created beforehand (preferably of the **Not in menu** type).

Softlink **481291**

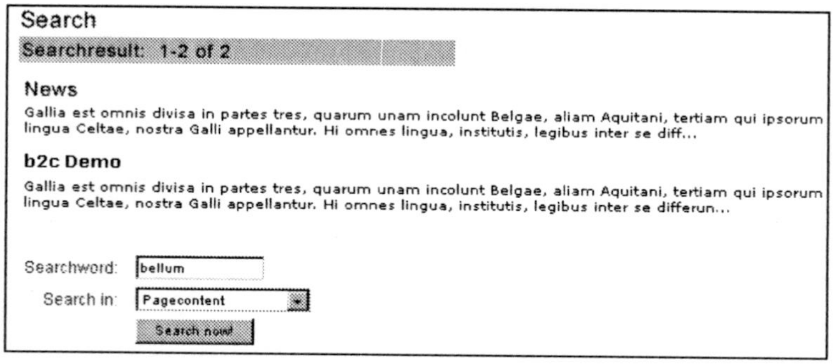

Figure 3.36

Input form with
search result on the
same page

Softlink **724882** Apart from the standard search, there is a more powerful variation, the *Indexed Search Extension*, which if necessary can be installed and used.

Login

Softlink **673847** Via the login form the (authorized) visitor reaches the areas in the front end reserved and protected for him. The login form is generated via the **Login** content type. A page can be defined as the **Send to page** via the Element Browser, to which the user is taken automatically after logging in. This assumes, of course, that front-end users and groups have been correctly set up and that the login form also "knows" where the user data is stored. In our example applications, B2B and B2E, the user data is located in the FEUser system folder.

Administrators can adjust this using TypoScript (fe_adminLib.pid = [uid]) or by specifying a second send to page with front-end user data. More information on front-end user systems and setting them up can be found in Chapter 4.11.

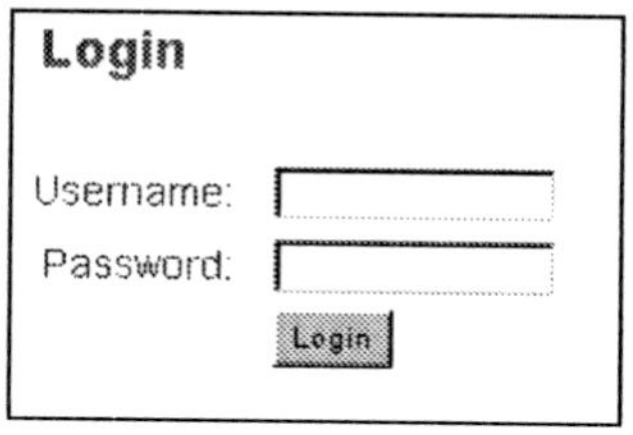

Figure 3.37

A simple login form

Textbox

The **Textbox** content type allows the editor to use predefined layout defaults for text passages. In the default configuration, text is inserted into a two-column table, where the left column can display images with various on icon). With these, files can be **Renamed, Information** can be displayed, and files can be **Copied, Cut,** or **Deleted.** At the bottom of the Details view you can have the clipboard or thumbnails displayed for images, by checkboxes [3]. The clipboard is always available in TYPO3 and allows you to move, copy, or delete files and contents. Even batch operations are possible with this. You can find more information on this in section 3.10.

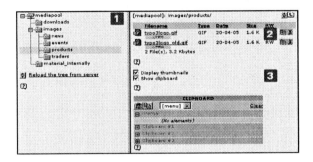

Figure 3.42

*Asset administration via the **File** | **File list** module: restricted access for the file mount mediapool*

The context-sensitive menu of the directory tree includes the actions **New** and **Upload Files.** You can create several folders at the same time via **New,** or create text files in the formats TXT, HTML, HTM, CSS, INC, PHP, PHP3, TMPL, JS, or SQL—but certain formats may be deactivated for security reasons. Using **Upload Files,** up to ten files can be uploaded simultaneously from the local network to the TYPO3 file system. When doing this, existing files can be overwritten, if requested, otherwise files with the same name are renamed by default with a sequential number.

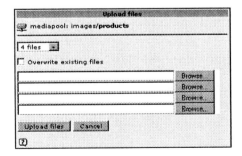

Figure 3.43

File upload of local-files to the TYPO3 file system

3.7.2 Inserting Assets into an Application

To upload files, you do not have to switch specially to the **File** module. Files can also be copied to the web server while pages are being created in the File Manager. The Element Browser can be used both to select existing files and to upload files [3] (overleaf).

*Softlink **525663***

105

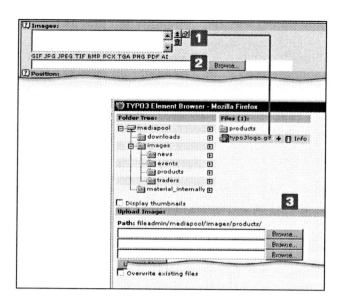

Figure 3.44

Linking files via
assets in the file
system [1] or one-off
via **Browse** [2]; the
steps shown are for
inserting an image
file in the **Image**
content element

You generally have two ways of handling file resources: selecting them from the file system via the Element Browser [1], or directly via the **Browse** button [2] (upload from the local workstation).

Depending on how the files were copied to the web server, they will be stored at different locations, which is of significance to their availability. A file in the file system is available for multiple use on the entire site through the Element Browser. This is not the case with a direct upload [2], because the file is stored in an internal system directory (uploads/), to which the editor has no access.

If the file is integrated several times via the Element Browser, TYPO3 recognizes this and numbers the image copies (automatically) with a unique combination of numbers (e.g. book.gif, book_01.gif etc.). The Rich Text Editor behaves in the same way when integrating graphics. The original file here (e.g. *.bmp) as well as the target format (e.g. *.jpg) are both stored and referenced as unique objects. This makes it impossible to mix files up, because unique data can be assigned to each record, and this does not get lost even if the original files are deleted from the file system. This function can be switched off via TypoScript (see Chapter 4.8).

Figure 3.45

t3-book.bmp was
integrated three
times in different
content elements

RTEmagicP_t3-book.bmp	332 KB	Bitmap
RTEmagicC_t3-book.bmp.jpg	3 KB	JPEG-Bild
RTEmagicP_t3-book_01.bmp	332 KB	Bitmap
RTEmagicC_t3-book_01.bmp.jpg	14 KB	JPEG-Bild
RTEmagicP_t3-book_02.bmp	332 KB	Bitmap
RTEmagicC_t3-book_02.bmp.jpg	14 KB	JPEG-Bild

3.8 Front-End Editing

In *front-end editing*, pages and contents are changed directly in the web site itself ("edit while you surf").

Softlink **615520**

For many users who, due to their jobs, only work occasionally on the system, this is certainly the simplest, quickest, most intuitive, and convenient method. The front-end editing mode is also highly suitable for specialized work steps, such as final text corrections. The administrator even has the possibility of restricting access of individual users and groups exclusively to front-end editing. After logging in, the user is then taken directly to the front-end.

If the editor is logged in to the back end, however, he or she is able to call pages in the front-end editing mode, via the context-sensitive menu or an appropriate button. As a rule his or her pages are displayed with small pencil icons [1] on all the content elements and processing bars [2]. Normal visitors do not get to see anything of this, of course.

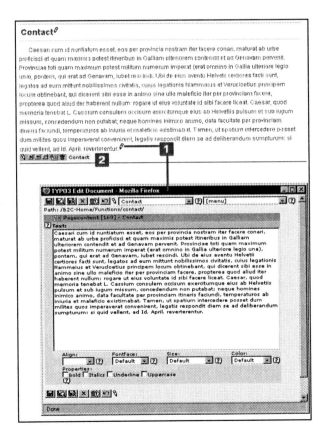

Figure 3.46

Front-end editing using the editing icons [1] and bar [2]

With the pencil icon, individual contents can be called in editing mode and are opened in a separate window. The editing bar also allows actions such as moving, hiding, and deleting the content, or new pages and content elements can be created.

A prerequisite for front-end editing is to have the correct configuration of permissions from the administrator. He or she needs to have activated both the template and the *Admin Panel* for the user or user group. With the help of the Admin Panel, the user can make settings in the **Editing** area, show or hide editing icons in the front end, or have a corresponding form field displayed.

Figure 3.47

Admin Panel in the footer of the front end

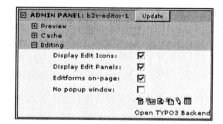

If front-end editing is enabled for the user, the pages are newly created and shown with editing icons and bars. Caching is not used in this. Although this slows down the delivery of pages slightly for the editor, there are no effects for the normal site user.

The front-end editing mode can be used as long as the user is logged in to the back end. If the session has been ended (or the editor logged out), the editing icons will no longer be shown.

3.9 The Rich Text Editor

Softlink **888606**

For the **Text** and **Text w/image** content elements, the editor has the *Rich Text Editor* (RTE) available. Depending on the configuration, the editor can edit text blocks in WYSIWYG mode ("what you see is what you get") and, for example, insert images by drag n drop or set links. When this is done, though, content and format details are no longer separated, since HTML tags are saved directly in the text. For this reason it is important that access to the RTE, and to the range of its functions, is specified very carefully. If an application is to adhere to rules of accessibility as defined by the W3C guidelines, with cascading stylesheets, for example, the RTE may not use any font tags, of course. The configuration is described in Chapter 4.8.4.

Softlink **788773**

The RTE is implemented in TYPO3 using ActiveX, and will therefore only work with the Internet Explorer on Microsoft platforms. Alternatively, you can use htmlArea, another Open Source project. The documentation can be found online here. If the editor is authorized to use the RTE, he or she can make personal settings (module: **User | Setup** or do this in the respective editing mode with the checkbox at the foot of the Details View).

If the RTE is activated, an editing bar with various icons is displayed in the **Text** form field.

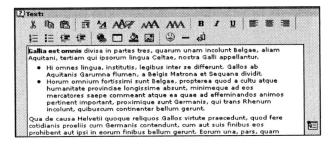

Figure 3.48

Rich Text Editor with all optionally available menu items

With the icon to the right of the text field, the RTE is opened in full picture mode. Changes to the original code can be examined with the **Source code** checkbox. For individual content elements the RTE can also be switched off with the corresponding checkboxes in the text entry field.

The functionality of most editing options is self-explanatory, and is shown separately with the rollover icon. For the sake of completeness, these are summarized in the following list. More complex functions are introduced separately afterwards.

Function	Shortcut	Description
Cut text	*Ctrl + X*	Text is cut out and stored in the buffer (also available via a context menu).
Copy text	*Ctrl + C*	The highlighted text is copied to the buffer (also available via a context menu).
Paste text	*Ctrl + V*	The text stored in the buffer is inserted at the position of the cursor (aso via context menu).
Paragraph type		A defined paragraph format can be selected for the highlighted text.
Character type		Classes are available for marking text passages, predefined by the administrator.

Table 3.2

Overview of RTE functions

Function	Shortcut	Description
Font Style		The highlighted text is shown in the selected standard font type. The display on the client side depends on whether that font type is installed there.
Font size		The highlighted text passage is given a font size from 1-7 in accordance with the HTML markup.
Text color		Depending on the configuration, there is either a color-picker or you have predefined colors.
Bold	Ctrl + B	The highlighted text is marked in bold (also via context menu).
Italic	Ctrl + I	The highlighted text is shown in italics (also via context menu).
Underlined	Ctrl + U	The highlighted text is underlined (also via context menu).
Align left		The block of text in which the cursor is placed is aligned to the left.
Centered		The block of text in which the cursor is placed is centered.
Align right		The block of text in which the cursor is placed is aligned to the right.
Numbering		Highlighted paragraphs are numbered sequentially.
Numbering signs		Highlighted paragraphs are given numbers with icons.
Decrease indent		Indentation of highlighted paragraphs is reduced or removed.
Increase indent		Indents highlighted paragraphs one or more times.
Insert link		Highlighted text passages within the text flow can be given links to other pages in the application.
Insert table		An assistant is available for inserting a simply structured table.
Background color		Background color is defined with a color picker or with predefined colors, depending on how the RTE is configured.

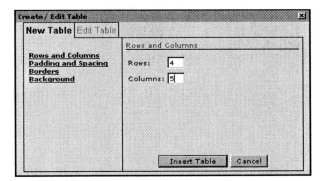

Figure 3.51

Assistant to create simple tables within the Rich Text Editor

3.10 Working Efficiently with TYPO3

Now that the back end, front-end editing, and standard content elements have been introduced, we will show you in this section how you can work practically with TYPO3, introducing the functions and working methods that will simplify and speed up your daily work, using a practical example.

3.10.1 Scenario

Our example is based on a content management scenario in which three different target groups from a TYPO3 installation are to be supplied with information:

1. *Business to Consumer* (B2C)

    End customers on a freely accessible web site; this part of the page tree will contain information intended for a broad audience. Our example involves a company with products, which are introduced on a separate page, as well as a news area on the start page, events, a list of dealers and standard contents such as Contact, Company logo, and Sitemap, summarized in the "Functions" area.

2. *Business to Business* (B2B)

    Partners and suppliers on a password-protected web site; this page contains extensive product information and sales-related materials for dealers.

3. *Business to Employee* (B2E)

    Employees in a protected intranet; this information forum for internal use contains organizational information for employees.

Although such a scenario is ideal for using the same content again in different locations, it is seldom implemented in this way in practice. For security reasons, intranet and internet web servers are always separated, so that the situation described here is only feasible if all web sites are created on the Intranet server, but the supply of the B2C und B2B web sites takes place on another web server in the Internet. More information on so-called "staging situations" can be found in Chapter 2.6.

3.10.2 Creating Page Structures

Softlink **189036**

In the first stage we will create the three web sites in the system.

Figure 3.52

Page tree as a result

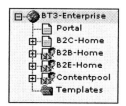

First a "Portal" page is created, and under this a "B2C Home" page. To create the subpages, we choose a quicker method. The **Web | Functions** menu contains a **Wizard** area, which is used to produce up to nine pages with a form. The wizard creates these pages as subpages, or after the currently selected page in the page tree. In our case, you first set up "B2C Home" without the wizard and then call this page in the **Web | Functions** module. There, select the wizard from the menu at the top right, and then the function **Create multiple pages**. The page titles are entered for the pages to be newly created; any fields not required are simply left open. The new pages are set up as the first subpages of the selected page, unless you specify, with the **Place new pages after the existing subpages** option, that they should be inserted after already existing subpages. With **Hide new pages** the pages are created as hidden pages, which should always be the case for web sites that are already publicly available.

The **Sort pages** function allows you to order the pages of the same level according to page title, subtitles, time of modification, and time of creation, or to reverse the current order.

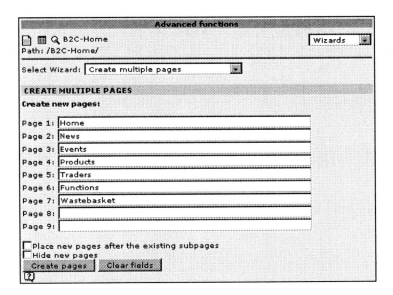

Figure 3.53

Wizard of the **Web | Functions** *module to effectively create and sort pages*

To create the B2B page tree, set the **Recursive Copy** option in the **User | Setup** module so that you copy at least one level when you save a page to the buffer. You now insert the copied page into "B2C-Home" by clicking again on the page icon of "B2C-Home" and adding it to the page tree with **Paste into.**

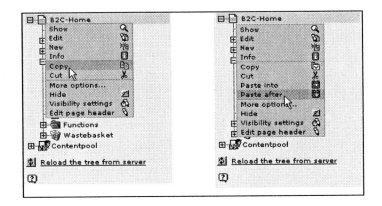

Figure 3.54

Copying and inserting a page

3.10.3 Serial Editing with the Buffer

It is often necessary to edit several pages or pieces of content in the same work process; the **Clipboard** is used for this, which displays the contents of the buffer and offers a number of editing options.

Softlink **965454**

It is activated in the List module with the **Show clipboard** checkbox at the foot of the Details View. If it is not already activated, you should also select the **Extended view** at the foot of the Details View. While the **Normal** [1] buffer can only take in one record at a time, the **Clipboards 1-3** [2] allow several pages or content elements to be included.

If the clipboard is activated, an extra icon appears in the List View for copying the relevant record to the normal buffer. If one of the **Clipboards 1-3** is activated, checkboxes appear after each element of the List View, making a multiple selection possible [3]. The information icon in the menu bar displays all the essential data for the record concerned.

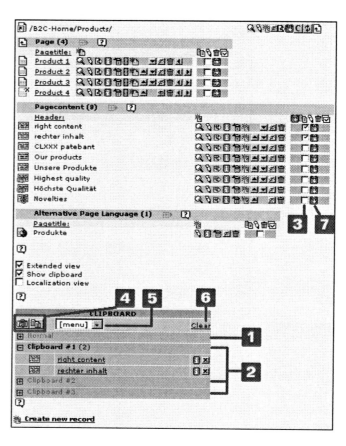

Figure 3.55

Clipboard in action: clipboard No. 1 is active, containing two content elements

With the photo icon, thumbnails of copied images are shown in the clipboard, and with the copy icon next to it you can choose between the mode for copying (orange icon) or moving (gray icon) for all elements [4]. The position where the elements should be inserted is defined with the corresponding icon in the List View (**Paste after; Paste into**) [7]. But the clipboard can also be used to open the records in it for editing, with the selection menu, or to delete them all permanently [5]. If there are several elements in the temporary buffer, they will all be displayed as edit forms, one after the other. If you only want to delete records from the temporary buffer, just click on the appropriate icon for each record, or on the button in the editing menu for the currently active clipboard [6].

Example

In our example, the first copy of the B2C tree in "B2B-Home" is renamed and two new pages are added to it: "Downloads" (sorted by "Dealers") and a SysFolder, "FEUsers" (sorted by "Functions"), to which the icon for front-end users was added in the page header with the option **Contains plugin**. With the clipboard activated, now select all the subpages of "B2B Home" in the List View and choose the **Edit marked** option.

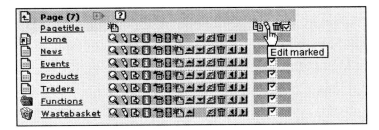

Figure 3.56

Selecting and editing options in the list view with activated clipboard

In the listing of forms in the title fields, you can now change the pages so that the following page tree is produced.

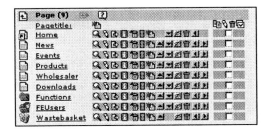

Figure 3.57

The page tree of B2B-Home after editing and adding two new pages

From the "Dealers" page, a "Wholesalers" page has now been created; in addition the shortcut has been moved from "Home" to the "B2B Home" (instead of B2C) page.

The B2E tree is still to be created; we will do this using the options for batch processing in the List View.

3.10.4 Editing Selected Fields

Softlink **729118**

The List View provides the best overview, and access as well, to records connected to a page, but it also has other functionalities, which might not be noticed at first. We recommend in general that you activate the **Extended View** and the **Clipboard**. For every data type, such as pages, the corresponding tables can be selected individually, to be viewed or edited, with the "**+**" icon in the area header [1].

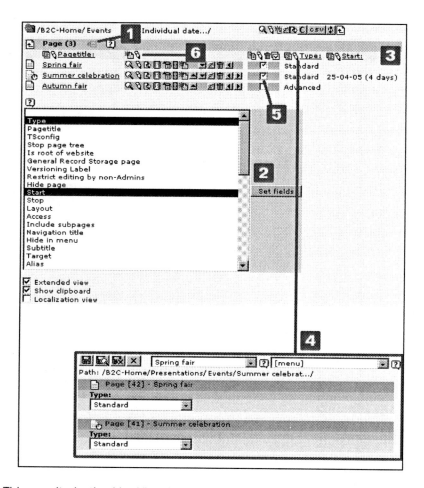

Figure 3.58

*In the **List** module, the corresponding **Type** fields are opened for editing via the **Page** table and the selection of two records*

This results in the List View being extended by a selection menu where individual fields can be selected for display [2]. In this figure the fields **Type** and **Start** have been selected [3]. By clicking on the title of the fields, you can sort up or down through the records in the selection. In this way you can quickly sort the news items alphabetically or by date of issue, for

If you open the whole data record of the page content, see that the values of the output data set are taken over [1] and to the comparison in the green selected areas [2] are preserved.

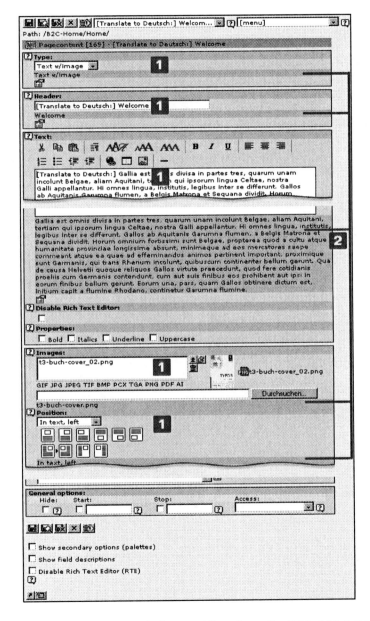

Figure 3.71

The whole data record

You can also start this translation workflow from the **Web | List** module directly. Moreover the check box **Localization view** can be activated. For missing translations of content elements the provision for providing the respective linguistic version is built in.

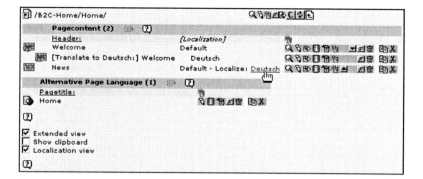

Figure 3.72

Missing and alternative translations

The module **Info | Localization overview** gives you the best overview about whole page branches and the current state of the translation workflows. New page titles of the alternative page language are added by selecting the checkboxes on the respective pages [1]. Page headers as well as contents can be edited. Further options such as **Hide default translation of page** [2] **or Hide page if no translation for current language exists** [3] are marked with different colors.

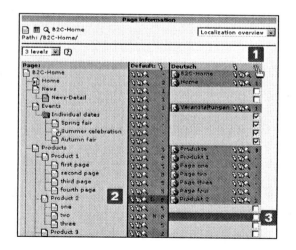

Figure 3.73

Overview of current state of translation workflows

4

TYPO3 for Administrators

4.1 Tasks and Targets of Administration

All tasks that do not involve installation and programming work for implementation on the one hand, and content production on the other, are assigned to the field of administration. This includes technical maintenance of the system as well as setting up, monitoring, and controlling the results of the content-production process. Opportunities to train to become a content manager have so far been rare, and most people involved in this field have not sought it out actively, rather it found them. And yet this is a business-critical task, because it is not only the image of the company which is maintained here, but also the company itself that is being managed. [1]

Seen in this light, "Content Management [...] is a part of both internal company information management and of knowledge management, and combines institutional aspects, company processes and technologies." http://www.nzz.ch/2003/05/23/em/page-article8TPZ8.html.

And yet the technology is only the vehicle here: "while the technology simplifies the creation, storage and dissemination of content, it is company processes and workflows which fundamentally enable the successful and profitable use of the technology." [2]

[1] People need to realize that the Web is no longer the thing about the thing; it is the thing itself. The site represents your organization. Content management is, indeed, managing the business." Suzanna Phelps-Fredette: "Content Management—How Can We Stop the Train Wreck?", transcript of a lecture at the IQPC Web Site Content Management Conference, San Francisco 2000, http://www.metatorial.com/papers/aha.asp

[2] Same source

The administrator plays the role of an architect who is permanently present, designing the information visible to the outside by organizing resources accordingly. Whether the work processes created for this have been designed by the administrator or by a consultant, either way the administrator must be highly familiar with the names and methods of the CMS used, in order to be able to influence the effect of the published information in terms of design, assessment, and optimization.

Unfortunately it is often forgotten, when a CMS is introduced, that the main expenditure lies in continuous content production. "While technology is obviously needed to implement a CMS, this investment is the simplest part of a CMS strategy." [3]

This experience has been widely documented and been shown to be true for nearly every CMS project. In addition to this, the introduction of a CMS always entails changes in new tasks for people and processes. Even where content was produced previously, widespread changes are probable: with its introduction, an improvement in existing processes should also be implemented, so that replanning and optimizing cannot be avoided.

The administrator thus stands at the center of the introduction and of the running operation; he or she is responsible for the processes involved. The work that needs to be done directly on the CMS involves creating the prerequirements for editorial work processes and portraying these with the means available in the system.

Actual content managers in the role of administrators watching over the system are frequently less technically-oriented employees, but they are usually responsible for the exterior image of the company, for marketing and PR or communication with customers (B2C), business partners (B2B), and employees (B2E). Most of their tasks in TYPO3 are appropriately supported by graphic wizards. These utilities cover a wide range of configuration options for the user interface and for assigning permissions to groups and users. Even where the use of system parameters is involved, namely with the TSConf system, a wizard is available to help those less technically well-versed to get started.

Consequently the administrator is also responsible for ensuring value creation from the CMS processes. The system can help here, both as a production environment and as an analysis tool. In this respect TYPO3 offers several internal information sources for statistical evaluations.

---

[3] Geoff Choo: "CMS strategy: Don't put the cart before the horse", TechRepublic Ins, 11 December 2001, ZDNet Australia: http://www.zdnet.com.au/insight/toolkit/weboperations/cms/0,39023923,20262306,00.htm

Apart from the predefined output options, there is also a powerful database interface where you can define specific queries yourself, which can be saved for later use.

This chapter introduces you to the basic problems faced, from the perspectives described, when preparing a content management environment, and illustrates the system of assigning permissions, various configuration options for the back end, as well as introducing tools for control and evaluation.

4.2 Planning and Implementing the Content Management Environment

It is a complex task to systematically define targets in new or existing processes using a content management application. This involves defining sources, frequency, and formats of contents, and planning and implementing the work steps associated with this to fulfil the editorial aims of the project.

One widespread method for analyzing, developing, and constructing such work processes and implementing them in a content management environment is the *Business Process Redesign* (BPR), which in combination with a *Rapid Application Development* (RAD), produces efficient project workflows and successful IT-supported business processes. We would like to briefly explain both these approaches below, providing a basis from which you can get to know these procedures better.

For our purposes it is sufficient to understand that every business process can be analytically dissected in the context of the BPR into a chain of elements. This analysis makes apparent the course of a specific task, with all its conditions, transformations, products, and decisions. This allows optimization potentials to be identified, which can frequently be sensibly supported by the use or modification of CMS technology. [4]

Deciding on a content management system is often the result of such a process analysis, which can serve here as a simple example of a fundamental optimization of the content production process: without CMS, the creation and maintenance of websites remains the preserve of experts with technical knowledge. The path that leads from the creation of information in the company down to communication with customers, employees, or business partners, has become considerably more effective and quicker through the use of CMS.

[4] An extensive theoretical representation with practical examples can be found in: Wil van der Aalst, Kess van Hee: "Workflow Management: Models, Methods and Systems", The MIT Press, Cambridge Massachusetts, 2002.

This is because the employees who have the necessary content knowledge available are themselves now in a position to publish this without any technical expertise. The business process for publishing information is simplified and accelerated.

Softlink **253617**

As a second example, a CMS could automatically replicate product data from a source that can be universally used, and display the annotations made by editors and then make the output available in websites, in the pre-printing stage, or also via Web services. Maintenance of core data would be optimized by the centralization and availability of enriched data in a kind of multipurpose information hub. A corresponding case example can be found via the softlink shown here.

Business processes should in general be result-oriented, realistic, and user-friendly. Where possible, information creation and processing should be combined, parallel activities merged, control mechanisms implemented, and information collected at source. [5]

These maxims can in many respects be adopted in a content management situation, for example by integrated companywide data storage in a single -source approach, by assigning user permissions intelligently and configuring the editing interface on a task-oriented basis, by transparent and simple procedures and continual performance reviews.

With TYPO3, processes planned in this way can be supported and displayed concretely through the permission system, by the optimized configuration of the editing interface, and by predefined workflows and commands. In addition, specialized system extensions can be developed and included, which improve this process support even more.

The methodical analysis and conception of the processes results in a description of the planned solution in a finely-detailed concept, which typically contains the following information:

- The site structure divided into topics

- The contents, sources, and formats (news, case studies, product datasheets, etc.

- The users involved, summarized in roles

- The work processes of these user roles in relation to the individual contents/formats along the information flow in the so-called content life cycle (see section 1.2.2)

[5] M. Hammer: "Reengineering Work: Don't Automate, Obliterate", Harvard Business Review, July-August 1990, S.104-112

4.3 Principles of Organizing Permissions in TYPO3

While the organization of content flows into the site structure and can be portrayed there directly, distinguishing individual users and permissions through analysis cannot be handled so intuitively, and requires knowledge of how the permission system works. This involves the following three fundamental issues:

Users and groups

> Global parameters can be assigned to these to control editing options.

Pages

> Access permissions for the roles "owner", "group" and "all others" can be defined for each page.

Controlling the editing interface

> The user interface can be configured on the page level or on the user r-/ group level.

In practice, the structure of the actual content is crucial in determining how it will be shown later as a page structure in a tree. The permissions of the employees involved are related to this page structure as far as work processes are concerned.

An analysis can be made, based on the type of tasks, of which functions are necessary for individual roles and which parts can be modified to simplify the user interface, and to lower the cost of training.

The result can be formally displayed in a matrix diagram with users and permissions. In many cases it will be sufficient to convert the corresponding settings directly in TYPO3, and to make these visible there by showing all affiliations via the **Tools | User Admin** module. This is a sensible and time-saving procedure, especially in the context of the Rapid Application Development approach described below.

This approach is based on the premise that it is crucial to the project's success to involve users with the relevant practical knowledge in the creation process. In software development, the method of Rapid Application Development (RAD) has been established for this purpose. This involves checking the conceptual approach of an IT project by regularly using prototypes of the system from an early stage, and in which users are intensely involved later on in testing and improving it. [6]

---

[6] James Martin: 'Rapid Application Development', Macmillan Publishing Co., Inc., Indianapolis, USA 1991; Wilhelm Hasselbring: 'Programming languages and systems for prototyping concurrent applications', ACM Comput. Surv. 32(1), 2000, p 43-79.

This approach ensures that planning and implementation remain closely linked, and that there will be no nasty shocks when putting theoretical ideas into practice in everyday situations.

TYPO3 is ideal for creating prototypes early on, for example to test the distribution of tasks with users and the organization of permissions in practice. A further positive result is that the users already become familiar with the options and functional principles, preparing them for the real work to come.

Because TYPO3 already enables you to introduce content and create page structures, even without a finished interface, you can start training immediately after installation and configuration. In this way, user orientation and the structure of content will become clear more quickly, and the insight gained can be used appropriately to design the interface, and for the production of applications.

4.3.1 Example Concept

The practical examples of this chapter are based on the following scenario. If you want to follow the individual steps in examples, it is important to know what the basic task is, and it is essential that you carry out the settings on pages and conditions as described in the example below.

Our example focuses on a situation in which the content management platform is to supply three websites. To the outside, the websites are distinguished by having three different domains, and have different, but related designs.

Portal

> The portal has content that is produced, maintained, and archived only for these pages by the relevant editors. In addition, the portal automatically includes content from the other websites that are present in the system.

Websites

> There is also a series of websites in the system that are edited by other editors. The websites in our example are aimed at different target groups and are named "B2C" (Business to Customer), "B2B" (Business to Business), and "B2E" (Business to Employee) accordingly.

> Each editor only has access to his or her own area and to the content pool (see following page) and produces news within a predefined workflow.

Products in the websites

> As an organizational unit beneath the website level, we are assuming that there are individual product areas, all of which are maintained by separate users (product managers) for this level.

Content pool/Media pool:

> Content that editors of individual websites can use for themselves is stored in a non-public area; they can also save content there for general use and/or for further processing. The content can be inserted from here with the **Insert record** content element, or be copied, depending on whether it will be further processed or not.

This means that at least one group is necessary for editing the portal and a group each for each of the websites. Assigning permissions in the system by means of workflows and actions enables the workflow of editors to be controlled for news in all sites and ensures that responsibilities for production and publication can be clearly assigned.

4.3.2 Implementation Steps

To set up the system, the following steps are now necessary, in the sequence specified:

1. Setting up a basic page tree to which permissions can be assigned

2. Setting up the user groups to which users can be assigned

3. Setting up users who can be assigned to groups

4. Setting up workflows and commands in any order you wish

Our example tree has the structure shown in Chapter 3.10.

In the next step we will create the user groups as the basis for the permissions system.

4.4 Back-End User Administration

Editors and authors work on content behind the scenes of the website. Their perspective is the so-called back end, which in many respects can be adjusted to the tasks of the individual participants—down to moving working options to the website itself.

4.4.1 Setting up User Groups

Permissions that are assigned equally to different users are defined in groups. Groups with fewer permissions become subgroups. This results in a hierarchy, like the one below:

Group A: Filemount a/

Subgroup A.1:   Filemount a/1/

Group A.1 receives all the permissions of group A, as well as its own permissions. If the group is a member of several other groups and these permissions contradict each other, then the overall positive permissions are valid. If group A does not have the permission to edit a page, but group B has this permission, a user belonging to both groups can edit the page.

The advantage of nesting groups is that all basic settings for users can be maintained in a small number of groups (just one in our case), so that specific settings in the corresponding record only need to be made for one group.

The user groups should be set up in our example as follows:

"Global" group

> Contains all the settings that should apply for all groups; in addition the script can be assigned read and write access for the entire file tree, and the actual access can be sufficiently set via the start points, which define the visible section. These start points are assigned by DBmounts. The "Global" group also contains the DBMount "Content pool".

"Portal" group

> Maintains the portal page and is responsible for the release of news from all levels of the workflow.

Groups for each website

> These contain only the assignment of the respective website branch ("B2C", "B2B", "B2E") of the file tree as well as the filemount for saving their own files.

"Products" group

> This group accesses a part of the website trees and also has its own filemount.

To create a user group, change to the List View and click on the name of your installation next to the globe at the top of the file tree, to reach the level named "Rootline" containing the system-wide records. You can add a new back-end user group with the link **Create new record**.

The form is divided into different areas:

Access Data

Enter the name of the group here. You can optionally configure the user group by specifying a domain in the **Lock to domain** field, so that the members can only log in to the system via a specific address, like www2.yourdomain.de/typo3. This is useful if different domains are pointing to your webserver or if you want to restrict access to TYPO3 to your intranet.

Access Lists

The **Access Lists** contain all options for setting the backend interface and access to every single input field and data area for groups. On selecting **Include Access Lists,** the form is reloaded. All entries that have just been made should therefore be saved. You will see a corresponding warning if you mark the selection field.

The Access List contains a selection menu listing all the input fields, each entry can be selected by clicking on it. To select various fields, click entries while holding down the ctrl-key. The individual selection fields are as follows:

Modules

The menu items on the left-hand page of the back end display are referred to as **modules.** An editor should see at least the elements **Web | Page, Web | List, File,** and **File | File list.**

It is useful to provide the possibility to individually adjust the back end, including the chance to change your own password, via **User | Settings.**

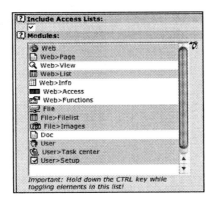

Figure 4.1:

After selecting **Include Access Lists,** the **Modules** section will appear after the form has been reloaded.

Tables (listing)

Select from this list the database tables that are to be shown to the user. The specified tables grow with the number of extensions installed, some of which also have tables available. After installation the permissions should therefore be checked, where appropriate, in this and in the next selection field.

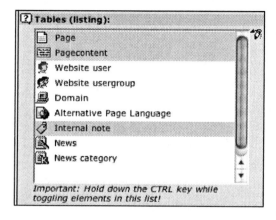

Figure 4.2:

Selecting the database tables that the user may see

Tables (modify)

Choose the database tables that should be made available to the user from this table.

Page types

Here you can specify which page types may be set up by the members of this user group.

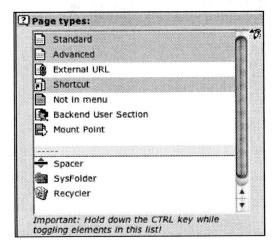

Figure 4.3:

Selecting the page types that the user may set up

Allowed excludefields

Using *excludefields*, you can define much more precisely than with the **Tables** settings exactly which input fields will be seen by a user group.

If this field has been defined as an excludefield, and is not explicitly allowed in this list, it will remain invisible to the user who is a member of the edited group.

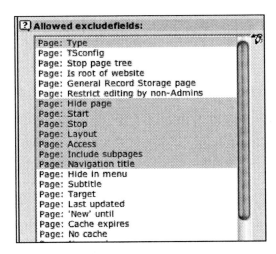

Figure 4.4:

Selecting the fields that the user will be shown for editing

Explicitly allow/deny field values

This option has been added in version 3.7.0 as a long-awaited answer to the problem of disabling content types for individual groups. Previously those could only be hidden via TSConfig-options.

Selecting any of the content types disables them for the active group. As an absolute minimum "Script" and "HTML" should be selected for security reasons.

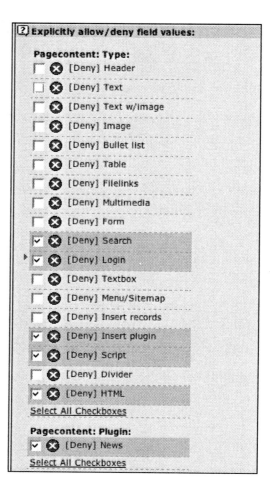

Figure 4.5:

Disabling content types for individual groups

Limit to Languages

The access of groups to language versions of the site can be limited here.

Custom Module Options

Back-end Module Extensions can add to this section with their own custom selection options.

DB Mounts

Database (DB) Mounts allow an entry point in the page tree to be assigned to the user. If the user belongs to several different groups, and an entry point is defined multiple times, then it will also be displayed to the user multiple times. You should therefore ensure that there are no redundant settings here covering different groups. In our example you should set up the groups as follows:

Group	File
Global	Content pool
Portal	Portal
Products	Products
B2C	B2C home
B2B	B2B home
B2E	B2E home

Table 4.1:

Example groups and associated filemounts

Filemounts/file releases

This refers to the directories in the file system assigned to user groups where users can store their data. These assignments are represented by means of so-called *filemounts* in the database. As records that are valid system-wide, the filemounts are saved in the Rootline, as are the users and groups. They can either be saved there or accessed in the group entry form on the right next to the selection field, via three further icons for "Edit", "Add", and "Show list".

To be able to define a filemount, the administrator must have set up corresponding subdirectories in the `fileadmin` directory, via the **File | List** module. The actual names of directories in the file system and the names of the filemounts are independent of each other. In our example we will give the following names to the previously created directories, in the **File releases** dialog:

Group	Filemount Label	Path
Global	Mediapool	mediapool/
Portal	All Files	files/
B2C	Files B2C	files/files_B2C/
B2B	Files B2B	files/files_B2B/
B2E	Files B2E	files/files_B2E
Product	Files P	files/files_p/

The name that is later shown to users is entered in the Label field. In the
Path field the file path is entered relative to the `fileadmin` directory
located in the web directory of your web server. Alternatively an absolute
path can be specified. In both cases the pathname must be terminated
with a slash.

Hide in Lists

This option serves to suppress the display of the group in the **User
| Tasks** module as well as in the **Web | Access** module. In this way
it can be avoided that users in the **User | Tasks** module send
ToDos or e-mails to global groups that were only setup for administrative purposes.

Subgroups

With the **Subgroups** option, the corresponding group can be
assigned to other groups as a subgroup whose permissions and
settings are inherited by the current group. In our example we will
assign the "Global" group as a subgroup to all groups, so that their
settings will be acquired.

TSConf

The final input field of the dialog enables configuration with
TypoScript. This area named **TSConf** is discussed in more depth
in section 4.8.

With **Save and close** the input is finished and the form is closed. If you
have used the **Include Access Lists** option when entering data, the user
group just edited is given a red icon in the List View. User groups in which
no further settings have been made are marked in blue.

4.4.2 Setting up Users

After the groups, it is now the turn for users to be set up, who can be assigned to these groups. The dialog for setting up users is different from that for groups only in terms of assigning permissions, with the options for configuring file access in the file module.

Users should always have their own user accounts, since apart from managing permissions, these can be used in many places in the system for working together and for administrative purposes.

- User actions can be traced by a log function.

- Users can communicate, via the **User | Tasks** module, using simple groupware functions (news, ToDos, notes).

- Users can make their own settings in terms of the display and function of the back end, or have customized work environments assigned to them by the administrator.

In the next step we add a user to each group, so that we can later test the configuration. Back in the Rootline view of the system, select **Create new record** and **Backend user**. These are the individual sections of the form:

Access Data

The first form section contains the input fields for user name, password, group affiliation, and the option to bind a user to one domain.

User names may only contain letters in lowercase, and spaces are not allowed. When you enter a password, it remains visible until it is saved for the first time, but is then stored as an MD5 hash in the database and is also transferred in this form to the back end when logging in to the web server. The consequence of this is that passwords that have been lost cannot be read out again, but must be newly assigned.

User Groups

Membership of user groups can be regulated via the selection field. The options on the right link the user dialog with the creation, editing, and display of user groups. The order in which the groups are specified is of significance in assigning permissions. New pages created by the user always belong to the first group in the list. This can be overwritten by TSConfig, just as the permissions of users, groups, and all others can be adjusted. An example of this can be found in section 4.8. The **Lock to Domain** option helps to ensure, in systems with several Internet domains, that users can only log in under their own domain.

Admin

The next section of the form contains the **Admin** option, which grants the user unrestricted permissions in the system. Where possible, this configuration should only be available to *one* user in the system, or at least be used very sparingly. With a few exceptions, a user equipped with administrator permissions is in a position to irretrievably destroy all content and settings.

User Data

In the next form block, user data should be entered; the user can change this data via the **User | Settings** module, although he or she has no access to the entire user record.

DB Mounts and Filemounts

The system of filemounts and DB mounts has already been described in section 4.4.1. While markings for **DB mounts** and **filemounts** are removed in the **Mount from Groups** option, the user is stopped from inheriting the group settings in this respect. In addition the permissions available to the user in terms of files in his or her filemount can also be influenced.

TSConf

Possibilities of user configuration via TypoScript are described in section 4.8.

With **Save and close** you exit the form, and the user is created. If you now leave the system and log in again as one of the newly created users, you can check your settings.

Example

Set up users for the groups "Portal", "B2C", "B2B", "B2E" as follows:

Table 4.3:

Example users

User	Group membership
Portal-editor	Portal
B2C editor 1	B2C
B2C editor 2	B2C
B2B Editor	B2B
B2E Editor	B2E

Setting up the previously mentioned product managers will be done later through the functionality of commands (see section 4.10).

4.5 Administration of Users with the Tools | User Admin Module

The **Tools** module contains an administration and analysis interface, in **User Admin**, which plays a significant role in the everyday work of the administrator. The tool helps to evaluate the current permissions situation by various criteria, and to make changes where necessary.

The current settings for an individual user or group (if you have previously selected groups for display) are shown by clicking on the user or group name. Access permissions in the page tree assigned to this user that are insufficient are also shown here. The other settings correspond to the listing shown overleaf. The options for editing records function in the same way as those in the list module.

A special feature is included in the **SU** option in the list of users. If you click on this icon for *Switch User*—similarly to the UNIX command of the same name—the current admin user switches to the user account selected. This is very useful for checking settings. However, there is no way back, apart from logging out and logging in again with your own login data. In this way the administrator can slip into any user role he wants, whatever the case, even if he or she doesn't know the current password of the user.

The following options are available for displaying users and groups in the evaluation overview, which can be used alone or in combination:

Option	Meaning
Filemounts	Comparision of users by directories assigned
Webmounts	Comparision of users by entry pages in the page tree
Default upload path	Path for file uploads from page elements
Main user group	First user group membership
Member of groups	Other user groups whose members are users
Page types access	Page types that users may create
Select Tables	Database tables that the users may view
Modify Tables	Database tables that the users may edit
Non-exclude fields	Fields that the user may edit
Explicit Allow/Deny	Page content elements the user may not insert
Limit to Languages	Language versions which group members may or may not edit
Custom Module Options	Permission settings added by a back-end module extension
Modules	Back-end modules accessible to users
TSConfig	TSConfig settings for this user
TSConfig HL	TSConfig settings for this user in highlight mode

Table 4.4

User and group display

If you have followed the entries mentioned in the previous sections, the user administrator will appear as follows after the **Main User Group** and **Member of Groups** have been marked:

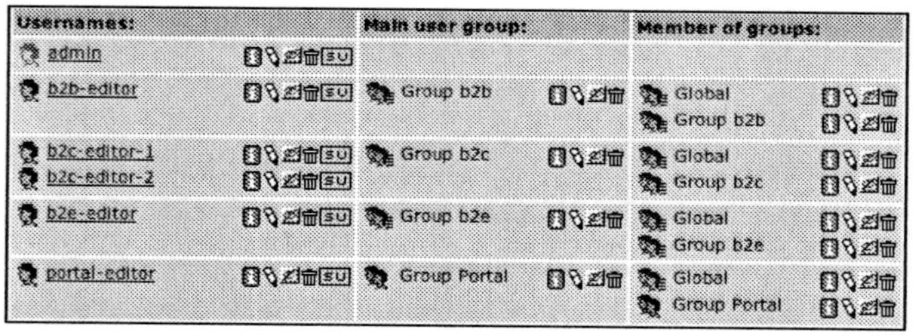

Figure 4.6:

Display of all group membership (right) and of primary group membership (middle)

With this division of users, it is easy to maintain settings via mutual base groups ("Global"), and at the same time assign completely separate work areas and separate page trees. To check settings for individual user groups and fine-tune them, you can slip into the respective roles with **SU** and check the range of functions available to the user concerned.

ATTENTION: to be able to edit pages, these must be released for access by the module described below.

4.6 Access Permissions on the Page Level

The access module allows you to assign permissions to users, groups, and all others in a similar way to the Linux file system. These permissions are initially set automatically when a page is created, irrespective of who has set up the page. The creator of the page is automatically its owner, and the group that is listed first in the list of groups in which he or she is a member is taken over here as the group. This value, as well as automatically assigned permissions, can be overwritten by TSConf and set individually (see section 4.8).

The **Web | Access** module always relates to the current position on the page tree when it is called, which is displayed in the top left corner. The **User overview** mode is active when it is run. This display mode shows the pages in the tree to a depth that can be configured. The **Permissions** mode available for selection shows the pages called with the permissions assigned to the owner, the group, and to all others.

After a page is called, on clicking on the pencil icon, a form appears that enables owner and group permissions to be assigned for this page. Finally you can determine the level of child pages down to which the current settings should apply.

Example

Change to the access module and click in the page tree on "Content pool". Clicking on the pencil icon there will take you to the editing form.

Assign this page and the pages lying below it to the "Global" user group and assign permissions as shown in the following figure. If you save your entries, you are returned to the user overview. Now select the page again for editing and reset the permissions just for this top page, by restricting the levels setting to the current page. In this way you have effectively created a situation in which users of a group can edit all subpages, but not the parent page, without you as the administrator having to edit the configuration for individual pages.

The final result should now look like this:

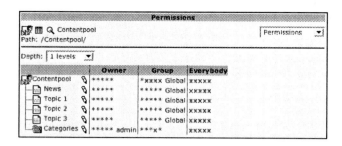

Figure 4.7:

Showing access permissions in the **Web | Access** *module*

In order to make all parts of the page tree also available to each of the users, it is best to assign all corresponding permissions to the "Global" group, except for the respective "home" pages and any other pages that should not be changed. The actual access has already been restricted by the entry points into the page tree for the respective groups.

4.7 Front-End Editing for Backend Users

One of the greatest advantages of TYPO3 has not even been mentioned yet: we refer to the possibility of allowing users to work directly on the website itself, entirely without, or as an alternative to, the back end. TYPO3 by default supports the possibility that users can edit contents in the preview after a page has been called, and add new pages. Using a simple extension, users configured in this way can also be moved directly to the website, that is, the so-called *front end*, and even work as "frontend-only" users.

A third possibility consists of guiding the editor by hyperlink from another page of your website to the login page and providing this link with a parameter that will take him or her, after logging in, back to the website with editing options, instead of into the back end. The back end therefore remains accessible for the editor, if required.

A corresponding link, which leads the user back to the start page of the website after authentication, looks like this:

```
<a href="typo3/index.php?redirect_url=../">Backend login
with redirection to the frontend</a>
```

The *Admin Panel* is the switchboard in the front-end editing module, a compilation of the most important editing functions in a simple user interface. Of course the Admin Panel and the options it provides can also be customized individually.

Administrators are automatically allowed to use *front-end editing*. To give a user this possibility as well, the following settings are necessary:

4.8 TSconfig—Options and Interface Control

TypoScript is not only used for writing templates. With the same syntax—except for the missing options of *Constants* and *Conditions*—values can be defined similarly to the Windows Registry for system configuration. This can be done on two different levels:

User TSConfig

Per user and per group, TSConfig can be used to influence the display of the back end globally, or just through individual back end modules.

Page TSConfig

On the page level, TSConfig can be usedto configure individual areas of a website accordingly.

A **User TSConfig** setting can be used to overwrite a configuration value of a page tree specifically to enable an administrator to have a different display, for example, than a user with a restricted task area.

Entering **Page TSConfig** properties in the header of a page will always apply these properties to all subpages of this page as well. To give administrators a chance of working quickly with this system, a tool was developed, called *TypoScript Property Lookup Wizard*.

4.8.1 TSConfig Wizard: TypoScript Property Lookup

If you click on the **TS** icon to the right of the input field in the page title or in the user or group form, an online help for all TSConfig options available here will open. This online reference is available in every TYPO3 installation, and the TSConfig wizard also allows you to take up values directly into the TSConfig input window.

It is very simple to use: one click on the linked value causes the value to be taken over in the **TSConfig** window of the main input dialog, and the wizard is closed.

If you click on "+" instead of the name, parameters are taken up in the entry window of the editor. With **Wrap**, brackets are placed around the parameter. **Indent** and **Outdent** are used to indent lines, in order to increase clarity.

4.8.2 User TSConfig

For each group or user, TypoScript offers a range of configurations using TSConfig. You cannot obtain an overview if you call the wizard in the form for editing users or groups. As with the object tree on the template level, we call this overview the **User** or **Page TSConfig** tree.

The various sections in the **User TSConfig** tree refer to the following configuration options:

admPanel

> Settings for the Admin Panel in the front end

Options

> Global settings for the back end

Setup

> Contains the branches **Default** and **Override**; the configuration options contained in the **User | settings** module can also be controlled here via TypoScript. Both branches then contain the same parameters, but differ in their effect. With **Default** you can, as the administrator, influence the default settings that the user finds in the module. If the user sets the option in this module to restore the default configuration, the system returns to the settings configured by **Default**. With the **Override** parameter, parameters can be preset for users in the **User | settings** module, which cannot be changed. This can be useful from the perspective of the administrator, to prevent the possibility of pages being deleted recursively, for example.

Mod

> The **Mod** area refers to the modules of the **Web** area. A series of parameters are available here for configuring the submodules of the **Web** module.

ATTENTION: the configuration options for the **Info** module are currently not functional!

Example

First we indirectly configure several viewing options for all groups, through settings in the "Global" group.

Because the layout uses only a middle and right column, the display of the left-hand and **margin** columns in the column view in the back end is pointless. With the following entry, the columns are selected for display:

```
mod {
   SHARED.colPos_list = 0,2
}
```

The columns are controlled as follows: Left=1, Normal=0, Right=2, Margin=3. In order to obtain a matching backend display for all users of this group, you can switch off the display of thumbnails in the back end, for example, and cause the user to be redirected to the **User | Tasks** module after logging in, instead of to the help page:

```
setup.defaults {
   thumbnailsByDefault = 0
   startInTaskCenter = 1
}
```

Settings for users can be viewed and compared in the **Tools | User Administrator** module with the **TSConfig** and **TSConfig HL** options. **TSConfig** calls up the same page view as the **Page TSConfig** browser of the **Info** module. **TSConfig HL** shows the values in the input syntax with colored highlighting.

4.8.3 Page TSConfig

Further options on the page level can be added to **User TSConfig**. The following options can therefore also be assigned to users and groups in their **TSConfig** fields. Conversely the options of **User TSConfig** cannot be entered in the pages. On the page level, the following areas are available:

TSFE

Contains an option allowing a user session to be transferred.

Mod

Controls the menus of the back-end modules, which can be influenced here

TCEMAIN

Concerns options that can be set for each system table, such as those for number of entries and time limits for the editing history; it also allows permissions to be assigned for a page tree independently of the user and group settings for creating pages.

TCEFORM

Refers to settings in the back-end forms; all input fields in the back end can be influenced by this.

RTE

The *Rich Text Editor* can also be adjusted via TSConfig. Because many options are not compatible with the design guidelines that apply for websites, this is normally restricted.

TCEMAIN Examples

TCEMAIN allows permission settings for creating new pages to be configured for groups or for pages. The entry in the homepage of a tree,

```
TCEMAIN.permissions.groupid = 4
```

specifies that new pages in this tree automatically belong not to the main user group, but to the "Global" group. The group is identified by its UID (in our example, "4") in the database. The UID is also displayed in the back end if you click on the information icon in the Extended List View or move the mouse over the icon in the List View.

With the same entry in the "Global" group, to which all other groups belong, all pages are made available to all others for editing, as long as they have access to them; in this way they do not have to be released specifically by the users of the group (or by the administrator) for users of a different group.

After new elements have been permanently assigned to a group, the permissions for this group can be set in terms of pages. The permissions.group key is used for this:

```
TCEMAIN.permissions.group = show, editcontent
```

The available values are **Show** (show in the back end), **Editcontent** , **Edit** (edit page header), **New** (create new subpages),and **Delete**.

When copying elements in the TYPO3 back end, automatic suffixes are added to the name. Thus "Page 1" becomes "Page 1 (copy)" after being copied and inserted. This feature can be switched off with:

```
TCEMAIN.default.disablePrependAtCopy = 0
```

A complete list of the **TCEMAIN** options can be found via the softlink shown here.

The TypoScript keys for influencing individual tables can be found via the softlink shown here.

TCEFORM Examples

With **TCEFORM**, all input forms can be influenced in terms of the display and naming of options. The notation used is as follows:

```
TCEFORM.[tablename].[fieldname].[TSConf_key] =
    value.
```

The TSConf keys and the values are defined in the reference under the softlink shown here.

First we exclude a number of content types from the selection of our "Global" user group, for security reasons:

```
TCEFORM.tt_content.CType.removeItems = search, login,
                div, script, html
```

In particular the elements `script` and `html` should always be suppressed in every installation, because they represent a serious security risk in the hands of experienced attackers who have gained access to the back end. But they are still available in the wizard, which is automatically displayed if you select the **Create new page content** option. We will therefore suppress the display of this wizard with the following entry in the "Global" group:

```
mod.web_layout.disableNewContentElementWizard = 1
```

In the default configuration (without extensions, which expand `tt_content`), the following elements can be selected, and are added with the expression in the "keys" line:

Table 4.6:

Elements in entry forms

German	English	TS key
Überschrift	Header	header
Text	Text	text
text m/ bild	Text w/image	textpic
Bild	Image	image
Punktliste	Bullet list	bullets
Tabelle	Table	table
Dateilinks	Firelinks	uploads
Multimedia	Multimedia	multimedia
Formular	Form	mailform
Suchen	Search	search
Login	Login	login
Textbox	Textbox	splash
Menu/Sitemap	Menu / Sitemap	menu
Datensatz einfugen	Insert record	shortcut
Plugin einfugen	Insert plugin	list
Script	Script	script
Trenner	Divider	div
HTML	HTML	html

The names in each of the elements can also be adjusted, by being overwritten. To do this, you must know the table and field names as they are written in the database. The field names are taken from the database structure, which you can call via **Module | Configuration**. The **$TCA array** contains all the fields of the database table, in the **tt_content** subitem, in which page content can be stored.

Headers can be overwritten with your own names in the following form:

```
TCEFORM.[tablename].[fieldname].[position] = value
```

The following line of TypoScript thus renames the standard header in the **header=type** field from "Layout1" to "Middle/Header".

```
TCEFORM.tt_content.header_ textbf{layout.altLabels.0}
    = Middle/Header
```

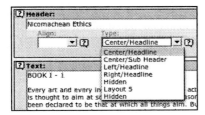

Figure 4.8:

Options from the header menu, with your own names

With the **removeItems** option, values can be completely excluded from the selection lists:

```
TCEFORM.tt_content.menu_type.removeItems = 3,4,5
```

An integer is added to the value, defining its position in the selection menu. The above line therefore hides the entries in the third, fourth, and fifth positions of the "Menu/Sitemap" page content element.

4.8.4 Adjusting the Rich Text Editor

The *Rich Text Editor* (RTE) is the WYSIWYG editor in the TYPO3 system, which provides users with various formatting options and several wizards, based on Microsoft Internet Explorer technology. In principle, all the options offered by Internet Explorer are implemented, even if most of these options in practice are not compatible with conventional design guidelines in terms of the layout. As a rule, the RTE range of functions is heavily restricted, and where required, can be adjusted to your own format specifications, which are fully configurable in the RTE.

The Rich Text Editor essentially has the following configuration interfaces:

1. Configuration of the input fields for which the RTE should be made available; the RTE can be given a different configuration for each of the input fields.

2. Switching on or off the editing options available in the menu bar.

3. Configuration of the options for formatting paragraphs and characters.

4. Influencing the transformation function for entries in the RTE when saving and for output from the database.

Restrictive RTE Configuration

Our first example is limited to a very plain variation, for the reasons described, but in our experience it is still the recommended configuration for most cases.

The RTE can be switched on or off for parts of the page tree via the corresponding **Page TSConfig** field.

First we configure the RTE so that it is only available in the **Text** and **Text w/image** content elements, even if extensions are installed that use the RTE:

```
RTE.default.disabled = 1
RTE.config.tt_content.bodytext.types {
  text.disabled = 0
  textpic.disabled = 0
}
```

In the next step we specify that all existing options, headers, and other formatting should no longer be included in the text field itself, but that only the standard formatting (to make restoring easier for the editor) and a formatting for quotes should be available. Suppressing headers in RTE fields is especially useful, because this forces editors to define text with various sections into separate content elements, which helps to improve clarity in editing and also allows other options, such as section menus, to come into play.

```
RTE.classes {
  highlight {
    name = Highlight
    value = font:bold; color:navy;
  }
  quote {
    name = quote
    value = font:italic 15px; margin-left:20px;
  }
}
  RTE.default.classesCharacter = highlight, quote
```

Via **User TSConfig** you can only configure which menu options are visible for the respective user or group in whose TSConfig field the entry is made. The options configured here are available to all members of the "Global" group, which is consequently all users of the system, with the following entry in the **TSConf** field for the group:

```
options.RTEkeyList = class, bold, italic, link
```

The editors can now see the the menu bar as shown in the following figure.

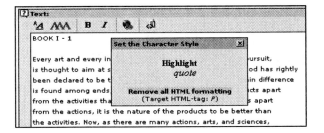

As you can see, the option to insert tables and images through the menu has also been suppressed. As an alternative there are special page content elements for this, which are easier to control in terms of a uniform appearance, and also preferable for reasons of clarity.

Extensive Configuration

The Rich Text Editor has several options in the default display that are not yet visible, and have to be added. These included a user object with which you can add your own definitions.

With the following entry—for example in the **TSConf** field of the system administrator—we can switch on all available elements of the RTE:

```
options.RTEkeyList = cut, copy, paste, formatblock,
class, fontstyle, fontsize, textcolor, bold, italic,
underline, left, center, right, orderedlist,
unorderedlist, outdent, indent, link, table, bgcolor,
image, emoticon, line, user, chMode
```

Below is an example for a classes configuration.

```
RTE.default {
  colors = color1, color2, noColor
  PROC.allowedClasses = left, right
  PROC.allowTagsOutside = IMG
  mainStyle_font = Verdana, sans-serif
  mainStyle_size = 12px
  mainStyle_color = #313031
  mainStyleOverride_add.P = font-family : Verdana,
                    sans-serif; font-size : 12px;
  mainStyleOverride_add.H1 = font-family : Verdana,
                    sans-serif; font-size : 18px;
  mainStyleOverride_add.H2 = font-family : Verdana,
                    sans-serif; font-size : 12px;
  inlineStyle.img = margin: 5px;
  hidePStyleItems = H3, H4, H5, H6, pre
  classesImage = middle, withoutmargin
  classesCharacter = red, middle, small, large,
                    gray, left
  classesParagraph = left
```

```
}

RTE.classes {
  withoutmargin.name = Normal, without margin
  withoutmargin.value = margin: 0;
  red.name = red
  red.value = color: red;
  middle.name = middle
  middle.value = display: block; text-align: center;
                 small.name = small
  small.value = font-size : 10px;
  large.name = large
  large.value = font-size : 14px;
  gray.name = gray
  gray.value = color: #636563;
  left.name = alignleft
  left.value = float:left; display: block;
}
```

The color selection can also be configured:

```
RTE.colors {
  corporate {
    name = BT3-Rot
    value = #BB0000
  }
  variant {
    name = Burgundy variation
    value = #6F0311
  }
}
RTE.default.colors = corporate, variation
```

Figure 4.10:

*Your own color
preferences in
the RTE*

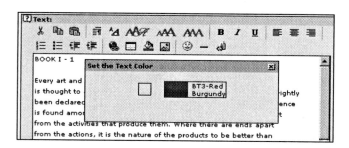

To restrict the color selection to the colors you have defined yourself, the default palette can be switched off as follows:

```
RTE.default.disableColorPicker=1
```

A user-defined object as an example with some useful characters that cannot be found on the keyboard:

```
RTE.default.userElements {
10 = Legal characters
10 {
  1 = ®
  1.description = Registered Trademark
  1.content = &reg;

  2 = ©
  2.description = Copyright
  2.content = &copy;

  3 = §
  3.description = Paragraph
  3.content = &sect;
}
20 = Currencies
20 {
  1 = yen
  1.description = Yen
  1.content = &yen;

  2 = pfund
  2.description = GBP
  2.content = &pound;

  3 = cent
  3.description = Cent
  3.content = &cent;
}

30 = Mathematical characters/functions
30 {
  1 = Power
  1.description = power superscript
  1.mode = wrap
  1.content = <sup>|</sup>

  2 = Index
  2.description = Index inferior character
  2.mode = wrap
  2.content = <sub>|</sub>

  3 = Degrees symbol
  3.description = degrees symbol
  3.content = &deg;
  }
}
```

Do not forget to enable the corresponding default element, if you have not
enabled all elements in the menu bar:

```
RTE.default.showButtons = user
```

The following figure shows the result:

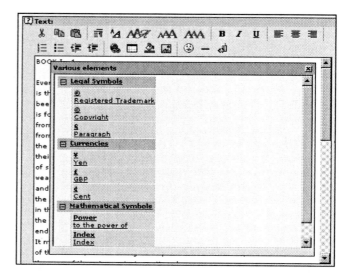

Figure 4.11:

Your own extensions via the user object of the RTE

The complete reference, with many further examples on configuring the RTE, can be found via the link shown here.

The influence of transformation for developers can also be configured via TypoScript using the options of the **PROC** key, as described by this softlink.

Alternatives

Restricting the RTE to the Internet Explorer from version 5 has caused many people to wonder about alternatives. Several different efforts have been made simultaneously to integrate htmlArea, itself another Open Source project into TYPO3. After one implementation has clearly taken the lead others have become obsolete and are marked accordingly in the Extension Repository and will (hopefully) vanish from the Archives soon. The definitive htmlArea Extension is by Stanislas Rolland. A complete documentation can be found online here: http://typo3.org/documenta-tion/document-library/rtehtmlarea/.

4.8.5 The Web | Info | Pages TSConfig Module

Now that your entries in the title forms of individual pages are hidden, it is not so easy to find out which values have been set at which points.

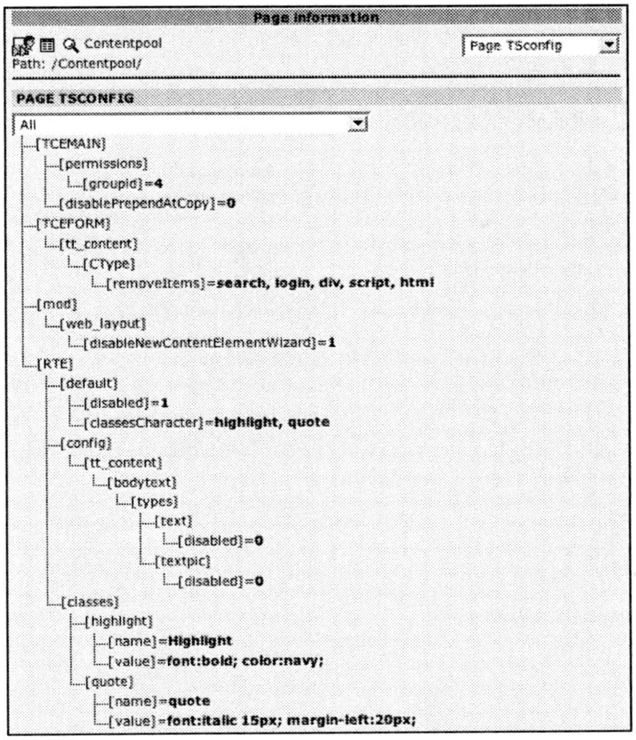

Figure 4.12:

Valid TSConfig settings for a random page on the page tree

The **Info** provides the **Pages TSconfig** function for this purpose. Here the active configuration is displayed for the currently selected page. You can choose to have all TSConfig entries displayed, or just individual areas.

4.9 Setting up Simple Workflows

In the view named "Rootline", which you are shown if you click on the name of your installation next to the globe at the top of the page tree, and select the List View, you can create records of all types.

If the workflow extension is installed you can now add a new workflow record to the end of the List View. If this and any other dependent extensions are not yet installed, first change to the *Extension Manager*. You will find the necessary notes on installing extensions in Chapter 6.

4.9.1 Workflow Configuration

Configuring a workflow requires an existing page tree and at least two different back-end user groups, with corresponding members. This module, which is currently quite simple, has three different roles: the task manager, who can initiate ToDos and assign users, the author, who writes new content, and the editor, who corrects this content and publishes it.

Publishing can be done here in different ways:

- By default, new content and pages are invisible, and remain hidden until they are released by an editor.

- New content and pages are created in a non-public part of the website, and after they are approved, are moved by the editor to a part of the website predefined in the workflow.

This makes it easy to put into practice the classical "dual verification" principle of editorial procedures. More complex workflows can be simulated by joining workflows together, but these options still leave a lot to be desired if TYPO3 is to assume a central role in a business process with the corresponding feedback loops.

In this respect there is a project which is being put into practice involving the integration of TYPO3 with a WfMC Standard compatible workflow editor and workflow engine compatible with the WfMC standard. When this is introduced, all the options for displaying more sophisticated workflows will be redesigned.

4.9.2 Example: News Workflow

The users of the "Portal" group should be able to assign users of the "B2C" group ToDos, by calling a predefined workflow in the **User | Tasks** module. To be able to create a workflow, the target page, the target user group, and the necessary extensions must be available.

Requirements: for our example, create a "News" page in the "Content pool" and add two subpages to it. The page on which the news is to be saved for displaying in the portal and in the websites, we will call "Live"; and the others where they were created and edited until being published in the workflow, we will call "Draft".

Now assign the following permissions to the newly created pages, using the **Web | Access** module:

"News":   only administrators

"Live":   only administrators

"Draft":   "Global" group, show page, edit page content

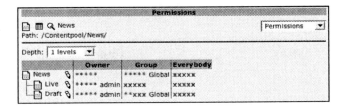

Figure 4.13:

Access permissions for the pages for news production

You must now add the "Draft" page for the "Portal" and "B2C" group to the **DBMounts**, so that both groups can see and edit the page. If you want the "Portal" group to be able to edit the article after publishing, you must give this group access permissions for the pages and also set them up as **DBMount** for this group.

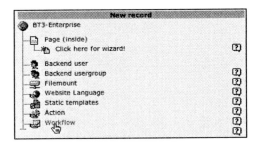

Figure 4.14:

Creating a new workflow in the Rootline

After installing the necessary extensions, a new record of the **workflow** type can be added in the Rootline of the system (List View on the top level of the page tree (see the preceding figure).

The **workflow** form consists of several sections:

The first part of the form contains the option of disabling the workflow. The second part contains the field for entering the title as it will later be shown to users. The description entered here is later visible in the Details View of the workflow.

The next form block now contains the basic settings for the workflow.

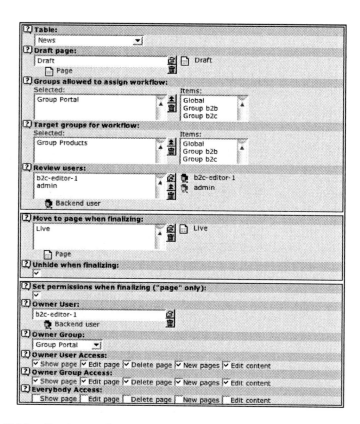

Figure 4.15:

Workflow form with entries for the new workflow

With **Table**, the target format of the workflow is defined. In its original state, and with an installed news extension, the following formats are available here: **News, News category, Page, Page content, Website users and groups, Domains, Alternative page languages**, and **Internal notes**. The **Draft Page** field calls the *TYPO3 Element Browser*, where you can select the page where the news elements are to be edited. Select the "Draft" page.

Groups specified in **Groups allowed to assign workflow** may start the workflow and assign it to the groups named in the **Target groups for workflow** dialog. This creates a new entry in the ToDo list of recipients.

Review Users are the users who can check and release work. Individual users should be chosen here.

In the next section you should choose if the entry should be moved with publication by the **Review User**, or be set from hidden to online.

If the workflow refers to pages, then further entry fields can be defined, by marking the **Set permissions when finalizing** option, for specifying the owner of the entry—together with the group and permissions for owner, group, and all others.

After this entry there is an option to set the "News" workflow in motion, in the **User | Tasks** module under **Tasks**. This appears to the target user as a new ToDo entry in his or her view of the **User | Tasks** module.

The actual workflow is processed by the status being changed to and fro. In this process, each step is recorded in the task protocol and displayed to the users involved. The task can then be escalated by any of the users and registered for release/publication. The actual release can only be made by the authorized user.

This has the consequence in our case that the news entry is no longer marked as hidden, and has been transferred to the "Live" page. After completion, the protocol only remains visible to the user who started the task.

The workflow is described from the perspective of the editor, in detail, in Chapter 3.4

4.10 Defined Procedures with Actions

Actions are less well known, and stand for a concept that is accordingly little used, but which has been available in TYPO3 since version 3.3.0. This approach implements predefined procedures, and these can be extended with your own actions. The actions are shown to users in the **User | Tasks** module (see the following figure).

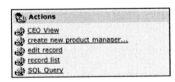

Figure 4.16:

Display of commands in the **User | Tasks** *module*

This function came about mainly as a way of giving administrators a chance to create restricted back-end user access. For this purpose, further useful standard action types were created.

4.10.1 Action Types

The following functions are predefined:

Create Back end User

>   Enables non-administrators to set up back-end users. To do this

a user must be set up that can be copied with its settings—the so-called *template user*. This is a very important function in situations where a large increase in back-end users is expected in a user group set up specially for this purpose; it can help the administrator to avoid not only errors, but also very monotonous work.

SQL Query

Provides a way of making predefined SQL queries available; to do this, a new action is first set up in the Rootline. Give this a name and assign it to one or more groups. The definition of the database query is then created in the **Tools | DB Check** module under **Full Search**, using the **Advanced Query** option. After you have set up a query, you can assign it with the **Save** option and by selecting the relevant action (**Save to Action**) from the selection menu. This action is now available to the members of the group specified. Remember that users must have access permissions for the table or page concerned.

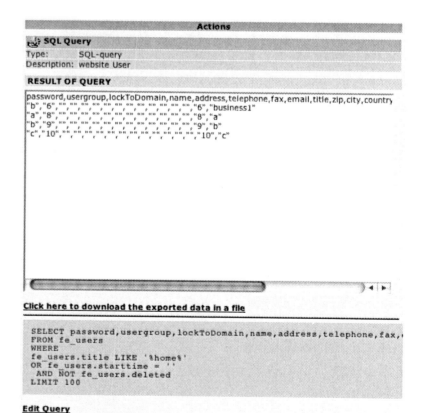

Figure 4.17:

*The **SQL Query** action is an example that displays data of front-end users*

Record List

The option for selecting a list of records under a specific page for display and editing; the options appear here as in the Extended List View. This is very useful to enable users to have a direct path for editing records—products, news etc.—after logging in.

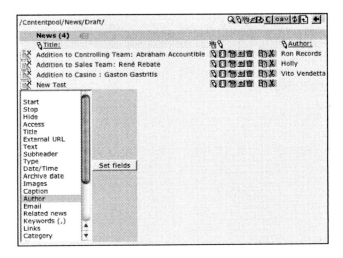

Figure 4.18:

Example of an action of the **Record List** *type*

Edit Record

Allows you to display a list of disparate records, which can then be called for editing. If required, a user who is only involved with a very small number of records, which rarely change, could in this way be put into a position of working effectively without the main **Web** module.

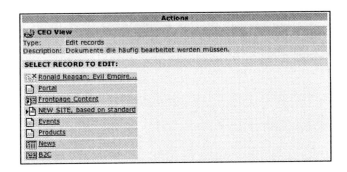

Figure 4.19:

List of records to be edited, called by an action of the **Edit Records** *type*

4.10.2 Example: Action for Setting up Users

With this type of predefined action, non-administrators can also set up users, an important function to get individual departments and teams in a large corporation, for example, involved in content production.

1. First the `sys_action` extension must be installed via the Extension Manager.

2. To be able to define an action for automatically setting up users, a user record must be available as a template. This so-called *template user* is copied by the action and given details such as user name, password, and entry point in the page tree. Set up a "product_template" user.

Actions are set up in the List View of the Rootline (**Web | Lists module/root**, which administrators can also call directly from the **User | Tasks** module). With **Create new record**, the **New record** dialog is called. Here, select **Action** as the type.

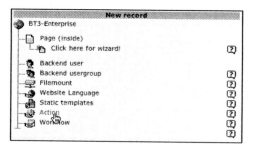

Figure 4.20:

Setting up the new action in the Rootline

In the input form, select the **Create Backend User** option and fill in the following fields (see the following figure):

Title/description

Enter a title and a description.

Assign Action to groups

Select groups that are later allowed to run the action via the Task Center. Select the "Portal" group.

User prefix

Here you can enter an expression, which is prefixed to the user name of all users set up with this action. In our case, enter "pm_" for "Product manager". These users are then grouped together in the list of back-end users and are easier to recognize.

The module provides the following functions:

Record Statistics

> This option analyzes all the entries in the database tables that are relevant for the administrator. **Marked-Deleted pages**: the first section shows basic data on the number of all unhidden pages, all hidden pages and deleted pages. This is useful because pages deleted in the TYPO3 back end are not deleted from the database; the deleted field in the pages table is merely set to the value "1". So if it was necessary in an emergency to restore a deleted page, this value can be reset to "0" via the *phpMyAdmin* database tool, to make the page visible again. Under **Document Types** the frequency of various page types is shown. The **Tables** area provides information on the number of existing entries, with the name of the table in the system in the middle column.

Total Page Tree

> The **Total Page Tree** option is particularly interesting in very large installations for viewing the entire file tree, without having to expand (and collapse again) many partial areas.

Database Relations

> This area performs an analysis of the database according to specific criteria.

- *Files with no references at all*: The system searches through files in the Uploads directory where all files that are loaded in the back end unspecifically to the server are stored. The files there are then checked to see if they are referenced from the database. If this is not the case, these files can and should be deleted, since they are no longer used and cannot be called by users in the back end, and they can also use up large amounts of hard disk space in big installations where users store images in this way on the server.

- *Files referenced from more than one record*: Database entries that are copied may have multiple references to a file in the Uploads directory. Such multiple links are analyzed and shown here.

- *Missing Files*: This option searches the database for links to files in the Uploads directory which no longer exist.

- *Select Fields/Group Fields*: This function searches the database for links in records to no longer existing records. *Select* and *Group* refer to different ways of displaying assignments of this type in TYPO3. *Select* is used for assignments of a predefined database table by selection fields (e.g., groups in the user dialog), *Group* is used for assignments that can contain content from various database tables (e.g. **Insert record**).

Full Search

Searches can be made here in the database, without having to go through phpMyAdmin.

- *Raw Search in all fields*: In simple mode, you can search through the entire database by entering an expression and sending it off. This is not recommended for very large databases or systems working under very heavy loads.

- *Advanced Search*: Offers a series of interesting options. The output of a search result is initially not restricted to the screen output, but can be changed with the following options: **Select Records** shows hits in a list where they can be immediately edited.

Count Results lists only the hit frequency.

Explain Query shows further parameters of the database query.

CSV Export shows the result as a comma-separated list with values in double quotes and commas separating results, and shown in rows. This is particularly useful if you want to process results further in spreadsheet programs, statistics programs and the like. The result appears in an entry window beneath which is an option for downloading.

XML Export shows the result in XML notation in an entry window, also with an option for downloading.

Make Query: After selecting the database table to be searched, table fields can be chosen in the selection field which are then added to the list of fields to be searched. The sections of the search can be specified beneath this. The table name is shown on the left, the operator in the middle, and the expression which is being sought on the right.

Possible operators are **Contains, Starts with, Ends with** and **Equals**. The checkbox to the right next to the input calls a selection of negative operators: **Does not contain, Does not start with, Does not end with, Does not equal**.

Each column has the options **Refresh, Remove**, and **Add**. Each further line also has functions to change the sort order and to formulate conditions. With the arrow right for indenting, you have the possibility to define conditions with the "and/or" operators.

Under the lines for defining queries there are three functions available for grouping the results. With **Group by**, results can be summarized according to groups arranged by fields, with **Order by** results can be displayed arranged by a field, with **Descending** the output is shown in descending order. With **Limit**, the number of results can be set.

Find Filename

This is a simple option to search by name through all the files in the filemount and in the TYPO3 source.

Searches can be made using regular expressions; a short introduction on these, with links to further resources, can be found via the softlink shown here.

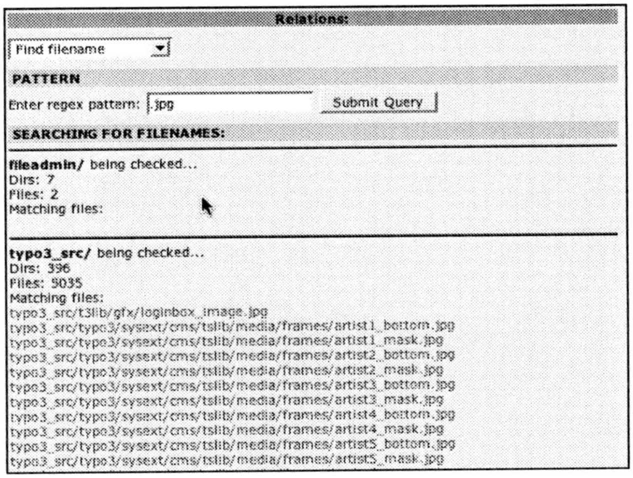

Figure 4.29:

Result of the file search

4.13 TYPO3 and Caching

As a CMS based on a database, TYPO3 generates HTML pages from many different sources. From HTML templates, via TypoScript from the database, down to page content from separate applications, pages are assembled when the page is called and transferred to the browser of the visitor. Because the functions of the PHP scripts and the necessary database queries put a heavy load on the webserver, TYPO3 saves pages that have been called and assembled for the first time in a buffer, the so-called cache. This cache takes a considerable strain off the database and web server, especially for large websites with a high amount of traffic.

Changes to the page cause the respective cache for this page to expire. Several functions are available to the administrator to delete this cache manually.

On the one hand there are two global functions to delete the entire cache, as well as the cache files of the TYPO3 configuration menu at the end of the page tree.

More options are provided by the **Web | Page** module at the end of the columns view. Here the cache of a page can be deleted manually, as well as a configurable number of child pages.

The **Cache and age** view in the page tree overview of the **Web | Info** module serves as a control instrument. Here you can check not only the current caches of the pages, you can also modify how long they are valid by clicking on the pencil at the top of the **Cache** column.

Figure 4.30:

*Setting the page cache via the **Web | Info** module*

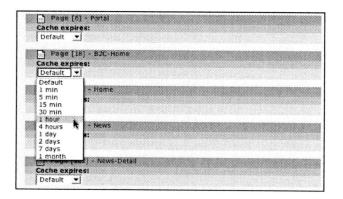

4.14 Digital Asset Management

4.14.1 Tasks and Aims of DAM

The *Digital Asset Management System* (DAM) is the response of the TYPO3 community to the need to have image material, documents, and other files (so-called assets), which are intended to enrich the text of the website, provided with metadata. In this context, a digital asset management system is a subsystem without any directly visible functions in the website; it serves to record, index, and manage files. In addition to this, however, it provides a simple interface for extensions that need to use this meta-information for functions in the back end or front end.

Another important innovation is the removal of an often criticized weak point in TYPO3: how to handle files when they are referenced from content elements. TYPO3 copies files that are to be published to a separate part of the system file tree, to protect these from being accessed by the user. If a user now deletes a file from the system via the back end, the function of contents displaying these files remains unchanged, and is protected from errors of the user. In many cases it may be desirable, however, to have direct access, to swap a file that is displayed at many locations in the website, for example. This is prevented by the protection function.

The DAM provides a way of configuring the handling of files individually, so that you can specify per file, group, or category whether the file should be copied to one of the temporary directories or if it should stay where it is and be included from there directly.

A simple application example for the DAM could be a picture gallery showing pictures, independently of where they are stored, and on the basis of a feature of the metadata, such as belonging to a specific category created for this purpose, or based on a keyword or file type occurring.

Another application could be the evaluation of the use of images from a pool of pay-per-view material, and which evaluates usage statistically and provides a corresponding billing interface in the back end.

4.14.2 Integration into TYPO3

The DAM is represented in the back end as a separate main module and is also integrated into the page tree. The DAM icon always calls the view of all categories and a list of file types. The **Media | List** submodule shows all files in a List View. In practice the **Media | List** and **Media | File** views should replace the **File | File list** standard module. Depending on the configuration, this is shown to the editor with all these views included, or is restricted to the DAM integration in the *TYPO3 Element Browser*. In this case, managing the image data is a task for administration.

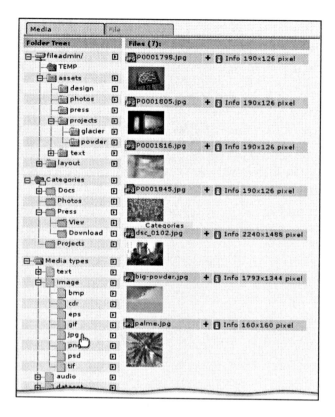

Figure 4.31:

The TYPO3 Element Browser with an installed DAM

The Media | List Module

The List View allows you to work with and on metadata in files that are already in the DAM, and in its function matches the standard **File | List** module. Editors use it to change existing metadata, makes selections, and save it. A simplified indexing system enables the metadata of already recorded assets to be edited en masse.

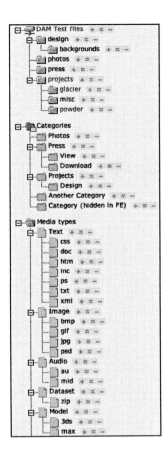

Figure 4.32:

Symbolic file tree of the DAM with three physical sections: physical directory structure, categories, and media types

As can be seen in this figure, there are three hierarchy trees in the navigation frame. The top one is a reproduction of the files in the filemount, the middle one shows a hierarchical tree of content categories. The lowest tree is generated automatically from the indexing system. Media objects are listed here, categorized automatically by their file type.

Clicking on the name of a tree section displays in the right-hand frame a list of media objects that have been indexed for this directory, category or mime type. The data of media objects can be edited in this list by clicking on the pencil next to the object concerned.

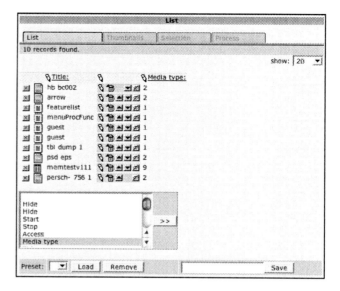

Figure 4.33:

List view of the DAM

Apart from the List View, three other views are available with their own functions after selecting a directory, a category, or a media type:

- *Thumbnails/overview*: Images—if available—are shown here as small previews.

- *Selection*: The current selection can be modified here. Individual files can be excluded from the selection, for example. In addition to this, the selection can be saved and exchanged among editors.

- *Process*: Already recorded files can be reprocessed here with modified or added metadata.

The Indexing Module

The **Indexing** module serves as an import dialog to provide new files with metadata and add them to the system. The DAM module creates a media object in the database for each file, which is consequently provided with meta-information. During indexing, the module, depending on the file type, automatically reads various default information into the database (e.g. image dimensions, file size, etc.). The indexing routine is designed to be expandable by means of so-called *services*, and in future could read out meta-information from PDF or Office files, for example.

The following working steps are required for indexing media data:

1. Upload the files to a subdirectory of fileadmin via the **File | List** module (or upload via FTP).

2. Import via **Media | Indexing**: selecting the directory to be indexed from the `fileadmin` hierarchy tree.

3. Follow the instructions of the indexing wizard, as shown in the following figures.

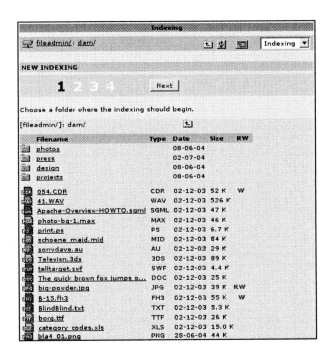

Figure 4.34:

Step 1 - Select the directory whose content is to be included in the DAM

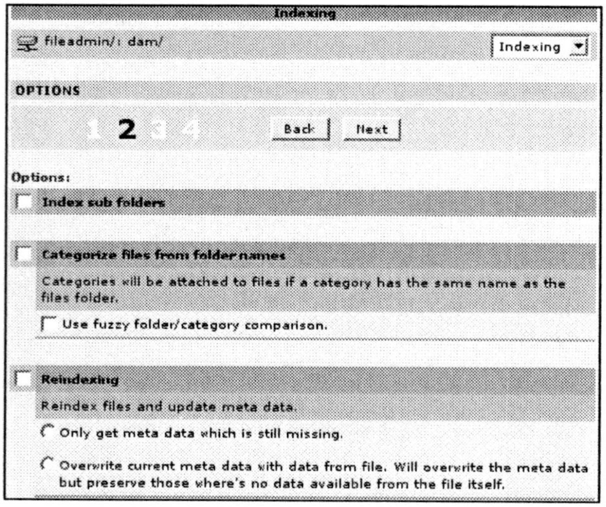

Figure 4.35:

Step 2 - select from the (expandable) list of options

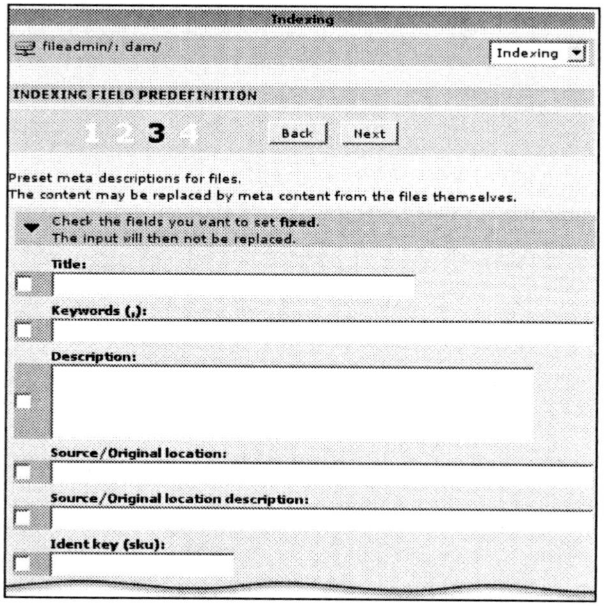

Figure 4.36:

Step 3 - Enter information for mass processing that you want to assign to all files to be proessed

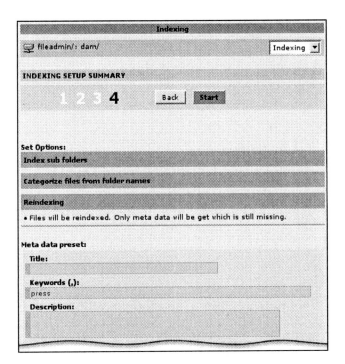

Figure 4.37:

Step 4 - Summary of your entries; these can be saved here as presets for further indexing procedures

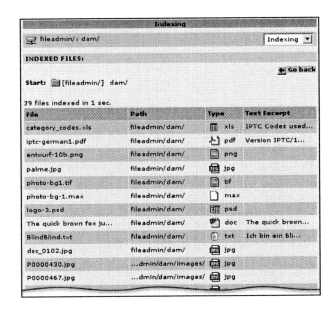

Figure 4.38:

Step 5 - Display of processed files

DAM Categories

The DAM module sets up a specific page as a directory in the page tree, where it stores its own records (media objects and DAM categories). Categories can be created, edited, and deleted here via the **Web | List** module. All the DAM media objects are also located on this page, although they can be edited more effectively via **Media | List**.

4.14.3 Prospects

The DAM fills a gap in terms of handling not database-based, but rather file-based information and resources, and will become an important tool, with improved management and increased security, especially where very large amounts of data and critical information are involved. With the DAM, many innovations are introduced into TYPO3 that are not directly involved with its function. The introduction of so-called services, as well as new display possibilities in the back end, are two such examples.

In terms of functions, the DAM provides the basis for extensions in the direction of document management functions; in particular linking it to the display and editing of OpenOffice documents could lead to many developments being initiated that will use TYPO3 increasingly for enterprise content management tasks. A further development approach that has moved closer due to the DAM is the introduction of a uniform handling of metadata for files (*assets*) and content in TYPO3. This is particularly necessary for the requirements of the Semantic Web.[7]

4.15 Administration: The Future

Several developments that TYPO3 will provide in future for administration can already be predicted, in the sense described at the beginning (in addition to the existing range of functions). An important step that is in store is the arrival of a complete versioning system in TYPO3. Based on this, the existing workflow module will be extended. In the medium term, the large dimensions of the workflow project, aimed at integrating external workflow engines, are quite significant. In the long term, the existing user administration system and the assignment of permissions will be heavily influenced by the requirements needed for operating a company portal, insofar as corresponding key workers can be found among the developers, and support can be found from sponsors.

---

[7] http://www.w3c.org/2001/sw/

The perspective of administration therefore has much influence on the future of the TYPO3 core; it represents the revolution on the way from a WCMS towards a broader and more fundamentally usable enterprise content management system.

5

TypoScript

5.1 The Role of the Developer

5.1.1 The Production Process

I think developers already know but are a little afraid to admit that writing software is a creative activity that requires a lot of interaction with the people who are going to use it-Richard Gabriel. [1]

However much time and effort is put into the preparation of a TYPO3-based communication platform, in the end it is the concrete steps of implementation that make the plan a reality. Only in the rarest cases does this process have only one possible solution. Designing practical user interfaces and functions always allows room for creativity, but also room for errors. The activity of programming is not only subject to the laws of the respective system, but must also create optimal starting points for the maintenance, extension, and correction of the code, through forward planning.

Two weak points that can very frequently lead to applications failing are closely involved with the role of the developer:

1. If the application's goal is not clearly defined to all those involved in the project, task descriptions will become focused on technical aspects of the software. However sophisticated the solutions may be, the success of an application usually depends on simple questions: Was a communication target clearly worked out and afterwards consequently put into practice? Was the software

[1] http://java.sun.com/features/2002/11/gabriel_qa.html

also tested by editors for user-friendliness and acceptance? Ultimately, every application lives from the content that editors can add quickly, and which they must manage. In other words: has the developer thought about the user?

2. Even the task of technical implementation is frequently underestimated. As the demands made on this implementation increase, it must be considered whether an implementation partner might be a more time-efficient and thus more cost-efficient solution, on the basis of their know-how for the application. In short: only someone who knows the conditions and possibilities of the system well can produce solutions that retain value in the long-term and, after a period spent maturing, can serve as the basis for further development steps.

This is not to say that the "tools of the trade" for creating new TYPO3 applications cannot be learned by anyone—that is precisely the aim of this book, after all.

5.1.2 Requirements and Overview

If you want to implement complex applications with TYPO3, a sound knowledge of TypoScript is a prerequisite. TYPO3 provides various standard out-of-the-box templates with which even a beginner can conjure up a website in a short time. These templates can be easily integrated and their appearance (colors, spacing, and logos) can be changed via wizards. But if you want to carry out modifications or implement functionality in accordance with the project requirements, a knowledge of TypoScript is needed. The basic principles of TYPO3's internal configuration language, TypoScript, and how it functions, are what this chapter is about. Some knowledge of HTML and how the World Wide Web functions is also required, of course.

Only if functionality that goes beyond the basic provisions of this system and the numerous freely available *extensions* is necessary, do you need a sound knowledge of PHP and the TYPO3 developer API. This subject is discussed in detail in Chapter 7.

This section of the book covers the following:

Section 5.2 introduces the concept of TypoScript. The template records and the possibility of cascading is discussed, syntax explained, and principles illustrated in the order of processing and the nesting of objects.

TS-objects, functions, data types, and the wrap concept are treated in more depth in section 5.3.

Numerous development tools and aids are introduced in section 5.4.

In its basic installation, TYPO3 already includes a series of standard templates. Section 5.5 gives you an overview and describes the areas in which individual templates are used in practice.

Sections 5.6 to 5.9 are dedicated to creating a base layout. Various template concepts are compared and implemented in an example scenario. Alternative content rendering concepts and template switching with `type/typeNum` also provide background information.

The navigation concept in TYPO3 involves varied menu types, based on text, graphics, layers, an image map, or selection menus. Its configuration is explained in section 5.10, using a number of specific examples.

Section 5.11 takes a closer look at important functions such as `stdWrap`, `optionSplit,` and the GIFBUILDER, which play central roles in TypoScript. Using `stdWrap` properties and conditions you can insert control structures into TypoScript. The GIFBUILDER allows a wide range of image manipulation.

Sections 5.12 and 5.13 deal with the implementation of a site with frames and allow a glimpse of the future with the topics of XHTML, accessibility, and TemplaVoila.

5.2 TypoScript—Basic Principles

5.2.1 What is TypoScript?

A content management system must be able to produce various different content in the desired form in each case, due to the separation of content and form. A frequently used procedure is to insert special *tags* (`<tagname>`) into an output *template* to control output. With its help, specific contents, functions, lists, or detailed views are integrated or transformed into the template displayed.

Softlink **387605**

At this point TYPO3 goes a crucial step further with the introduction of *TypoScript* (TS), because in TypoScript you can create the output template yourself, allowing for far greater control of the output format and layout than would be possible with simple HTML templates.

With the information defined in TypoScript, not only can dynamic content be inserted into a template, but it is also possible to influence the appearance of the output (*front end*) in its details. The base layout can be generated entirely with TypoScript, or be taken from an HTML file. For navigation you can use a menu based on texts, graphics, layers, Flash, or a simple selection menu. Menus can be generated dynamically and each menu's appearance can be determined individually. You can create graphics from texts and images in run time or control the layout and the contents of the output, independent of time or users. Even the behavior of the back end for individual users and groups is controlled via TypoScript. As mentioned in Chapter 4, you can specify, for example, which editing functions are available to the editor in the Rich Text Editor.

TypoScript takes over the role of mediator between information and functions that are implemented in the core of TYPO3 by means of PHP, or added through extensions. In this way, TypoScript can be seen as an intermediate layer for transmitting information to system functions.

To avoid misunderstandings, we would like to make clear what TypoScript is *not*, before getting to work defining what it is. For the technically minded, section 5.2.3 has more in-depth information.

TypoScript is neither a programming language nor a script language, so it cannot be compared with Java, PHP, or JavaScript. It is not possible to use loops (`for`, `while`,...), for example. TypoScript serves as an "information carrier". You don't have to learn any new, and above all, proprietary languages. TypoScript itself is not run at any time.

If TypoScript is not a script language, then what is it? One description that you should keep in mind whenever you want to test TypoScript to the limits, is as follows:

TypoScript has a syntax with which hierarchical information can be defined in a tree structure through simple ASCII text. In this way any information can be passed on by TypoScript as the interface to the system. But only the objects and properties queried by the system influence the behavior of the back end and front end. And only the objects and properties described in the documentation for the current version of TYPO3 are available.

Users of Windows operating systems are perhaps familiar with the hierarchical structure of system information in the Registry, which arranges values logically as objects.

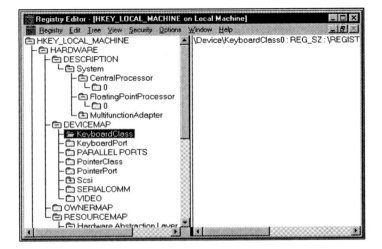

Figure 5.1:

Diagram of the hierarchy of objects and their values structured by the Registry editor

Similarly, individual objects configured with TypoScript are arranged in a tree structure. The **TypoScript Object Browser** (**Web | Template** module) template tool represents this hierarchy in a graphical user interface.

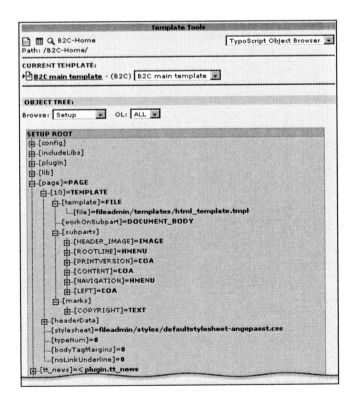

Figure 5.2:

TypoScript Object Browser displays nested objects and values

5.2.2 TSref

Softlink **342678** At this point we would briefly like to remind you of the TypoScript reference TSref; it is a kind of bible for those who work daily with TypoScript, because in it, you can find precise descriptions of all available objects, properties, and functions. You should always have the reference close to hand if you are working with TypoScript! The TSref is available online at TYPO3.org and can be downloaded in OpenOffice format or as a PDF. If you don't have the TSref yet, now is the time to download it!

5.2.3 Digression: TypoScript and PHP

To acquire a better understanding of the technical background, the following section explains the relationship between TypoScript and PHP. Alternatively you can move on directly to section 5.2.4.

Even if in theory you can create output using PHP in any form at all, as a rule TYPO3's own *TypoScript Front-end Engine* (TSFE) is used when a website is called up via the file index.php (tslib/index_ts.php). It evaluates the information in the individual template records in the page tree of the website. [2]

The objects and values of the template records, structured by the TypoScript intermediate layer, are processed here by PHP.

- The information is placed by the system, using the t3lib_TSparser (t3lib/class.t3lib_tsparser.php) class, into a multi-dimensional PHP array. This is available in certain applications and functions in TYPO3.

- If information is passed on to the PHP array that is not utilized by functions of TYPO3 classes, it behaves like variables created in PHP that are not queried. They are ignored, but this does not lead to any output errors.

An example to clarify this: In the abstract TypoScript code below, information parsed by PHP is placed in a multi-dimensional array.

```
myObject.property1 = value_x
myObject.property2 = value_y
myObject.property2.property3 = value_z
```

In PHP the array would be created directly, as follows:

```
$TS['myObject.']['property1'] = 'value_x';
$TS['myObject.']['property2'] = 'value_y';
```

---

[2] The detailed front-end rendering process is described in section 5.7 and 7.5.1.

```
$TS['myObject.']['property2.']['property3'] =
'value_z';
```

or alternatively:

```
$TS = array(
  'myObject.' => array(
    'property1' => 'value_x',
    'property2' => 'value_y',
    'property2.' => array (
      'property3' => 'value_z'
    )
  )
)
```

An array can also be displayed with TYPO3's own `debug()` function, which creates the following output:

Figure 5.3:

Display of the abstract TS code with the TYPO3 debug() function

TYPO3 provides a tool for displaying and editing TypoScript, the *TypoScript Object Browser*. This displays the example code in the following way:

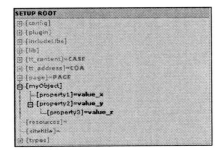

Figure 5.4:

Display of the abstract TS code in the TypoScript Object Browser

Example: HRULER

The interplay between TypoScript and PHP can be illustrated by the very simple HRULER content object (cObject) that draws a horizontal line. Let's take a look at the following TypoScript template:

Softlink **762761**

```
page = PAGE
page.typeNum = 0
page.20 = HRULER
page.20 {
  lineThickness = 10
  lineColor = #e6e6e6
```

```
        spaceLeft = 100
        spaceRight = 100
}
```

The third line is of interest, where a TypoScript object of the HRULER type is defined, to which configuration parameters are added in the following lines. The TypoScript values of the lineThickness, lineColor, spaceLeft, and spaceRight properties are placed by PHP into an array. The PHP HRULER() (tslib/class.tslib_content.php) function is then available for processing. Here is the PHP function: [3]

```
function HRULER ($conf) {
    $lineThickness = t3lib_div::intInRange($this->
                    stdWrap($conf['lineThickness'],
                    $conf['lineThickness.']),1,50);
    $lineColor = $conf['lineColor'] ? $conf['lineColor'] :
                'black';
    $spaceBefore = intval($conf['spaceLeft']);
    $spaceAfter = intval($conf['spaceRight']);
    $content = '';

    $content.=' <table border="0" cellspacing="0"
                cellpadding="0" width="99%"><tr>';

  if ($spaceBefore) {
    $content.='<td width="1"><img src=".$GLOBALS['TSFE']->
        absRefPrefix.'clear.gif' width=".$spaceBefore.'"
        height="1" alt=""/></td>';
  }
    $content.= '<td bgcolor=".$lineColor.'">
        <img src=".$GLOBALS['TSFE']->
        absRefPrefix.'clear.gif' width="1"
        height=".$lineThickness.'" alt="" /></td>';

  if ($spaceAfter) {
    $content.='<td width="1"><img src=".$GLOBALS['TSFE']->
        absRefPrefix. 'clear.gif' width=".$spaceAfter.'"
        height="1" alt=""/></td>';
  }
    $content.= '</tr></table>';

    $content = $this->stdWrap($content,$conf['stdWrap.']);
    return $content;
}
```

This results in an output of a horizontal line with a width of 10 pixels and with the color #e6e6e6. It is indented on the left and right by 100 pixels.

---

[3] To display a horizontal line, TYPO3 uses a table, since an <HR> tag could not be sufficiently controlled via CSS in older browsers.

This example clearly illustrates the capabilities, but also the limits, of TypoScript. TypoScript offers developers a secure interface for configuring existing functionality, making errors in handling PHP impossible and guaranteeing correct HTML code in the output.

At the same time, a look at the above function shows that the developer determines that when the HRULER object is used, a horizontal line will be drawn using a table construction. This property is not included in the parameters for this special object.

This paradigm applies in principle to every TypoScript object: its parameterization can be explained from the parameters that utilize one or more PHP functions.

5.2.4 TypoScript Templates

TypoScript templates determine how the TypoScript Front-end Engine will ultimately set up the output, that is, which contents will be read from the database, whether an HTML template will be used, where contents will be inserted, and so on. In addition, the transformation of database content for the front-end output is controlled by the TypoScript template. In general this means which font families, font sizes, colors, and spacings are used in the website output.

Softlink **917652**

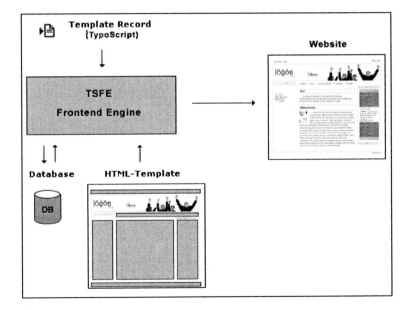

Figure 5.5:

An overview of the front-end rendering process

TypoScript templates control the following areas when generating output:

- Cache

- Logging/statistics

- HTML header details

- Page types (e.g. print output)

- Base layout

- Content elements (appearance and function)

- Creating links

- Integration of extensions and PHP scripts

TYPO3 provides predefined templates for most areas, so that developers do not have to specify all definitions required for the output—such as creating links, for example—for every website.

Before these concepts are explained, here are some small exercises using TypoScript, to help you familiarize yourself with the basics of TypoScript.

5.2.5 Hello World!—The First TypoScript Template

In order that TYPO3 creates any output at all, a TypoScript template is necessary. If this is missing, the error message "No template found!" will be displayed when the page is called up in the front end.

Figure 5.6:

A missing TypoScript template

TypoScript templates are set up as records in the page tree. There are two types of templates: *root templates* and *extension templates*. The difference is that root templates are marked as Rootlevel and form the basis for a website, whereas extension templates can be found anywhere in the page tree and extend or modify the root template. Template records can thus be cascaded via the page tree, which means that TypoScript can add templates together or overwrite them.

There are two ways of creating a new template: by clicking on one of the page icons in the page tree you can create a record of the **Template** type via the context menu and the **New** item. It is immediately assigned to the selected page and can also be edited like other records.

The second way is with the **Template | Info/Modify** module. Select the page on the page tree that you intend to be the root page of a website (e.g. "Home"). If no template is yet assigned to the page, this is indicated and you can create one in the **CREATE NEW WEBSITE** form area with the **Create template for a new site** button. Optionally, a **Standard Template** could immediately be integrated here via the selection menu, to be used for the website. But more on this later.

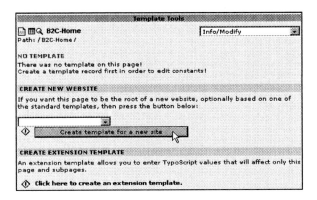

Figure 5.7:

New TypoScript template with the **Template | Info/Modify** module

Assuming you have set up your first root template with **Create template for a new site**, TYPO3 will have created a template record with the title "NEW SITE". It already contains seven lines of TypoScript code in the **Setup** field. This TypoScript setup defines the output in the front end produced by a page with the text "HELLO WORLD!".

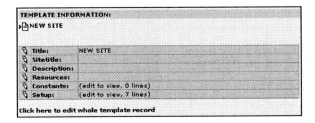

Figure 5.8:

Template record displayed in the **Template | Info/Modify** module

It is possible to edit the entire record via the link in the footer or to open a selection of the most important fields with the assigned icons.

The **Setup** field contains the following details:

```
# Default PAGE object:
page = PAGE
page.typeNum = 0
page.10 = TEXT
page.10.value = HELLO WORLD!
```

If you only edit individual fields, the cache of the record will be deleted when you save, and the current details will be taken into account when rendering the page. If you edit the whole record, updating is achieved by the **Clear all Cache** button at the foot of the module area or in the front end via the Admin Panel. If details are not shown immediately when developing a site, this does not necessarily mean that there are input errors. In such cases you should clear the cache.

If the whole template record is opened via the **Click here to edit whole template record** button, an overview is shown in form fields of all existing information so far. It is noticeable that through the action **Create template for a new site, Rootlevel** was set in the template, and it thus serves as a starting point for a website. In addition, details of **Constants** and **Setup** that may have been set until now in the page tree and in TypoScript templates, are ignored by checking the clear boxes. These three settings enable new websites to be defined from any point within a page tree.

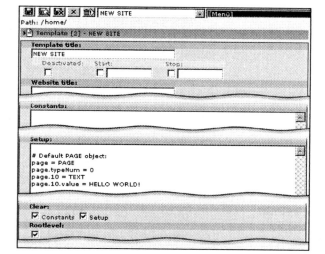

Figure 5.9:

Partial view of the template record

If the page is now called up in the front end, you will see the following output:

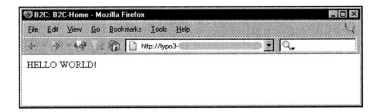

Figure 5.10:

Output in the frontend

Add one line to the TypoScript configuration as shown below, with the
`<strong> </strong>` tags to highlight the text.

```
# Default PAGE object:
page = PAGE
page.typeNum = 0
page.10 = TEXT
page.10.value = HELLO WORLD!
page.10.wrap = <strong>|</strong>
```

The front-end output now shows "HELLO WORLD!" in bold:

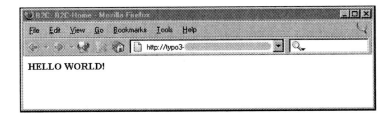

Figure 5.11:

Front-end output after the modied configuration

The possibilities of TypoScript go far beyond what this small example has
shown. But first, the function of the template record will be illustrated.

5.2.6 Cascading Templates

In the following example a second template, "my content", will be created
in addition to the "NEW SITE" template. This can be done, for example,
through the **Template | Info/Modify** module with the **Create an extension
template** option.

In an extension template the **Rootlevel**, **Clear Constants**, and **Clear Setup**
flags are not set by default. Such a template can be placed anywhere in
the page tree. This makes it possible on the one hand to set TypoScript
for specific page trees, since the template will automatically become
active on the page and its subpages. On the other hand, templates can
also be placed in SysFolders, to keep them there as libraries and to
integrate them into other template records. In this way, templates can be

better structured, individual functionalities can remain modular as components, and code can be reused.

In both cases a nesting of template records takes place. This procedure of nesting templates is also called *cascading*.

Integrating the "my content" template into the "NEW SITE" main template is done via the **Include basis template** field in the template record. The entire "NEW SITE" template record must be open for editing. The "my content" template is selected and integrated with the Element Browser.

Figure 5.12:

Integrating a basis template in "NEW SITE"

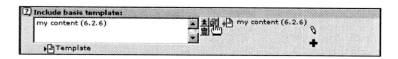

The hierarchy of the templates can be controlled in **Template Analyzer**. If you select the main template, its dependencies are shown in a tree-like structure. The order, from top to bottom, corresponds to the order in which individual templates are processed by the TypoScript front-end Engine.

Figure 5.13:

*Template Analyzer in the **Web | Templates** module*

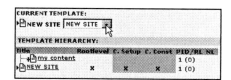

As an example, the `temp.myContent` object is defined in the "my content" template.

```
temp.myContent = TEXT
temp.myContent.value = A text output
```

Through integration, this object is now available in the "NEW SITE" template and can be used there.

```
page.20 < temp.myContent
```

5.2.7 Template Records

Softlink **917198** As illustrated in the previous section, a template record is absolutely essential for generating the front-end output. An individual template record can contain the following information:

Template title

In the **Template title** field the name of the template by which it is displayed in the overview of the back end is defined. You can choose any name you like. But since many different template records are frequently used, a name that makes the functions defined in this template record clear should be used. In the extended fields **Deactivated, Start**, and **Stop**, the template can generally be deactivated or used on a time-dependent basis, in the same way as other records within TYPO3.

Website title

The title of the overall website is specified in the **Website title** field. In the default configuration it is inserted in the header of the front-end output inside the HTML before the respective page title, and displayed in the title bar of the browser window:

```
<title>B2C: Products</title>
<title>[Website title]: [Page title]</title>
```

Constants

In the **Constants** field you set values for constants that replace the corresponding constants in the **Setup** field. Constants represent values set once or globally, which should be easy to manage in the entire application (font size, fonts, background colors,...). They should not be confused with variables as they are known from programming languages. Constants are replaced in the order in which they are entered, and can overwrite each other.

Setup

This field contains the actual TypoScript setup code, which defines both the appearance and behavior of the application. Constants (changeable properties or global values) in the **Setup** field are substituted by the values of the **Constant** field.

Resources

This field can contain assets such as images, masks, Truetype fonts, stylesheets, HTML, and text documents. The field can be referenced with TypoScript through the `resource` data type. When copying a template, the assets of the **Resources** field are also copied and numbered sequentially. `logo.gif` becomes `logo_01.gif`, for example. It is therefore advisable to set references to resources with a wildcard (`logo*.gif`).

Clear and Rootlevel

The subitems **Clear Constants, Clear Setup** and **Rootlevel** form a functional group that needs to be seen in the context of cascading templates.

Rootlevel

The **Rootlevel** defines the point inside a page structure that is to be the starting point (root) of a new application (website). The properties of each template are inherited by all subpages (child pages) in the page tree. If new templates are set in individual page areas, their properties are added together hierarchically with those of the overlying pages (parent pages). In this way values can be reset on lower levels overriding those of the parent templates.

The root template serves as the starting point for all TypoScript configurations for an application until a template sets a new Rootlevel. A root template is marked with a blue arrow in its icon.

Clear Constants and Clear Setup

By means of these checkboxes, cascading of **constants** or the **setup** within the page tree can be stopped. A template defined in this way does not inherit any **constants** or **setup** properties from templates in the page tree lying above.

Include static

TYPO3 in its basic installation provides a series of standard templates (*static templates*). These include not only functional configuration packages for representing content elements, but also complete out-of-the box templates with border layouts, as examples for your own use. The various types of standard templates are introduced in section 5.5.

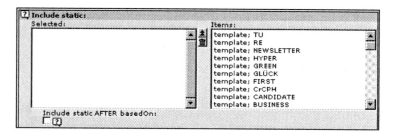

Figure 5.14:

Selecting standard templates

If you have included several standard templates from the selection, you can determine the order in which they are processed by clicking on the double arrow icon. They are deleted with the garbage can icon.

The **Include static AFTER basedOn** checkbox inverts the order in which basis templates (see below: **Include basis template**) and standard templates are processed by the TypoScript Engine. In the default setting, basis templates are processed after standard templates. This normally makes sense, because you can overwrite values in the standard templates with your own values.

In the example shown, a basis template and the standard **content (default)** template are integrated by the root template. The TypoScript configurations that contain loaded extensions (**default TypoScript from Extensions**) behave like standard templates. The Template Analyzer shows a summary of the order in which the individual templates are processed from top to bottom and added together.

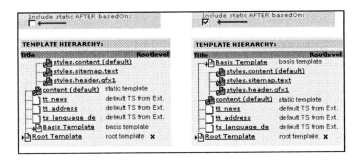

Figure 5.15:

Template Analyzer shows the effect of the Include static AFTER basedOn option

Include static (from extensions)

Extensions can also contain standard templates. They are integrated in the **Include static (from extensions)** form area. TypoScript configurations containing the extension from `ext_typoscript_*.txt` (**default TypoScript from Extensions**), however, are automatically loaded during installation. Examples of extensions that contain standard templates are `Office Displayer` and `CSS Styled Content`.

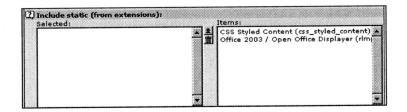

Figure 5.16:

Integrating the standard template of the extension with a mouse click

Include basis template

Basis templates represent personal libraries with which the developer can organize the TypoScript code on a modular basis. Basis templates allow TypoScript to be managed in a clearer way and allow code encapsulated according to functionality to be used effectively for further projects. They represent their own template records whose root flags and clear flags are not set. Basis templates can in turn include their own basis templates, in which case a cascading structure is created. They are given an icon with a green "plus" sign.

In the example shown, a template with the name Basis Template was integrated with the root template.

Figure 5.17:

Integrating a base template

Static template files from T3 Extensions

For TypoScript code containing extensions, (**Default TypoScript from extensions**) the order of integration is also important. In combination with the **Include static AFTER basedOn** selection, the **Static template files from T3 extensions** selection field offers numerous possibilities for cascading templates.

Default (Include before if Root-flag is set)

With this default setting the standard templates of the extensions are inserted before the root template. This is useful because you can then override values from the extension templates with the root template. The difference between this and the next configuration is that the extension templates are only integrated beforehand if **Rootlevel** is set.

Always include before this template record

If the choice has been made, the standard templates of the extensions are read in directly before the corresponding template. The interesting thing here is that the template from extensions can only be modified in this way.

Never include before this template record

This option prevents the standard templates of extensions from being read in directly before the corresponding template. This means that although the template of the extension is active, it cannot be modified by a separate TypoScript setup.

In the following example, a basis template (`basic -- st Green`) was integrated into the root template (`main template`). This in turn merely integrates a standard template (`template; GREEN`). The News (`tt_news`) extension is also installed, which includes its **own** standard TypoScript code. The order in which it would be sensible for them to be read in is: first the standard templates, and then the template for the extensions, since it might overwrite values in the standard templates, then the basis template, to override values of the predecessors, and finally the root template.

In the first case, the default setting **Default (Include before if Root-flag is set)** is left as it is, both for the root template and for the integrated basis template. The TypoScript of the `tt_news` extension is read in after `basic-st Green` and before `main template`.

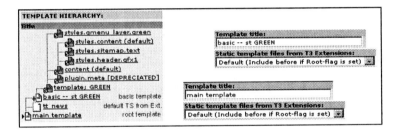

Figure 5.18:

Static template files from T3 extensions: example 1

If the setting **Always include before this template record** is enabled and the default setting is retained for the root template, the TypoScript code for the `tt_news` extension is read in twice—which does not make much sense.

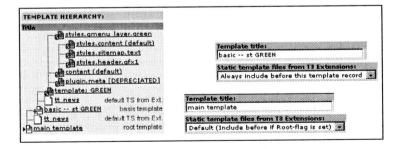

Figure 5.19:

Static template files from T3 extensions: example 2

In the last case, the **Never include before this template record** setting for the root template prevents TypoScript code from the extensions from being read in directly before `main template`. On the other hand the basis template forces data to be read in directly before `basic-st GREEN`.

Figure 5.20:

*Static template files
from T3 extensions:
example 3*

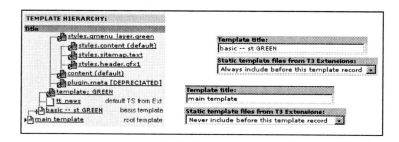

Template on next level

This selection field provides a simple way of integrating a template which should be valid for all following pages in the next levels. Because of this, not every following page on the next level needs to be assigned to its own template record. Layout changes for individual page areas can thus be implemented quickly.

Description

A description of the template and its functionality helps you or third parties to find their way more quickly into the project at a later point in time.

Back-end Editor Configuration

Softlink **626488**

The field provides a way of passing on predefined styles to the CSS editor. It is rarely used, and is currently not being maintained.

5.2.8 Constants and Setup

The two most important fields of a template record are **Setup** and **Constants**. **Setup** contains the TypoScript setup, that is, the TypoScript that defines all the configurations controlling the appearance and behavior of the website. This is processed during the rendering process.

The **Constants** field on the other hand passes on easy-to-handle values or global values, namely constants, to the setup field. This procedure provides you with an overview when modifying values for individual page areas. Used in the right way, you can, for example, change a color value used across several templates, from a central location, instead of having to search through all the templates used.

The notation corresponds to the normal TypoScript syntax: in the setup field the constants are enclosed by {$ and }.

In the following example, "Hello TYPOS!!" is displayed in the front end.

Constants:

```
myText.Content = Hello TYPOS!!
```

Setup:

```
page = PAGE
page {
   typeNum = 0
   10 = TEXT
   10.value = {$myText.Content}
}
```

If no corresponding constants are defined in the **Constants** form field for the constants queried in the setup, then {$myText.Content} would be displayed in the front end.

The object hierarchy of the TypoScript entries for the **Setup** and **Constants** fields can be represented clearly in the TypoScript Object Browser (**Web | Template** module). To do this, select the page in the page tree whose TypoScript setup you want to display, and select the mode with **Browse: Constants** or **Setup**.

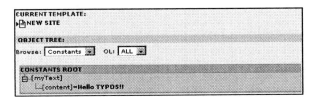

Figure 5.21:

Displaying constants in the Object Browser

Passing on content through constants for dynamic pages does not make much sense, of course. It is more interesting to use constants for values such as text formats, colors, image properties, etc., that is, for values that are repeatedly used in an application, and should be easy to modify.

5.2.9 Elements and Concepts

The NEW SITE template created with the **Template | Info/Modify** module contains the following lines, which display an HTML page in the front end with the text "HELLO WORLD!":

```
# Default PAGE object:
   page = PAGE
   page.typeNum = 0
   page.10 = TEXT
   page.10.value = HELLO WORLD!
```

In abstract form, the details can be translated to:

```
# Comment
    myObject = OBJECTTYPE
    myObject.PROPERTY = value_1
    myObject.subObject = OBJECTTYPE
    myObject.subObject.PROPERTY = value_2
```

By means of introduction, the terms will be named using an example, and then will be defined more precisely.

```
# Default PAGE object:
```

The first line represents a comment, and is therefore ignored by TYPO3.

In the following line `page` is defined by the "=" operator as an object of the PAGE type.

```
page = PAGE
```

The name `page` can in principle be freely chosen. But some names are reserved by convention for specific basis objects. While `page` is used for normal content pages, the name `plugin` is reserved for plugins (extensions).

```
page.typeNum = 0
```

An object has *properties*, to which values can be assigned. `typeNum` is a property of the PAGE object type, which is assigned the value 0 here. The character sequence `page.typeNum` defines the *path* for the property.

The following line defines `page.10` as an object of the TEXT type. In TypoScript, numerical lists (*arrays*) are frequently used. In this case the numerical list is a property of the PAGE object type. For objects of the PAGE type, this list can in turn also take in objects. Here 10 is defined as an object of the TEXT type. `page.10` is the object path to this object.

```
page.10 = TEXT
```

Bear in mind that such lists do not always take in objects; this depends on which data type the list belongs to. Relevant information can be found in the TypoScript reference TSref and in the corresponding extensions.

```
page.10.value = HELLO WORLD!
```

The `value` property of the `page.10` object is assigned the value HELLO WORLD!.

Here are the concepts once again, explained in detail:

Object types

TYPO3 provides a whole range of predefined object types for use in your own TypoScript template. Examples of these are PAGE, TEXT, and IMAGE. Most object types create front-end output; these are also named *cObjects* or *Content Objects*. Other object types are used for general configuration purposes.

Objects

page was defined as an object of the PAGE type. Because page is in the top level of the hierarchy, it is also referred to here as a *top level object*. These can have almost any name you want. Already reserved naming conventions, such as lib, config, constants, styles, or temp are documented in the TSref (see soft link).

Softlink **110843**

The page object could also be named monday, but descriptive names help to increase the overall clarity. If you want to define a page with frames, the name frameset might be a good choice.

Properties

Object types, and therefore objects of the respective type have precisely defined properties, which are described in the TSref. Only these properties are taken into account by the objects. The following line has no effect whatsoever, because the PAGE object has no value property.

Softlink **839954**

```
page.value = Hello World!
```

No error is created, however, because TypoScript does not run at any point.

The properties of an object itself have a specific data type. page.typeNum for example is of the int type, which means that only whole numbers are valid as values. The types and their valid parameters can be found in the TSref.

Operators

The individual operators are introduced a little later. One of these, for example, is the assignment operator "=".

Path and object path

Objects and properties can be addressed with their paths. The path is assembled from the overlying objects and properties, separated by a dot.

page.10 is the object path to the corresponding object; page.10.value is the path to the value property for this object.

5.2.10 The Syntax

As a rule of thumb, the notation can be summarized as follows:

[*objectpath*].[*property*] [*operator*] [*value*]

The following syntax rules apply for TypoScript setup:

- Objects and properties are separated by a dot, which at the same time defines the hierarchical dependency.

- TypoScript differentiates between upper and lower case.

- Constants have the form {$name} and are replaced with a value before the TypoScript setup is processed.

- For object names and properties, only the characters A-z, a-z, 0-9, the minus character "-", and the underscore "_" are used.

- The text from the beginning of the line to the operator forms the path to the object or the property. It may not contain spaces.

- The order of processing for object properties is defined by the object itself; it is not defined by the order of the lines in the TypoScript setup.

- Numerical lists (page.10, page.20) are processed in ascending order.

Constants

The syntax rules for the setup also apply to constants, with the following restrictions:

- Constants are not objects, and consequently have no properties; therefore no functions such as stdWrap or if are available. They are nevertheless organized hierarchically.

- The =< reference operator is not available.

- Multiple line values cannot be used in the same way as in the setup with ().

Values

The following rules apply for a value:

- It is not enclosed by quotation marks.

- It begins after the operator and ends with a new line.

- Multiple line values can be used with the help of ().

- Spaces before and after the value are removed when it is passed on.

Comments and Comment Blocks

/, #, /*, */

Comments can be added to document TypoScript. If you are not too familiar with programming techniques, we can only recommend to you at this point that you include sufficient comments in your projects for you to be quickly able to find your way again in your code, even after a long interval.

One-line comments are marked by / or #, and must precede the contents.

```
# Default PAGE object:
/ a different comment
```

Multiple line comment blocks begin with /* and finish with */ at the beginning of the final comment line. The completion mark is important, because the following code will otherwise also be treated as a comment.

```
/*
a multiple line comment
is inserted here.
*/
```

Operators

{}

The { } operators help you to write TypoScript more clearly and compactly by enabling you to nest several properties together.

The following example exactly matches the previous example setup.

```
page = PAGE
page {
  typeNum = 0
  10 = TEXT
  10 {
    value = HELLO WORLD!
  }
}
```

This is introduced with a curly bracket, {. All other details after the operator in the same line are ignored during *parsing*. The first hierarchically subordinate property must follow in the next line. The indentation only improves readability. The nesting of properties is concluded with the } operator. It must be the first character of a line, with the exception of empty spaces.

()

> The round brackets () enclose values, which can continue over several lines. This is very useful if a text is to be taken over that is already in structured form, or if values are to be shown more clearly, for the sake of better legibility.

The TypoScript example has been slightly changed below, to illustrate this use. The 10 object was defined as an HTML content object. The page.10.value property is passed on as HTML code, which was created in an HTML editor, for example.

```
page {
  typeNum = 0
  10 = HTML
  10.value (
   <table width="100%" border="0"
      cellspacing="0" cellpadding="0">
   <tr>
    <td width="25%" align="left" bgcolor="#003366"><span
       style="color:#FFFFFF">Small example:</span></td>
    <td width="75%" align="center" bgcolor="#84A1E5">
      <span style="color:#FFFFFF">Input of multiline
      values</span></td>
   </tr>
   </table>
   )
}
```

The front-end output appears as follows:

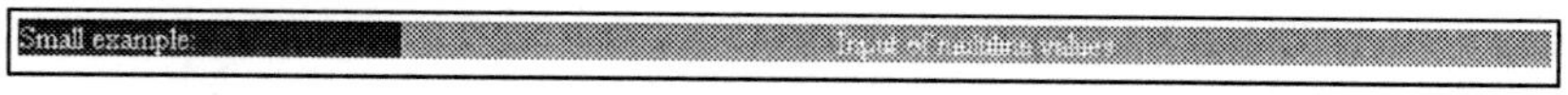

Figure 5.22:

The ( ) operators

=

> The equals sign, =, stands for an assignment. An object is defined by assigning it to an object type. A value is assigned to a property. The entire string of a line after the operator is treated as a value. Empty spaces before and after it are removed.

```
page.10.value = HELLO WORLD!
# corresponds to
page.10.value=HELLO WORLD!
```

< (Copy)

With the < operator, one path can be copied into another. Individual properties or whole objects can be copied. When this is done, both the properties and the values of an object are copied. Objects, properties, and values that already exist in the destination path are overwritten.

Now two new objects are assigned to the "HELLO WORLD!" example. `page.15` is defined as an HTML content object, and a "break" is set as the output value. The `page.10` object is copied into `page.20`. Inside the curly brackets, the object path can also be accessed using the syntax `20 < .10`.

```
page = PAGE
page {
  typeNum = 0
  10 = TEXT
  10.value = HELLO World
  15 = HTML
  15.value = <br />
  20 < page.10
# or alternatively:
# 20 < .10
}
```

Because there is an identical TEXT object in `page.20`, the front-end output now creates the text twice:

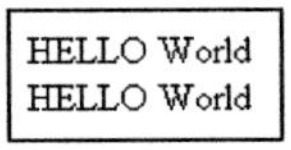

```
HELLO World
HELLO World
```

Figure 5.23:

Copying an object path with the < operator

Individual objects and their hierarchy can be illustrated and controlled graphically in the TypoScript Object Browser (**Web | Template | TypoScript Object Browser | [Template name]**).

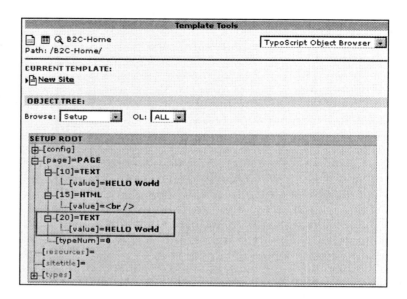

Figure 5.24:

TypoScript Object
Browser: the proper-
ties of the 10 object
were transferred to
the 20 object

=< (Referencing)

In conjunction with the = operator, < does not copy the object path, but makes a reference to it. Referencing is only possible with objects, not with properties. Please note that apart from this one exception, only one operator is allowed in TypoScript.

The following example illustrates the different ways in which copying and referencing work:

```
# The objectXY object
objectXY = TEXT
objectXY {
  value = Hello TYPOS??
  textStyle.color.default = red
}
page = PAGE
page {
  typeNum = 0
  # Object 10 references the object objectXY
  10 = < objectXY
  10.value = Hello TYPOS!! (reference)
  15 = HTML
  15.value = <br />
  # the current objectXY object is copied
  20 < objectXY
  20.value = Hello TYPOS!! (copy)
}
# A property of the objectXY object is changed later
objectXY.textStyle.color.default = blue
```

In the front end, the text of the copy is shown in red and that of the reference, in blue (but in view of the black and white illustration below, you will just have to take our word for it...):

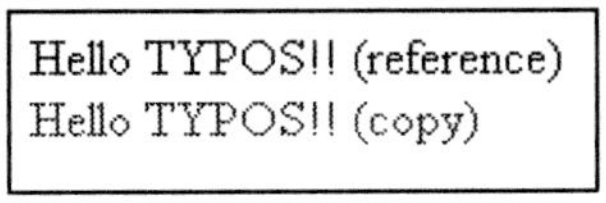

```
Hello TYPOS!! (reference)
Hello TYPOS!! (copy)
```

Figure 5.25:

A comparison of referencing and copying

The `page.10` object points here with the `=<` operator to the previously defined `objectXY` object. Since this is a reference to the `objectXY` object, it is taken on by the `page.10` object while the TypoScript setup is being processed. In this way it can be used many times and in different places in the object tree, and is always up-to-date, since changes to the referenced object are valid for all references.

In the TypoScript Object Browser you can check to see how the TypoScript setup will be put together. The text "Hello TYPOS!! (reference)" will be shown in blue in the front-end output, since `textStyle.color.default` in the `objectXY` object was subsequently overwritten. It is also interesting that properties of the reference can be overwritten locally, in this case with `page.10.value`. A copy in the `page.20` object path does not take on the change in the text color. The properties and values of `objectXY` were copied when the TypoScript code was read in, which was before the text color was set to blue. The overwritten text "Hello TYPOS!! (copy)" therefore appears in red.

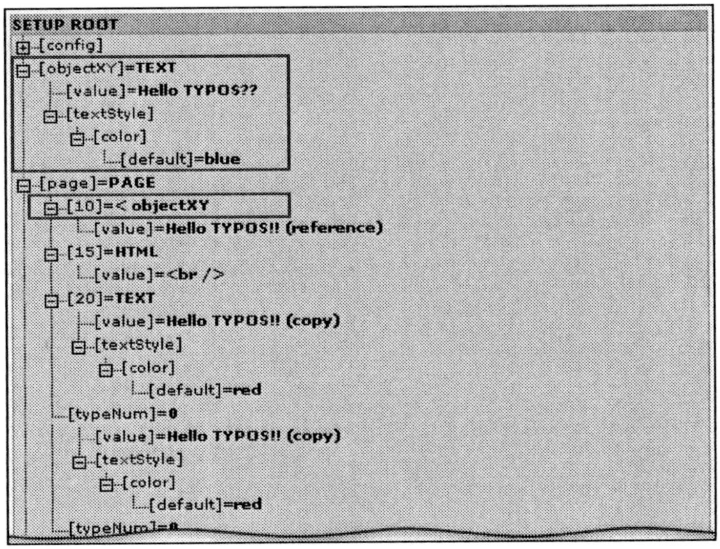

```
SETUP ROOT
[+]-[config]
[-]-[objectXY]=TEXT
    |---[value]=Hello TYPOS??
    [-]-[textStyle]
        [-]-[color]
            |...[default]=blue
[-]-[page]=PAGE
    [-]-[10]=< objectXY
        |...[value]=Hello TYPOS!! (reference)
    [-]-[15]=HTML
        |...[value]=<br />
    [-]-[20]=TEXT
        |---[value]=Hello TYPOS!! (copy)
        [-]-[textStyle]
            [-]-[color]
                |...[default]=red
    |---[typeNum]=0
        |---[value]=Hello TYPOS!! (copy)
        [-]-[textStyle]
            [-]-[color]
                |...[default]=red
    |---[typeNum]=0
```

Figure 5.26:

TypoScript Object Browser: the 10 object points with a reference to objectXY

221

>

The > operator deletes all objects and properties existing so far from the respective path.

In the following example the `page.20` object is deleted again.

```
page = PAGE
page {
  typeNum = 0
  10 = TEXT
  10.value = HELLO World
  15 = HTML
  15.value = <br />
  20 = TEXT
  20.value = Hello TYPOS!!
  20 >
}
```

Only the first text is displayed:

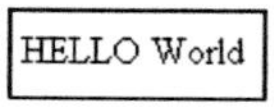

Figure 5.27:

"Hello TYPOS!!" has been deleted

HELLO World

Conditions

Softlink **270225**

Conditions in TypoScript are enclosed by the [] characters, written on their own line, and cannot be placed inside properties nested with { }. Conditions are defined that must be fulfilled for the following TS code to be valid. In this way it is possible, for example, to restrict instructions to specific browsers or user groups.

If the conditions are identified as fulfilled during parsing, the parser continues interpreting the TypoScript code. Otherwise it will ignore it until the condition has been removed.

Conditions are dealt with in more detail in section 5.11. Here we are just interested in the syntax. In the following example, the condition [browser = netscape] means that the page.10 object is only set if the calling browser identifies itself as Netscape. [END] (alternatively: [GLOBAL]) marks the end of the condition.

```
page = PAGE
page.typeNum = 0

[browser = netscape]
page {
  10 = TEXT
  10.value = HELLO World
  10.wrap = |<br />
```

```
}
[END]

page {
   20 = TEXT
   20.value = Hello TYPOS!!
}
```

If several conditions are defined in one line, they are linked by OR, that is, as soon as a condition is valid, the following TypoScript code is also valid. AND links cannot be implemented yet with TypoScript conditions.

In the following example different text is displayed by the `page.20` object if the request is from Netscape or if the operating system is Linux.

```
[browser = netscape] [system = linux]
page.20.value = You're a Linux or Netscape user
[END]
```

The [ELSE] condition is regarded as fulfilled if a condition set before this is not fulfilled. It must also be terminated with [END] or [GLOBAL].

```
page = PAGE
page.typeNum = 0
[browser = netscape]
page {
   10 = TEXT
   10.value = output for the Netscape browser
}
[ELSE]
page {
   20 = TEXT
   20.value = output for all other browsers
}
[END]
page {
   30 = TEXT
   30.value = output for all browsers
   30.wrap = <br />|
}
```

The Firefox browser, for example, can be identified as a Netscape browser, and produces the following output:

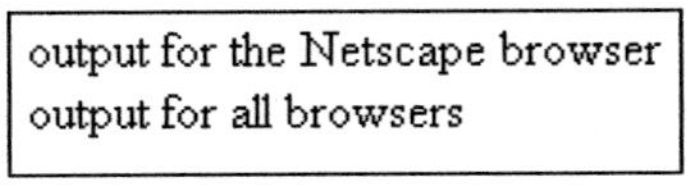

output for the Netscape browser
output for all browsers

Figure 5.28:

Condition [browser = netscape] fulfilled

It must be noted that conditions cannot be nested. So the following example would *not* work.

```
[browser = netscape]
page.20.value = You're a Netscape user
[system = linux]
page.20.value = You're a Linux and Netscape user
[END]
[END]
```

Includes

TypoScript libraries can also be included as external text files. The instruction for this must be on a separate line, but unlike conditions, it can be set within nested properties. It is already processed and inserted before parsing begins.

The following example shows the integration of an external file with the help of the `<INCLUDE_TYPOSCRIPT>` instruction.

```
page = PAGE
page.typeNum = 0
page {
   10 = TEXT
   10.value = Output 1
   10.wrap = |<br />
<INCLUDE_TYPOSCRIPT: source="FILE:
                         fileadmin/typoscript/include_1.txt">
   30 = TEXT
   30.value = Output 3
}
```

The external file `include_1.txt`, which was stored in the file system under `fileadmin/typoscript/`, contains these settings:

```
20 = TEXT
20.value = Output 2 (integrated via Includes)
20.wrap = |<br />
```

This produces the following output in the front end:

Figure 5.29:

TypoScript integrated
via Includes

```
Output 1
Output 2 (integrated via Includes)
Output 3
```

5.2.11 Order of processing

To be able to utilize TypoScript, you must understand the order in which TypoScript is processed.

1. TypoScript constant instructions are read in from top to bottom,

and conditions are taken into account.

2. Constants are substituted in the TypoScript setup in the same order in which they were set up.

3. TypoScript setup instructions are read in from top to bottom.

4. Conditions are evaluated as they are read in.

5. Copies of objects and properties using the < operator are made while parsing takes place. This means, of course, that only the configuration of an object available at the time of the copy is copied. If changes are made to the output object in the following lines, these are not applied to the copy already created.

6. The TypoScript code is processed and references are resolved.

As you can see, the order of TypoScript instructions during parsing is relevant, since the reoccupation of properties in copies and output objects has no effect on the other object concerned in each case. On the other hand, the order during processing does not play any role.

- Properties are *not* processed in the sequence in which they are created in the template. Rather, the object itself defines when it will evaluate a property.

- Objects are processed in the order of the numerical lists in which they are defined.

The following examples will therefore create identical output; it is obvious that the first variation is by far the clearest.

Example 1:

```
page = PAGE
page.typeNum = 0
page.10 = TEXT
page.10.value = I am an
page.15 = HTML
page.15.value = <br />
page.20 = TEXT
page.20.value = example text!
```

Example 2:

```
page = PAGE
page.typeNum = 0
page.143 = HTML
page.143.value = <br />
page.377 = TEXT
page.377.value = example text!
page.23 = TEXT
page.23.value = I am an
```

225

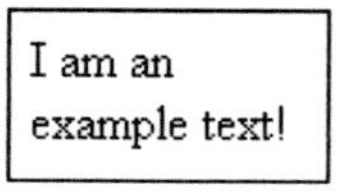

Figure 5.30:

Front-end output of
examples

> I am an
> example text!

5.2.12 Nesting of Objects

Another essential principle of TypoScript is its ability to nest objects. So far you have seen how objects create contents and display them in the sequence specified in a numerical list. The following TypoScript setup is such an example:

```
page = PAGE
page.typeNum = 0
page.10 = TEXT
page.10.value = I am a
page.10.wrap = |<br />
page.20 = TEXT
page.20.value = small
page.20.wrap = |<br />
page.30 = TEXT
page.30.value = example text!
```

This produces the following output:

```
I am a
small
example text!
```

The general assumption is that each object in turn gives up its content, so that the output gradually accumulates in the front end. This is only partially correct: objects always pass on content or data created to the object that has integrated them. In the above example, the HTML objects pass on their contents to the overlying PAGE object. Only when all the objects of page have been processed does this return the contents created, after which they are then displayed.

This nesting can be continued downwards for as many layers as you like, since many object types possess properties that can take in objects. The following setup, for example, creates the same output as the above example:

```
page = PAGE
page.typeNum = 0
page.10 = COA
page.10 {
  10 = COA
  10 {
```

```
    10 = COA
    10 {
       10 = TEXT
       10.value = I am a
       10.wrap = |<br />
    }
    20 = TEXT
    20.value = small
    20.wrap = |<br />
  }
  20 = TEXT
  20.value = example text!
}
```

The identical setup in a notation without brackets looks like this:

```
page = PAGE
page.typeNum = 0

page.10 = COA
page.10.10 = COA
page.10.10.10 = COA

page.10.10.10.10 = TEXT
page.10.10.10.10.value = I am a
page.10.10.10.10.wrap = |<br />

page.10.10.20 = TEXT
page.10.10.20.value = small
page.10.10.20.wrap = |<br />

page.10.20 = TEXT
page.10.20.value = example text!
```

To acquire an understanding of the TypoScript setup, you must know that the COA object type, like the PAGE object type, can take in objects in a numerical list. The procedure is as follows: with page.10 a COA object is called, which in turn, first as page.10.10, calls a COA object, and so on. Eventually a first (TEXT) content object is called up with page.10.10.10.10, which actually creates an output, namely "I am a ". All objects in COA page.10.10.10 have now been processed. The COA object has received the content generated from the embedded TEXT object, which it now passes onto the parent COA page.10.10. This processes its object list, calling the next TEXT object page.10.10.20. The content generated is appended to the content that the COA has received from the child COA, and after the object list has been processed, it is passed on to the calling COA page.10 object. The procedure is repeated until all objects have been processed, the PAGE object receives the contents, and they are displayed.

This nesting can be illustrated by adding the following to the setup:

```
page.10.10.stdWrap.case = upper
```

Now this output is produced:

```
I AM A
SMALL
example text!
```

The COA object `page.10.10` receives the instruction, with `.stdWrap.case=upper`, to convert its contents to upper case. The object itself does not create any content at all, but in a nested hierarchy, two TEXT objects are embedded whose contents are received by the COA, thus converting the content to upper case.

So tree hierarchies of objects can be created with TypoScript, where on the one hand the levels are processed in turn, but on the other, the order of processing is simultaneously dependent on the hierarchy. In this way you end up with a powerful configuration tool for the output in the front end.

5.3 TS Objects, Functions, and Data Types

5.3.1 Data Types

Softlink **253434**

The data types used by TYPO3 are very varied and to a large extent not comparable to the data types of programming languages. Although there are data types such as int, string, and boolean, there are also things like degree and pixels. Just like int, these are also integer values, with the difference that degree defines a number of degrees and pixels a number of pixels. As you can see, the data types help to further describe what sort of data can be expected from a property. Sometimes the functionality of a property only becomes clear through the data type. The complete list of data types can be found using the soft link here.

One special feature lies in the fact that a number of data types are actually functions. So far we have shown you how TypoScript is used to set configuration parameters. Apart from the Conditions, this is a purely static procedure. But with the functions available, TypoScript acquires dynamic capabilities and can process and modify data.

Here is a very simple example:

```
page.10 = HTML
page.10.value = kasper
page.10.value.case = upper
```

`value` is in the `HTML` object type and of the `stdWrap` data type. This function knows the `case` property and can be configured with the `upper` value to convert the output to upper case.

TypoScript provides a number of similar functions, which will be described below in more detail. It is these functions in combination with object types in particular that transform TypoScript into a powerful tool.

The data types are listed in the TSref in the reference tables of properties for individual objects. In the assignments, not only data types can be found, but also values such as `->select` or `->filelink`.

In these cases, functions can usually be reached via properties of the same name, or predefined objects of the specified type are available (e.g. TLO `config`). In the following figure you can see how the `if` and `stdWrap` properties point to the corresponding functions.

Softlink **924038**

Property:	Data type:	Description:	Default:
setCurrent	string /stdWrap	Sets the "current"-value.	
key	string /stdWrap	This is the	
default	cObject		
Array	cObject		
stdWrap	->stdWrap		
if	->if	if "if" returns false nothing is returned	
[tsref:(cObject).CASE]			

Figure 5.31:

The CASE object type integrates the stdWrap and if functions

If `+calc` was added to a data type value in the TSref, then calculations can be carried out with the value. The `+-/*` operators used in this have no priorities and are processed in the order in which they appear.

Softlink **034017**

As can be seen in figure 5.31, the property is of the `string/stdWrap` data type. For pieced-together data types like this, you can specify a value (`string`) or use the specified function (`stdWrap`). You can also combine both.

Softlink **695668**

5.3.2 The Wrap Concept

A *wrap* is a very important concept in many TypoScript objects. It represents a string that is split into parts by the "|" (*pipe*) character. If the object has the wrap property, it is enclosed by the value of the wrap.

The TEXT object `page.10` with the value `Hello World` is enclosed in the example by the `<strong>|</strong>` wrap:

```
page.10 = TEXT
page.10.value = HELLO WORLD!
page.10.wrap = <strong>|</strong>
```

The result is a text highlighted in bold: `<strong>HELLO WORLD!</strong>`

Spaces, markers for tabs, and line breaks before and after the individual parts of the wrap are removed when it is passed on.

5.3.3 Functions

Softlink **991290**

As already described, several data types take on a special capacity. They are used equally by many content objects and provide universal functionalities for them. On the PHP level they are implemented by independent functions, which is why they are also listed as functions in the TSref. They fit in seamlessly, however, with other TypoScript data types into the syntax of objects and properties. But they can only be used if properties are of the corresponding data type, since they are called up explicitly on the PHP level. The TSref documents which property is of which data type.

Please bear in mind that functions are not available for constants.

stdWrap

This function plays a very important role in TYPO3. Depending on how it is used, data can be imported, controlled, and manipulated by it. Many of the functions below can be used from `stdWrap`. So if the data type of a property is `stdWrap`, powerful tools are available for processing its contents.

imgResource

This function defines the source of an image file, subjects the image to simple processing steps, and creates the required HTML code for its output. The function is available under the properties belonging to the `imgResource` file type of the same name.

imageLinkWrap

This function allows an image to be edited with the advanced features of the graphic library (GIFBUILDER). In addition you can set a simple link (`typolink`) or a zoom link with the `showpic.php` script to open the image in a separate JavaScript window.

numRows

With this functionality you can determine the number of records in a table or in a Select query.

select

with this function an SQL query can be formulated that will be displayed by the CONTENT cObject. Hidden or deleted records, or ones restricted in visibility by start/stop rules or front-end user groups, are not taken into account in this process.

split

This function splits a text content on the basis of a specific character or letter, and processes the resulting sections with further functions or content objects. This is helpful, for example, if a menu is to have multiple colors.

if

The if function imitates the classical IF control structure. If the subordinate conditions are all met, the contents of the child object remain as they are. Otherwise FALSE is returned and the contents of the object are deleted.

typolink

typolink sets a link around the content passed on. This function should always be used where possible instead of "hard-coded" links, not least because this supports the simulation of static HTML files.

textStyle

The somewhat aging textStyle function defines the appearance of text areas when using FONT or other HTML elements. The modern alternative to this would be to use CSS definitions.

encapsLines

This function inserts paragraphs, for example, into HTML tags for the output. Tags such as P or DIV are added when parsing, and not saved with the content in the database, so that the content remains "clean".

tableStyle

The content is enclosed by a TABLE tag with tableStyle. Various design details can be defined here. The function is useful, for example, in the planning of the basic layout table, especially for setting up pure TypoScript templates.

addParams

Using this function, additional attributes (parameters) can be passed to HTML elements of existing cObjects.

filelink

With `filelink` a file name is converted to a download link. Path details, attributes such as alternative text or title, and icons are added. Advanced features of this function can count the number of downloads or disguise the actual location, for reasons of security.

parseFunc

An extended postprocessing of the contents is possible with this function. You can, for example, replace markers inserted in the text, define rules for using or substituting HTML elements, or start a recursive processing of nested HTML blocks, while bringing in further functions. In this way you can wrap contents or search terms so they are more easily identified, and determine how links or ordered and unordered lists are generated, or which tags may or may not appear in contents.

makelinks

`makelinks` generates complete HTML links from simple web or e-mail addresses that appear in the content.

tags

You can use this function to define your own abstract tags. They are saved in the database and are substituted in the output, where required, by various HTML elements that really exist. This function is used in conjunction with `parseFunc`. One example of user-defined tags in TYPO3 is the `<LINK>` element, which is replaced during parsing with a proper HTML link.

HTMLparser

The `HTMLparser` function separates the entire HTML input into single HTML elements and their attributes. In doing this, defined rules are applied for the interplay of elements and attributes. The function is especially useful for manipulating imported or alien HTML contents, and when working with the Rich Text Editor.

HTMLparser_tags

`HTMLparser_tags` is called by the above-mentioned `HTMLparser` function. It defines precise rules for attributes of each single HTML element.

5.3.4 Content Objects (cObject)

Softlink **207606**

Content Objects or *cObjects* is what TypoScript is all about: they create output from data, using a TypoScript setup. Although other methods of data input and output are possible, in general content objects are used to transform the data of the content types that are available in the back end (**Text, Image, Insert plugin,...**) and saved in the database, for output in the front end.

An array with current data, which can be accessed, is assigned to every cObject while it is being processed. This is usually the data of the current record. If a **Text w/image** content type is rendered, for example, the data entered (for example the heading on the file names of the inserted images) is available to the TypoScript setup that displays this content element, because the fields of the record can be accessed (cf. section 5.11.3).

In the examples so far, we have just used the TEXT, HTML, and HRULER cObjects. But TYPO3 has a large number of possible cObjects.

Example: cObject FILE

Softlink **036048**

The cObject FILE integrates content elements from the file system up to a maximum size of 1024 kB. A special feature is that image resources of the types JPG, GIF, JPEG, and PNG are displayed with an `<img>` tag. All other formats are parsed and their contents displayed unprocessed.

In the following example `page.10` is defined as a FILE cObject. The `file` property (data type: `resource`) points to an image in the GIF format. The `page.20` object is also defined as a FILE cObject, but points to a file in the TXT format. As a result the file is parsed and its content displayed.

```
page = PAGE
page {
   typeNum = 0
   10 = FILE
   10.file = fileadmin/images/layout/logo.gif
   20 = FILE
   20.file = fileadmin/documents/text1.txt
}
```

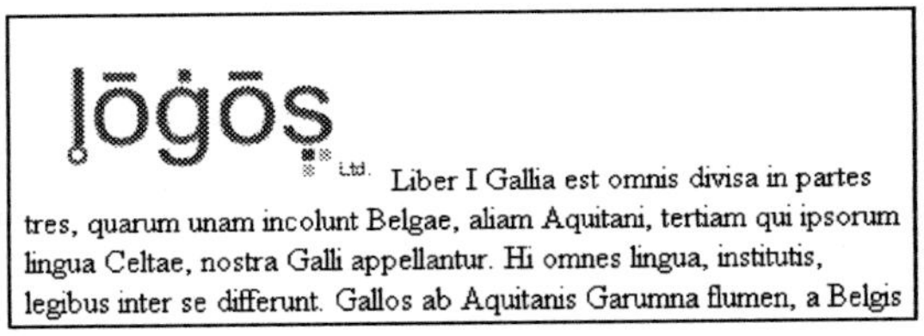

Figure 5.32:

Accessing the file system with the FILE cObject (output in the front end)

An Overview of cObjects

HTML

HTML is used to display HTML content. The value property is of the stdWrap data type, with which properties of the function of the same name are available.

Example:

```
10 = HTML
10.value = this is an HTML object
10.value.case = upper
```

TEXT

TEXT is very similar to the HTML cObject and is used to display non-formatted texts. The properties of the stdWrap function are addressed by the basis of the object, however, which is not the general rule.

Example:

```
10 = TEXT
10.value = this is a text object
10.case = lower
```

COBJ_ARRAY (COA, COA_INT)

The COBJ_ARRAY cObject (alternatively: COA) comprises various objects in a numerical list, in one array. If you create an object of the COA_INT type, it behaves exactly like the USER_INT object: it is rendered non-cached!

Example:

```
temp.myObject = COA
temp.myObject{
   10 = HTML
   10.value = <table border=1 cellspacing=5
              bgcolor=grey><tr><td>
   20 = TEXT
   20.value = A cObject, created with COA.
   30 = HTML
   30.value = <td><tr></table>
}
```

FILE

With the FILE cObject you can access the file system and integrate text, images, or HTML files, for example.

Example:

```
10 = FILE
10.file = fileadmin/html/html-inhalt1.htm
```

IMAGE

Images can be integrated with the IMAGE cObject. The file property of the imgResource data type enables access to the file system or to the resources of the template record.

Example:

```
10 = IMAGE
10.file = header_dealers*.gif
20 = IMAGE
20.file = fileadmin/images/layout/header_products.gif
```

IMG_RESOURCE

The IMG_RESOURCE cObject returns only the reference to the image without an <img> tag.

Example:

```
10 = IMG_RESOURCE
10.file = header_dealers*.gif
10.stdWrap.wrap = <table width="400" border=0
                   cellspacing=15
background="|"><tr><td>Our Dealers<td><tr></table>
```

CLEARGIF

The CLEARGIF cObject inserts a transparent GIF image that can be used as a placeholder.

Example:

```
10 = CLEARGIF
10.height = 15
```

CONTENT

With the CONTENT cObject you can display the contents of the database. The Select query is restricted to tables that begin with tt_, tx_, ttx_, fe_, or user_. To display the records, an appropriately configured TLO is necessary with the name of the table that defines the output. The tt_content table, for example, is preconfigured in the Content (Default) standard template.

Example: output of the contents of the current page and the "Normal" column:

```
10 = CONTENT
10.table = tt_content
10.select {
  pidInList = this
  orderBy = sorting
  where = colPos=0
}
```

RECORDS

With the RECORDS cObject, records from the database can be displayed. This is comparable to the **Insert record** content type. Records from inaccessible pages (hidden, time-restricted, or access-protected pages) can normally not be selected as long as the dontCheckPid option is not set.

Example: here the address records with UID 2 and 3 are read out.

```
10 = RECORDS
10 {
  source = tt_address_2,3
  tables = tt_address
  conf.tt_address = < tt_address.default
}
```

HMENU

With this cObject you can generate a hierarchical menu. The (1 / 2 / 3 /...) property determines which menu object should be rendered by the different levels.

Example:

```
10 = HMENU
10.1 = TMENU
...
```

CTABLE

The CTABLE cObject creates an HTML table whose contents cell is surrounded by four further cells. Content can be assigned to each of these cells.

Example:

```
10 = CTABLE
10 {
  tableParams = border=0 width=500
  c.10 = CONTENT
  ...
  rm.10 = HMENU
  ...
}
```

OTABLE

This HTML table is used to add an offset to the contents, that is, they are offset from the upper left corner.

Example:

```
10 = OTABLE
10 {
  offset = 10,70
  tableParams = border=0 width=100
  10 = TEXT
  10.value = Content
}
```

COLUMNS

With this cObject you can create a table for which you can specify the number of columns, parameters, number of rows, width, column spacing, and the width of the common dividers.

Example:

```
10 = COLUMNS
10 {
  1 = CONTENT
  ...
  2 = CONTENT
  ...
  gapWidth = 30
  gapLineThickness = 1
  if.isTrue.numRows < .1
  if.isTrue.ifEmpty.numRows < .2
  totalWidth = 500
}
```

HRULER

This simple cObject draws a horizontal line, for which you can specify the thickness and color of the line, and its spacing to the left and right.

Example:

```
10 = HRULER
10 {
  lineThickness = 1
  spaceLeft = 20
}
```

IMGTEXT

The IMGTEXT cObject helps to arrange images and texts. It is normally used to generate the **Text w/Image** content element.

The images are placed in a table, which is positioned before or after the text, and to the left or right of it.

Example: the extensive IMGTEXT object of styles.content (default) is replaced.

```
temp.imagetext = IMGTEXT
temp.imagetext {
  text < tt_content.text.20
  imgList.field = image
  textPos.field = imageorient
  imgPath = uploads/pics/
  imgObjNum = 1
  1.file.import.current = 1
  maxW = 150
  border = 1
  textMargin = 10
}

tt_content.textpic.20 >
tt_content.textpic.20 < temp.imagetext
```

CASE

CASE provides functionality in case distinction similar to the switch construction in PHP. If the key property matches the name of another property of the object array, then this object is displayed.

The naming of the cObject can be freely chosen but the reserved words key, default, stdWrap, and if cannot be used. If the key property is not defined, then the default object is used instead.

Example: for the **Text** content type, layout 2 is displayed, with a heading with lowercase letters.

```
temp.stuff = CASE
temp.stuff.key.field = CType
temp.stuff.default < lib.stdheader
temp.stuff.text < lib.stdheader
lib.stdheader >
lib.stdheader < temp.stuff
lib.stdheader.text {
  10.2.case = lower
}
```

LOAD_REGISTER

The register is an internal temporary memory in TYPO3. The variables stored there are globally available and are read out, saved, or overwritten at various points during parsing. With LOAD_REGISTER, temporarily saved values can be overwritten by the system through your own definitions, in order to influence the process of content generation. The temporary memory is organized as an array and can take in properties and their values.

Example: the time of the last update of the page is overwritten with a fixed date:

```
10 = LOAD_REGISTER
10.SYS_LASTCHANGED.data = date: U
```

RESTORE_REGISTER

This object undoes the changes in the internal system register made by LOAD_REGISTER. The original register array is restored. If the registry changes are only supposed to have an effect at a specific point, and then need to be replaced again with system values, it is appropriate to use RESTORE_REGISTER.

Example:

```
20 = RESTORE_REGISTER
```

FORM

The FORM object is responsible for the output of forms. Using this, forms can be defined both directly in TypoScript (e.g. the system's own mail and login forms) and in the back end of the system by editors.

Example: login form

```
temp.loginform = FORM
temp.loginform {
  dataArray {
    10.label = Username:
    10.type = *user=input
    20.label = Password:
    20.type = *pass=password
    30.type = logintype=hidden
    30.value = Login
    40.type = submit=submit
    40.value = Login
  }
  layout =   <tr><td>###LABEL###</td><td>
            ###FIELD###</td></tr>
  stdWrap.wrap = <table>|</table>
  hiddenFields.pid = TEXT
  hiddenFields.pid.value = 123
}
```

SEARCHRESULT

The SEARCHRESULT cObject controls the output of the hit list via the **Standard, Advanced,** and **Not in menu** page types, as a result of a database-based TYPO3 search. Apart from the values for tables and fields to be included in the search, the appearance of the list is determined. The search terms are supplied by an added form with special URL parameters. Database queries are performed in the background and the result list is returned. The search terms are retained in the register described above, so that terms found can, for example, be color marked by other functions.

USER and USER_INT

These content objects are the recommended instrument for integrating your own PHP scripts. The object calls a PHP function or method of a class, and any individual configurations can be passed on here. Nearly all front-end plugins are based on these objects.

The USER_INT object is used especially if dynamic functionalities are involved that cannot or should not be cached. If the user sends a newsletter registration, for example, this data must be dynamically processed for it to be saved in the database.

Example:

```
includeLibs.alt_xml = media/scripts/xmlversionLib.inc
10 = USER
10.userFunc = user_xmlversion->main_xmlversion
```

PHP_SCRIPT

PHP_SCRIPT serves to integrate simple PHP scripts. A disadvantage here is that the caching functionality of the page has to be completely switched off, causing noticeable delays when calling the page and increasing the load on the server.

To integrate your own scripts, you should, where possible, make use of USER or USER_INT. This option is ignored if $TYPO3_CONF_VARS["FE"]["noPHPscriptInclude"] = 1; is set in localconf.php.

PHP_SCRIPT_INT

In contrast to PHP_SCRIPT, this variation does have some improvements in caching, but causes problems in debugging and with global variables. USER or USER_INT should be used instead.

PHP_SCRIPT_EXT

With this object, integrating scripts takes place outside the TypoScript environment. A significant performance advantage is gained in doing this, but the processing is to a large extent "missed" by TYPO3. USER or USER_INT should be used instead.

TEMPLATE

You can load an HTML template with this cObject. In contrast to FILE you can limit the output of the HTML file to specific areas. You can specify which content will replace which placeholders.

Example:

```
page.10 = TEMPLATE
page.10 {
  template = FILE
  template.file = fileadmin/templates/test.tmpl
  workOnSubpart = DOCUMENT
  subparts {
    HELLO = TEXT
    HELLO.value = this text replaces the subpart
                "HELLO"
  }
  marks {
    TESTMARKER = TEXT
    TESTMARKER.value = this text replaces the
                    "TESTMARKER" marker
  }
}
```

MULTIMEDIA

This cObject gives you a way of integrating various multimedia files. Some possible file types are: TXT, HTML, HTM, CLASS, SWF, SWA, DCR, WAV, AU, AVI, MOV, ASF, MPG, and WMV.

Depending on the file type, you can specify various parameters to be applied to the file.

Example:

```
10 = MULTIMEDIA
10.file = fileadmin/video/test.avi
10.params.width = 200px
```

EDITPANEL

In the context of the "front-end editing" concept, editing options for the page can be made available in the front end to users logged in to the back end.

Example:

```
temp.editPanel = COA
temp.editPanel {
  10 = EDITPANEL
  10 {
    allow = toolbar,hide,move,delete
    label = current page:<B>%s</B><br /> you can
    create a new subpage here,<br/> or edit or move
    the page.
    line = 5
  }
  20 = EDITPANEL
  20 {
    newRecordFromTable = tt_news
    line = 0
    label = New page contents<br /> you can create a
                                    news article here
  }
}
```

5.3.5 Top Level Objects

Softlink **110842**

To create an output page, the page object has been used so far, which was assigned to the PAGE object type. Here the page object represents a *top level object* (TLO). It lies in the top level of the object hierarchy. You could also say: it is at the far left in the TypoScript setup. TypoScript uses a range of TLOs that can have an influence on the application. In the "setup" area of the TSref, predefined TLOs are listed, together with the properties and objects that they integrate (e.g. FE_TABLE, FRAMESET, FRAME, META, CARRAY). Several toplevel objects such as config, constants, and FEData do not first have to be defined by being assigned a data type, since they are already predefined.

types

Data type: readonly

Reserved for internal use (class.t3lib_tstemplate.php); type=99 is reserved for plain text display, for example.

resources

Data type: readonly

resources is used internally to store resources for the template hierarchy in a comma-separated list.

sitetitle

Data type: `readonly`

Reserved for internal use to parse the current title of the website from the templates.

config

data type: `->CONFIG`

Global configuration values for page generation, caching, debugging, link handling, etc. are defined with **config**; these values are saved with cached pages, which means that they are also available if a page is called from the cache.

constants

data type: `->CONSTANTS`

This defines constants that replace correspondingly marked text passages in the contents for the whole site. This is done when passing the contents with the `parseFunc` function. Example:

```
constants.WEBMASTER_EMAIL = webmaster@my-company.com
```

FEData

data type: `->FE_DATA`

`FEData` configures how `GET` and `POST` data sent by users via the front end is handled. `FEData` is an old concept and is hardly used by extensions anymore. Example: guestbook.

includeLibs

data type: `array of strings`

With this you can integrate PHP files that have their own function libraries into TYPO3, so that these functions can then be accessed. Note that the `PAGE` object provides properties with the same functionality (`page.includeLibs`). But these properties are inserted after the TLO `includeLibs` and can overwrite values in the TLO. Example:

```
includeLibs.gmenu_foldout =
                    media/scripts/gmenu_foldout.php
```

plugin

Plugins from extensions are inserted into the TLO `plugin`. Loaded plugins can be found via their extension key as subobjects in `plugin`.

tt_*

The TLO `tt_*` is used to render contents from tables. The normally used `content (default)` standard template contains a corresponding definition for the `tt_content` table, thus controlling the rendering of most content elements.

temp

The TLOs `temp` and `styles` are used for code libraries that you can copy during parsing. They are not stored with the template in the cache, however, but are deleted/emptied before the template is cached! Use `temp` to store your own temporary data.

styles

Behaves in the same way as `temp`, but is not available for your own use, and is used by the included default templates instead.

lib

Serves to define code libraries to which references are made.

...

data type: PAGE

The title can be named as you please. But it is recommended that you use the title `page` for the definition of the TLO of the PAGE type.

....

data type: any type

Define your own TLOs and assign them to the corresponding data types.

The TLOs used and the hierarchy of objects can be displayed clearly in the TypoScript Object Browser:

Figure 5.33:

Top level objects of the template, displayed in the TypoScript Object Browser

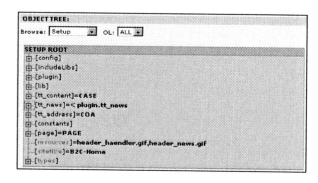

Examples

config

A number of options are globally configured with `config`. If you set `config.simulateStaticDocuments = 1` in the setup of the TypoScript template, for example, the dynamically created output of the front end is simulated as static pages. [4]

With `config.cache_period = 432000` you set the page's cache life to five days.

```
config {
  simulateStaticDocuments = 1
  cache_period = 432000
}
```

constants

With the TLO `constants` you can define constants for the entire application. This enables you, using the `parseFunc` function and its `constants=1` property, to replace the corresponding place-holders with text. If the parser finds the constants of the `###WEBMASTER_EMAIL###` example in the content of the application, then `webmaster@my-company.com` is displayed as a link.

```
constants {
  WEBMASTER_EMAIL = <a href="mailto:webmaster@
    my-company.com">webmaster@my-company.com</a>
}
```

lib

The TLO `lib` is intended for libraries of reusable code that can be referenced. A text like the one in the example is not really ideal for this, of course!

```
lib.welcomingText = TEXT
lib.welcomingText {
  value = TypoScript is simply great.
  wrap = <p> | </p>
}

page = PAGE
page {
  typeNum = 0
  10 = TEXT
  10.value = Hello Typos!
  20 = < lib.welcomingText
}
```

---

[4] For the prerequisites, see TSref.

temp and styles

Softlink **110841**

The top-level objects `temp` and `styles` are peculiar in that they are removed from the setup after they have been parsed by TypoScript. This means that it is not possible to use a reference to the `temp.myObject` object, since `temp` no longer exists during processing of the setup.

The reason for this is that all TypoScript values are generally stored in the `cache_hash` database table after they have been read in, to increase performance. If certain parts of TypoScript need to be stored temporarily, the top-level objects `temp` and `styles` are intended for this. Their objects, properties, and values can then be copied to different points in TypoScript and reused. After parsing, however, they are deleted, which keeps the cached pages slimmed down. The toplevel object `temp` is intended for your own general objects, while `styles` was reserved for the standard templates (static templates) included in TYPO3.

5.4 Development Tools

TYPO3 provides a number of tools for the developer to make programming with TypoScript easier. On the one hand the **Web | Template** module in the back end makes a large range of functions available, and on the other, the **Admin Panel** can be embedded in the front-end output, providing additional help utilities.

5.4.1 Info/Modify

The **Web | Template | Info/Modify** module can show you a list of existing templates in the page tree. To do this, select the Rootline as the current page by clicking on the title of the globe in the page tree. The list shows the pages with templates, and whether these are root or extension templates.

The module also helps in setting up new templates, if the current page selected is one without a template. If required, you can select a static template.

In addition you have the possibility of skipping to the template that is closest to the current page.

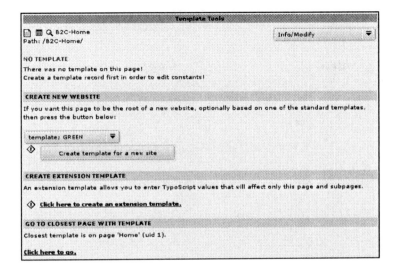

Figure 5.34:

Info/Modify can be used to create new templates

If you have selected a page with a template, the template can be edited, in which case you can select individual fields or the entire record. If you edit single fields, the TS wizard (see next section) is also available. In addition, the cache is automatically deleted.

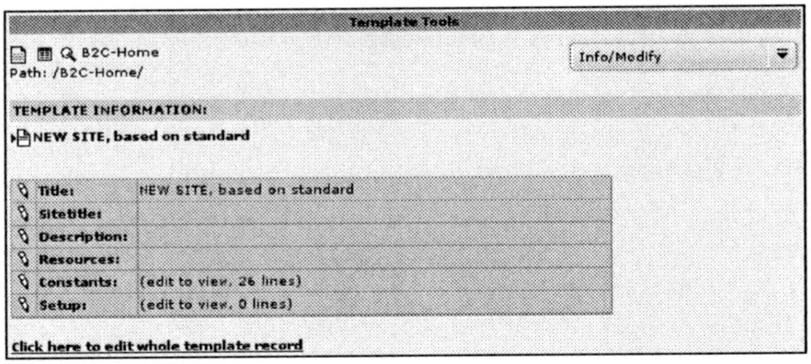

Figure 5.35:

Editing functions for existing template records

5.4.2 TS Wizard

Just as editing is supported by wizards for the entry of content for content types such as **Table** or **Form**, there is also a wizard for TypoScript, with which object types and properties can be browsed through and selected.

In the following figure you can see how a TS setup was opened for editing with the **Web | Template | Info/Modify** module. With the TS wizard icon, the wizard is opened in a separate window.

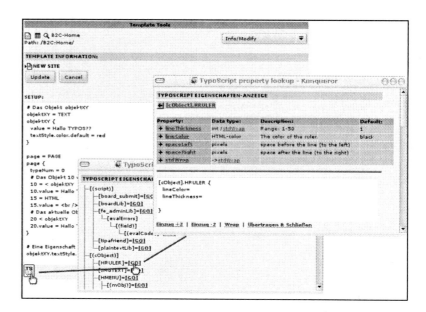

First the list of object types is displayed, each of which can be opened in a details view with the **[GO]** link. In this example the HRULER cObject is opened. The details view shows the properties of the object type with its data types, description, and default values. If you click on the name of a property, the wizard closes and the property is included in the input form. In the example, the desired properties were first collected in the entry field of the wizard, with a click on the "**+**"-icons. Then the properties were enclosed with the object type, using **Wrap**. Finally if you click on the **Transfer & Close** link, the code is taken over.

Softlink **090547** Even if the wizard cannot replace the TSref completely, it still has most information available, so that you don't have to worry about it all the time. The data displayed is created directly from the TSref OpenOffice document. Even the properties of extensions are read out from the respective documentation. You can find out how you need to prepare your extension documentation for this from the soft link here.

5.4.3 TypoScript Object Browser

The TypoScript Object Browser (**Web | Template | Object Browser**) has already been used a few times in the previous sections to display TypoScript setup. Apart from just showing constants or the setup, the Object Browser also provides functions for testing conditions and for browsing through and displaying constants in the setup. In addition to this, properties can be edited with the Object Browser.

The Object Browser always works on the basis of the currently selected page or the template contained in it. However, in addition to the data of the current template, all the accumulated template data from the Rootline is also shown. The TypoScript active in the front end when the current page is called is shown. If conditions are defined in the template, these can be activated individually, so their behavior can be tested.

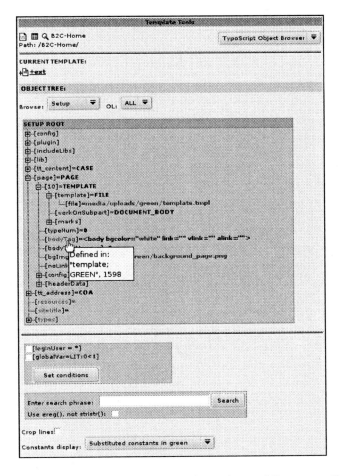

Figure 5.37:

TypoScript Object Browser in the **Web | Template** *module*

The search function searches through the values of the properties and displays the search results in color. If the **Use ereg()** option is selected, regular expressions can be used.

As shown in the preceding figure, constants can be highlighted in the setup, so that you can choose whether the original constants should be displayed, or the replaced values.

If you click on the name of a path element (e.g. **property**), you can edit this with the following form:

When you do this you have the chance to edit the value, add a property, or delete the selected element with **>**.

The modified or added TypoScript is written to the current template, whereby the text line is always attached at the end. It may therefore be the case that after a while a confusing mass of code collects, which has to be sorted out by hand. But this editing option with the Object Browser is a great help, not least because the TS wizard is also available here.

5.4.4 Template Analyzer

The **Web | Template | Template Analyzer** module has already been mentioned in connection with cascading templates, since among other things, it displays the hierarchy of the active template.

The Template Analyzer shows the logical hierarchy of the template for the currently selected page—the templates used for front-end rendering.

In addition to this, the table shows whether **Rootlevel, Clear Constants**, or **Clear Setup** is set for a template—as well as the page ID and the level (Rootlevel) on which the template is located. The last column shows the IDs of templates that were integrated with **Template on next level**.

In the following figure, you can see how **Clear Constants** is set in the template with the title "One Extension Template", and therefore constants defined in previous templates are deactivated.

If you click on the title of a template, its active code is displayed. In this example we can see the code of the "Main Template" template. Constants are not shown, although some are defined in the template. The reason for this is that we are on a page in which the "One Extension Template", which has **Clear Constants** set, is active. The constants are therefore deactivated and are not shown.

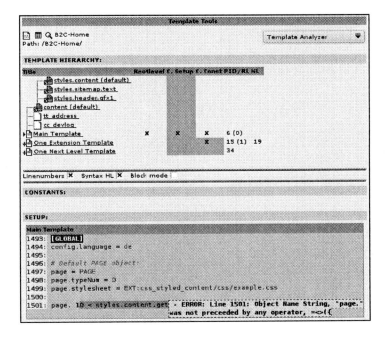

Figure 5.39:

Template Analyzer shows the hierarchy and code of individual Templates

Checking the Syntax

TypoScript cannot be tested to see if a non-existent object is addressed or if properties and values were wrongly named. Minor typing errors are frequently to blame if the desired result is not achieved. You can only check to see if entries are syntactically correct.

From TYPO3 version 3.6.0, **Syntax highlighting** is available to developers under **Template Analyzer**.

In the above example an empty space was inserted into the object path. The syntax highlighter then complains that the space after the object path is not followed by an operator.

5.4.5 Constant Editor

As described in section 5.2.8, constants are used in the template record to pass easy-to-handle or global values to the `setup` code. These constants can optionally be edited in a simple and clear manner with the *Constant Editor* (**Web | Templates | Constant Editor**). In this way standard templates, which configure complete web pages, make it very easy for the user to change the appearance and functionality of the site using constants.

Standard templates in particular can be conveniently configured with the Constant Editor. In the following figure, a screenshot of the template is shown, as well as a description.

Figure 5.40:

Constant Editor editing the GREEN standard template

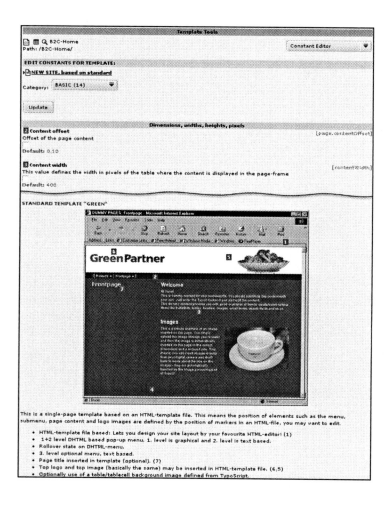

The Constant Editor returns the preset values (default) for the selected template. If individual values are to be overridden, the checkboxes for the constants must be activated and the form must be reloaded. They are now set in the form fields and saved in the `Constants` field of the selected template record.

Highlighting Constants for the Constant Editor

If you also want to make your constants changeable with the Constant Editor, additional information on the constants is necessary, such as descriptions and value ranges.

For this purpose the constant definitions must be preceded by comments with specific syntax rules.

Example:

```
# cat=temp.myText; type=string; label= My Text
  myText.myTextInput = Hello World!
```

TYPO3 basically ignores comments when parsing templates, but not the Constant Editor. It divides groups up into categories, on the basis of additional data in the special comments, and displays them with a descriptive text (the label) for editing, according to their type.

Syntax rules for comments: *Softlink* **969386**

- The comment is set in the line before the constant involved.

- Each comment line is divided by semi-colons into separate parameters.

- Each parameter consists of a key and a value, separated by an equals sign. TYPO3 provides the following keys: `cat` (category and possible subcategory), `type` (type of constant), and `label` (explanatory text).

The following template, `my text`, serves as an example. The template defines the text and its presentation with the help of constants.

Input in the `constants` field of the `mytext` template:

```
# cat=mytext/ctext/a; type=string;
        label= My TextmyTextInput = Hello World!
# cat=mytext/ctext/b; type=typo;
        label= My fontmyTextFont = Verdana
# cat=mytext/ctext/d; type=color;
        label= My text colormyTextFontColor = red
# cat=mytext/ctext/c; type=small;
        label= My text sizemyTextFontSize = 32
```

Input in the `setup` field of the `mytext` template:

```
temp.myContent = TEXT
temp.myContent {
  value = {$myTextInput}
  textStyle.face.default = {$myTextFont}
  textStyle.size.default = {$myTextFontSize}
  textStyle.color.default = {$myTextFontColor}
}
```

The constants can easily be changed in the Constant Editor, via the additional data for third parties. The following figure shows the current values of the `myText` template and of the `temp.myText` category.

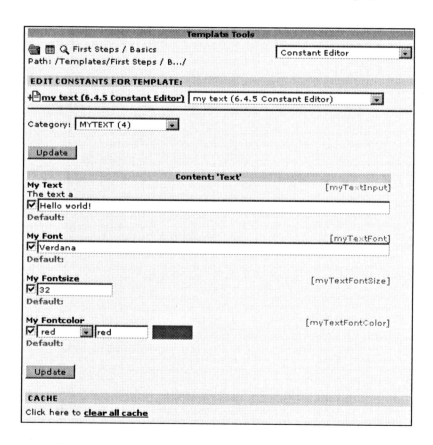

Figure 5.41:

Constants of the myText template in the Constant Editor

Parameters

Categories (cat)

Categories can be freely chosen, and bundle together various constants. This is why it is sensible to choose general terms that encompass a grouping. It is also possible to use the following preset categories for standard templates.

basic

The `basic` category bundles constants that are of great significance for the template layout. They are some of the basic constants you will probably always be configuring, and include dimensioning and image files, and allowing various properties to be activated.

menu

Menu settings are dependent on the type; they include font files, sizes, and backgrounds.

content

Constants that influence the display of content elements.

page

General configurations regarding the page such as meta tags, link destinations, etc.

advanced

Advanced functions that are rarely used.

plugin.*

Constants for individual plugins (extensions).

Example: `plugin.meta`

Subcategories

Subcategories arrange the constants of a category in the Constant Editor according to areas, and are added to the category with /. Only those constants defined in the list are available. All the others are automatically shown under the `Others` subcategory. You can specify the order in which the constants are listed by adding a letter from `a-z`. If none is specified, `z` is taken as the default value.

Example:

```
# cat=basic/enable/b; type=string;
        label= My constants
```

255

Possible subcategories:

enable

For constants that are used to switch basic functions of the template on or off.

dims

For dimensions of all kinds, such as pixels, width, height of images, frames, etc.

file

Bundles constants that define files such as background images, fonts, etc.; further options concerning the file can be specified here.

typo

For typography and related constants.

color

Helps to summarize color definitions; however, many colors are also included in other categories, with related options.

links

For use with links; typically, `target` is specified for this.

language

Language-specific options.

`cheader, cheader_g, ctext, cimage, cbullets, ctable, cuploads, cmultimedia, cmailform, csearch, clogin, csplash, cmenu, cshortcut, clist, cscript, chtm`

These subcategories are based on the predefined content elements of TYPO3 such as text, heading, image etc.

Field type (type)

With `type` you specify the field type, which defines the editing options for the user interface of the Constant Editor.

int [low-high]

A whole number; optionally the value range can be specified.

Example: `int [0-10]`

int+

Positive whole number

color

> HTML-coded colors

wrap

> A wrap can be edited with this

offset [L1,L2,...,L6]

> Comma-separated list of whole numbers; you can specify up to six titles as comma-separated parameters in square brackets. The defaults are the titles x,y.

options [item1, item2, ...]

> Selection field with titles/values, in which single elements are separated by commas; title and value are separated by =.
>
> > Example: `options [label1=value1, label2=value2]`

boolean [truevalue]

> Boolean value; optionally the value for "true" can be specified. The default value is 1.

comment

> Boolean value; selected = "", not selected = "#"
>
> This type can be used to comment out, and thus deactivate, TypoScript code with the help of a constant.

file [ext-list /IMAGE_EXT]

> Helps to select file resources; it is possible to upload directly, to load files into the **Resources** field of the template record. Optionally this selection can be restricted to specific data types. To do this, a list of allowed data types, e.g. `[ttf]` or `[txt,html,htm]` (without spaces), is specified in the list. You can also enter `[IMAGE_EXT]`. In this case the default image file types are allowed.

string

> Text input field.

Header and description (label)

> With the help of the `label` type, a header and a descriptive text can be specified. The header and descriptive text are simply separated by a colon:

```
# cat=mytext/ctext/a; type=string;
  label= My Text: The text appears on the right...
myTextInput = Hello World!
```

Description for categories (TSConstantEditor)

You can also define a general description for individual constant categories. This is used for example to explain the standard templates using a screenshot and additional description.

The additional data is defined in the constants TLO `TSConstantEditor`. This allows you to assign numerical icons to individual constants and to integrate an image–usually a screenshot.

Please note that `TSConstantEditor` is defined in the `Constants` field of the template. Use of the terms "TLO" or "object" and "property" for constants is not, strictly speaking, correct, since these are not objects. But we will use the terms here just for the sake of simplicity.

Example:

```
TSConstantEditor.mytext {
  header = my text
  description = my text is a demo // it contains ...
  bulletlist = List item 1 // List item 2 // List item 3.
  image = gfx/szenario-1.png
  1 = myTextInput,Text
  2 = myTextFont,Color
}
```

Here is a summary of the properties of `TSConstantEditor`:

header

Data type: string

Header for the description; this is shown in capitals.

description

Data type: string

Description of the template itself; new lines are implemented with //.

bulletlist

Data type: string

Displays a bulletlist; individual items are separated with two slashes, //.

image

> Data type: image
>
> You can optionally insert an image to illustrate the connections. Enter the numbers of the constants that you are describing on the picture, and position where they will be visible in the front end. The image must be stored in the `gfx/` directory of the `Constant Editor` module (`tstemplate_ ceditor`), or integrated with the resources field of the template record.

Array, 1-20

> List of constant names
>
> Red-numbered icons are assigned to the listed constants in the Constant Editor via the numerical list. They establish the connection to the specified image.

5.4.6 Admin Panel

Apart from the functions for editors, the Admin Panel also provides information for the TypoScript developer. During rendering, TSFE logs the rendering process; the log can be displayed in the Admin Panel.

If the Admin Panel is configured accordingly [5], the following options are offered in the **TypoScript** section:

Tree display

> If this option is activated, the output is displayed as a tree.

Display all times [6]

> This option shows the time in milliseconds needed to render the page elements.

Display messages

> Additional explanations and error messages are shown in the rendering log, which is switched on with this option.

Track content rendering

> Information on the rendering of contents is shown here. Output is restricted to general information and PAGE objects.

---

[5] Setting up the Admin Panel is described in section 4.7.

[6] Up to TYPO3 version 3.6 this option was wrongly described as "always show". Other options are also described more clearly in version 3.7.

Display content

> If this option is active, the generated content can also be displayed. In this way you can look directly at the HTML code for the corresponding TS object.

Explain SELECT queries

> SQL queries are shown with this option and analyzed using the SQL EXPLAIN instruction. Due to the introduction of the DB abstraction layer in version 3.6, this does not function, but it was also used very little in Version 3.5.

Force TS Rendering

> If this option is deactivated, it is possible that the page will be loaded from the cache. So if you want to test your TypoScript template, the option should be activated.

In the output of the Admin Panel, various elements of the rendering process are highlighted in color in the details column. Messages are shown in black, error messages in red with a preceding icon, file contents (HTML templates) in green, and generated content in blue. TS objects embedded inside generated content are shown at the corresponding positions in red, enclosed by square brackets.

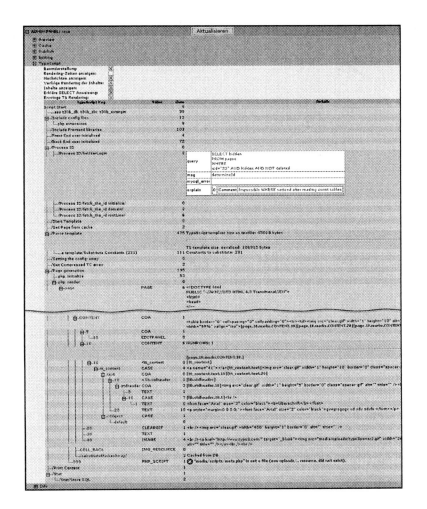

Figure 5.42:

TypoScript area in the Admin Panel for displaying the front-end rendering process

5.4.7 Import and Export of TYPO3 pages

TYPO3 provides a quite unassuming function in the context menu, in **t3d Import and Export**, that can also be very helpful for the developer, for example, to import and export templates as files. In addition it is possible to export entire page trees with contents, including directly integrated media such as *TYPO3 documents* (t3d file), and import them back into other TYPO3 applications.

t3d Export

The export of records is called with the **More options ... | Export to .3d** context menu. First you select the page in the page tree from which the export should be started.

The following form serves to specify the extent of the export, which can involve entire page trees or just single pages.

Figure 5.43:

*Calling the t3d
export from the
context menu*

The configuration for the export is specified in the top area of the user interface. Various properties and functionalities are available.

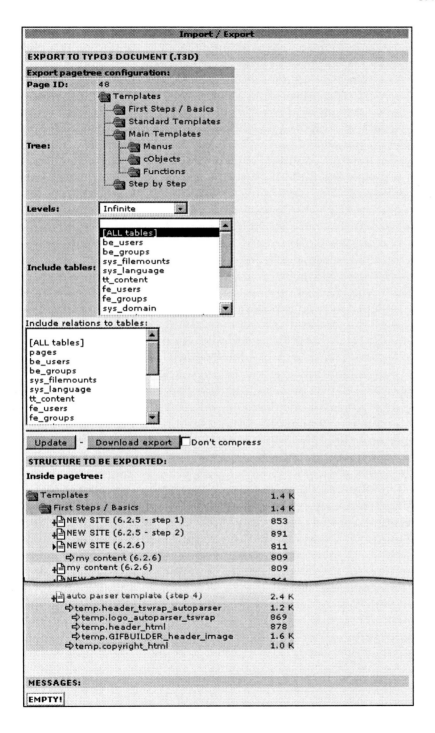

Figure 5.44:

Determining export properties

Page ID

> Page ID of the page from which the export should be performed.

Tree

> The page tree to be exported, which is selected via the start page and the level depth.

Levels

> The depth of the levels to be exported (beginning with the start page selected) can be specified in a selection menu.

Include tables

> Here you can decide what content of database tables located in the section of the page tree selected should be included in the export.

Include relations to tables

> If the records contain relations to records outside the page tree selected, you can define here which tables should be included.

The selected configurations are applied with the **Update** button . The structure of the records selected for export is shown in detail in the lower area. If relations are lost, they are marked with **Lost relation**. If the details are correct, the export is started with the **Download export** button. [7]

t3d Import

The import of data via a TYPO3 document is in turn called from the context menu with the menu item **More options... | Import from .t3d**. The starting point is the page on the page tree from which the data should be integrated. Since an import via the Rootline (globe) is not possible, you can start an import via any page, for example, and then move the imported page tree.

---

[7] If you experience difficulties in downloading, we should point out a bug in Internet Explorer 5.5 which tries to save the page of the back end as a download.

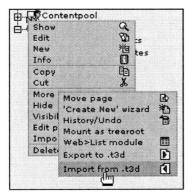

Figure 5.45:

Calling the t3d import via the context menu

The TYPO3 document (`.t3d`) must be located directly in the `fileadmin/` directory to be imported. You can upload a file directly to this directory with the form displayed, so that it is available for selection for import through the selection menu. **Preview** shows a preview of the records to be imported.

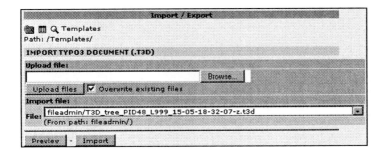

Figure 5.46:

Import interface for a TYPO3 document

5.5 Standard Templates (Static Templates)

Every TYPO3 package already contains records in the `static_template` table that are only readable from the back end, but not directly change-able. These are the so-called *standard templates*, also known as *static templates*. You can have the standard templates listed using the **Web | List** module, for example, if you select the Rootline (globe) in the page tree.

Softlink **546011**

The standard templates supplied represent the library and can be used in your own websites. They provide complete site templates; but they also contain some basic individual TypoScript components such as content (default), which define and format the output of content elements.

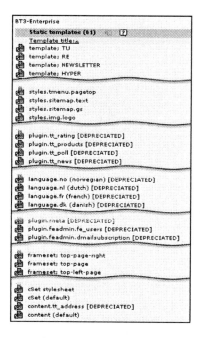

Figure 5.47:

*Standard templates
contained in the
TYPO3 basic installa-
tion listed by the
Web | List module*

A number of templates are marked with the label [DEPRECIATED], which means they are considered to be old or out of date, and are only included for reasons of backward compatibility. In particular, most plugin.* templates have become redundant since the introduction of the extension system, as corresponding templates are supplied with the extensions.

To use the templates, insert them with the **Include static** field into the template record.

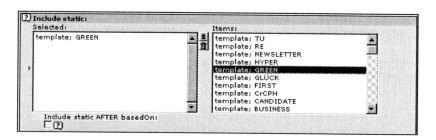

As already mentioned, extensions can include their own templates. In this way it is possible that they offer standard templates, which can be selected in the template record under **Include static (from extensions)**. In their function, these correspond to the templates available via **Include static**. Even entire website templates can be made available in this way. An example of this is the `Green` template, which was implemented as an extension and can be found in the TER for download.

The standard templates are assigned to various categories, depending on the application field, and given corresponding prefixes (`template`, `plugin`, `content`,...). An overview follows of the individual categories.

5.5.1 content (default)

This is the most used standard template. As a rule it not only forms the basis for websites and other standard templates, but also defines the basic processing and representation of content entered in the front end. The template applies corresponding content objects to the records of the `tt_content` table, depending on which content type was specified by the editor (the `CType` table field). The template is based on `styles.content.default`, in which individual content types are defined in detail. In addition, `styles.sitemap.text` and `styles.header.gfx1` are also included as basis templates.

The template remains at the heart of TYPO3, although more recent developments have gained prominence. `content (default)` uses TypoScript not only for display but also for program logic, which is not actually the core task of TypoScript. But the demands made on TypoScript have changed, in particular through the increasing acceptance of CSS-based layouts and the need to have access for those with disabilities to Internet sites. It is intended that the code will be slimmed down and that more competence be delegated to CSS or extension functionality. This concept has been continued in the successor template from the extension of the same name, `css_styled_content`.

Many of the standard templates are merely code components integrated into a larger context. These connections between the individual templates can be viewed in the Template Analyzer.

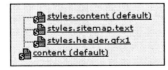

Figure 5.49:

Content (Default) and the integrated basis templates in the Template Analyzer

5.5.2 styles.*

```
styles.content (default)

styles.tmenu.pagetop

styles.sitemap.text

styles.sitemap.gs

styles.img.logo

styles.hmenu.tu (EXT1)

styles.hmenu.tu

styles.header.gfx1

styles.gmenu_layer.green

styles.gmenu.first (EXT1)

styles.gmenu.first

styles.gmenu.bug
```

This type of template menu provides code fragments for other standard templates. Many of these templates are used in the site templates (`template.*`), which can be seen from the suffix used, e.g. `styles.hmenu.tu`, `styles.gmenu.bug`. Others such as `styles.sitemap.text` and `styles.header.gfx1` are used in the `content` (default) template. The components have been stored in separate templates so that they can be re-used in other standard templates. They provide preconfigured page objects such as menus, sitemaps, headings, and logos.

styles.content (default)

The `styles.content` (default) template deserves special mention; it contains a selection of predefined TypoScript objects for use in other templates, in particular for basic content rendering in the `content` (default) template. The most well-known example from this template, often used in practice, is `styles.content.get`, which selects the contents entered in the back end in the `Normal` column for display:

```
styles.content.get = CONTENT
styles.content.get {
  table = tt_content
  select.orderBy = sorting
  select.where = colPos=0
  select.languageField = sys_language_uid
}
```

You never need to switch the template on separately, as long as you are using the `content (default)` template, with which it is automatically integrated. Many settings can be configured in this template with constants (module: **Template | Constant Editor | Content**).

5.5.3 cSet.*

`cSet (default)`

`cSet stylesheet`

cSet (default)

This was introduced as a further step towards effectiveness in creating websites; it continues to be used frequently in practice, although it has been overtaken to a large extent by `cSet stylesheet`, and more recent concepts such as the `CSS styled content` extension make it completely superfluous. The template only contains definitions of constants. The core idea of the template is to bundle individual definitions from `styles.content.default` and to make available new, global constants for these. This makes it possible, for example, to define the font for all content objects with one entry. The definitions bundled in this way can be easily adjusted in the Constant Editor, in the `CSET` category.

cSet stylesheet

This is a more modern alternative, but here the focus is on the use of cascading stylesheets (CSS), which was summarized in a separate file (`media/scripts/defaultstylesheet.css`). After changing the link to a newly created CSS file in the `fileadmin/` directory

```
# Example input in the constants field
content.stylesheet.file = fileadmin/styles/default
                          stylesheet-modified.css
```

the existing CSS definitions can be applied and individually adjusted. In contrast to `cSet (default)`, this template not only contains constants, but also changes several settings in the setup. In particular, `<font>` tags are removed and the headings replaced by native HTML headers (h1-h6), and `<br />` is replaced by `<p> </p>`.

5.5.4 frameset;*

```
frameset; top-page-right

frameset; top-page

frameset; top-left-page

frameset; top / left-page

frameset; page-bottom

frameset; left-page

frameset (+); top / left-adr-page
```

These documents for frameset-based websites are in part used in the site templates described below. The name implies which layout will be implemented; `frameset; top-page-right` for example means: one frameset at the top, a central content frameset (`page`), and a frameset to the right. The size of individual framesets can be set with constants. Some of the frameset templates can also be nested. The template with (+) does not generate a complete page, for example, but serves as an extension for another frameset template. The frameset templates above all have a didactic value, since they make it easier to understand the handling of framesets in TypoScript. In practice, however, layouts are often used that are not covered by these documents.

5.5.5 template;*

Templates with this prefix are optional out-of-the-box templates for displaying the website. They are all based on the `content (default)` standard template for rendering content.

Make sure that your desired standard template is listed at the top of the included standard templates. Adjustments can be easily made with the Constant Editor.

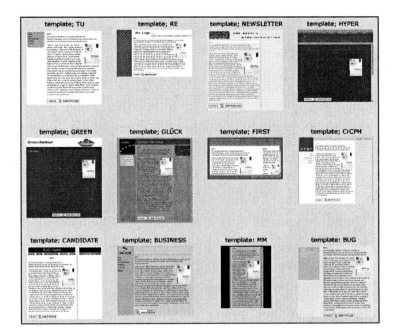

Figure 5.50:

Example page displayed with different standard site templates

The available templates are ideal not only for examples, but also for websites that need to be brought online "in a hurry". The examples are quite ancient and are based either on pure TypoScript templates, on the integration of HTML templates, or on frames. A project group has been formed within the TYPO3 community with the aim of creating new templates with a fresh design, taking into account accessibility. The templates available until now will then be moved to an extension.

The current out-of-the-box templates and their functionality:

TU

TU is a template without frames. You can specify a head image and the background color for the page. The graphic menu on the left side has two levels; it changes the text color for rollover and in an active state. You can add background pictures to individual menu items and define their TrueType font, text color, and size, as well as the offset. There is also an option to insert graphics before and after the menu (so-called clear.gifs as placeholders).

RE

This template is based on frames. The upper frame contains a graphical menu of the first level, the left frame, a graphical menu of the second level. The third frame contains the page contents. You can define the states `Normal`, `Rollover`, and `Active` for the menu items (background images and colors, text color, etc.). If you wish, you can define a background image for each frame and position a graphic beneath the left menu.

NEWSLETTER

This is a template for a page without menus. As the name suggests, it is intended for sending a newsletter as an HTML e-mail, with the `Direct Mail module` extension. It is based on an HTML template file, which determines the layout of the page. You have a choice of one or two columns. The head logo is not defined in this HTML template, but is configured directly via TypoScript.

HYPER

`HYPER` is a frame-based template, consisting of the head with a DHTML layers menu and a single column frame for the contents. The page title is shown in a picture, and you can specify a logo for the head region. The appearance of pages is influenced by stylesheets.

GREEN

This one-page template is based on an HTML template. This means that all elements such as main menu, submenu, head image, logo, page title, and page content are positioned in this file with the corresponding markers. You can modify the HTML template just as you wish. The menu is a DHTML-based popup-menu in which the first level is graphics-based and the second level is text-based. Optionally you can have another text-based menu shown in the third level. If you want you can choose to show the page title beneath the menu. Background images for tables and tables cells can be defined with TypoScript.

GLÜCK

This standard template is based on a three-column table. The first level of the text-based menu is in the left-hand column, the second level in the right-hand column. Both columns are optional, i.e. they can be switched off via TypoScript. You can define a logo, background image, and contents for each column. Margins, widths, and alignments can be adjusted in detail. The page background and page color can also be defined. This template is configured entirely with TypoScript.

FIRST

`FIRST` is a frame-based template in which the frames `Menu`, `Bottom`, and `Page frame` are nested in another frameset, which centers the page in the browser. The menus are arranged graphically on two levels. A further, separate general menu from a directory can be found in the `bottom` frame. You can define the background color and dimensions for each of the three frames, or optionally integrate another column with news from a specified page.

CrCPH

`CrCPH` is a single-page template based on an HTML template file. TypoScript is used less here. You can modify large parts of the layout to your requirements by editing this template file with your preferred HTML editor. The two text-based menus are also defined directly in the HTML template.

CANDIDATE

`CANDIDATE` is a single-page template with two content columns and a text-based menu with one level, placed beneath the head image in the main column. The page title (or the subtitle, if it exists) appears on the head image. But you can also switch it off. You can deactivate the right-hand column, or have it shown on the left-hand side instead. You can also place the head image over both columns, or vary this image in certain branches of the website. The first image is displayed for the whole branch, which is assigned to the page on the first level. The width and color of the space between the two columns can be specified or reduced to zero.

BUSINESS

`BUSINESS` is a frame-based template with a very simple two-column layout. The menu is in the left-hand frame, and the page content in the right-hand frame. You can define background images for each frame and set the width for the left-hand frame. The menu is text-based and shows two levels. The font tags can be adjusted to your requirements for both levels. In the second level you have the option of placing graphics in front of each menu item, which can be changed on rollover. In the page head, the page titles of the overlying pages are shown for the first and second levels of the current page; as with the menu, you can define the font tags of this page title. It is possible to draw a line beneath the page title, the color of which you can define.

MM

`MM` is a single-page template with an imagemap-based menu in the head area. You can define background images and color, as well as the border width and color. Additionally you can specify contents for an optional second column, and determine its background color and images, as well as other standard headers and text properties. You can add an offset between the two columns, and the background color and image can be freely chosen. For the imagemap menu, the following configuration options are available: background color, TrueType font, text color, size, and spacing in the image.

BUG

BUG is a frame-based template. Three frames are available: top, left, and right. All frames can be configured in terms of their size and background color. In the top frame it is possible to include a graphic, in the left-hand frame you can specify the layout for the graphical menu: background image for the entire menu and for individual menu items, rollover effects (for text color and/or graphics before or after the page title), TrueType font, text color, size, shadowing, spacing.

5.5.6 plugin.*

```
plugin.tt_rating [DEPRECATED]
...
plugin.tt_board_list [DEPRECATED]
plugin.tipafriend [DEPRECATED]
plugin.postit1
plugin.meta [DEPRECATED]
plugin.feadmin.fe_users [DEPRECATED]
plugin.feadmin.dmailsubscription [DEPRECATED]
plugin.alt.xmlnewsfeed (89)
plugin.alt.xml (96)
plugin.alt.wap (97)
plugin.alt.print (98)
plugin.alt.plaintext (99)
plugin.alt.pda (95)
```

Plugins are responsible for the display and functionality of special, mostly dynamic contents in the front end, and normally contain their own PHP functions. The standard templates with the `plugin.` prefix can be divided into two groups. One group is responsible for embedding special contents and functions into the general content flow, e.g. `plugin.tt_news` or `plugin.feadmin.fe_users`. The second group (`plugin.alt.*`) generates complete pages that are processed and displayed differently to normal content pages. Depending on whether a printed version, text version, XML version, or WAP version for mobile phones is involved—content is displayed differently in each case. While the print version, for example, is only implemented with TypoScript modifications, a totally different rendering engine is used for the XML plugin. Through this capacity to display existing content in several alternative formats, the functionality of `plugin.alt.` templates is moving towards cross-media publishing.

Nearly all plugins from the first group are identified with DEPRECATED, because when the Extension Manager was introduced, all templates were moved to corresponding extensions. These templates should not be used for new projects. But they are still to be found in the list of standard templates, for reasons of backward compatibility.

5.5.7 temp.*

`temp.tt_board (shared) [DEPRECATED]`

`temp` templates are helper templates that serve as components or "code snippets" for other templates. `temp.tt_board (shared)` is part of the function of the forum plugin and is the basis for two more templates: `plugin.tt_board_list` and `plugin.tt_board_tree`. It is responsible for the general display and functionality of the TYPO3 Forum. The two other forum templates for displaying lists and trees use the basic settings for this helper template. All three templates are out of date, as they have been moved to the `Message board, twin mode` (tt_board) extension.

5.5.8 content.tt_*

`content.tt_address [DEPRECATED]`

This is a method used to directly output records from tables, in this case `tt_address`. The addresses output do not require a plugin with PHP functionality, but are formatted with the simple use of TypoScript objects. It is also out of date because it was replaced by the template for the `Address list` (tt_address) extension.

5.5.9 (example)

`records (example)`

This example template shows, like the `content.tt_address` template, how the output of content from extended tables (tt_address, tt_links, tt_news, etc.) can be rendered by the simple use of Typoscript. It should not be used in projects, but serves merely as an example of usage.

5.5.10 language.*

language.no (norwegian) [DEPRECATED]

language.nl (dutch) [DEPRECATED]

language.fr (french) [DEPRECATED]

language.dk (danish) [DEPRECATED]

language.de (german) [DEPRECATED]

The language templates help to configure various languages, and are another ancient feature of TYPO3. There is hardly any use left for this type. The reason for this is not only that they were moved to extensions. Even there they are no longer up-to-date, because the entire language control is now stored in special files in the individual extensions. In earlier versions of TYPO3 they served the purpose of supplying translations for plugins and individual content objects, such as login forms or search forms; they are included now for reasons of backward compatibility.

5.6 Base Layout—Template Concepts

When developing a web application with TYPO3, you are faced with the choice of which method to use. Depending on your knowledge as a web developer, and on the requirements of the project or customer, the important thing here is to decide if the base layout should be based on HTML tables or cascading stylesheets (CSS), whether frames will be involved, etc. These decisions should be made independently of TYPO3, since all options are open to you with the CMS.

In the next step you decide on which method will be used to implement the requirements of the base layout and to mark the contents with TYPO3. There are several ways to do this, which makes it difficult to retain an overview and make the right choice when coming into contact with TYPO3 for the first time.

The individual template methods are briefly characterized below and then each implementation is introduced.

5.6.1 Standard templates (static templates)

TYPO3 provides you with complete out-of-the-box website templates, as so-called standard templates. Their appearance and functionalities are already set, but can be adjusted to a certain extent with constants. Above all they are regarded as very good references to study working with TypoScript examples, but they can also be used productively, of course. But if CI guidelines for professional fields and individual requirements need to be considered, the developer will quickly reach the limits of standard templates in terms of being able to adjust them.

5.6.2 Pure TypoScript Templates

The entire base layout of a website can be determined completely with the help of TypoScript, without having to use external HTML files. With this method you can work in two ways:

1. It is possible to quickly specify a table layout, using the cObject CTABLE, which will divide a website into areas such as topMenu, leftMenu, rightMenu, bottomMenu, and content-cell.

2. The layout can be controlled entirely via CSS, by wrapping all the page elements with the <div> HTML tag. This technique is ideal for implementing accessibility-compatible websites.

Layouts that are controlled by tables or stylesheets can now also be implemented by integrating HTML templates. Pure TypoScript templates could have some advantages:

- All information controlling the output is located in one place, and is not stored in external HTML files. This provides clarity and full control.

- The HMTL code can be constructed on a very modular basis using TypoScript with constants and setup. This makes it particularly easy to carry out area-specific modifications to a site.

- TS templates cascade and HTML templates do not. So you can nest a layout template and spread it over various templates, or overwrite parts of the page tree.

Especially for layouts that are implemented via CSS and do not use tables, the use of an external HTML template is hardly necessary any longer, or has no advantages, since the individual areas of the basic layout are only marked with <div> tags, and everything else is controlled via CSS.

5.6.3 TypoScript and HTML Templates

Even though the methods of pure TypoScript templates are extremely flexible, and thus efficient, models usually gain acceptance due to their simplicity. For this reason developers will also be given the opportunity of integrating external HTML templates through the TEMPLATE cObject. The concept is one of substituting special areas of the HTML template, located with markers (subparts and marks) with contents from the database.

Advantages of integrating HTML templates:

- From the point of view of the web developer, they can be implemented very quickly, with little preparation time needed.

- The base layouts can be made with external editors.

- When working in a team, content designers and TYPO3 developers can work in parallel if content areas and functionality have been specified right at the beginning.

5.6.4 Template Auto-Parser

Softlink **591606**

TYPO3 would not be TYPO3 if it did not continually try to improve and simplify editing procedures. The Template Auto-Parser extension is such a development. Using this it is possible to parse HTML templates to be included, and thus have the corresponding subparts marked automatically. They are identified with the id of HTML elements such as <div>, <span> and <td>. Moreover all parts of the stylesheets and images in the HTML template are updated to the correct folder within the file system of fileadmin/. Working with the Template Auto-Parser is documented in depth in section 5.9.2 as well as in the tutorial, "Modern Template Building, Part 1" (see soft link).

Pros and cons of the Template Auto-Parser:

- The user focus of the method is aimed principally at agencies and web developers from the field of HTML design. Results are achieved quickly without subparts having to be marked by hand. But the subjective feelings of the TYPO3 developer are that the Template Auto-Parser takes over "control" of the proceedings to some extent.

- If roles are swapped during development, there will be no danger that the screen designer will accidentally remove markers designating subparts in the HTML template.

5.6.5 TemplaVoila

The newest method of template integration is called *TemplaVoila*. This is
just one of several extensions (TemplaVoila!), which arose in the context
of a rather large project for the Dassault Systemes group in France. It is
currently still at the alpha stage, and a large amount of development is
still to be done. But even at this point in time it is worth taking a look at
the concept and its outlook, if only as a means of comparison to other
solutions.

Softlink **003992**

TemplaVoila promises to implement the design within minutes (instead of
days) provided that an HTML template is available. The area for the page
content is divided into zones that can contain different formats of content
elements. This technique replaces the organization of content via
columns otherwise used in TYPO3. For this purpose, the already great
wealth of options for template management has been complemented by
a new one. It provides the developer with a GUI for a graphic-based definition of content elements, by selecting HTML design files (point and click).

Advantages of TemplaVoila:

- This approach opens up a new flexibility for the structuring and
  composition of content blocks and zones, with all the advantages
  of a CMS and the usual extensive control over the design.

- New content elements can be made very quickly using templates
  and used immediately without having to be programmed.

- Control rules can be defined with the system to determine possible combinations of content elements.

TemplaVoila is still in the development stage. Technical concepts until
now linked closely to the organization of content via columns, such as
multi-language capability through a page tree, still need to be implemented.

But TemplaVoila promises some great advantages for the future. The
concept is illustrated more closely in section 5.13.3.

For all those who want to try out and use TemplaVoila now, in its current
state, we refer to the very detailed tutorial "Futuristic Template Building".

5.7 Content Rendering Concepts

Irrespective of how you have implemented the base layout, there are
various possibilities of rendering the content. The rendering methods for
displaying content for the front end are not at all restricted to HTML.

Content can also be displayed as simple text or as XML. But even HTML has been transformed over time, so that XHTML and accessibility are important keywords nowadays.

Here TYPO3 offers a number of solutions, and you can develop others yourself. Obviously the base layout must match the format of the content, and where necessary it is omitted (for example with pure text output).

For a basic understanding of content rendering we must take a step back at this point. As you already know, TypoScript itself is not a programming language, but merely serves to determine the order of processing of PHP functions to be called, together with their parameters. If you define an object of the TEXT type, the function with (in this case) the same name, TEXT(), in the PHP script tslib/class.tslib_content.php, is called while the TypoScript setup is being processed, and the corresponding output generated. The rendering functions contained in the script were developed at a time when the use of CSS was unthinkable, because browsers could either not support CSS at all or the implementation was so full of errors that it was advisable not to use it. So there has been a certain evolution of rendering concepts in TYPO3, which is not yet complete, and will certainly continue as long as technology in the Web continues to change.

The various HTML rendering variations are defined in the following already familiar standard templates:

content (default)

cSet Stylesheet

css_styled_content

content (default) is the oldest content rendering template and uses <font> tags for output. The cset stylesheet template represents a transition to rendering using CSS, which merely redefines the values of content (default) so that, for example, no <font> tags are used anymore. Nevertheless the functions from class.tslib_content.php are used for rendering, but they frequently use tables for positioning, and other techniques which would be more sensible to do with CSS. For this reason the css styled content extension was developed. This also uses the rendering functions from class.tslib_content.php, but does replace a number of functions with its own ones.

The development of css styled content is not yet finished, but can already be used for your own projects.

Apart from the HTML output, TYPO3 offers several other predefined alternative formats that can be used for the following standard templates:

```
plugin.alt.xmlnewsfeed (89)
```

```
plugin.alt.xml (96)
```

```
plugin.alt.wap (97)
```

```
plugin.alt.print (98)
```

```
plugin.alt.plaintext (99)
```

```
plugin.alt.pda
```

The names already hint at what formats will be created using these templates. Frequently the templates own scripts are used for the output, and hardly any use is made any more of the functions from `class.tslib_content.php`.

5.8 Switching Templates with type/typeNum

It is frequently desirable to create front-end output in several different variations or formats. A common example of this is offering a variation for printing. But it is also possible to offer locally used content via XML feed to other websites.

In order that different variations of a page can be used at the same time, TYPO3 provides a system with which several page templates can be defined and one single template chosen for rendering.

The following TypoScript template should help to illustrate this concept:

```
temp.content = TEXT
temp.content.value = HELLO WORLD!
temp.content.wrap = <h1>|</h1>
page = PAGE
page.typeNum = 0
page.10 = COA
page.10 {
   10 = IMAGE
   10.file = media/uploads/typo3power1.gif
   20 < temp.content
}
plaintext = PAGE
plaintext.typeNum = 99
plaintext.config.disableAllHeaderCode = 1
plaintext.10 = COA
plaintext.10.stdWrap.stripHtml = 1
plaintext.10 {
10 < temp.content
}
```

The content to be displayed (HELLO WOLRD!) is defined with the `temp.content` object, which is used in the two following page setups `page` and `plaintext` to make the content available. As you will see later on, typically `styles.content.get` is used to retrieve the contents from the database.

So in `page` and `plaintext`, two templates exist for page output. `page` defines the normal HTML output and also contains a small base layout, namely the output of the TYPO3 logo before the actual content.

In the front end, the following HTML output is generated (abbreviated):

```
<!DOCTYPE html
PUBLIC "-//W3C//DTD HTML 4.0 Transitional//EN">
<html>
  <head>
    <title>test plaintext</title>
    <meta http-equiv="Content-Type"
         content="text/html; charset=iso-8859-1" />
    <meta name="generator" content="TYPO3 3.8 CMS" />
  </head>
  <body bgcolor="#FFFFFF">

  <img src="media/uploads/typo3power1.gif" width="186"
         height="43" border="0" alt="" title=""/>
    <h1>HELLO WORLD!</h1>
  </body>
</html>
```

The `plaintext` template on the other hand should display the same content as normal text without HTML markup. It should be pointed out that TYPO3 offers a better option with the `plugin.alt.plaintext (99)` standard template for outputting pure text, and that this template is just used here as an example. As you can see, it contains a different base layout (without a logo). Moreover, `config.disableAllHeaderCode=1` is set for the PAGE object, which stops the output of the HTML header, and with `stdWrap.stripHtml=1` all HTML code is removed from the contents created within the COA object. And this template really does only generate the output HELLO WORLD!

But how can the `plaintext` template be addressed or selected? The key lies in the `typeNum` values.

```
page.typeNum = 0
plaintext.typeNum = 99
```

If you call the page in the front end and append the parameter `type=99` to the URL (e.g. `http://www.example.org/?id=36&type=99`), TYPO3 selects the matching template that contains the 99 value in the `typeNum` property. In this way, any output variation can be used. The same mechanism is used for frames. This is explained in more depth in section 5.12.

The numbers specified in brackets in the `plugin.alt.*` standard templates are the `typeNum` values used.

5.9 Creating TypoScript Templates

Because the foundations for working with templates and TypoScript have now been laid, we can demonstrate the practical development of site templates below. For this purpose, we will use the BT3 scenario that was already set up in section 3.10. What needs to be done now is to give an appearance in the front end to the applications of the scenario. Because the example contains several sites, we will use this to introduce the various possibilities of template development. A template was supplied by the screen designer as a base layout that already has the basic structure and a number of the functionalities to be integrated.

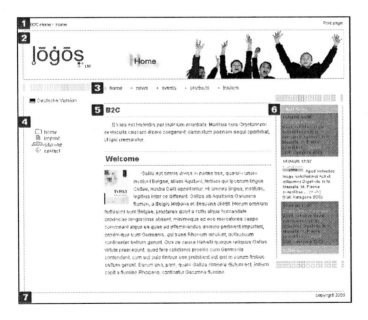

Figure 5.51:

The graphic template

The page has several elements:

1. In the header of the application, a Rootline menu should show the path of the current page from the respective root page. A link calls the print version.

2. The header shows the logo, replaceable images, depending on the area, and the title of the current page.

3. Below this is a horizontal main navigation.

4. The sub-navigation and meta-menu items (such as "Home", "Print", "Sitemap", and "Contact") are located in a column on the left.

5. The area for the actual page content is placed in the middle and is open-ended at the bottom.

6. Optionally, a number of site areas should show additional information or news in a column on the right.

7. A footer with a copyright sign, for example, concludes the application visually.

Softlink **821706**   If you want to work through the examples, you can download the templates and required assets via the softlink, as a TYPO3 document (t3d) and a tar archive, and integrate them into your application.

Also have the TSref ready at hand, or open the TS wizard in the back end (see section 5.4.2), with which you can conveniently browse through the object definitions.

Template Structure

To be able to show as much as possible in the examples, and also to provide you with material to reconstruct the examples, the individual templates are constructed in a very modular fashion. We have used cascading templates here. Various function components are gradually developed and integrated into parent templates. This enables you to work efficiently and use the templates many times in different examples.

The cascading of templates can be done in two ways:

*   Traditionally, further templates are integrated within one template, using **Include basis template**. This procedure was also used in the standard templates supplied by TYPO3.

*   In addition it is possible to nest templates via page areas, that is, to place a template on a page, thus activating it automatically. This is used either to overwrite values for individual areas of the website or to configure a specific functionality for these areas.

An overview of the templates that are distributed across an application can be obtained from the Rootline (click on the name of your installation next to the globe and select the **Web | Template** module). If you have reconstructed all the examples, it should look like the following figure.

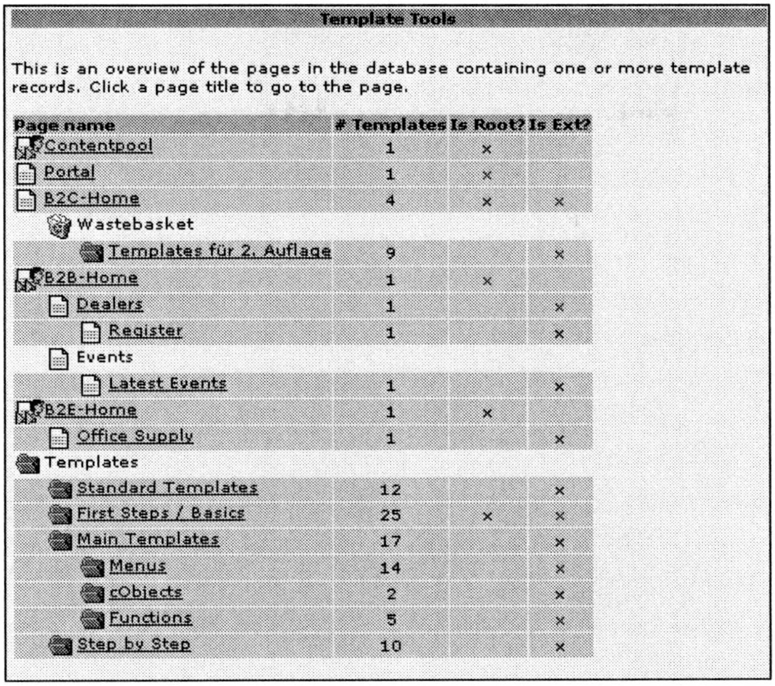

Page name	# Templates	Is Root?	Is Ext?
Template Tools			
Contentpool	1	x	
Portal	1	x	
B2C-Home	4	x	x
Wastebasket			
Templates für 2. Auflage	9		x
B2B-Home	1	x	
Dealers	1		x
Register	1		x
Events			
Latest Events	1		x
B2E-Home	1	x	
Office Supply	1		x
Templates			
Standard Templates	12		x
First Steps / Basics	25	x	x
Main Templates	17		x
Menus	14		x
cObjects	2		x
Functions	5		x
Step by Step	10		x

This is an overview of the pages in the database containing one or more template records. Click a page title to go to the page.

Figure 5.52:

Template overview from the Rootline

We have defined only the **Website title** in each of the root templates of the site ("Portal", "B2C", "B2B",...), the so-called "main templates" (B2C main template, B2B main template,...). The actual TypoScript configuration and inserting standard templates is done in the respective basis templates. We have also done this on the page level. As can be seen in the above figure, templates are created, for example, in the "Dealers" or "Events" pages of the "B2B" website. These also allow for further configuration, via **Include basis template.** The individual basis templates used in this chapter are all located in the templates system directory and its subdirectories. This procedure allows you to quickly insert, swap, and test different methods, demonstrated via the template records.

The following figure shows an example of cascading templates, starting from the "B2C" site.

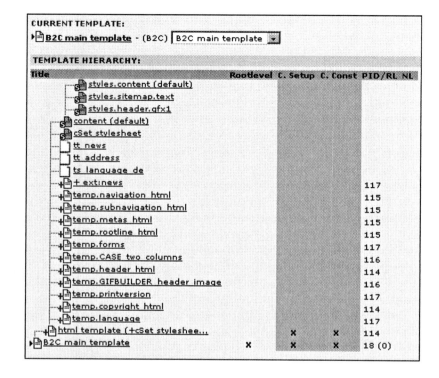

Figure 5.53:

Template hierarchy
in the Template
Analyzer

5.9.1 TypoScript and HTML Templates

Softlink **905945** We would like to illustrate the use of HTML files for the base layout, based on the "B2C" site. Integrating external HTML templates into the TypoScript template is a simple and frequently used method.

We will explain the following:

- How the HTML document must be prepared

- How it is inserted with the TEMPLATE cObject

- How certain marker areas of the template are addressed

- How dynamic content is displayed in the front end

- How to use code libraries

The HTML Template

The HTML template can be created with any HTML or text editor. In our first example we will implement the site for the "B2C" area, which is based on an HTML template. This uses a table layout, is built without frames, and corresponds to the graphic template in Figure 5.51. In doing so, the entire layout of the site, including the function and content areas, will be designed to give the TypoScript developer clear instructions for the implementation.

In the next step the areas whose contents or functionalities are to be dynamically replaced by TYPO3 will be defined. This involves menus, buttons, individually changeable texts, and the content area.

To identify these areas for TYPO3, special placeholders are required in the HTML template. Two types of placeholders are available for this: *subparts* and *markers*.

Subparts

- Subparts are always used in pairs and enclose sections of the HTML template that are completely replaced by the output of the TypoScript configuration.

- The name of the subpart is enclosed by ###; distinction is made between upper and lower case.

- Subparts themselves can be surrounded by HTML comments.

- Before content objects of the individual subparts are generated, all subparts of the array are loaded into the register, so that you can access them if required.

  Example:

  ```
  <!--###CONTENT### start -->
  ...
  <!--###CONTENT### stop -->
  ```

Marker

- Markers are only used singly, not in pairs, and are replaced by the output of the TypoScript configuration.

- The name of the marker is enclosed by ###, and distinction is made between upper and lower case.

- Markers cannot be set in HTML comments, since these are not removed.

  Example:

  ```
  ###COPYRIGHT###
  ```

Preparing the HTML Template

Because HTML headers and `<body>` tags are usually created by TYPO3 from the front end, only the part of the HTML template inside the `<body>` tags should be used. Subpart markers are inserted into the HTML code for this purpose.

```
<body>
<!--###DOCUMENT_BODY### start -->
...
<!--###DOCUMENT_BODY### stop -->
</body>
```

The HTML template should also be prepared in such a way that all image paths refer to the directories in the file system in which they are stored, relative to the root directory. They should also be accessible from the **File | Filelist** module (e.g. `fileadmin/images/...`). This means that if you place the HTML file in the root directory of the website and access it, the embedded images must be visible. You can therefore also access `clear.gif`, which can be found in the root directory.

Figure 5.54:

HTML template called via the root directory

Prepared in this way, the HTML draft for the template now appears as follows (abbreviated). Here the contents that should have been substituted have been removed, to make it easier for us to read the document. With the exception of the `###COPYRIGHT###` marker, only subparts were used.

```
<!DOCTYPE HTML PUBLIC "-//W3C//DTD HTML 4.01
Transitional//EN">
<html>
<head>
<title>Untitled</title>
<link rel="stylesheet" type="text/css"
     href="fileadmin/styles/
     defaultstylesheet-modified.css">
</head>
<body>
<!--###DOCUMENT_BODY### start -->
<table width="800" border="0" cellspacing="0"
                              cellpadding="0">
<tr>
...
```

```
</tr>
<tr>
  <td> </td>
  <td height="32" colspan="5" align="left"
      valign="middle">
   <table width="785" border="0" cellspacing="0"
       cellpadding="0">
    <tr>
     <td width="650" align="left" valign="middle">
     <!--###ROOTLINE### start -->rootline
     <!--###ROOTLINE### stop --></td>
     <td width="135" align="right" valign="middle">
     <!--###PRINTVERSION### start -->Print version
     <!--###PRINTVERSION### stop --></td>
    </tr>
   </table>
  </td>
</tr>
<tr>
...
</tr>
<tr>
  <td width="15"><img src="clear.gif" width="1"
    height="1" alt="" border= "0"></td>
  <td width="1" bgcolor="#CCCCCC"
      background="fileadmin/images/layout/
      1px_gray.gif"><img src="clear.gif"
      width="1" height="1" alt="" border="0"></td>

  <td width="197" colspan="2" align="left"
    valign="middle">
    <img src="fileadmin/images/layout/logo.gif"
        width="177" height="82" alt=""
        border="0"></td>

  <td width="586" align="right">
  <!--###HEADER_IMAGE### start -->Header
  <!--###HEADER_IMAGE### stop --></td>
  <td bgcolor="#CCCCCC" background="fileadmin/
    images/layout/1px_gray.gif" width="1">
    <img src="clear.gif" width="1" height="1"
    alt="" border="0"></td>
</tr>
<tr>
...
</tr>
<tr>
  <td> </td>
  <td colspan="3" height="40">
      <img src="fileadmin/images/layout/
      balken_gelb.gif" width="166" height="18" alt=""
      border="0"></td>
  <td colspan="2" height="40">
```

```
    <!--###NAVIGATION### start -->Main navigation
    <!--###NAVIGATION### stop --></td>
  </tr>
  <tr>
    <td> </td>
    <td bgcolor="#CCCCCC" background="fileadmin/images/
      layout/1px_gray.gif"> <img src="clear.gif"
      width="1" height="1" alt="" border="0"></td>
    <td align="left" valign="top">
    <!--###LEFT### start -->Subnavigation
    <!--###LEFT### stop --></td>
    <td> </td>
    <td align="left" valign="top">
    <!--###CONTENT### start -->Content
    <!--###CONTENT### stop --></td>
    <td width="1"><img src="clear.gif" width="1"
      height="1" alt="" border="0"></td>
  </tr>
  <tr>
  ...
  </tr>
  <tr>
    <td height="18" colspan="6"
        align="right">###COPYRIGHT###</td>
  </tr>
  <tr>

    <td height="10" colspan="6" align="right"> </td>
  </tr>
</table>
<!--###DOCUMENT_BODY### stop-->
</body>
</html>
```

In the following figure you can see the template again in a schematic diagram. This is for a typical layout based on tables, with transparent GIFs (dotted) as placeholders. The areas with subparts are marked with broken lines.

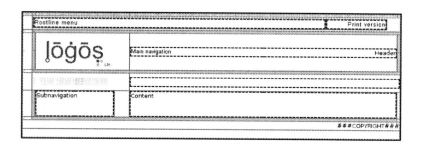

Figure 5.55:

Schematic diagram of the areas of the HTML template

In this example, the subparts and markers were set generously, so that only the base layout was left in the core. This creates content areas that can still be structured using TypoScript. This has the advantage that you can change the appearance of individual dynamic areas at any time via TypoScript objects and also—specifically in our case—that code libraries can be used again across various templating methods.

The HTML template must now be stored in the file system of the TYPO3 application in a directory beneath `fileadmin/....` If it is placed in the root folder, the image references will no longer function; but since the HTML template is displayed with `index.php` as part of the front-end output in the root directory of the website, the references will work.

Creating the Template Record

As already described, we are using cascading templates in the examples, which are inserted by a root template.

In the `Templates/Main Templates/` system directory, create a new template record, `html template`, and insert it in the root template for the "B2C Home" page (`B2C main template`) as the basis template. `html template` represents the actual definition of the page template and includes the `content (default)` template as well as individual code libraries as basis templates.

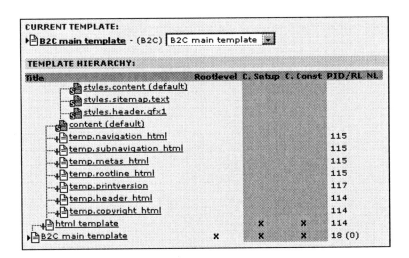

Figure 5.56:

Future nesting of the TS templates in the Template Analyzer

In the setup of the `html template` TS template, the TLO `page` will be defined as a page by assigning it as the `PAGE` object type, already demonstrated in section 5.2. The property transferred by this, `typeNum`, is assigned the value `0`. Since our site is not based on frames, this is sufficient.

```
page = PAGE
page.typeNum = 0
```

Other properties such as `bodyTagMargins` and `noLinkUnderline` specify that the `<body>` tag generated by TYPO3 is displayed with the parameters `leftmargin="0"`, `topmargin="0"`, `marginwidth="0"`, `margin-height="0"`, and that links created in the content are not underlined.

```
page.bodyTagMargins = 0
page.noLinkUnderline = 0
```

If you now call a page from the "B2C" site you will see that the TS template functions. Although nothing is yet displayed, the correct parameters have been assigned to the `<body>` tag in the source text.

cObject Template

To now insert the HTML template, the `PAGE` object type is used to take up content objects in a numerical list (array). `page.10=TEMPLATE` defines an object of the `TEMPLATE` object type in the object path `page.10`. The `template` property that the object `page.10` now has is then defined as an object of the `FILE` object type, and through the `file` property, refers to the HTML template in the file system.

```
page.10 = TEMPLATE
page.10 {
  template = FILE
  template.file = fileadmin/templates/html_template.tmpl
}
```

With this, the HTML template is already displayed in the front end, but the subparts and markers are not yet replaced.

It is a good idea to reconstruct the definition of the `TEMPLATE` object, for example by opening the TS setup with the **Web | Template | Info/Modify** module and using the TypoScript wizard, described in section 5.4.2, to set the properties for the `TEMPLATE` object type. There it is also clear that the `template` property can take in a cObject.

Addressing Subparts and Marks

First the area of the HTML template that is to be used for the TYPO3 output is defined. Since TYPO3 creates its own header and `<body>` tag, this is the subpart `###DOCUMENT_BODY###`, set in the HTML template inside the `<body>` tag. This encloses the area of the template to be interpreted, and whose subparts and marks are to be replaced. It is addressed with the `workOnSubpart` property and the name of the selected

DOCUMENT_BODY subpart as the value. The subparts and marks properties of the page.10 object represent lists of cObjects with the names of the corresponding subparts and markers. To test if the individual placeholders are correctly addressed, they are defined below as objects of the TEXT type, and each of them is assigned an output text as the value.

```
page.10 = TEMPLATE
page.10 {
  template = FILE
  template.file = fileadmin/templates/html_template.tmpl
  workOnSubpart = DOCUMENT_BODY
  subparts.HEADER_IMAGE = TEXT
  subparts.HEADER_IMAGE.value = area for header image
  subparts.ROOTLINE = TEXT
  subparts.ROOTLINE.value = rootline
  subparts.PRINTVERSION = TEXT
  subparts.PRINTVERSION.value = print button

  subparts.CONTENT = TEXT
  subparts.CONTENT.value = the content area

  subparts.NAVIGATION = TEXT
  subparts.NAVIGATION.value = area for main navigation
  subparts.LEFT = TEXT
  subparts.LEFT.value = area for subnavigation and
                        metas (e.g.legal information)
  marks.COPYRIGHT = TEXT
  marks.COPYRIGHT.value = footer with copyright
}
```

If a page of the "B2C" site is called now in the front end, it can be seen that all the subparts and marks have been replaced with the corresponding texts.

Figure 5.57:

Placeholders of the HTML template have been replaced

Inserting Dynamic Content

Now the content for the respective pages should be displayed, of course. Because content (default) as well as styles.content (default) were inserted as basis templates in the TS template html template, this is simple, because it means that the predefined styles.content.get object is available.

Extract from styles.content (default):

```
styles.content.get = CONTENT
styles.content.get {
  table = tt_content
  select.orderBy = sorting
  select.where = colPos=0
  select.languageField = sys_language_uid
}
```

With the help of the styles.content.get object, the contents of the tt_content table in the Normal (colPos=0) column are queried and rendered with the content (default) standard template, because a corresponding TS setup is defined there for the individual content types. The setup is located under tt_content.*, and due to the identical name, is used automatically by the CONTENT object to render the tt_content table.

Now the styles.content.get object is also copied to page.10.subparts.CONTENT, whereby the contents of the Normal column of the current page are rendered and inserted in the subparts with the name CONTENT. The content to be displayed is put in a table by the wrap property of the CONTENT object type.

```
page.10 {
  ...
  subparts.CONTENT < styles.content.get
  subparts.CONTENT.wrap =<table width="586"
                          cellspacing="0" cellpadding=
"0" border="0"><tr><td>|</td></tr></table>
  ...
}
```

Please note that CONTENT in the object path page.10.subparts.CONTENT is only the name for the subpart marker in the HTML template; this does not mean that it is automatically an object of the CONTENT type. But in fact, page.10.subparts.CONTENT is defined as a CONTENT object with a copy of the styles.content.get object.

The individual pages of the "B2C" application now reproduce the content of the current page in the front end.

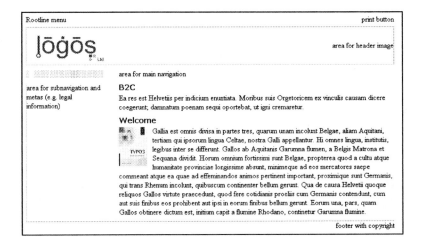

Figure 5.58:

Content is displayed dynamically

To format the content output, the cSet (default) and cSet Stylesheet standard templates simplify marking with the Constant Editor. Both bundle individual style definitions from styles.content.default with constants, making global changes easy to carry out. The difference between the two is that cSet (default) performs the markings using traditional HTML formatting, while cSet Stylesheet uses cascading stylesheet definitions that are stored in a separate file. Depending on which method you prefer, the appropriate standard template must be integrated as basis template after content (default) in the html template TS template. We have illustrated both variations in turn.

cSet (default)

If cSet (default) is inserted, the default values can be changed with the Constant Editor. In the example, standard values of the CSET category such as background color, fonts and sizes for various content elements, and headers are overridden.

```
# adjusted constants of the cSet standard template
# (default)
cSet.pageColor = white
cSet.tableCellColor = #E6B800
cSet.color = #666666
cSet.color1 = #0000CC
cSet.color2 = #E6B800

cSet.fontFace = Arial
cSet.fontFace.text = Arial

cSet.size1 = 1
cSet.size2 = 2
cSet.size3 = 3
```

The changes are saved by the Constant Editor in the `Constant` field of the currently selected template.

cSet Stylesheet

The standard template access is a stylesheet file supplied by the TYPO3 base installation under `media/scripts/default-stylesheet.css`. Copy this file and store it in a directory in the file system under `fileadmin/`. Then specify the new path in the `CONTENT` category in the Constant Editor.

Figure 5.59:

Inserting the new CSS file

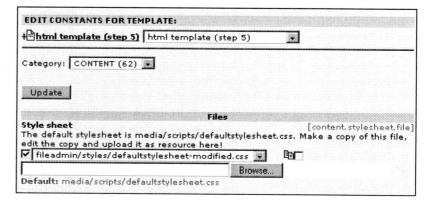

The new value of the constant is written in the `Constants` field of the TS template:

```
# adjusted constants of the cSet standard template
# stylesheet
content.stylesheet.file = fileadmin/
                defaultstylesheet-modified.css
```

You can now modify styles in the CSS file, or add new ones. Modifications can be carried out either with a special CSS editor or directly with TYPO3 (**File | Filelist**).

Stages of Construction with Cascading Templates

The TS template now inserts the HTML template and displays the contents maintained by the editors in the back end. However, it still contains several placeholders, which so far only contain text for test purposes. These will be individually replaced with code libraries and inserted as a basis template. The menus will all be discussed together in their own section.

The Image in the Header

First an image should be added to the HEADER subpart, which, depending on the area of the page tree, can be specified by the editors through the **Files** field of the corresponding pages. To do this, a separate temp.header_html TS template is created that defines the temporary object header_image of the IMAGE object type.

```
temp.header_image = IMAGE
```

In order to specify the location from which the images are to be read, the file.import property determines the directory where the images are stored via the **Files** field. The file property belongs to the imgResource data type. This in turn is a function containing the import property.

```
temp.header_image.file.import = uploads/media/
```

The folder where the images are located is now specified, but not where the images are to be displayed. The import property belongs to the path data type, but it has the stdWrap function available, and therefore the data property of the getText data type. This enables values from the data stored internally by TYPO3 (PHP array) to be read out, including those images that are assigned to individual pages. So data = levelmedia:1, slide reads out data of the levelmedia type from the first level in the page tree; the slide parameter has the effect that TYPO3 goes from the current page in the page tree to level 1, until an image is found and displayed.

```
temp.header_image.file.import.data =
                        levelmedia:1, slide
```

The stdWrap function will be looked at in more detail, but we have seen here how powerful it is, just by reading out data. The important thing at this point is that, if you have worked through the example with us, you will already have an understanding of handling the TSref (see Figure 5.62).

You now only need to insert the prepared images into the respective page headers (page type: **Advanced**) of the first level via the **Files** field.

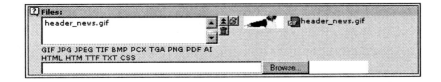

Figure 5.60:

Image file inserted in the page header

In the html template TS template the temp.header_image object path is passed to the HEADER_IMAGE subpart so that the object just defined can also be used.

297

```
subparts.HEADER_IMAGE < temp.header_image
```

In the front end, various images, depending on the page area, are now displayed in the header of the application, via the three lines of TypoScript code.

Figure 5.61:

Output in the front end

The Text in the Footer

In the footer of the application there is editable text reproducing the copyright. A separate TS template is also created here (`temp.copyright_html`) and inserted as a basis template in the `html template` template record.

```
marks.COPYRIGHT < temp.copyright_html
```

The code component `temp.copyright_html` generates an object with the same name, of the `TEXT` object type. Its `value` property is passed a constant as a value, and the output of the object is wrapped with an HTML `<font>` tag.

```
temp.copyright_html = TEXT
temp.copyright_html {
  value = {$copyright}
  wrap = <font face="Arial,Helvetica,sans-serif,
               sans-serif" size="1" color="#666666"
               class="copyright">|</font>
}
```

298

IMAGE:

Property:	Data type:
file	imgResource

Datatype reference

Datatype:	Examples:	Comment:
resource	*From the resourcefield:* toplogo*.gif *Reference to filesystem:* fileadmin/picture.gif	1) A reference to a file from the resource-field in the template. You can write the exact filename or you can include an asterisk (*) as wildcard. It's recommended to include a "*" before the fileextension (see example to the left). This will ensure that the file is still referenced correct even if the template is copied and the file will have it's name prepended with numbers!! 2) If the value contains a "/" it's expected to be a reference (absolute or relative) to a file on the file-system instead of the resource-field. No support for wildcards.

imgResource	Here "file" is a imgResource:
	file = toplogo*.gif
	file.width = 200
	
	GIFBUILDER:
	file = GIFBUILDER
	file {
	   ... (GIFBUILDER-properties here)
	}
		1) A "resource" (see above) + imgResource-properties (see example to the left and object-reference below)
		Filetypes can be anything among the allowed types defined in the configuration variable $TYPO3_CONF_VARS['GFX']['imagefile_ext'] (localconf.php). Standard is pdf,gif,jpg,jpeg,tif,bmp,ai,pcx,tga,png.
		
		2) GIFBUILDER-object

imgResource:

imgResource is properties that is used with the data type imgResource.

Property:	Data type:	Description:
import	path / stdWrap	*value* should be set to the path of the file with stdWrap you get the filename from the data-array **Example:** This returns the first image in the field "image" from the data-array: .import = uploads/pics/ .import.field = image .import.listNum = 0

stdWrap:

Property:	Data type:	Description:
Get data:		
data	getText	

Datatype reference

Datatype:	Examples:	Comment:
getText	*get content from the $cObj->data-array* *[header]:* = field : header	This returns a value from somewhere in PHP-array, defined by the type. The syntax is "type : pointer"
	= leveluid : 0 *Gets the value of the user defined field "user_myExtField" in the root line (requires additional config in TYPO3_CONF_VARS to include field!)*	**leveltitle, leveluid, levelmedia:** [levelTitle, uid or media in rootLine, 0- , negative = from behind, " , slide" parameter forces a walk to the bottom of the rootline until there's a "true" value to return. Useful with levelmedia.]

Figure 5.62:

Reading the TSRef

Now a value must be passed to the constant in the `Constants` field of the TS template:

```
copyright = Copyright &copy; 2005
```

The front end now displays the closing text.

It is not obligatory to use the `copyright` constant, but you should be able to change the copyright sign using the value of a constant.

The application is extended further in sections 5.10 and 5.11.

5.9.2 The Template Auto-Parser

Use of the *Template Auto-Parser* is demonstrated in the "B2E" area of the website. It is similar to the integration of HTML templates in the way it is used, except that here the marking of subparts and markers, as well as the resolving of image and resource paths, is taken over by the `Template Auto-Parser (automaketemplate)` extension. It must already be installed and loaded. You should also install the `CSS styled content (css_styled_content)` extension, which will be used instead of the `content (default)` standard template.

The HTML Template

In order to bring some variation into the application, the layout of the HTML template in the "B2E" area is not based on tables, but is marked with the help of `<div>` tags whose appearance is defined entirely by cascading stylesheets (CSS). [8] These few `<div>` tags can also be created with TypoScript, as shown in section 5.9.3. The Auto-Parser recognizes areas if it finds the `id` parameter in HTML elements such as `<div>`, `<span>`, and `<td>`. The HTML template was prepared accordingly and stored in the file system. If they are included, images, etc. should be stored in subdirectories, relative to their links. The paths to external files such as images do not need to be adjusted in the HTML template.

Softlink **544119**

```
<!DOCTYPE HTML PUBLIC "-//W3C//DTD HTML 4.01
                              Transitional//EN">
<html>
<head>
<title>Untitled</title>
<link href="fileadmin/styles/auto-parser-template.css"
            rel="stylesheet" type="text/css">
</head>
<body>
  <div id="rootline">rootline</div>
  <div id="header">
  <div id="logo"}>logo</div>
  <div id="headerimagetext">headerimagetext</div>
</div>
  <div id="navi">navi</div>
  <div id="middle">
  <div id="subnavigation">subnavi</div>
  <div id="content">content</div>
</div>
  <div id="printversion">printversion</div>
  <div id="footer"></div>
  <div id="copyright">Copyright &copy; 2005</div>
</body>
</html>
```

Configuring the Template Auto-Parser

The hierarchy of the template matches that of the "B2C" area. An `auto parser template` basis template is assigned to a `B2E main template` root template where the actual page is defined. The latter incorporates the `CSS styled content` standard template for rendering the contents, via **Include static (from extensions)**.

---

[8] Of course the efficiency of this method only becomes apparent with more complex HTML templates.

When you have installed the `Template Auto-Parser` extension, you will see a new `tx_automaketemplate_pi1` object of the USER object type under the TLO `plugin`.

```
CURRENT TEMPLATE:
▶ B2E main template

OBJECT TREE:
Browse: Setup ▾    OL: ALL ▾

SETUP ROOT
  ⊞ [config]
  ⊞ [includeLibs]
  ⊟ [plugin]
      ⊟ [tx_automaketemplate_pi1]=USER
          ⋯ [userFunc]=tx_automaketemplate_pi1->main
          ⊞ [content]=FILE
          ⊞ [elements]
      ⊞ [tx_rlmpofficeimport_pi1]=USER
  ⊞ [lib]
```

Softlink **363442** The Template Auto-Parser can be addressed and configured with this. The possible options can be found in the documentation on the extension (see softlink). Add the following to the setup of the TS template `auto parser template`:

```
###    Configuration of the auto template parser:    ###
plugin.tx_automaketemplate_pi1 {
  content = FILE
  content.file = fileadmin/templates/
                 auto-parser-template.tmpl
  elements {
    BODY.all = 1
    BODY.all.subpartMarker = DOCUMENT_BODY
    HEAD.all = 1
    HEAD.all.subpartMarker = DOCUMENT_HEADER
    HEAD.rmTagSections = title
    DIV.all = 1
  }
}
```

With the `content` property you can configure in the Template Auto-Parser which HTML template will be used. It is then instructed, with the `elements` property, to wrap all HTML tags found of the `<body>`, `<head>`, or `<div>` type with subparts. In all HTML elements of the `<body>` and `<head>` type, a `subpartMarker` (in capitals) is set so that they can be addressed below via the TEMPLATE cObject. Because the title of TYPO3 is generated dynamically, the `<title>` tag is removed with `elements.HEAD.rmTagSections`

=title. If the relative paths to images and resources of the HTML template are to be adjusted to the TYPO3 environment from the root directory, a prefix to the folder in the file system can be specified. This was not done in the example, because only the CSS file is involved, and the reference already points to the correct directory.

```
#Prefix all relative paths with the value:
plugin.tx_automaketemplate_pi1.relPathPrefix
    =fileadmin/template/
```

Creating the Page

To create the page, the TypoScript code in this case is constructed in more modular fashion, by creating objects in the `temp.*` object path. The `headerTemplate` object of the TEMPLATE object type is created to integrate the HTML header data. Its `template` property is given the `plugin.tx_automaketemplate_pi1` object as a reference.

The `workOnSubpart` property specifies that the object only refers to the area of the HTML template that was enclosed by the DOCUMENT_HEADER placeholder.

```
### cObject for header ###
temp.headerTemplate = TEMPLATE
temp.headerTemplate {
  template =< plugin.tx_automaketemplate_pi1
  workOnSubpart = DOCUMENT_HEADER
}
```

In the previous example, an HTML file already containing markers was read in by an object of the FILE type, and passed to the TEMPLATE object for processing. Similar things take place with the Template Auto-Parser, with the difference that the `plugin.tx_automaketemplate_pi1` plugin sets the markers automatically due to the configuration, also adjusting file references in the process. You can therefore assign an `id` to the blocks in the HTML file and then access it in the TS setup, without having to insert markers by hand.

In the same way the `mainTemplate` object is now created, except that it refers to the area of the HTML template enclosed by the DOCUMENT_BODY placeholder. Individual subparts are again supplied with output text, for test purposes. The subparts are addressed with the same name (observing upper and lower case) as the `ids` of the HTML template.

```
### cObject for body ###
temp.mainTemplate = TEMPLATE
temp.mainTemplate {
  template =< plugin.tx_automaketemplate_pi1
  workOnSubpart = DOCUMENT_BODY
```

```
subparts.rootline = TEXT
subparts.rootline.value = rootline
subparts.printversion = TEXT
subparts.printversion.value = printbutton
subparts.header = TEXT
subparts.header.value = area for header image
subparts.navi = TEXT
subparts.navi.value = area for main navigation
subparts.subnavigation = TEXT
subparts.subnavigation.value = area for subnavigation
        and metas (e.g.legal information)
subparts.content = TEXT
subparts.content.value = content area
subparts.copyright = TEXT
subparts.copyright.value = footer with copyright
}
```

The pages created in the final phase, and the temporary objects are copied to the object path `page.headerData.10` and `page.10`.

```
## Create page ###
page = PAGE
page.typeNum = 0
page.noLinkUnderline = 0
page.headerData.10 < temp.headerTemplate
page.10 < temp.mainTemplate
```

The application called in the front end already shows the base layout controlled via CSS, and the corresponding subparts with their test contents.

Figure 5.65:

Front-end output in the current stage of construction

If you look at the source code for the front-end output, you will see that the link to the CSS file in the header remains intact, and that a number of placeholders for subparts can still be found.

```
</head>
<body bgcolor="#FFFFFF">

<div id="rootline">rootline</div>
<div id="header">area for header image</div>
<div id="navi">area for main navigation</div>
<div id="middle"><!--###middle### begin -->
    <div id="subnavigation">area for subnavigation and metas (e.g. legal information)</div>
    <div id="content">content area</div>
<!--###middle### end --></div>
<div id="printversion">printbutton</div>
<div id="footer"><!--###footer### begin --><!--###footer### end --></div>
<div id="copyright">footer with copyright</div>

</body>
</html>
```

Figure 5.66:

Parts of the output in the source code

If creating subplot markers is only desired for certain `ids`, you can config-ure the Template Auto-Parser accordingly.

```
plugin.tx_automaketemplate_pi1.DIV.id {
    rootline = 1
    printversion = 1
    ...
    copyright = 1
}
```

Stages of Construction with Cascading Templates

So far only example text was displayed using this template. Below, TS objects will be developed for specific areas, displaying appropriate content, which can be inserted into the main template.

Displaying Page Content

The output of the `Normal` content column has already been shown with the `content (default)` standard template (with the predefined `styles.content.get` object). The CSS `styled content` standard template used in this template also contains the same object, and can be used accordingly.

```
temp.mainTemplate = TEMPLATE
temp.mainTemplate {
    ...
    subparts.content < styles.content.get
    ...
}
```

Creating the Header

In contrast to the example in section 5.9.1, the logo is not contained in this HTML template. We now have to define this using TypoScript together with the image in the header. This is why an object is created, of the same name and of the COA object type, in the template you have created yourself, named `temp.header_tswrap_autoparser`.

305

The COA cObject (also called COBJ_ARRAY) can contain several objects in a list. In this way the 10 object generates an image (object type: IMAGE) that is localized in the file system via the file property.

```
temp.header_tswrap_autoparser = COA
temp.header_tswrap_autoparser {
  10 = IMAGE
  10.file = fileadmin/images/layout/logo.gif
```

The logo should contain a link to the homepage of the website. This can be done with the stdWrap function, which provides the IMAGE object type as a property.

It integrates the typolink function, which states (through its parameter property) which data the link should be created from. Here a link is made to the page with the ID 75.

```
10.stdWrap.typolink.parameter = 75
```

The parameter property is of the string/stdWrap data type. As an alternative, it is possible to automatically find out the ID of the root page of the website (level=0) with the data property of the stdWrap function.

```
10.stdWrap.typolink.parameter.data = leveluid:0
```

The image and the link are then enclosed, by the wrap property of the stdWrap object, with a <div> tag, which deals with the positioning of the logo via CSS.

```
10.stdWrap.wrap = <div id="logo">|</div>
```

20 is created as the second object of the COA by the already existing temp.header_image object being copied to this object path. temp.header_image originates from the temp.header_html TS template of the example in section 5.9.1, and is simply re-used.

To do this, the template must be included as a basis template in the auto parser template template record. In addition, the desired images must be selected in the corresponding pages of the first level, via the **Files** field.

Since this application is based on CSS, the object is then wrapped with a <div> tag.

```
# simple image, without GIFBUILDER
20 < temp.header_image
20.wrap = <div id="headerimage">|</div>
}
```

The Text in the Footer

In order to display the copyright at the bottom of the page, using the `temp.copyright_html` TS template, you include it as a basis template and copy the object to `temp.mainTemplate.subparts.copyright`. The only difference is that the text should not be wrapped with a `<font>` tag. For this reason the `wrap` property is deleted with the `>` operator.

```
temp.mainTemplate = TEMPLATE
temp.mainTemplate {
   . . .
      subparts.copyright < temp.copyright_html
      subparts.copyright.wrap >
   . . .
}
```

The template has now reached the same level of development as the previous example. Creating menus and special functions is described later on. But first we will show you in the next section how base layouts are constructed without external HTML files.

If you enjoy working with the Template Auto-Parser, we would once again like to point out to you the very extensive tutorial, "Modern Template Building, Part 1" (see softlink).

5.9.3 Pure TypoScript Templates

In the final method for creating TS templates, we will manage without including HTML templates, and create the base layout entirely with TypoScript.

We will show you two examples of this, using the layout of the "B2B" application, one with the wrapper concept, with `<div>` tags, and the other with the `CTABLE` cObject. The templates are cascaded in the same way as in the "B2C" and "B2E" applications. A basis template, `ts wrap template` or `ts CTABLE template`, is assigned to a root template `B2B main template`. You define the actual page and integrate the `content (default)` and `cSet stylesheet` standard templates, as well as other TS code components, according to the level of development.

Working with Wrap

If we refer back to the example of the Template Auto-Parser, the HTML template integrated there can also be created entirely with TypoScript. In this way, when parsing the output, no use is made of an external HTML file marked with placeholders. Work replacing subparts and markers is unnecessary, since all HTML markings required are defined in the TS template.

In the `ts wrap template` TS template, again make a `page` TLO of the PAGE object type and specify with the `bodytag` and `stylesheet` properties how the `<body>` tag should appear, and where the CSS file is to be found in the file system.

For all contents of the page, create the relevant contents via a numerical list and enclose them with `<div>` tags through the `wrap` property. The appearance of the site is also controlled here with cascading stylesheets (CSS).

```
page {
  10 = TEXT
  10.value = rootline
  10.wrap = <div id="rootline">|</div>
  ..
}
```

Already created and reusable code components of the `temp.header_tswrap_autoparser` and `temp.copyright_html` TS templates are included in the template record with the **Include basis template** field, and its properties are passed on to the respective objects in the numerical list.

```
20 < temp.header_tswrap_autoparser
20.stdWrap.wrap = <div id="header">|</div>
```

So far only content of the `Normal` column was displayed. A second fixed content area is integrated here with the `60` object, which displays the content of the `Right` column via the predefined `styles .content.getRight` object of the `styles.content` (default) standard template.

```
60 < styles.content.getRight
```

The `60` object is now of the CONTENT object type. In order to enclose the content with `<div>` tags, which is done in the output with CSS, the `stdWrap` function and its `wrap` property are used.

```
60.stdWrap.wrap = <div id="right">
        <div id="rightcontent">|</div>
        <div id="rightfooter"> </div></div>
```

The wrap is set with the `stdWrap` function, because the following property also needs to be set:

```
60.stdWrap.required = 1
```

If the `required` property is set, `stdWrap` will only process the other set properties if a value is passed to `stdWrap`. In this case it means that the wrap is only displayed if the CONTENT object `page.60` generates output—that is, if there is content in the right-hand column. In the front-end output, a framework is only displayed via CSS if content also exists in the `Right` column.

The setup of `ts wrap template` in its current stage of development:

```
page = PAGE
page.typeNum = 0
page.bodyTag = <body bgcolor="#FFFFFF" leftmargin="0"
                topmargin="0" marginwidth="0">

page.stylesheet = fileadmin/styles/ts-template-wrap.css

page {
# Top
  ## rootline
  10 = TEXT
  10.value = rootline
  10.wrap = <div id="rootline">|</div>
  ## Header
  20 < temp.header_tswrap_autoparser
  20.wrap = <div id="header">|</div>
  ## Main Navigation
  30 = TEXT
  30.value = area for main navigation
  30.wrap = <div id="navi">|</div>

# Left / Submenu
  40 = TEXT
  40.value = area for subnavigation and metas (e.g.
                                legal information)
  40.wrap = <div id="subnavigation">|</div>

# Content
  50 < styles.content.get
  50.stdWrap.wrap = <div id="content">|</div>

# Right
  60 < styles.content.getRight
  60.stdWrap.wrap = <div id="right">
         <div id="rightcontent">|</div>
         <div id="rightfooter"> </div></div>
  # the framework in DIV elements is only displayed if
  # content exists
  60.stdWrap.required = 1

# Printversion
  65 = TEXT
  65.value = printbutton
  65.wrap = <div id="printversion">|</div>

# Footer
  ## simple placeholder to enable a CSS line break
  ## (clear: both)
```

```
70 = TEXT
70.value = <div id="footer"></div>
## Copyright note
80 < temp.copyright_html
80.wrap = <div id="copyright">|</div>
}
```

Working with CTABLE

Simple table layouts can be created quickly with TypoScript using the CTABLE cObject. This creates a standard table with up to five cells. One cell for the contents (c) can optionally be surrounded by the cells for a left margin (lm) and a right margin (rm) as well as a top (tm) and bottom margin (bm).

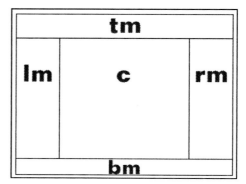

Even though the layout for the example site is not ideal for conversion with CTABLE, since it contains several lines and frames, it can still be managed. In the ts CTABLE template basis template, again define the page TLO with the properties used so far, typeNum, bodyTagMargins and noLinkUnderline.

```
page = PAGE
page.typeNum = 0
page.bodyTagMargins = 0
page.noLinkUnderline = 0
```

In this example we divided up the layout into several objects with the *numerical list* property of the PAGE objects type. The 2 object should now create a table that positions the Rootline menu and the button for the print version. The CTABLE object type is assigned to it, via which all properties of the cObjects are made available. First additional parameters in the table are set with the tableParams properties, and with offset the distance from the top left corner is set to 0.

```
###### rootline #######
page.2 = CTABLE
page.2 {
  tableParams = border="0" cellpadding="0"
               cellspacing="0" width="785" offset = 0,0
```

The c, lm, rm, tm, and bm properties are of the CARRAY +TDParams data type, that is, they represent a numerical list of cObjects. Your own parameters can be passed to the table cells themselves.

The c content cell for the future Rootline menu is now temporarily defined as an object of the TEXT type; a placeholder text is defined with its value property.

```
c.10 = TEXT
c.10.value = this creates the Rootline menu
```

The content of the cell is centered:

```
c.TDParams = valign="middle"
```

The left cell lm takes in a cObject of the CLEARGIF object type and serves as a utility to fix the table to a height of 32 pixels.

```
# Height of rootline
lm.10 = CLEARGIF
lm.10.height = 32
```

A placeholder text is also set for the right column rm, for the link to the print version of the page.

```
rm.10 = TEXT
rm.10.value = printbutton
rm.TDParams = valign="middle" align="right"
}
```

The objects page.10, page.20, page.30, and page.40 are defined as further tables. The contents cell page.10.c will display the logo and area image in the header of the page, and consists of several objects in the form of a numerical list (COA).

```
###### header ######
page.10 = CTABLE
page.10 {
  tableParams = border="0" cellpadding="0"
               cellspacing="0" width="785"
  offset = 15,0
  # Logo
  c.10 = COA
  # Positioning table for logo and Header_Image
  c.10.5 = HTML
  c.10.5.value = <table border="0" width="768"
     cellspacing="0" cellpadding="0">
```

```
                    <tr><td width="197">
c.10.10 = IMAGE
c.10.10.file = fileadmin/images/layout/logo.gif
c.10.TDParams = align="left" valign="top"
                    bgcolor="white"
c.10.15 = HTML
c.10.15.value = </td><td align="right">
c.10.20 < temp.header_image
c.10.30 = HTML
c.10.30.value = </td></tr></table>
```

The framework is implemented by the cells `page.10.1m`, `page.10.tm`, `page.10.rm`, and `page.10.bm`, which display objects of the IMAGE type.

```
# framework for the header
lm.10 = IMAGE
lm.10.file = fileadmin/images/layout/1px_gray.gif
lm.TDParams = align="left" valign="top"
                bgcolor="#CCCCCC" height="125" width="1"

tm.10 = IMAGE
tm.10.file = fileadmin/images/layout/1px_gray.gif
tm.TDParams = align="left" valign="top"
                bgcolor="#CCCCCC" height="1" width="785"

rm.10 = IMAGE
rm.10.file = fileadmin/images/layout/1px_gray.gif
rm.TDParams = align="left" valign="top"
                bgcolor="#CCCCCC" height="125" width="1"

bm.10 = IMAGE
bm.10.file = fileadmin/images/layout/1px_gray.gif
bm.TDParams = align="left" valign="top"
                bgcolor="#CCCCCC" height="1" width="785"
}
```

`page.20` displays the main navigation.

```
###### Navigation ######
page.20 = CTABLE
page.20 {
  tableParams = border="0" cellpadding="0"
          cellspacing="0" width="785" offset = 15,0
  c.5 = HTML
  c.5.value = <table border="0" width="785" height="40"
          cellspacing="0" cellpadding="0"><tr><td
  width="197">
  c.10 = IMAGE
  c.10.file = fileadmin/images/layout/balken_gelb.gif
  c.10.params = hspace="0" vspace="0"
  c.15 = HTML
  c.15.value = </td><td>
  c.20 = TEXT
```

```
   c.20.value = area for main navigation
   c.TDParams = align="left" valign="middle"
               bgcolor="#FFFFFF" height="40"
   c.30 = HTML
   c.30.value = </td></tr></table>
}
```

Table page.30 positions the submenu and the content area via page.30.1m and page.30.c. They are encompassed by the HTML objects page.25, which displays the gray line on the left-hand page, and page.35.

```
###### Subnavigation and Content ######
#Framing table for left and right lines
page.25 = HTML
page.25.value = <table border="0" cellspacing="0"
          cellpadding="0"><tr><
          td width="15"><img src="clear.gif"
          width="15" height="1"
          alt="" border="0"></td><td width="1"
          bgcolor="#CCCCCC"
          background="fileadmin/images/
          layout/1px_gray.gif"><img src="clear.gif"
          width="1" height="1" alt=""
          border="0"></td><td>

page.30 = CTABLE
page.30 {
  tableParams = border="0" cellpadding="0"
            cellspacing="0" width="767"
  offset = 0,0
  c.10 = COA
  c.10.5 = HTML
  c.10.5.value = <table border="0" cellspacing="0"
                cellpadding="0" width ="586"><tr>
  c.10.10 < styles.content.get
  c.10.10.wrap = <td align="left" valign="top">|<br />
            <br /></td>
  c.10.25 = HTML
  c.10.25.value = </tr></table>
  # space so that the cell is also included if content
  # is missing
  c.10.stdWrap.ifEmpty =  
  # offset to copyright sign
  c.20 = HTML
  c.20.value = <br /><br />
  c.TDParams = align="right" valign="top"

  lm.10 = TEXT
  lm.10.value = area for subnavigation and
             meta-information (imprimatur, etc.)
  # height, so that the content is at least 400 pix
  # high, even if content is missing.
  lm.TDParams = width="197" align="left"
```

313

```
                        valign="top" height="400"
   }

   # end of framing table
   page.35 = HTML
   page.35.value = </td></tr></table>
```

The footer of the output with the copyright is created by the `page.40` table object.

```
   ###### Copyright ######
   page.40 = CTABLE
   page.40 {
      tableParams = border="0" cellpadding="0"
                    cellspacing="0" width="785"
      offset = 15,0

      c.10 < temp.copyright_html
      c.TDParams = align="right" valign="middle"
              bgcolor="#FFFFFF" height="18"

      tm.10 = IMAGE
      tm.10.file = fileadmin/images/layout/1px_gray.gif
      tm.TDParams = align="left" valign="top"
              bgcolor="#CCCCCC" height="1" width="785"

      bm.10 = CLEARGIF
      bm.10.height = 30
   }
```

You can see that the listing has become quite large, and that CTABLE is better suited, for a simpler layout, to create this clearly using a table.

All template methods have now been introduced, and which one you will use to design your application depends on your preferences and skills. In the next section, menus will be introduced that automatically display the current page tree as a means of navigation.

5.10 Menus

Menus handle not only the navigation concept in your website, but also provide important design elements. With TYPO3, many different types of menus can be created. Functionalities for creating menus based on text, graphics, layers, an imagemap, or selection menus are already included, and can be addressed via TypoScript, where various logical menu structures are possible.

In the front end, menus are created dynamically via the hierarchy of pages in the page tree. If you create a new page in the back end, for example, it is automatically shown in the relevant menu once it is released.

Inside menus, the page types **Standard, Advanced, External URL, Shortcut,** and **Mount Point** are generally displayed, provided no restrictions are set by TypoScript. The **Spacer** placeholder must be defined separately for it to be displayed. The page types **Not in Menu, SysFolder,** and **Recycler** are not included.

Level

Because normally only a sitemap displays all the pages of a website, a definition must be made in most menus as to what page the menu is to start on and where it is to finish. One way of defining this exists in the so-called *levels*. The Rootline of the website, as the first level, corresponds to level 0, the next level to level 1, and so on.

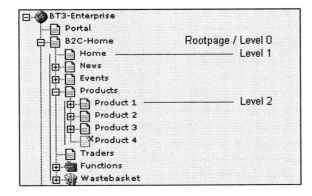

Figure 5.68:

Levels in the page tree

The Rootline

An important concept frequently used in the context of menus in TYPO3 is *Rootline*. The term is also used to name the lowest level in the page tree. You can display standard templates, for example, in the **Web | List** module, by selecting the Rootline (globe). Rather confusingly, this term has another meaning for menus. Here the Rootline is a list of pages, obtained by moving down to the root page, starting from the current page. In Figure 5.68, the Rootline of the "Product 2" page would be: Product 2, Products, B2C Home.

We will show below how our various menu types are configured with TypoScript. Inside the BT3 example application, they are saved as individual template records in the `Templates/Main Templates/Menus/` SysFolder. For display in the individual websites, "B2C", "B2B", and "B2E", the desired menus are included in the respective main template as basis templates. The existing placeholder texts in the main templates are replaced by the corresponding objects.

Example: in the "B2C" website, the main template `html template` defines the page. In the template record here, integrate the menu you have created, with **Include basis template**.

Into the `page.10.subparts.NAVIGATION` object path, which until now showed a placeholder text,

```
page.10 {
  ...
  subparts.NAVIGATION = TEXT
  subparts.NAVIGATION.value = area for main navigation
  ...
}
```

the menu object is now copied. Be careful that it is the object of the menu that is copied, and not the template record, which usually has the same name in the examples.

```
...
subparts.NAVIGATION < temp.navigation_html
...
```

The menu would now already be visible on the website. But first it must be created.

5.10.1 cObject HMENU—Common Properties of Menus

Softlink **460074**

Whatever menu you want to show on your website, they are all created with the HMENU (*hierarchical menu*) cObject.

Here is a simple example creating a menu for the pages of level 0, in which the entries are shown beneath each other, because in each menu item a wrap is used with a `<br />` tag.

```
temp.navigation = HMENU
temp.navigation.entryLevel = 0
temp.navigation {
  1 = TMENU
  1.NO.allWrap = |<br />
}
```

HMENU takes on the task of gathering the page information. The actual rendering of the menu entries is performed by subobjects, which are included in a numerical list. In contrast to the PAGE or COA object type, the numbering has a special significance. The properties 1, 2, 3, etc. stand for the corresponding levels. The `entryLevel` property specifies the level in the page tree, seen from the Rootline, from which you start counting the levels for the menu. The above TS setup will therefore create a menu with one level of depth, starting from level 0.

In the example, by the way, a menu object that creates simple text links is used in TMENU. As already mentioned, other menu types are also supported by TYPO3.

```
temp.navigation.1 = TMENU
# the second level of the menu is a graphical menu
temp.navigation.2 = GMENU
```

The following menu types are available in TYPO3:

TMENU

Displays a text-based menu.

GMENU

GMENU stands for "graphical menu". Images are generated automatically from individual page titles.

GMENU_LAYERS/TMENU_LAYERS

GMENU_LAYERS and TMENU_LAYERS add further properties to the corresponding GMENU or TMENU menu object and display it with DHTML layers. Because of different interpretations of the standards by various browser versions, the menu objects cannot be used for older browsers, and can only be used to a limited extent for new ones.

GMENU_FOLDOUT

GMENU_FOLDOUT extends the GMENU menu object. It creates a menu for two levels, which folds out or back in without the page having to be reloaded.

IMGMENU

The IMGMENU menu object creates an ImageMap.

JSMENU

JSMENU creates a classical foldout menu.

Apart from the `entryLevel` property, HMENU has several other properties that control menu output. The number of menu entries can be specified with the `minItems` and `maxItems` properties, for example, and with `begin` you can define the first menu entry. With `excludeUidList`, you can also exclude certain pages from inclusion in the menu.

special is a powerful property that helps you define menus with a different structure from the page tree. Menus can be created that display the Rootline, show pages with specific keywords, or list subpages from selected pages. All possible options are discussed in section 5.10.8.

Softlink **401761**   The menu objects themselves (TMENU, GMENU,...) have a number of states in common, but also have their own specific ones. They all have the addParams state for example, which passes on further links to the menu link.

Softlink **478459**   With the exception of JSMENU, the other menu objects of the series TMENU, GMENU, and IMGMENU also share states that accept menu items. NO (normal) represents the normal case, which always has to be defined as the default configuration. All other states must be activated if they are to be used, and their behavior must be defined individually.

NO

The menu item in the normal NO state. The definition is obligatory.

IFSUB

The IFSUB status is active if the menu item has subpages.

ACT

The menu item has the ACT status if it is located in the Rootline of the current page.

ACTIFSUB

If the menu item is located in the Rootline of the current page, and if it has subpages to be displayed in a menu, then it has the status ACTIFSUB.

CUR

The current page has the status CUR.

USR

The status USR applies to pages for which access is restricted by front-end user groups. It overrides the states IFSUB, ACT, and CUR.

SPC

The SPC status applies specifically to the **Spacer** page type and is used especially for the structuring of menus. SPC has no rollover functionalities, since it is not linked.

USERDEF1

> The states USERDEF1 and USERDEF2 can be defined in a separate script (see the properties HMENU/special = userdefined or .itemArrayProcFunc).

USERDEF2

> See USERDEF1.

[RO]

> With this, a variation for mouse rollovers can be created for a menu item. The RO status is not available for many objects, and must be added to the reference for the respective object.

Individual menu items are introduced below, using the example application. Only some of the available properties will be used. Consult the TSref to obtain an overview of all the other properties.

5.10.2 Text Menus (TMENU)

TMENU creates a text-based menu from the page or navigation title of the page header. The titles are automatically linked. The appearance is configured by you. The advantage of text-based menus is mainly their fast loading times.

Softlink **623534**

We would like to point out a special feature concerning the TMENU menu object: the properties before and after have the same properties as stdWrap. But the field property above it is not directly available. This is due to an error in the design, which has been left in for the sake of backward compatibility in TYPO3. For this reason, you should avoid it and use the data property instead (e.g. before.data=page:title).

Example: "B2C" Main Navigation

For the "B2C" site, a TS template with the name temp.navigation _html is created for the main horizontal navigation, and uses the TMENU menu type.

The states of the menu items are shown by font colors and various icons in front of the title. The front-end output of the figure shows the active "home" page and the rollover, via the "events" menu item.

Figure 5.69:

The main navigation
as a **TMENU** for
one level

The menu is defined using the HMENU cObject and entryLevel=0 property.

```
temp.navigation_html = HMENU
temp.navigation_html.entryLevel = 0
```

The object path temp.navigation_html.1 is assigned the TMENU menu type.

```
temp.navigation_html.1 = TMENU
```

First the behavior of the NO status is specified. ATagBeforeWrap defines that the link will be placed around the wraps; linkWrap encloses the text with the <font> tag, including the CSS class. With the case=lower property of the stdWrap function, the text is displayed in lower-case. An image is placed in front of each link with beforeImg. If it should also be linked, beforeImgLink=1 must be set. For the TMENU, a rollover state is activated with RO=1 and the accompanying image is replaced through the beforeROImg property.

```
temp.navigation_html.1 {
  NO {
    ATagBeforeWrap = 1
    linkWrap = <font face="Arial,Helvetica,sans-serif,
        sans-serif" size="2" color="#666666"
        class="navi_no"> |   </font>
    stdWrap.case = lower
    beforeImg = fileadmin/images/icons/navi_no.gif
    beforeROImg = fileadmin/images/icons/navi_ro.gif
    RO = 1
  }
```

The behavior of the menu items in the ACT state (which means that they are located in the Rootline of the active page) is ascertained by copying from the NO object. Only the linkWrap and beforeImg properties are overwritten, to give them a different color value or a different CSS class and another image for the active state, via the wrap. The state must be activated via ACT = 1.

```
  ACT < .NO
  ACT {
    linkWrap = <font face="Arial,Helvetica,sans-serif,
        sans-serif" size="2" color="#333333"
        class="navi_act"> |   </font>
    beforeImg = fileadmin/images/icons/navi_act.gif }
    ACT = 1
}
```

Integrate the TS template and temporary object in the main template of the "B2C" site, and inspect the output in the front end.

Example: "B2B/B2E" Main Navigation

The "B2B" and "B2E" sites are based on `<div>` tags, the layout of which is controlled entirely by cascading stylesheets. They are particularly suitable for accessibility websites. In accordance with this, the main navigation for the two sites is created with the `temp.navigation_autoparser_tswrap` TS template.

Instead of the `<font>` tags, each menu item is wrapped as a list entry with `wrapItemAndSub=<li>|</li>`. The whole menu is enclosed by the HTML tag for lists, `wrap=<ul>|</ul>`. The rest of the procedure is the same as the "B2C" main navigation. The properties of the NO state are passed on by copying to the ACT state, and just one CSS class is set for the link, using parameters (`ATagParams=class="navi-active"`).

```
temp.navigation_autoparser_tswrap = HMENU
temp.navigation_autoparser_tswrap.1 = TMENU
temp.navigation_autoparser_tswrap.1 {
  wrap = <ul>|</ul>
  NO {
    wrapItemAndSub = <li>|</li>
    stdWrap.case = lower
  }
  ACT < .NO
  ACT.ATagParams = class="navi-active"
  ACT = 1
}
```

Now you just need to define the appearance of the menu via the CSS file included in the main template. Open the corresponding file with the **File | Filelist** module and edit the required styles.

```
ul {
  margin: 0;
  padding: 0;
}
#navi li, #rootline li {
  display: inline;
  margin: 3px;
}
#navi a:link, #navi a:visited {
  padding: 0 5px 0 10px;
  background: url(../images/icons/left.gif)
            no-repeat left; text-decoration: none;
  color: #666;
}
...
```

The output in the front end is the same as that for the "B2C" application.

Example: "B2C" Subnavigation

A TMENU is implemented in the `temp.navigation_html` template for the subnavigation. The respective menu items in the first and second levels are arranged via a table layout and separated by various separating lines. The active state of the first level is made clear by writing the page title in capitals. For the second level, small icons are displayed in front of the titles.

In the front end, the subnavigation for two levels and rollover appears as in Figure 5.70.

The subnavigation is to start at level 1, which is achieved with `entryLevel=1`.

```
temp.subnavigation_html = HMENU
temp.subnavigation_html.entryLevel = 1
```

The meta-pages "home", "print", "sitemap", and "contact" in the Functions SysFolder can be excluded from display by giving the `excludeUidList` property a corresponding list of page IDs. However, it is better to simply set up the pages as **Not in menu** type.

```
temp.subnavigation_html.excludeUidList =
                         122,121,120,119
```

Level 1 of the menu is defined as TMENU.

```
temp.subnavigation_html.1 = TMENU
```

The level is wrapped with a three-column table that defines the format.

```
temp.subnavigation_html.1.wrap = <table width="170"
     cellspacing="0" cellpadding="0" border="0"><tr>
     <td width="7"><img src="clear.gif" width="7"
```

```
height="1" alt="" border="0"></td>
<td width="11"><img src="clear.gif" width="11"
height="1" alt=""border="0"></td>
<td width="152"><img src="clear.gif" width="152"
height="1" alt=""border="0"></td></tr>|</table>
```

The NO and ACT states are configured so that each menu item is displayed, via the allWrap property, as a separate table row and with the separating line as an image. With the wrapItemAndSub property, the submenu items of level 2 would also be included, but this is not wanted.

```
temp.subnavigation_html.1 {
NO {
 linkWrap = <font face="Arial,Helvetica,sans-serif,
          sans-serif"size="2" color="#666666"
          class="subnavi_no">    |</font>
 stdWrap.case = lower
 allWrap = <tr><td> </td><td colspan="2">
  <img src="fileadmin/images/layout/subnavi1_line.gif">
  <br /> |</td></tr>
 ATagBeforeWrap = 1
}
  ACT < .NO
  ACT.stdWrap.case = upper
  ACT = 1
}
```

The second level of the menu is also defined as TMENU. The menu items of the second level are given their own icons and enclosed by an HTML layout with the allWrap property.

```
temp.subnavigation_html.2 = TMENU
temp.subnavigation_html.2 {
 NO {
   linkWrap = <font face="Arial,Helvetica,sans-serif,
            sans-serif" size="2" color="#666666"
            class="subnavi2_no"> |</font>
   stdWrap.case = lower
   allWrap =<tr><td colspan="2"> </td><td>
            <img src="fileadmin/images/layout/
            subnavi2_line.gif"><br /> |</td></tr>
   beforeImg = fileadmin/images/icons/subnavi2_no.gif
   beforeROImg = fileadmin/images/icons/subnavi2_ro.gif
   RO = 1
   ATagBeforeWrap = 1
 }
 ACT < .NO
 ACT.beforeImg =
       fileadmin/images/icons/subnavi2_act.gif
 ACT = 1
}
```

Include the TS template in the main template of the "B2C" site and again inspect the result in the front end.

5.10.3 Graphical menus (GMENU)

Softlink **193130**

GMENU is similar to TMENU in the way it functions, except that it creates a linked image from every page or navigation title, via the internal TYPO3 function of the GIFBUILDER. This structural freedom increases the loading times of the application, however, since all menu items and their states must be included as images.

Example: "B2C" Subnavigation

As the second variation, a simple graphical menu is created with the `temp.subnavigation_html_gmenu` TS template, for the subnavigation of the "B2C" site. The first level arranges the menu items aligned to the left and places two lines around them. The second level is aligned to the right and marked with a line on the right border. The active pages are highlighted in color (see Figure 5.71).

Figure 5.71:

Subnavigation as a **GMENU** for two levels

Create the HMENU cObject with `entryLevel=1` and define the first level of the menu as GMENU.

```
temp.subnavigation_html_gmenu = HMENU
temp.subnavigation_html_gmenu.entryLevel = 1
temp.subnavigation_html_gmenu.1 = GMENU
```

First the properties of the NO object are specified; in GMENU objects, this is, by definition, of the GIFBUILDER type.

```
temp.subnavigation_html_gmenu.1 {
  NO {
```

Each menu item is wrapped with a `<br />` tag. The size of the image, *Softlink* **023806** `XY=150,40`, and the background color, `backColor=white`, are defined by the properties of the `GIFBUILDER` function.

```
wrap = |<br />
XY = 150,40
backColor = white
```

Individual objects of the GIFBUILDER are created via a numerical list, each item of which is defined as the GifBuilderObj type. So the menu item of the first level consists of several objects.

The 7 and 8 objects each create a GifBuilderObj of the BOX type, which overlap because of the hierarchy.

```
# gray box
7 = BOX
7.dimensions = 16,18,120,20
7.color = #DFDFDF
# white box
8 = BOX
8.dimensions = 16,18,119,19
8.color = #FFFFFF
```

Because the `dimensions` properties differ by one pixel, you just see a gray line in the horizontal and vertical planes.

The 10 object is a GifBuilderObj of the TEXT type and contains the `stdWrap` data type. This is used to read the page title to be displayed, with `10.text.field=title`. The `fontFile` property points to the TrueType character set to be used for creating the images, and which needs to be loaded into the file system beforehand, under `fileadmin/....` Font size and color are defined via the `fontSize` and `fontColor` properties, spacing is defined with x/y coordinates, and text alignment, with `offset` and `align`.

```
10 = TEXT
10.text.field = title
10.fontFile = fileadmin/fonts/VERDANAB.TTF
10.fontSize = 11
10.fontColor = #FFFFFF
10.offset = 30,31
10.align = left
```

The `niceText` property, which displays smaller letters more clearly, does not always work as intended, depending on the ImageMagick version included, and makes demands on server resources to create the images.

```
#10.niceText = 1
```

With the GifBuilderObj of the SHADOW type, a shadow is created, whose position can be set with the coordinates of the `offset` property, and its focus and transparency can be defined with `blur` and `opacity`.

```
# shadow for the text
10.shadow.offset = 1,1
10.shadow.blur = 80
10.shadow.opacity = 40
```

The GifBuilderObj TEXT does not have any `bold` property, but you can simulate this by passing on the text a second time (`20<.10`), or by using `iterations=2`.

```
# simulate bold text --> the font gets clearer
20 < .10
}
```

Another possibility, which usually looks better, consists of including a real bold font (`10.fontFile=fileadmin/fonts/VERDANAB.TTF`).

For the RO=1 (rollover) state for menu items, only the font color is replaced.

```
RO < .NO
RO {
   10.fontColor = #FFCC66
   20 >
   20 < .10
}
RO = 1
```

The menu item with an active state, ACT is stored with another GifBuilderObj BOX.

```
ACT < .RO
ACT {
   # shadow
   5 = BOX
   5.dimensions = 18,20,120,20
   5.color = #D3D3D3
}
   ACT = 1
}
```

Level 2 of the menu for the second level first takes on all the properties of level 1, by copying them.

```
temp.subnavigation_html_gmenu.2 = GMENU
temp.subnavigation_html_gmenu.2 <
         temp.subnavigation_html_gmenu.1
temp.subnavigation_html_gmenu.2 {
NO {
```

The size of the image to be created is overwritten.

```
XY = 150,24
```

The 7 and 8 properties (gray and white box) are deleted.

```
7 >
8 >
```

A new GifBuilderObj of the BOX type is created as an 8 object, with a width of 1 pixel and a height of 24 pixels.

```
# right line
8 = BOX
8.dimensions = 136,0,1,24
8.color = #DFDFDF
```

Several properties are overwritten in the GifBuilderObj 10 of the TEXT type.

```
10.offset = -25,16
10.fontSize = 10
10.align = right
20 < .10
}
```

The RO state of Level 2 takes over the properties of the NO object and only overwrites the font color.

```
RO >
RO < .NO
RO {
    10.fontColor = #FFCC66
    20 >
    20 < .10
}
RO = 1
```

The active ACT state takes over all properties of the RO object.

```
ACT < .RO
ACT = 1
}
```

The menu is now finished. Integrate the TS template and the temporary object in the main template and check the result in the front end.

5.10.4 Layer-Based Menus (TMENU_LAYERS / GMENU_LAYERS)

The TMENU_LAYERS and GMENU_LAYERS menu objects function on top of TMENU or GMENU and extend their properties. Both create a navigation for several levels, via DHTML layers and JavaScript. For this, you must integrate their functionalities with media/scripts/tmenu_layers.php

Softlink **620108**

script and/or `media/scripts/gmenu_layers.php`. When selecting the menu, bear in mind the issue of browser compatibility. Older browsers in particular do not support the latest versions of the *W3C Document Object Model* (DOM), or only support it to a limited extent.

Softlink **599829** Up-to-date browsers such as Opera 7 do support more recent versions of the DOM. If you want to use `TMENU_LAYERS`, it is advisable to modify the corresponding JavaScript functions in the file `/media/scripts/ jsfunc.layermenu.js` (see softlink).

Example: "B2C" Main Navigation

For the main navigation of the "B2C" site, a graphical layer menu is created in the `temp.navigation_html_gmenu_layers` TS template.

If you roll over the menu items of the first level, the selection of the subpages in a layer should be visible. It remains there if a page of the second level is active. The icons in front of the menu items and the font color change on rollover and in an active state.

The result can be seen in the following figure.

Figure 5.72:

Main navigation as **GMENU_LAYERS**

First integrate the functional library, `gmenu_layers.php`, and create a hierarchical menu as a temporary object (`HMENU`). The first level will be defined as the `GMENU_LAYERS` menu object.

```
includeLibs.gmenu_layers =
                    media/scripts/gmenu_layers.php
temp.navigation_html_gmenu_layers = HMENU
temp.navigation_html_gmenu_layers.1 = GMENU_LAYERS
```

After this the behavior of the layer is determined.

With the `layerStyle` property, the CSS attributes are assigned to the `<div>` tag used. In this case the y-position is fixed to 195 pixel. With `lockPosition` the layers are locked in place, and do not follow the mouse pointer. Select `x` for horizontal and `y` for vertical menus. `xPosOffset` defines the offset of the layer from the menu item on the x-axis. The property refers—depending on whether `lockPosition` is set or not—either to the top left corner of each menu image or to the position from which it was activated.

```
temp.navigation_html_gmenu_layers.1 {
   layerStyle = position:absolute;left:0;top:195;width:
             10px;VISIBILITY:hidden;
   xPosOffset = -215
   lockPosition = x
```

The `expAll=1` property of the GMENU menu object should be set in all cases, so that the second level can also be seen on rollover. Otherwise the layer navigation will not work.

```
expAll = 1
```

With the `displayActiveOnLoad` property you can ensure that the layer menu remains visible, even for an active page in the second level.

```
displayActiveOnLoad = 1
```

Now level 1 of the menu is defined, as already demonstrated in the example of the graphical subnavigation for the "B2C" site, as GMENU. First, we set the normal state NO:

```
NO {
   backColor = white
```

The size of individual menu items is automatically calculated, in this case, with the GIFBUILDER property XY, from the length of the images in the GifBuilderObj array. The `x,y +calc` data allows this access, and sets the values for X to `[10.w]+40` pixels and for Y to 30 pixels.

`[10.w]` stands for the width w of object 10 in the numerical list, to which 40 pixels are added. The height of the object could be addressed via `[10.h]`.

```
XY = [10.w]+40, 30
```

The other properties are already known. Two overlying GifBuilderObjs 5 and 7 of the BOX type are created. The 10 object reads out the title of the page and formats it.

```
5 = BOX
5.dimensions = 2,15,5,1
5.color = #666666

7 = BOX
7.dimensions = 4,13,1,5
7.color = #666666

10 = TEXT
10.text.field = title
10.text.case = lower
10.offset = 14,18
10.fontFile = fileadmin/fonts/ARIAL.TTF
10.fontSize = 12
```

```
        10.fontColor = #666666
}
```

The RO state for the rollover is activated, the properties of the NO object are taken over, and a few color values are overwritten.

```
RO < .NO
RO {
  5.color = #E6B800
  7.color = #E6B800
  10.fontColor = #E6B800
}
RO = 1
```

The active state of the menu items should display a yellow frame around a minus sign. To do this, two overlaying squares (yellow and white) are added as new GifBuilderObjs 1 and 3 of the BOX type to the numerical list, and the 7 object is deleted (plus becomes minus).

```
ACT < .NO
ACT {
  # box around the sign: yellow or white square
  1 = BOX
  1.dimensions = 0,11,9,9
  1.color = #E6B800

  3 = BOX
  3.dimensions = 1,12,7,7
  3.color = white

  # no |
  7 >
}
  ACT = 1
}
```

The second level of the menu shows the individual menu items as a GMENU in the layer. It does not hide any new properties and is used here just for purposes of practice.

```
temp.navigation_html_gmenu_layers.2 = GMENU
temp.navigation_html_gmenu_layers.2.wrap = |<br />
temp.navigation_html_gmenu_layers.2 {
  NO {
    backColor = white
    XY = 120, 19

    # left and bottom line
    5 = BOX
    5.dimensions = 0,0,1,19
    5.color = #CCCCCC
    7 = BOX
    7.dimensions = 0,18,120,1
```

```
    7.color = #CCCCCC
    10 = TEXT
    10.fontFile = fileadmin/fonts/ARIAL.TTF
    10.fontSize = 11
    10.text.field = title
    10.text.case = lower
    10.offset = 12,10
    10.fontColor = #666666
}

RO < .NO
RO.10.fontColor = #E6B800
RO = 1

ACT < .NO
ACT.10.fontColor = #E6B800
ACT = 1
}
```

Observe the menu in the front end, expand the individual submenus on rollover, and keep them open for active subpages.

5.10.5 GMENU_FOLDOUT

The GMENU_FOLDOUT menu object is restricted to two levels and generates a navigation that opens dynamically, via JavaScript. For the first menu level you must use a graphical menu, while for the second level you can choose between a graphical and a text-based menu. The functionality is integrated with the script media/scripts/gmenu_foldout.php. Do not forget the restricted compatibility for older browsers when using this type of navigation.

Softlink **623360**

Example: "B2C" Subnavigation

As an example, the subnavigation of the "B2C" site is examined, which so far has been implemented as a TMENU. Create a new TS template, temp.subnavigation_html_gmenu_foldout. This should result in individual submenu items in the first level opening when clicked on. The layout is the same as that for the text menu, and appears as shown in the following figure.

Figure 5.73:

Subnavigation as a
GMENU_FOLDOUT
for two levels

The two levels of the menu are implemented with the GMENU menu object. First you should integrate the required function library, gmenu_foldout.php via includeLibs.

```
includeLibs.gmenu_foldout =
media/scripts/gmenu_foldout.php
```

Define a temporary object as a cObject of the HMENU type. With entryLevel=1, the menu starts in the first level of the website. For the first level, the GMENU_FOLDOUT menu object is defined.

```
temp.subnavigation_html_gmenu_foldout = HMENU
temp.subnavigation_html_gmenu_foldout.entryLevel = 1
temp.subnavigation_html_gmenu_foldout.1 = GMENU_FOLDOUT
```

In order for the subpages in the second level to be shown always, you need to activate the expAll property of the menu object. menuOffset positions the first menu level to the top left corner of the page. With the subMenuOffset property, the offset of the subitems to the respective main menu item is defined. The background color is defined with the menuBackColor property, and width and height with menuWidth and menuHeight respectively.

```
temp.subnavigation_html_gmenu_foldout.1 {
  expAll = 1
  menuOffset = 17, 202
  subMenuOffset = 14,25
  menuBackColor = white
  menuWidth = 164
  menuHeight = 800
```

If you want the submenu to close when another main menu item is called, stayFolded=0 should be set. The speed with which the submenu opens dynamically can be defined via the number of steps; foldSpeed=1 immediately shows the final state. With displayActiveOnLoad=1, submenus are opened automatically if the current page is located in this submenu.

```
stayFolded = 0
foldSpeed = 6
displayActiveOnLoad = 1
```

The normal state NO for the first level is defined. The background color and size for it are specified.

```
NO {
   backColor = #FFFFFF
   XY = 164, 22
```

The 3 object of the numerical list inserts an image as a GifBuilderObj IMAGE, which visually highlights the individual menu items.

```
3 = IMAGE
3.file = fileadmin/images/layout/subnavi1_line.gif
3.offset = 3
```

The 10 object reads out the title of the page and formats it.

```
10 = TEXT
10.text.field = title
10.text.case = lower
10.offset = 29,15
10.fontColor = #666666
10.fontFile = fileadmin/fonts/ARIAL.TTF
10.fontSize = 11
}
```

The active state ACT again takes over the properties of the NO object, and only changes the details insofar that the page title is displayed in capitals (case=upper).

```
ACT < .NO
ACT {
   10.text.case = upper
}
ACT = 1
}
```

In the same way the second level of the temp.subnavigation _html_gmenu_foldout.2 menu is defined. Here, in contrast to level 1, you have a choice between a TMENU and a GMENU. The GMENU was used in the example, and its RO and ACT states are marked with separate icons.

```
temp.subnavigation_html_gmenu_foldout.2 = GMENU
temp.subnavigation_html_gmenu_foldout.2 {
   NO {
      XY = 150,18
      backColor = white

      3 = IMAGE
      3.file = fileadmin/images/layout/subnavi2_line.gif
```

```
                    3.offset = 5

                    10 = TEXT
                    10.text.field = title
                    10.text.case = lower
                    10.offset = 24,13
                    10.fontColor = #666666
                    10.fontFile = fileadmin/fonts/ARIAL.TTF
                    10.fontSize = 11
                  }
              RO < .NO
              RO {
                    12 = IMAGE
                    12.file = fileadmin/images/icons/subnavi2_ro.gif
                    12.offset = 15,2
                  }
              RO = 1

              ACT < .RO
              ACT {
                    12.file = fileadmin/images/icons/subnavi2_act.gif
                  }
              ACT = 1
          }
```

Insert the TS template and the temporary object into the main template of the "B2C" site and check the output in the front end. It can be a bit annoying that the pages are reloaded through the call each time the submenu opens. You can avoid this by creating pages in the first level of your application that also have subpages, such as the **Shortcut** page type, without their own contents.

The dontLinkIfSubmenu property causes the second level of the menu to be opened if it has subpages, but not to be linked. The loading process is omitted.

```
              ...
              dontLinkIfSubmenu = 1
```

Pages without subpages are linked as normal.

5.10.6 ImageMaps (IMGMENU)

Softlink **610406** The IMGMENU menu object generates an image with an imagemap from the background image and the page title of a menu level to be displayed. For individual menu items, sensitive areas are set with `<area>` tags, creating links to the individual pages. The menu items consist of GIFBUILDER objects that can be structured as you like. For the individual states, NO, ACT, SPC, etc., GIFBUILDER creates separate images in each case.

Example: "B2C" Main Navigation

For the "B2C" site, any variation of the main navigation will be implemented with the IMGMENU menu object, via a new temp.navigation_imgmenu TS template. The following output should be generated in the front end.

Figure 5.74:

Main navigation as an **IMGMENU**

The menu represents the main navigation, which is why it starts in the Rootlevel: entryLevel=0. The maxItems property specifies that up to six menu items can be shown.

```
temp.topmenu = HMENU
temp.topmenu.entryLevel = 0
temp.topmenu.maxItems = 6
```

The menu only has one level, defined as IMGMEMU. The background image on which the title is displayed is specified with the main property of the GIFBUILDER data type.

Softlink **023805**

As has already been shown, the individual objects of the GIFBUILDER are generated as a numerical list, to each of which a GifBuilderObj is assigned as the data type. With the 10 object, a GifBuilderObj of the IMAGE type is now created, which links to the desired base image with the file property.

```
temp.topmenu.1 = IMGMENU
temp.topmenu.1 {
    main.10 = IMAGE
    main.10.file = fileadmin/images/layout/bg_imgmenu.gif
```

The original size of the image is ascertained through the XY properties, and with reduceColors, the color palette of the image is scaled down to 16 colors, thus reducing the file size.

```
main.XY = [10.w], [10.h]
main.reduceColors = 16
```

You define the starting point of the menu from the top left corner of the image, with dWorkArea.

```
dWorkArea = 12,22
```

The normal state of the menu is defined. The distrib property specifies the distance between menu items. The 10 object in the list reads out the title of the page as a TEXT GifBuilderObj and defines its display.

```
NO {
  distrib = textX+25, 0
  10 = TEXT
  10.text.field = title
  10.fontSize = 12
  10.fontColor = #666666
  10.fontFile = fileadmin/fonts/ARIAL.TTF
  10.niceText = 1
  10.offset = 2,0
```

With `imgMap`, you can access a property of the GIFBUILDER that enables an image map for the image file to be created from the TEXT GifBuilderObj. The `explode` property enlarges the sensitive area by the x/y-coordinates.

```
  10.imgMap.explode = 3,2
```

The plus sign before each menu item is implemented via two GifBuilderObjs of the BOX type.

```
  # |
  20 = BOX
  20.dimensions = -5,-6,1,5
  20.color = #666666
  # -
  30 = BOX
  30.dimensions = -7,-4,5,1
  30.color = #666666
}
```

The active state ACT takes over all the properties of the NO object. Object 20 in the numerical list is deleted (plus becomes minus), and a border is created with the objects 40, 50, 60, and 70.

```
ACT < .NO
ACT {
  20 >
  #- below
  40 = BOX
  40.dimensions = -9,0,9,1
  40.color = #666666
  # - above
  50 < .40
  50.dimensions = -9,-8,9,1
  # | left
  60 < .40
  60.dimensions = -9,-8,1,9
  # | right
  70 < .40
  70.dimensions = -1,-8,1,9
}
ACT = 1
}
```

The menu is finished. Integrate the `temp.navigation_imgmenu` TS template and the `temp.topmenu` temporary object in the main template and test the output in the front end.

5.10.7 JavaScript Menus (JSMENU)

The `JSMENU` menu element sets up a navigation in which pages are selected through selection menus that are dependent on each other. Each selection menu represents a website level. The most important feature of this menu, compared to a simple selection menu, is that the lower levels are filled with corresponding entries that depend on the higher level currently selected, without the page having to be reloaded in the browser. A `JSMENU` can show up to five levels (five selection menus).

Softlink **421175**

Example: "B2B" Main Navigation

In this example, a variation is created for the main navigation of the "B2B" site with the `temp.navigation_tswrap_jsmenu` TS template. The following figure shows the finished menu when the "Product 1" subpage is selected.

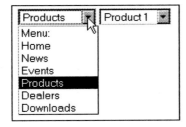

Figure 5.75:

The main menu as a **JSMENU**

Define the temporary object `temp.jsmenu_tswrap` as an `HMENU` cObject and define the first menu level as a `JSMENU`.

```
temp.jsmenu_tswrap = HMENU
temp.jsmenu_tswrap.1 = JSMENU
```

The number of levels to be displayed is defined with the `levels=2` property.

```
temp.jsmenu_tswrap.1 {
   levels = 2
```

With the numerical list you define the behavior of individual levels. For level 1 the selector box is distinguished from the following selector boxes using a wrap with an empty space. If you want to select the active page in advance, then set the value `showActive=1`. If no page is selected, then the first selector box normally has no value. A label can be given to the respective selection menu with the `firstLabel` property.

```
1 {
  wrap = |  
  showActive = 1
  firstLabel = Menu:
}
```

The values of the first level are passed on to the second one, and only the label is overwritten.

```
2 < .1
2.firstLabel = Submenu:
}
```

The menu is finished, and you can include it in the main template of the "B2B" site.

5.10.8 ".special" Menus

Softlink **743914**

The `HMENU` cObject by default displays the page structure as a tree, but can be made to generate other structures with the `special` property. A so-called Rootline menu, for example, shows the pages of the Rootline. A simple setup will look like this:

```
temp.navigation = HMENU
temp.navigation.entryLevel = 0
temp.navigation.special = rootline
temp.navigation {
  1 = TMENU
  1.NO.allWrap = | / 
}
```

This produces the following output:

```
B2C-Home/ Products/ Product 2/
```

The `special` property determines what special structure the HMENU should create. The following types are available. The properties for each of the menu types can be taken from the TSref.

directory

The `directory` type generates a menu from the subpages of the specified page IDs or from the current page.

list

With `list` you can create a menu for specific pages, determined by their IDs.

updated

If you want to show pages depending on whether they have been updated or not, you can do this with updated.

rootline

The path from the root page to the currently active page normally helps the user to retain an overview of complex applications. This rootline menu is generated through the rootline type.

browse

The browse type allows you to browse through pages in different ways (previous, next,...).

keywords

The keywords type creates a menu of pages that match the current page with one or more keywords in the page header. This makes it easy to show related pages.

userdefined

With the userdefined type you can also control menus with your own PHP script. The TSref contains a detailed example of this.

Example: Directory

Almost every application has pages that are not meant to be shown in the context of the main navigation. In the "BT3" example application, this applies to the meta-menu items "Home", "Imprint", "Sitemap", and "Contact". They should always be present, and they are stored here in the Functions SysFolder for the page tree. Here the directory menu type can be used for the display.

The menu should be structured as shown in the following diagram, and be placed beneath the subnavigation on the left-hand page.

Figure 5.76:

Meta-information, created with the special.directory property

Create your own temp.metas_html TS template for the "B2C" site and define an HMENU as a temporary object. The special property is assigned the desired menu type with the directory value. The value property defines the page IDs to which the menu refers. Because the value refers to the page IDs of the Functions SysFolder, a constant was set as the value, which you have to define accordingly for your application.

```
temp.metas_html = HMENU
temp.metas_html.special = directory
temp.metas_html.special.value = {$metas.pid}
```

The menu itself can be configured as you please, and in the example is configured as a TMENU. It is formatted by a table.

```
temp.metas_html.1 = TMENU
temp.metas_html.1 {
  wrap = <br /><br /><br /><table width="170"
        cellspacing="0" cellpadding="0"
        border="0">|</table><br /><br /><br />
  NO {
    linkWrap = <font face="Arial,Helvetica,sans-serif,
      sans-serif" size="2" color="#666666"
      class="metas"></font>
    allWrap = <tr><td><img src="clear.gif" width="10"
      height="1" alt=""border="0"></td>
      <td align="left" valign="top">|</td></tr>
    ATagBeforeWrap = 1
```

Individual images in front of the pages are read out via import.field=media (the **files** field in the page header of the corresponding pages).

```
    # get the image from the page (files field in
    # pages of the type advanced)
    beforeImg.import = uploads/media/
    beforeImg.import.field = media
    beforeImg.import.listNum = 0
  }
}
```

For the "B2B" and "B2C" sites based on <div> tags, the following variation is produced with the temp.metas_autoparser_tswrap TS template:

```
temp.metas_autoparser_tswrap = HMENU
temp.metas_autoparser_tswrap.special = directory
temp.metas_autoparser_tswrap.special.value =
                                    {$metas.pid}
temp.metas_autoparser_tswrap.1 = TMENU
temp.metas_autoparser_tswrap.1 {
  noBlur = 1
  wrap = <ul id="metas">|</ul>
  NO {
      wrapItemAndSub = <li>|</li>
      beforeImg.import = uploads/media/
      beforeImg.import.field = media
```

```
                    beforeImg.import.listNum = 0
              }
       }
```

Now insert the meta-navigation, with **Include basis template**, into the corresponding main template, and replace the placeholder texts by copying the corresponding temporary objects. Because both the subnavigation and the meta-information are to be shown together in a subpart or in a `<div>` tag, the COA cObject can be used for integration.

Example "B2C":

```
page.10 {
   ...
   subparts.LEFT = COA
   subparts.LEFT.10 < temp.subnavigation_html
   subparts.LEFT.20 < temp.metas_html
```

Example "B2B"/"B2E":

```
page {
   ...
   # Left / Submenu
   40 = COA
   40.10 < temp.subnavigation_autoparser_tswrap
   40.20 < temp.metas_autoparser_tswrap
   40.stdWrap.wrap = <div id="subnavigation">|</div>
```

Example: Rootline

A rootline menu is included in the header of the example application. It shows the user the current path. The page titles displayed are linked. Its implementation should appear as in the following figure.

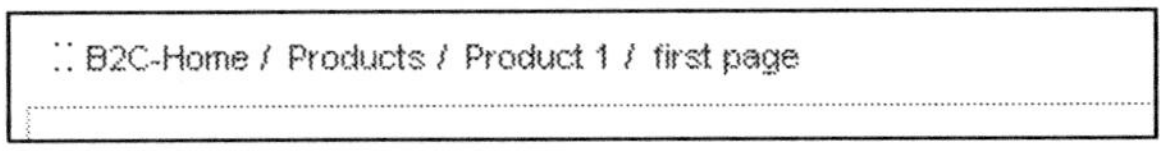

:: B2C-Home / Products / Product 1 / first page

Figure 5.77:

The Rootline menu shows the path of the current page

First define an HMENU with the `special=rootline` property.

```
temp.rootline_html= HMENU
temp.rootline_html.special = rootline
```

With the `range` property you can specify the level with which it should begin and end. If you omit the end value (or set it to -1), the entire path is displayed. With -2, the current page is not included, with -3, two levels are not included, etc. Note that you may not use spaces in the value.

```
temp.rootline_html.special.range = 0|-2
```

The menu itself is created in the example as a text-based TMENU. The wrap around the whole menu specifies that two colons are displayed in front of the menu items. The normal state NO is provided with a `<font>` tag through `linkwrap`.

```
temp.rootline_html.1 = TMENU
temp.rootline_html.1 {
  wrap =   ::|
  target = _top
  NO {
    linkWrap = <font face="Arial,Helvetica,sans-serif,
          sans-serif" size="1" color="#666666"
          class="rootline">|</font>
```

A peculiar feature here is that the individual menu items are separated with a slash. But this is not placed after the last menu item, unless `allWrap=/` is set.

Softlink **819809** The solution lies in the use of the `optionSplit` function, which makes available all the properties and values of the menu objects. `optionSplit` is mainly used if values are to be set for a whole series of elements. For menus, one value is normally defined for many menu items. If `optionSplit` is used, the value is parsed by the function, and depending on the definition, different values are assigned to the elements. It is interesting at the current point in time that three values, separated by the `|*|` syntax, are passed on with the `allWrap` property. The last menu item here is not wrapped with the backslash. Syntax and rules of priority in the function are explained later on, in section 5.11.1.

```
# optionSplit: "/" after every item except for the last
  allWrap = |*| <font face="Arial,Helvetica,
        sans-serif,sans-serif" size="1"
        color="#666666"class="rootline">|
         / </font> |*| |*|
  ATagBeforeWrap = 1
  }
}
```

Finally, here is the variation of the rootline menu from the TypoScript template `temp.rootline_autoparser_tswrap` for the "B2B" and "B2E" sites. Individual menu items are displayed in the form of a numerical list, and formatted with CSS.

```
temp.rootline_autoparser_tswrap = HMENU
temp.rootline_autoparser_tswrap.special = rootline
temp.rootline_autoparser_tswrap.special.range = 0|-2
temp.rootline_autoparser_tswrap.1 = TMENU
temp.rootline_autoparser_tswrap.1 {
  wrap = <ul>:: |</ul>
  noBlur = 1
  NO {
    linkWrap= <li>|</li>
```

```
      # optionSplit: "/" after every item except for the
      # last
      allWrap = |*|  | / |*|  |*|
   }
}
```

Insert the Rootline menus and test the output in the front end.

In the current state of construction, the "BT3" application is almost complete. All the menus are set up and integrated. Just a few functionalities are missing, such as the print version. These will be added in the next section. In addition, more cObjects will be introduced and functions will be described in more detail.

5.11 TypoScript in Detail

5.11.1 The optionSplit Function

The `optionSplit` function is available in TS properties marked with the data type of the same name, and is often used in menu objects. It enables distinctions to be made in cases where one value is set for several elements, and passing on different values to individual elements.

Softlink **819808**

Syntax

The rules are simple, but become more complex when combined.

|*|

> Divides values into the main areas *First*, *Middle* and *Last*

||

> Divides the main areas into a maximum of the first, second, and third sub-area.

1 Values are set by their priority, in the sequence: *Last, First, Middle*.

2 If the *middle* value is empty (" "), the last part of the *first* value is repeated.

3 If the *first* and the *middle* values are empty, the first part of the *last* value is repeated before the *last* value.

4 The values of the *middle* main area are repeated.

Example: COLUMNS

With the COLUMNS cObject, a table with several columns and assigned content can be created. It contains, among other things, the gapBgCol property of the HTML-color / stdWrap +optionSplit data type. It defines a background color for individual gaps between the table cells. By accessing the optionSplit function, it is now possible to specify different colors for individual gaps.

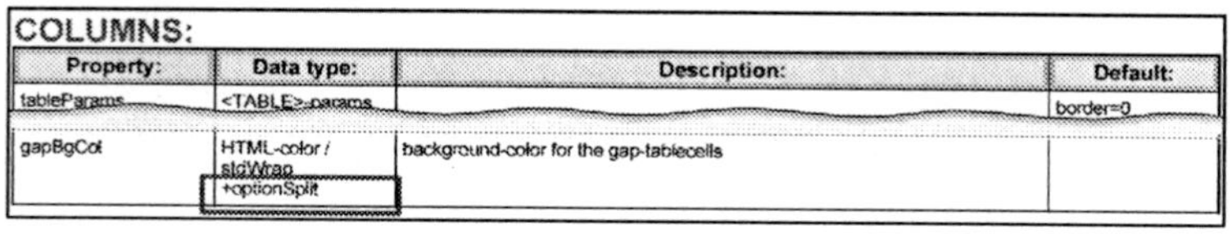

Figure 5.78:

From the datatype you can see when optionSplit is available

COLUMNS:			
Property:	Data type:	Description:	Default:
tableParams	<TABLE>-params		border=0
gapBgCol	HTML-color / stdWrap +optionSplit	background-color for the gap-tablecells	

A table with seven columns, and thus six gaps, is quickly configured. The tableParams and totalWidth properties set parameters in the <table> tag and a width of 500 pixels. The gap and line thickness between columns are specified with gapWidth and gapLineThickness, and the number of columns set by rows. Finally, content is assigned to individual columns.

```
10 = COLUMNS
10 {
   tableParams = cellspacing="0" cellpadding="0"
                 border="0"
   totalWidth = 500
   gapWidth = 30
   gapLineThickness = 1
   rows = 7
   gapBgCol = red
   1 = TEXT
   1.value = column1
   ...
   7 = TEXT
   7.value = column7
}
```

One interesting property we would like to demonstrate using optionSplit is gapBgCol, which so far has only been given the value red: all gaps are a uniform red (we have highlighted the colors in the following figures).

Figure 5.79:

Value: red

If three values are passed on with `optionSplit`, based on the main areas:

```
gapBgCol = red |*| green |*| yellow
```

then the *first* space is red, the *last* one yellow, and all others repeat the value of the *middle* space (rule 4).

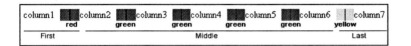

Figure 5.80:

Value: red || green |*| yellow*

The repeat of the *middle* value (rule 4) can best be seen if it is divided into sub-areas.

```
gapBgCol = red |*| green || fuchsia |*| yellow
```

Here the colors green and fuchsia are set for the *middle* area, and, depending on how many elements exist, are shown alternately.

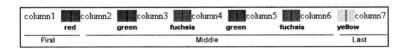

Figure 5.81:

Value: red || green || fuchsia |*| yellow*

The main areas *First* and *Last* can also be subdivided with separate values. The *first* area is given three values, the *middle* area one, and the *last* one, two values.

```
gapBgCol = red || aqua || grey |*| green |*| yellow
           || fuchsia
```

In the output, all gaps are displayed with their corresponding colors.

Figure 5.82:

Value: red || aqua || grey || green |*| yellow || fuchsia*

For the *First* and *Last* main areas, set three values each (or reduce the number of columns with the `rows` property):

```
gapBgCol = red || aqua || grey |*| green |*| yellow
           || fuchsia || aqua
```

Now the sequence in which the main areas are processed is applied, since for seven columns, only six gaps exist. First the values for the *Last* main area are set, then those for the *First*, and finally those for the *Middle* (rule 1). The value of the *Middle* main area is no longer considered, since all gaps have already been defined by the *Last* and *First* areas.

Figure 5.83:

red || aqua || grey || green |*| yellow || fuchsia || aqua*

If no value is assigned to the *Middle* main area,

```
gapBgCol = red || grey |*||*| yellow
```

the last value of the *First* main area is repeated (rule 2). Note that there should not be a space between the dividers. In the example, the value "grey" is repeated for the gap.

Figure 5.84:

Value: red || grey |||*| yellow*

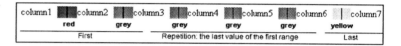

If the *First* and *Middle* main area is not filled with values, the first value of the *Last* main area is repeated (rule 3).

```
gapBgCol = |*||*| yellow || fuchsia || aqua
```

In the example, first the values of the *Last* main area are set. The remaining gaps will take the color yellow as the first value of the *Last* main area.

Figure 5.85:

Value: |||*| yellow || fuchsia || aqua*

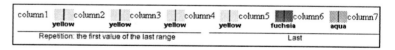

The `optionSplit` function has already been used for the rootline menus of the `temp.rootline_html` and `temp.rootline_autoparser_tswrap` TS templates. A special feature of this is that it is applied to all objects of the `GIFBUILDER` before the individual menu items are created. The same applies for the `allWrap` property used.

```
temp.rootline_autoparser_tswrap.1.NO {
    ...
    # optionSplit: "/" after every item except for
    # the last
    allWrap = |*|  | / |*|  |*|
    ...
}
```

The `allWrap` property is given three values:

- The *First* area is empty |*|.

- The *Middle* area contains, the wrap `| / |*|` as a repeating value.

- The *Last* area contains an empty space, which is why a final `|*|` divider is set. Otherwise the empty spaces at the beginning and end of the entire string would be removed, according to the TypoScript rules.

The `optionSplit` function may look rather complex at first, but it is also very powerful, and you can assign different values to a series of elements without any additional programming. For menus in particular, `optionSplit` is a utility that it would be hard to do without.

5.11.2 Working with Images and the GIFBUILDER

Softlink **788778**

If TYPO3 is installed with the recommended graphic libraries, you can carry out extensive image manipulation using the GIFBUILDER function. Graphical menus in particular access this and automatically create images in GIF format from the individual menu items. But they can also produce headers with individual fonts as an image. In this way, layout 5 of the headers for content elements is created as a graphic, with the `content (default)` standard template and `styles.header.gfx1` integrated as a basis template. The `Textbox` content element also accesses the GIFBUILDER.

GIFBUILDER Objects (GifBuilderObj)

The GIFBUILDER functions as a series of general properties such as `XY`, `offset`, or `reduceColors`, which specify the size of the image, a general gap for all objects from the top left corner of the image, and the reduction of the GIF image to a specific number of colors. A work area is created inside the image with the `workArea` property. The actual objects are generated in a numerical list of `GifBuilderObj`. Be careful: in the TSref, references to individual objects are set exclusively to GifBuilderObj, and not to `cObjects` with the same name, such as TEXT or IMAGE.

The following GIFBUILDER objects can be used directly or through other GifBuilderObjs:

TEXT

The GifBuilderObj TEXT creates an image from text. Via the `stdWrap` data type and `getText` you have the possibility of reading the text out separately.

347

SHADOW

As a GifBuilderObj, SHADOW is a property of TEXT, and creates a shadow. If it stands alone, a link must be made to the TEXT object to which it refers, via textObjNum.

EMBOSS

The same thing applies to the EMBOSS GifBuilderObj. It creates two offset copies behind the TEXT object, producing the character of a relief. Using properties, these can be given different colors, made softer, or more transparent.

OUTLINE

The GifBuilderObj OUTLINE is also a property of TEXT. It strengthens contours and can only be influenced by color value and intensity. The result is usually not too good. It is better to use a shadow with a strong intensity.

BOX

BOX creates a rectangle whose size and alignment can be defined.

IMAGE

The GifBuilderObj IMAGE of the imgResource data type can be referenced to an image, or you can even use the GIFBUILDER function, via which all GifBuilderObjs are available to it.

EFFECT

With EFFECT it is possible to rotate the image, to turn it upside down, to set grey values, change the gamma values, etc. Values are added with the value property and separated with the pipe symbol, "|".

WORKAREA

If you set a new WORKAREA in the numerical list of the GifBuilderObjs, the following objects will refer to the newly set work area (e.g. with the offset property).

CROP

CROP can restrict the display of the image to partial areas. This GifBuilderObj sets the workArea to the new dimensions of the image.

SCALE

SCALE scales the image with the `width` and `height` properties to a new size. This GifBuilderObj also sets the `workArea` to the new dimensions of the image.

ADJUST

With ADJUST you can correct the tone values of the image by defining the input and output grey values. If you have to correct the gamma values, use the GifBuilderObj EFFECT. The properties here are also listed via `value` and separated by the pipe sign, "|".

[IMGMAP]

IMGMAP is not a GifBuilderObj, but is used in conjunction with TEXT to create an ImageMap for a GIF file. It is used for the IMGMENU menu object.

+calc

If `+calc` is added to the data type of a property in the TSref, calculations can be performed with the value. The operators used here, `+`, `-`, `/`, and `*`, do not have any priorities and are processed in the same order in which they are set. However, for the GIFBUILDER you can also refer to values of other objects. This makes it possible, for example, to calculate the width and height of the overall picture, depending on GifBuilderObjs such as TEXT or IMAGE.

```
...
XY = [100.w]+160 , [100.h]+5
```

For the image dimensions, this means:

```
XY = [width of the GifBuilderObj 100]+160 pixel,
     [height of the GifBuilderObj 100]+5 pixel
```

.niceText

The *Freetype* library, integrated in the GDLib and used by PHP, does not always support satisfactory anti-aliasing in all versions. The `niceText` property helps display small letters more clearly. It provides a workaround by causing TYPO3 to render text in double size on a mask, which is then downscaled to the correct size. In doing so, the *combine* ImageMagick function is used to place (to mask) the text onto the background. This procedure puts a large demand for resources on the server to create the images, but provides better results, depending on the ImageMagick version used. But since the images are not newly created for each call, but only on the first call after the cache has been emptied, you must decide at what point you want to use niceText. Please note that niceText, depending on the versions of GDlib, Freetype, and ImageMagick used, can produce different results, so that your graphical menu on the live server may possibly look different to the one on the production server.

Example: The Image in the Header

Softlink **016166**

In the section "Stages of Construction with Cascading Templates" onwards, an image had already been inserted in the header area of the output. The IMAGE object type used for this can use two different methods for integrating images, with its file property of imgResource data type.

- It references a file in the file system or the **Files** field in the page header.

- It uses GIFBUILDER, a function that allows you to create an image combining several graphic objects such as images, text, or boxes.

The first method was demonstrated in the temp.header_html TS template.

Working with the GIFBUILDER function will now be illustrated using the temp.GIFBUILDER_header_image TS template. If you want to follow and reconstruct the example, you will find it in the Main Templates/ cObjects SysFolder.

The header should not only display the current image that was included in the page headers, as was the case until now, but also include the title of the current page as a graphic. The text is given a shadow and the first letter is highlighted in color.

Figure 5.86:

Including the graphic as a GIFBUILDER object

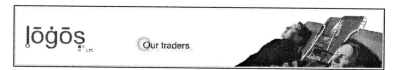

First we create a temporary object, which is defined as an IMAGE cObject. Through the file property of the imgResource data type, a new image is created with the GIFBILDER function.

```
temp.header_image_gifbuilder = IMAGE
temp.header_image_gifbuilder.file = GIFBUILDER
```

First the size of the image is determined with XY.

```
temp.header_image_gifbuilder.file {
  XY = 588,125
```

The object 10 in the numerical list of GifBuilderObj is of the IMAGE type and gets the respective images, which were assigned to the partial page tree, from the **Files** field of the page header. The slide parameter causes the page tree to be searched from the current page down to level 1, until the first image has been found.

```
10 = IMAGE
10.file.import = uploads/media/
10.file.import.data = levelmedia:1, slide
```

The object 10 is positioned with the offset property in relation to the top left corner of the overall image (or, if workArea is set, to the work area).

```
10.offset = 199,0
```

Next the yellow first letter of the page title is created. The object 18 is defined as a GifBuilderObj of the TEXT type. Its text property is of the stdWrap data type and first tries to read the subtitle of the page, via text.field = subtitle. If none is there, the title is used instead.

```
18 = TEXT
18.text.field = subtitle // title
```

The case and crop properties specify that the text will be written in capitals, but only the first letter will be displayed.

```
18.text.case = upper
18.text.crop = 1
```

The object 18 is also positioned in the overall picture with offset; it is assigned a font size and color.

```
18.offset = 62,90
18.fontSize = 40
18.fontColor = #FFCC33
```

The niceText property improves the font reproduction.

```
18.niceText = 1
```

The TEXT GifBuilderObj accesses the EMBOSS GifBuilderObj via its emboss property. The two copies of the letter offset by the value of the offset property are filled with the same color value; blur makes them softer and opacity controls transparency.

```
18.emboss {
  highColor = #FFCC33
  lowColor = #FFCC33
  offset = 2,2
  blur = 99
  opacity = 50
}
```

In the same way, the whole text is generated as object 20.

```
20 = TEXT
20.text.field = subtitle // title
20.offset = 75,85
20.fontSize = 20
20.fontColor = #333333
20.niceText = 1
```

Here the TEXT GifBuilderObj, via shadow, accesses the SHADOW GifBuilderObj and produces a silver shadow. It has an offset to the top left corner of the 20 object, via offset; with blur it is softened, with opacity it is set to 60% transparency, and with intensity its brightness is defined.

```
20.shadow {
    color = silver
    offset = 7,8
    blur = 70
    opacity = 60
    intensity = 15
  }
}
```

You can extend the example just as you please, of course. With the mask property of the IMAGE GifBuilderObj, the image is given a black and white mask.

Figure 5.87:

Mask placed over the image

Add the following line to the TypoScript configuration:

```
10.mask = fileadmin/mediapool/material_intern/
          gifbuilder-mask.png
```

Only those parts of the image covered by the white areas of the mask will be visible for the GIFBUILDER object 10; the black areas will be invisible.

Figure 5.88:

The header image with the mask

Alternatively you can add a new GIFBUILDER object 15. It is a GifBuilderObj of the IMAGE type, which creates a separate picture with the GIFBUILDER function. With the XY property, the size of the image is again specified, and referenced to the image in the file system with its GIFBUILDER object 100.

Figure 5.89:

The image shows the TYPO3 logo on a gray background

```
15 = IMAGE
15.file = GIFBUILDER
15.file {
  XY = [100.w]+160 , [100.h]+5
  100 = IMAGE
  100.file = fileadmin/mediapool/material_intern/
             typo3logo.gif
```

With the offset property, the logo is positioned in the newly created image.

```
100.offset = 160, 5
```

The background of the image is set to transparent with transparentBackground = 1. The same result is achieved via transparentColor = #CCCCCC with the gray color value of the logo.

```
      transparentBackground = 1
      transparentColor = #CCCCCC
}
```

This results in the TYPO3 logo being seamlessly integrated into the header image.

Figure 5.90:

A combination of several images in one

You can see that there are no limits to working with the GIFBUILDER

353

function. Ultimately, it is your creative ideas alone that will determine the result.

5.11.3 The stdWrap Function

The stdWrap function plays a central role in TypoScript and also mirrors the concept of TS. Much use has already been made of it in the examples. Its functionality grew out of the wrap concept and the fact that TypoScript is not a programming language, and therefore cannot handle control structures (apart from conditions) on its own.

With its collection of properties and functions that supply data, change or edit contents, as well as functions that enable conditional processing, stdWrap is the "Swiss Army Knife" for the TypoScript developer.

The properties and functions of stdWrap can be used anywhere an object property of the stdWrap data type exists. Frequently objects also have a property with the name stdWrap, which makes precisely this function available.

The properties of stdWrap are separated into the three areas Get data, Override/Conditions, and Parse data, depending on their purpose. Please note that the properties are processed in the same order as they are listed in the TSref.

Get data

The Get data area of the properties is used to make data available or to read it out. This can be for a title page, the current date, a cObject, a number of rows from a database query, a file list of a directory, or a global variable. The most important properties are data, field, current, cObject, and filelist.

data

Reads out values from different PHP arrays, with the syntax Type:pointer, such as data records.

Example: ... .data = page:title

field

Usually returns the contents of a database field from the current data record, as a value.

Example: ... .field = title

current

Sets the access to the current content of the data register, as a Boolean value. The data register is an internal buffer in TYPO3 where current values are stored for certain functions. The variables stored there are available globally and are read out, saved, or overwritten at various points during processing.

cObject

Loads the content of a content object.

Example: ... .cObject = IMAGE

filelist

Reads a file directory and supplies a list of files. The following parameters must be separated with the pipe sign |:

1. Path

2. Comma-delimited list (without spaces) of possible file types (gif,jpg...)

3. The order of sorting: name, size, ext, or date

4. r inverts the order of sorting

5. If this switch is set (not empty), the file list is created with the complete path, and not just with the file name

   Example: ... .filelist = fileadmin/img/|jpg,png|name||1

As an additional aid, you can have the list of the current data record displayed directly in the front-end output, with the stdWrap debugData property.

Figure 5.91:

Output of the current
data record in the
front end

$cObj->data:	
uid	47
pid	18
tstamp	1087374477
sorting	128
deleted	0
perms_userid	1
perms_groupid	1
perms_user	31
perms_group	27
perms_everybody	0
crdate	1081438117
cruser_id	1
title	Home
doktype	2
TSconfig	
treeStop	0
author	
author_email	
nav_title	
content_from_pid	0
mount_pid	0
alias	
nav_hide	0
mount_pid_ol	0
currentValue_kidjls9dksoje	index.php?id=18

Override/Conditions

The properties in this area are used to override and compare values. Among other things, you can set a new value that is dependent on other values. The most important properties are:

override

Overwrites the value of an object if the value of `override` is not empty "" or 0. Whether the original object already has a value or is empty is irrelevant here.

ifEmpty

Passes a new value to an object if its value until now is empty "". 0 is treated here as a value.

listNum

Extracts the desired value from contents that are separated by commas

trim

Removes empty spaces, tab spaces, and line breaks

required

If the current value is empty "", the calling object is used. `stdWrap` properties that follow this are not taken into consideration.

if

> Includes the `if` function of the same name. It is used to query if one or more conditions are met, and values are set depending on this.

fieldRequired

> If the given field of the current data record is empty, the current value is also emptied.

Parse data

The `Parse data` area defines properties for processing data. A wide range of string operations is possible here. HTML content can be filtered via the `HTMLparser` function, and certain tags can be removed. With `split`, the contents can be split into individual values, on the basis of specific characters, and processed. Other functions that are included via properties are `encapsLines`, `addParams`, `textStyle`, `tableStyle`, `filelink`, and `typolink`.

Get data and Parse data

As `stdWrap` properties of the `Get data` function area, `field` and `data` have already been used in the examples so far.

field

With `field`, the subtitle or title of the pages

```
...
NO {
  10 = TEXT
  10.text.field = subtitle // title
```

or an image from the **Files** form field in the page header was read out for individual menus.

```
NO {
  # get the image from the page
  beforeImg.import = uploads/media/
  beforeImg.import.field = media
```

data

The `data` property was used to obtain the image in the page header not only from the current page, but to search through the rootline down to the top level until the first image has been found.

```
temp.header_image = IMAGE
temp.header_image.file.import = uploads/media/
temp.header_image.file.import.data =
                                    levelmedia:1, slide
```

Properties of the `stdWrap` object from the `Parse data` area have already been used in the first steps in section 5.2. This simple example displays the text in upper case, with the `case` property:

```
page.10 = HTML
page.10.value = kasper
page.10.value.case = upper
```

Example: Print Version

In the example application, the print version is missing. A button that optimizes the relevant page for printing should be included. The base layout is omitted in the print version, and only the content is formatted via CSS styles. The page is called with the URL parameter `&type=98`, which is reserved internally as `typeNum=98` for the print version. In order to create the link for the print view, properties are used from the areas `Get data` and `Parse data` of the `stdWrap` object.

Create a new TS template. You will find it in the examples under the name `temp.printversion` in the `Main Templates/Functions/` SysFolder. Here the button for printing is generated, and a page is also defined that is responsible for the output.

First you create a temporary cObject of the `COA` type.

```
temp.printversion = COA
temp.printversion {
```

The button is created with the `wrap` property over the entire object.

```
wrap = <a href="|" name="Printversion"
    title="Printversion" target="_blank"
    class="printversion">{$printlabel}</a>
```

However the current URL with the `&type=98` parameter is missing from the button. For this purpose the `10` property in the numerical list of the `COA` is defined as a `TEXT` cObject.

```
10 = TEXT
```

As a special feature of the `TEXT` cObject, the `stdWrap` properties are directly addressed from the basis of the object, which does not match the standard behavior of other objects. In order to now obtain the URL of the current page, the `data` property is used.

The property has the `getText` data type, which means it is able to read out values from different arrays made available by the system, using the syntax `Type:Pointer`.

The current address can be determined with the `getIndpEnv` type and the `REQUEST_URI` pointer.

Softlink **293098**

```
10.data = getIndpEnv:REQUEST_URI
```

In the array there is now a value such as `/index.php?id=18`. It can be further processed with the `wrap` property, in order to add the `&type=98` parameter.

```
10.wrap = |&type=98
```

Note that this is only a simple example to create the link for the print output. If you use the TS option `config.simulateStaticDocuments`, this and the following example will not work—they are used more to display the `stdWrap` properties. An extension to create corresponding links correctly is available in the TER.

Softlink **463307**

A second possibility is to use the `split` property. With this, the value can be split up into individual parts via the properties of the `split` function of the same name. [9]

`10.split.token=/` sets the string to be used as a divider. `/index.php?id=18` is now split into two values. The first one is empty, and the second one contains the string after the `index.php?id=18` divider. `10.split.cObjNum` of the `cObjNum +optionSplit` data type is used as a pointer to cObjects in a numerical list.

These objects (1, 2, 3,...) are called to process the split values. Which object is called for which split value is defined by `cObjNum`. If `cObjNum=1` is set, each split value is passed to the `1` object for processing.

`optionSplit` can also be used to have each individual split value

---

[9] This would not make sense in the example, since only one value is processed; it is just used here to demonstrate the `split` function.

processed by a different object. The exact way that optionSplit functions is explained in section 5.11.1. In the following setup, the 2 object, which adds the type parameter to the split value taken over with current=1, is only called for the last value (index.php?id=18) All other split values are processed with the 1 object, which sets an empty value with override=.

```
    /* Demonstration of the split function
    10.split.token = /
    10.split.cObjNum = 1 |*| 1 |*| 2
    10.split.1.override =
    10.split.2.current = 1
    10.split.2.wrap = |&type=98
    */
}
```

The result matches the first and shorter variation.

You now need to define the template for the page output in the print format, with typeNum=98. Switching templates, using type/typeNum, was already discussed in section 5.8.

```
# different page template for the 98 type
# (=print version)
alt_print = PAGE
alt_print {
   typeNum = 98
```

Inline CSS style details define the format of the output.

```
CSS_inlineStyle = body, p, h1, h2, h3, h4
                { font-family: Arial, Verdana,
                sans-serif; font-size: 11pt; }
                h1, h2, h3, h4
```

Finally the content of the Normal column is displayed.

```
    10 < styles.content.get
}
```

Override/Conditions

As we already hinted at the beginning, it is possible to link properties to conditions. stdWrap properties that override values or set conditions have also been used already in the examples.

listNum

For the temp.metas_html menu that shows meta-information, the first image from the array was addressed with the listNum=0 property when images were read from the page header. Even if there are several images in the `files` field, only this one is displayed.

```
NO {
   beforeImg.import = uploads/media/
   beforeImg.import.field = media
   beforeImg.import.listNum = 0
```

ifEmpty

For the base layout of the `ts CTABLE template` TS template, an empty space was passed on (` `), with the `ifEmpty` property, so that the table is still displayed even if it has no content.

```
page.30 = CTABLE
page.30 {
   ...
   c.10 = COA
   c.10.5 = HTML
   c.10.5.value = <table border="0" cellspacing="0"
                    cellpadding="0" width="586"><tr>
   c.10.10 < styles.content.get
   c.10.10.wrap = <td align="left" valign="top">|<br />
                    <br /></td>
   c.10.25 = HTML
   c.10.25.value = </tr></table>
   c.10.stdWrap.ifEmpty =  
```

Example: Using Two Columns

Until now, only the content of the `Normal` column has been displayed in the main templates. Only the `ts wrap template` TS template was included permanently in the base layout as the `Right` column. One solution to the optional use of a second column could be to create two different TS templates that are included in the page tree, depending on requirements. But since not all pages should be shown in two columns, a more flexible solution is needed, which only creates the right-hand area in the template if contents are actually available.

This will be demonstrated here using the `auto parser template` TS template. To do this, several objects are created in the `temp.*` object path. First the `styles.content.get` object is copied to `temp.inhalt`, so that this can be used to query the contents of the `tt_content` table in the normal (`colPos=0`) column.

```
# left content
   temp.inhalt < styles.content.get
```

The second temporary object `temp.right` reads out the contents of the `Right` column (`colPos=2`) with the previously made

361

`styles.content.getRight` object.

```
### right content ###
temp.right < styles.content.getRight
```

The `stdWrap.required` property terminates further processing of `stdWrap` if the object has not produced any content, which in this case is the content read out from the right-hand column. If content exists in the right-hand column, then this is enclosed by a `<div>` tag for positioning on the page, using the `stdWrap innerWrap` property.

```
temp.right.stdWrap.required = 1
temp.right.stdWrap.innerWrap = <div id="right">
                    <div id="content_right">|
         </div><div id="rightfooter"></div></div>
```

The content of the `Normal` column is placed in front of this with the `preCObject` property and also wrapped in a `<div>` tag.

```
# placing the left content as cObject before the right
# content
temp.right.stdWrap.preCObject < styles.content.get
temp.right.stdWrap.preCObject.wrap =
                    <div id="content_left"> | </div>
```

The setup `temp.right` now defines an object that displays the contents of the `Normal` and `Right` columns, provided the contents are generated in the right-hand column; otherwise nothing at all is displayed. The `Normal` column is provided here with the `content_left` ID instead of `content` in the `<div>` tag, which means that the column can be set more precisely via CSS than for a single column output.

The output of the `temp.inhalt` object is overwritten by the `temp.right` object if content exists in the right-hand column. This is done by the `stdWrap override` property.

`override` itself has the `string/stdWrap` data type, and so it can display a string or data via properties of the `Get Data` function group of `stdWrap`.

```
temp.inhalt.stdWrap.override.cObject < temp.right
```

The content of the `temp.inhalt` object is finally copied to the subpart.

```
temp.mainTemplate = TEMPLATE
temp.mainTemplate {
  ...
  subparts.content < temp.inhalt
}
```

This results in the base layouts being divided into two content areas, if content exists in the `Right` column.

Figure 5.93:

Output in the front end

You can see that the stdWrap function is a powerful tool for reading content, following control structures for comparisons, and finally for processing content. If the range of functions is not sufficient for your purposes, there is also the possibility of having content processed with your own PHP functions, with the preUserFunc and postUserFunc properties.

5.11.4 Conditions

Softlink **315080**

Conditions have already been introduced. These conditions must be fulfilled in order for the TS code that follows them to be considered. These queries represent another control structure that you can use. You may recall that if several conditions are set, only the first condition to be true is taken into account. They are terminated with [END] or [GLOBAL]. Conditions cannot be set inside the { } operators, that is, inside nested properties. The [ELSE] condition is automatically fulfilled if the condition set before it was not fulfilled.

Conditions can also be combined, as the following example shows, where the enclosed TS code is only processed if the calling system can identify itself as a Linux system, or is located in the IP range of 145.153.102.*.

```
[system = linux][IP = 145.153.102.*]
...
[END]
```

No conditions have been used so far in the examples. We will briefly introduce the conditions listed in the current TSref, and afterwards show how they are put to use in practice in the example application.

Overview

Softlink **501292** The following overview names all the conditions that you can set. The exact values can be found in the TSref.

browser

Syntax: [browser =browser1 , browser2 ,...]

[browser = msie] applies to all MS Internet Explorer versions

[browser = msie, opera] applies to all MS Internet Explorer and Opera browsers

[browser = opera7] applies to all Opera 7.xx browsers, including Opera 7.1 etc.

Note that browsers can also be identified under other names, so that the request will then not lead to the desired result.

version

Syntax: [version =value1 , >value2 , =value3 , <value4,...]

This condition queries the browser version. The values are floating-point numbers, with "." as the decimal separator. The version number can be supplied with three operators:

- = The value must match exactly. [version = 5.5]

- > The version must be larger than the specified value. [version = > 5.5]

- < The version number must be smaller than the specified value. [version = < 5.5]

system

Syntax: [system=system1,system2]

The character string is compared with the first part of the system identification and returns the condition as true if they match.

[system = win9] matches Win95 and Win98

[system=win,mac] matches Windows and Mac operating systems

device

Syntax: `[device=device1,device2 ]`

The condition is true if the character string matches the output device (`pda`, `wap`, `grabber`, `robot`).

useragent

Syntax: `[useragent=agent ]`

A check is made to see if there is a match with the variables `getenv("HTTP_USER_ AGENT")`. The wildcard * can be used at the beginning and/or at the end of the string.

`[useragent=Lotus-Notes/4.5(Windows-NT)]` matches `HTTP_ USER_ AGENT "Lotus-Notes/4.5(Windows-NT)"`

`[useragent = Lotus-Notes*]` also matches this.

language

Syntax: `[language =lang1,lang2,...]`

The variable `getenv(HTTP_ACCEPT_LANGUAGE)` is compared with a given value; with an exact match the query is fulfilled.

IP

Syntax: `[IP =ipaddress1,ipaddress2,...]`

The variable `getenv("REMOTE_ADDR")` is checked for a match with the given value. This can contain the wildcard *, or just consist of one, two, or three parts:

`[IP = 145.*.*.*]` matches all IP addresses that begin with 145.

hostname

Syntax: `[hostname =hostname1,hostname2,...]`

The value as a comma-separated list of domain names must match the variable `getenv("REMOTE_ADDR")`. Wildcards * are allowed, but may not be used in a string.

`[hostname = YourDomain.*.com]` is correct

`[hostname = YourDomain*.com]` is wrong

hour

Syntax: `[hour =hour1,>hour2,<hour3,...]`

The values (in 24-hour format), separated by sliding commas, are compared with the current hour on the server.

Possible operators are =, >, and <.

minute

Syntax: [minute =...]

The specified minute (0-59) is compared with the current minute on the server.

dayofweek

Syntax: [dayofweek =...]

The day of the week (from 0/Sunday to 6/Saturday) is compared with the day of the week on the server and returns "true" if the two match.

dayofmonth

Syntax: [dayofmonth =...]

The day of the month (1 to 31) is compared with the current day on the server.

month

Syntax: [month =...]

The months (from 1/January to 12/December) are compared with the current month on the server.

usergroup

Syntax: [usergroup =group1-uid,group2-uid,...]

The condition is fulfilled if the front-end user logged in is a member of the specified user group. The wildcard * covers all user groups set up, which can be determined by the global variable gr_list.

loginUser

Syntax: [loginUser =fe_users-uid,fe_users-uid,...]

The uid of a front-end user logged in is checked for a match with the given whole number. The wildcard * can be used to query if the user really is logged in.

treeLevel

Syntax: [treeLevel =levelnumber,levelnumber,...]

If one of the given whole numbers matches the current level inside the Rootline, then the condition is fulfilled. 0 matches the Rootlevel, 1 matches the first menu level. [treeLevel = 2,3]

PIDinRootline

Syntax: `[PIDinRootline =pages-uid,pages-uid,...]`

The condition is met if the current page matches one of the specified `pids`, or if one of its subpages is involved. Only then is the following TypoScript code executed. In order to assign a different color value to the headers in various areas of the page tree, you can use the following code:

```
[PIDinRootline = 37]
content.wrap.header1 = <h1 class="blue">|</h1>
[END]
[PIDinRootline = 16]
content.wrap.header1 = <h1 class="red">|</h1>
[GLOBAL]
```

Page 37 and its subpages are given the blue style, page 16 and its subpages, the red style.

PIDupinRootline

Syntax: `[PIDupinRootline =pages-uid,pages-uid,...]`

See `PIDinRootline`. The difference is that the ID of the current page is not included in the comparison.

globalVar

Syntax: `[globalVar=var1=value,var2<value2,var3>value3 ,...]`

The condition is met if the value of the variable matches the value of the corresponding system variable. Multiple variables are separated by commas.

Possible operators are: >, <

`[globalVar = GP:L=3]` applies, for example, to the URL

`...index.php?id=45&L=3.`

globalString

Syntax: `[globalString=var1=value,var2=*value2,var3= *value3*,...]`

As `globalVar`, with the difference that values are compared as a string. The wildcard * can also be added at the beginning or at the end.

`[globalString = HTTP_HOST=www.mysite.com]` and

[globalString = HTTP_HOST=*.mysite.com] both match the value http://www.mysite.com.

userFunc

Syntax: [userFunc =user_match(checkLocalIP)]

With userFunc, your own PHP functions can be used for checking.

Example: Extending the Print Version

The button used so far in the temp.printversion TS template to call the print version works very well, but only as long as you do not create static URL addresses with the TS option config.simulateStaticDocuments.

This is why the template will be extended below. Depending on the URL type, the string is edited and given various parameters.

For the existing temp.* object, first the 10 object is reconfigured for static URL addresses.

```
temp.printversion = COA
temp.printversion {
  wrap = <a href="|" name="Printversion"
         title="Printversion" target="_blank"
         class="printversion">{$printlabel }</a>
# simulate Static Version, all included link parameters
# will also be processed.
  10 = TEXT
  10.data = getIndpEnv:REQUEST_URI
```

The URL read out via the stdWrap property is split into individual strings with the listNum.splitChar property and the "." as a value. With listNum=0, only the first element of the value is taken into account, and is wrapped with |.98.html. (The whole thing works if you have included the parameters with config.simulateStaticDocuments_pEnc_onlyP as an MD5 hash when creating the static URL address.)

```
  10.listNum.splitChar = .
  10.listNum = 0
  10.wrap = |.98.html
}
```

The already existing temp.printversion.10 object is now given a Condition and only processed if this is met.

globalString queries whether the server variable ENV:REQUEST_URI has the value /index.php*. The wildcard * is used to check the string just for the start value /index.php.

```
# "normal" version, for pages with index.php, with
# parameters where required, e.g.: ?id=3434&L=1

[globalString = ENV:REQUEST_URI = /index.php*]
```

If the condition is met, the current `temp.printversion.10` object is deleted and redefined, as in the previous version.

```
temp.printversion.10 >
temp.printversion {
  10 = TEXT
  10.data = getIndpEnv:REQUEST_URI
  10.wrap = |&type=98
}
```

The `condition` is concluded with `[GLOBAL]`.

```
[global]
...
```

The page template remains unchanged. The print version can now be used for both variations.

Example: Language Selection

TYPO3 is very well suited for multi-language applications. We have already shown how the editor can maintain the content of several languages in the back end. These should now be selectable via a language selection in the front end, a link that calls the page with the parameter &L=[sys_language_uid], and in front of which a small flag for the chosen language is placed.

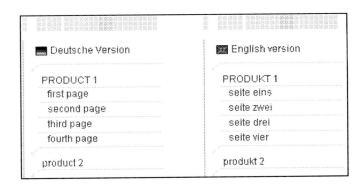

Figure 5.94:

Language switch: English is active, German can be chosen (left) and vice versa (right)

This can be implemented via an included PHP script; but it can be done more simply with TypoScript.

In the setup of the newly created `temp.language` TS template, English is first defined as the default language (`sys_language_uid=0`) for the `config` TLO with the `language=en` property.

```
# Setting up the language variable "L" to be passed
# along with links
config.linkVars = L

# English as default language, sys_language.uid = 0
config.sys_language.uid = 0
config.language = en
config.locale_all = en_UK
```

If the URL contains the parameter `L=1`, the language with ID 1 (`sys_language_uid=1`), that is, German, is defined as the alternative language. Since this is not a global definition, the GET/POST data is checked with the condition `[globalVar=GP:L=1]` to see if the condition is met.

```
# German language, sys_language.uid = 1
[globalVar = GP:L = 1]
config.sys_language_uid = 1
config.language = de
config.locale_all = de_DE
[GLOBAL]
```

The actual link is created as a temporary object via the COA cObject. The 10 object of the TEXT object type should provide the alternative language, depending on the language currently selected. This is why `value` is set as a constant. A table that formats the output is placed around the whole object with the `stdWrap` `outerWrap` property. It contains the flag of the alternative language, which is also included as a constant.

```
temp.language = COA
temp.language {
  10 = TEXT
  10.value = ${languageVersion}
  10.outerWrap = <table width="160px"
          bgcolor="#FFFFFF" border="0"
          cellpadding="1" cellspacing="0"><tr>
          <td width="12px"><img src="clear.gif"
          width="10px" height="26px" alt="" /></td>
          <td width="16px"><img src="{$flagSmall}"
          width="14px" height="11px" border="0" />
          </td><td width="170px">|</td></tr></table>
```

With the `stdWrap` `typolink` property, a link is generated around the 10 object. The `parameter` property determines the current ID. With `additionalParams`, the third constant is added as a value to the `&L` additional parameter. `AtagParams` adds a CSS class to the `<a>` tag.

```
10.typolink {
    parameter.data = page:alias // TSFE:id
    additionalParams = &L={$foreignLanguageID}
    ATagParams = class="lang"
  }
}
```

You now just need to define the correct constants for the link, depending on the current language. If this is the defined default language, English (`[globalVar=GP:L=0]`), no condition is required, and the parameter for the link is set with `foreignLanguageID` to 1. The text and the flag icon are specified with `languageVersion` and `flagSmall`.

Constants:

```
foreignLanguageID = 1
languageVersion = Deutsche Version
flagSmall = fileadmin/images/icons/flagde.gif
```

If the current language is one other than the default language English, that is, the parameter `L` of the current URL has a value `>0` (`[globalVar=GP:L>0]`), then set a condition with the `globalVar` condition in the **constants** field and redefine the constants.

```
[globalVar = GP:L>0]
foreignLanguageID = 0
languageVersion = English version
flagSmall = fileadmin/images/icons/flaguk.gif
[global]
```

Insert the language switch into the relevant main template and check the result in the front end. You will see that everything works in a simple way with pure TypoScript.

5.12 Working with Frames

Even if working with frames is no longer considered best practice, we want, for the sake of completeness, to demonstrate how frame-based sites can be implemented with TYPO3.

Using frames you can divide the browser view into various freely definable segments. Each segment forms separate pages of a web application, which can call each other via links and the `target="Name of the Frames"` attribute. An HTML file with the following code includes the pages `top.htm`, `menu.htm`, `content.htm`, and `bottom.htm` via a nested frameset.

```
<!DOCTYPE HTML PUBLIC "-//W3C//DTD HTML 4.01
    Frameset//EN"
```

```
"http://www.w3.org/TR/html4/frameset.dtd">
<html>
<head>
<title>The Title</title>
</head>

<frameset rows="205,*,50" framespacing="4"
      frameborder="1" bordercolor="#000000">
<frame src="top.htm" name="top" frameborder="0"
      scrolling="no" marginwidth="0" marginheight="0">
<frameset cols="195,*">
<frame src="menu.htm" name="menu" frameborder="0"
      scrolling="no" marginwidth="0" marginheight="0">
<frame src="content.htm" name="content" frameborder="0"
      scrolling ="no" marginwidth="0" marginheight="0">
</frameset>
<frame src="bottom.htm" name="bottom" frameborder="0"
      scrolling="no" marginwidth="0" marginheight="0">
</frameset>
</html>
```

If the page is called in the browser, it will clearly show the individual frames. Content is provided by individual pages.

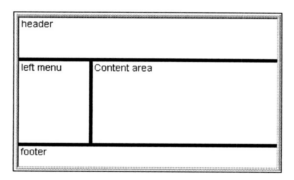

Figure 5.95:

Output of the HTML example in the browser

5.12.1 Creating Frames

Softlink **234280**

To create a site with frames in TYPO3, you must define a number of pages in a TS template.

```
myframeset = PAGE
top = PAGE
menu = PAGE
content = PAGE
bottom = PAGE
```

Each of the pages is assigned to a separate value via the `typeNum` property.

```
myframeset.typeNum = 0
top.typeNum = 1
menu.typeNum = 2
content.typeNum = 3
bottom.typeNum = 4
```

A content object of the TEXT type is created for each of the individual pages, with the exception of `myframeset`.

```
top.10 = TEXT
top.10.value = header
menu.10 = TEXT
menu.10.value = left menu
content.10 = TEXT
content.10.value = content area
bottom.10 = TEXT
bottom.10.value = footer
```

You can already call pages individually in the browser via the `id` and the corresponding `type` parameter. The concept of template switching using `type`/`typeNum` has already been introduced in section 5.8.

Figure 5.96:

Addressing individual pages with the type parameter

If you call a page without the `type` parameter, it will be set to the default value `0`, thus calling the `myframeset` template. This is now defined as a frameset, in order to construct the HTML example. As a top-level object of the PAGE object type, `myframeset` has the `frameset` property of the FRAMESET object type. It creates the `<frameset>` tag and the respective frames or framesets nested in each other, via the individual objects of the numerical list. For the sake of clarity, their attributes were standardized as constants and moved to the **constants** field.

Constants

```
frameSetParams = border="1" frameborder="1"
                 framespacing="0"
frameParams = scrolling="auto" frameborder="1"
        border="1" framespacing="0" marginheight="0"
        marginwidth="0"  noresize
```

Setup

The number and size of frame rows and columns is specified with the rows and cols properties; params is set as a constant.

```
myframeset.frameSet.rows = 205,*,50
myframeset.frameSet.params = {$frameSetParams}
```

The frames and the nested framesets are now defined via the numerical list. The 10 object is of the FRAME object type, and its obj property is a pointer to the top pages already created as TLOs. The attributes of the frame for the params property are also passed on as constants here.

```
myframeset.frameSet {
  10 = FRAME
  10 {
    obj = top
    params = {$frameParams}
  }
```

The 20 object is of the FRAMESET object type and represents a frameset within a frameset. With the objects 24 and 26, two frames are created in this way, and display the pages menu and content in the middle frameset.

```
  20 = FRAMESET
  20.cols = 195,*
  20.params = {$frameSetParams}
  20 {
    24 = FRAME
    24 {
      obj = menu
      params = {$frameParams}
    }
    26 = FRAME
    26 {
      obj = content
      params = {$frameParams}
    }
  }
}
```

Finally the frame 30 is created, which includes the bottom TLO.

```
  30 = FRAME
  30 {
    obj = bottom
    params = {$frameParams}
  }
}
```

If you again call the page in the browser without the parameter, the output will match that of the HTML example.

5.12.2 The Example Site with Frames

To create the example site with a frameset, we have chosen a simple division into three vertical frames in the `ts wrap template (frames)` TS template. In the middle content area `content`, the left menu, the actual content, and the right column are integrated. This makes it easier to address individual target frames with the menus. On the left they all have the attribute `target="content"`. The result is shown in the following figure. `border` was set to `1` in order to highlight the individual frames.

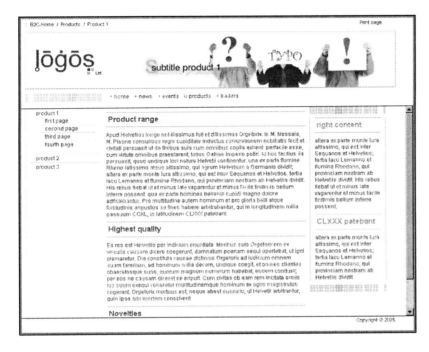

Figure 5.97:

Output of the example site with frames

So that you do not have to keep on repeating the same frame parameters, they have again been set as constants and defined in the **constants** field.

Constants

```
frameSetParams = border="1" frameborder="1"
        framespacing="0" frameParams = scrolling="auto"
        frameborder="1" border="1" framespacing="0"
        marginheight="0" marginwidth="0" noresize
```

In the setup, four pages are generated as TLOs of the `PAGE` type; each of them is assigned its own `typeNumber` with `typeNum`.

Setup

```
myframeset = PAGE
top = PAGE
content = PAGE
bottom = PAGE

myframeset.typeNum = 0
top.typeNum = 1
content.typeNum = 2
bottom.typeNum = 3
```

For page objects that are intended to display content, the CSS file is inserted with the stylesheet property, which is responsible for formatting the output.

```
top.stylesheet = fileadmin/styles/ts-template-wrap.css
content.stylesheet = fileadmin/styles/
                          ts-template-wrap.css
bottom.stylesheet = fileadmin/styles/
                          ts-template-wrap.css
```

The frameset itself is called via the myframeset TLO with the typeNum=0 property. It is again defined with the frameSet object and its properties. The number and size of the frames is determined with rows; params integrates the attributes as constants from the **constants** field. The separate frames themselves are generated as objects of the numerical list.

```
myframeset.frameSet.rows = 205,*,50
myframeset.frameSet.params = {$frameSetParams}
myframeset.frameSet {
  10 = FRAME
  10 {
    obj = top
    params = {$frameParams}
  }
  20 = FRAME
    20 {
    obj = content
    params = {$frameParams}
  }
  30 = FRAME
  30 {
    obj = bottom
    params = {$frameParams}
  }
}
```

The frameset is already complete, and only the content for individual pages still needs to be included. At this point we will assign the pages top, content, and bottom by copying temporary objects that still need to be created.

```
top.10 < temp.top
content.10 < temp.content
bottom.10 < temp.bottom
```

To define the content, we can take advantage of the fact that existing TS templates can be used repeatedly. The menus and functionalities included in the following listing, must, of course, be included in the template record with **Include basis template**. The same applies for the content (default) basis template, which is integrated with **Include static**.

Each of the temporary objects is defined as a COA. They must be placed at the beginning of the setup so that they already exist when individual page objects are parsed.

The desired TS objects are copied to the individual objects in the numerical list and wrapped with <div> tags. The menus are adjusted here at the same time and 10.1.target, for example, is set to the content page. If you are not sure about addressing properties for nested objects, the **TypoScript Object Browser** will be of further help to you.

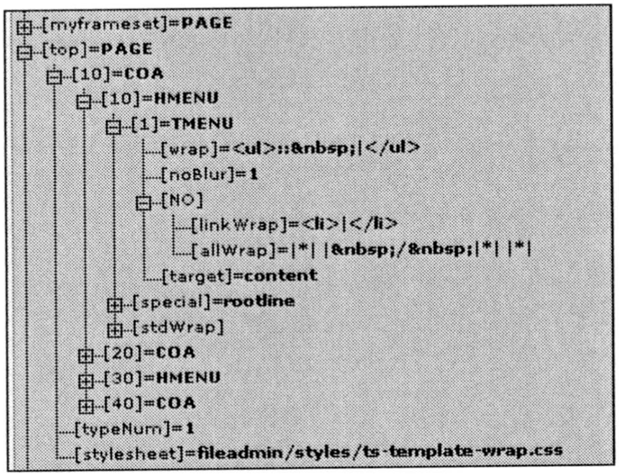

Figure 5.98:

TypoScript Object Browser

temp.top summarizes the contents for the top frame. The rootline menu (10), the button for the print version (40), the header image (20), and the main navigation (30) are displayed.

```
temp.top = COA
temp.top {
    ## Rootline Menu
    10 < temp.rootline_autoparser_tswrap
    ## adjust menu
```

```
10.1.target = content
10.stdWrap.wrap = <div id="rootline">|</div>
## Header
20 < temp.header_tswrap_autoparser
20.stdWrap.wrap = <div id="header">|</div>
## Main Navigation
30 < temp.navigation_autoparser_tswrap
## adjust menu
30.1.target = content
30.stdWrap.wrap = <div id="navi">|</div>
# Print Version
40 < temp.printversion
40.stdWrap.wrap = <div id="printversion">|</div>
}
```

Objects for the contents of the subnavigation (100), meta-information (200), the Normal column (20), and the Right column (30) are copied to the temp.content object for the content frame. You can see that within the COA temp.content the object 10 of the numerical list was in turn defined as COA.

```
temp.content = COA
temp.content {
  # Left / Submenu + Metas
  10 = COA
  10 {
    100 < temp.subnavigation_autoparser_tswrap
    ## adjust menu
    100.1.target = content
    100.2.target = content
    200 < temp.metas_autoparser_tswrap
    200.1.target = content
  }
  10.stdWrap.wrap = <div id="subnavigation">|</div>
  # Content-Left
  20 < styles.content.get
  20.stdWrap.wrap = <div id="content">|</div>
  # Content-Right
  30 < styles.content.getRight
  30.stdWrap.wrap = <div id="right">
                    <div id="rightcontent">|</div>
                    <div id="rightfooter"> </div>
                    </div>
  30.stdWrap.required = 1
}
```

The temporary object temp.bottom for the bottom frame takes over the properties of the temp.copyright_tswrap_autoparser object with the 20 object, to display the copyright sign at the footer of the application.

```
temp.bottom = COA
temp.bottom {
```

```
# Footer
10 = TEXT
10.value = <div id="footer"></div>
## Copyright
20 < temp.copyright_tswrap_autoparser
20.wrap = <div id="copyright">|</div>
}
```

Finally the target frames are defined in the `constants` field so that the forms and content links address the correct frame. They are inserted via `content (default)` as constants with the default value `page`, and can also be edited with the `Constant Editor`.

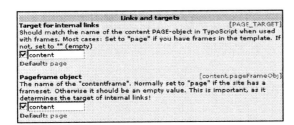

Figure 5.99:

Attributes for links are set to content

Constants

```
PAGE_TARGET = content
content.pageFrameObj = content
```

This should suffice for the example on frames. If you view the result in the front end, it will be the same as those of the other example sites. Some functionalities still need to be adjusted. The Rootline Menu, for example, does not yet show the path of the current page, but you could make this into one of your first tasks.

5.13 Future and Prospects

5.13.1 XHTML and Accessibility

The need to separate content from design not only contributed to the creation of content management systems, but also influenced the under-

---

[10] HTML is derived from SGML, which was developed as a pure mark-up language. XML originated from this, and in turn efforts are being made to re-establish XHTML as a pure mark-up language.

lying technologies. HTML was originally developed as a markup language [10] with layout elements, to bring structure into documents (to split up documents), to embed other media such as images into the text flow, and to enable documents to be connected via links.

The rapid spread of websites, especially in the commercial area, had an influence on the fact that design became more important as a means to differentiate or customize websites. For a long time tables intended for list type content were used for this purpose, as the main design tool. More and more tricks like this were used to implement layouts with HTML to meet the expectations of a visual medium.

Many tricks and workarounds, as well as the dialects of different browsers, have led to the consistency of HTML syntax being heavily compromised, and as a consequence, the ability of programs such as browsers for the disabled to logically interpret it. The WWW consortium headed by the HTML developer Tim Berners-Lee made several attempts to meet design demands by extending HTML specifications and making them more consistent, at the same time standardizing syntax and allowing less room for interpretation by browsers.

The basic idea behind HTML, and even its predecessor SGML, was to precisely separate form and content. [11] Cascading stylesheets (CSS) were developed fairly early on as a technology suitable for this, but in practice their acceptance by browser manufacturers and web developers was very slow.

The change in ideas in recent years has been accelerated by the following facts:

- The maintenance of content and changes to the design require a large amount of work, because the two are interwoven.

- Documents are unnecessarily large and use up valuable bandwidth and loading time.

- Output to alternative devices is not possible, or possible only with large modification costs.

- New technologies such as XML were developed, which are considerably more flexible and efficient.

- Laws have been passed in many countries that prescribe

[11] "Many credit the start of the generic coding movement to a presentation made by William Tunnicliffe, chairman of the Graphic Communications Association (GCA) Composition Committee, during a meeting at the Canadian Government Printing Office in September 1967: his topic—the separation of information content of documents from their format." From: Charles F. Goldfarb, "The Roots of SGML, a personal recollection", http://www.sgmlsource.com/history/roots.htm

the separation of form and content as a component of accessibility information, at least for websites of public institutions or authorities.

XHTML plays an important role as a specification and as the successor to HTML, and forms the connection between HTML and XML. With the introduction of XHTML at the latest, design elements were to a great extent removed from the language. Where possible, design should be controlled exclusively by CSS, to achieve stricter separation of content and design. In addition, fault tolerance is also heavily reduced. The stricter syntax means that browsers need to use less resources for error correction, and they can therefore function extremely efficiently on many different devices, down to smartphones.

Advantages of standard conformity in general, and XHTML in particular:

- **Low costs**: shorter loading times and server loads, better performance; simplification of website maintenance due to more nimble code, and the separation of content and design.

- **Investment security**: standard conformity ensures compatibility to newer output devices and extendibility to other XML-based languages.

- **Longer range**: improved accessibility from different platforms, browsers, and assisting technologies; not least, a better positioning with search engines.

From the last mentioned point, it becomes clear why XHTML and accessibility are often mentioned in the same breath: the *Web Content Accessibility Guidelines* (WCAG) or the German *Barrierefrei Informationstechnologie-Verordnung* (BITV), assume a standard conformity, because this enables a broader technical support of assistive technologies such as screen readers, voice browsers, and Braille line readers for people with physical disabilities. So by complying with (X)HTML standards, we are already halfway towards a content accessible website.

Softlink **895351**

In version 3.6.0, TYPO3 conforms with "XHTML1.0 Transitional". All the source code of the core was cleaned up in this respect and adjusted to the newer standard. The extensions are initially not involved in this, and will be brought up to date gradually by the respective authors.

These are the essential reforms of XHTML1.0:

- Well-formed: Elements may not overlap and must display closing tags.

- Element and attribute names must be written in lowercase.

- Attribute values must always be placed in quotation marks, e.g.

`border="0"`. Attributes may not appear in minimized form, but must be written out in full, e.g. `checked="checked"` instead of just `checked`.

- Empty elements must be terminated, e.g. `<br />` or `<br></br>`.

- The content of script and style elements must follow a specific syntax or better, be moved to external script or style documents.

Softlink **570674**   You can check whether your webpages are XHTML conformant or not with the (X)HTML validator of the WWW Consortium (see softlink). The techniques for generating accessibility-compatible webpages described in the following section work in harmony with XHTML and should be seen in this context.

Softlink **728651**   These are the most important TypoScript definitions concerning XHTML, which are set via `config`:

doctype

Data type: string

Example: `xhtml_trans | xhtml_frames | xhtml_strict | xhtml_11 | xhtml_2 | none`

Declaration of the document type. Shows to which standard the browser should comply.

doctypeSwitch

Data type: Boolean/string

Example: `1`

Is used to set the XML prolog under the Doctype declaration—a workaround for some browsers.

xmlprologue

Data type: string

Example: `none`

Serves to remove the prolog `<?xml version="1.0" encoding="utf-8"?>`

htmlTag_setParams

Data type: `string`

Sets attributes of the `<html>` tag; when the `doctype` is set, every thing is already correctly defined. This property can be used for any inconsistencies.

htmlTag_langKey

>Data type: string

>Example: `en{-US}`

>Enables the language value to be set for the `xml:lang` and `lang` attributes in the `<html>` tag, if `config. doctype= xhtml` has been set.

htmlTag_dir

>Data type: string

>Example: `rtl | ltr`

>Sets the direction of the text flow, e.g. for Arabic or Hebrew.

removeDefaultJS

>Data type: boolean/string

>Example: `external | 1`

>JavaScript is either moved elsewhere or removed completely.

inlineStyle2TempFile

>Data type: boolean

>Example: `1`

>The inline style definitions are moved to separate files.

xhtml_cleaning

>Data type: string

>Example: `all | cached | output`

>Provides a workaround, e.g. for extensions.

5.13.2 Accessibility

In Germany, for example, the BITV (Barrierefreie Informationstechnik-Verordnung Ordinance on Barrier-Free Information Technology) came about as a consequence of the Act on Equal Opportunities for Disabled Persons. The BITV applies initially only to Government Offices. On a Federal level, this Ordinance has to a large extent been put into practice. By the end of 2005, all Federal and many State institutions must have accessibility websites, accessible for the physically impaired.

The primary aim is to provide physically impaired people with equal possibilities of accessing information. Even those with minor impairments, such as being short-sighted or color-blind, should benefit from this. A further positive side effect is the general improvement in the usability of websites, which is for the good of all.

Here is a summary of these guidelines, in accordance with the most recent accessibility guidelines of the W3C Consortium WCAG2.0 (not yet officially released).

Accessibility websites must, for people with disabilities, be:

- Perceptible (alternative content such as `alt` attributes for images)

- Usable (with a wide range of devices and physical restrictions, navigable, orientation aids)

- Comprehensible (language, abbreviations)

- Robust (conform to standards)

In practice, these guidelines concern all those involved in contributing to the creation of a TYPO3-based website: core code developers, extension developers, website developers, and editors. Much has already been done in the core, but there remains much to be done for extensions. But a great deal of responsibility lies in the hands of web developers and editors.

The most important practical adjustment for web developers is the banning of layout control from (X)HTML. One of the consequences of this technique is managing without tables as a layout method. Both basic layout and highlighting and other design techniques are primarily implemented on the CSS level. HTML merely takes over the structuring of the document, which is why the source code of all accessibility pages looks surprisingly similar.

Example: On a conventional HTML page, many web developers mark headers with elements such as `font-size` and `font-weight`. A screen reader does not know what to do with such markups. But if the headers are marked with `h1-h6` elements, screen readers recognize them as such, and for better orientation in a large document, for example, might only read out the headers at first.

Apart from the properties already mentioned above regarding standard conformity and declarations, there are also a number of special control options on the TypoScript level that concern accessibility. Here are a few examples:

The following settings should switch off the JavaScript function in menus, in order to prevent the ugly border around linked images that can be seen when they are clicked on.

```
noBlur = 1
```

The function is quite harmless in itself. Unfortunately it has the effect that you can no longer navigate with the tab keys, so it must be removed.

The link from form labels to the respective form elements must be clearly structured. XHTML provides a `label` element for this. With the form property

```
accessibility = 1
```

we activate the functionality that automatically create labels and links them to the corresponding input elements. An example of the result:

```
<label for="email">Your Email:</label>
<input type="text" id="email" name="email" />
```

Inconsistencies with the predominant language can be specified in the TypoScript code:

```
parseFunc.short.Browser = <span xml:lang="en"
                          lang="en">Browser</span>
```

This results in better legibility when using screen readers.

Inside menus, you can use

```
accesskey = 1
```

to create attributes for defining access keys that enable navigation with keyboard commands. The practical use of this HTML attribute is controversial. In TYPO3, keyboard shortcuts are created with the first letter of the respective menu items. This is a particular problem because many keyboard shortcuts are already reserved by the operating system and the browser. The opinion is widespread that merely the numbers 0 to 9 should be used as access keys for offering central navigation options. This functionality cannot be implemented by this TypoScript property, however, which is why its use is not recommended.

Missing Adjustments in the TYPO3 Core

Complex HTML tables and complex forms that meet the Accessibility Guidelines cannot yet be displayed. In such cases the web developers/administrators should store the correspondingly prepared contents statically as HTML content in TYPO3.

It can be assumed that standard conformity and accessibility will play a more important role in creating websites in future; the effects of this on TYPO3 are being investigated by the TYPO3 Accessibility Project.

Softlink **563588**

5.13.3 TemplaVoila

Softlink **003991**

A number of new concepts are introduced in TYPO3 with TemplaVoila [12], which in their interaction represent not just a new template system. Apart from the possibility of preparing HTML templates from a back-end module, new content types can be created that can be used flexibly, and are not restricted by the structure of a database table. In addition, the concept of columns is torn up; areas can be defined so that they only accept certain content types, which is supported by a new page module.

As already mentioned, the development of TemplaVoila is not yet complete, but the extension is nevertheless a powerful tool, which has already proven itself in production situations, and which will be introduced here in an overview. A more detailed introduction can be obtained by the softlink to the tutorial "Futuristic Template Building".

Even if TemplaVoila may seem to fit like a glove into the application, it consists of many different components, some of which can be used on their own. To illustrate the new possibilities, the components will be introduced separately, but TemplaVoila must nevertheless be seen as the sum of its parts.

Visual Template Mapping

A fundamental function of TemplaVoila is the convenient processing and integration of HTML templates. The function is similar to the Template Auto-Parser, except that the areas that are to be used or replaced in the template can simply be chosen by mouse click, using a back-end module.

---

[12] The name is intended as a pun on the fact that an HTML template can be created in TYPO3 in a very short time. The correct name ought to be "Templat Voilà", which comes out in translation as: "there's your template already!"

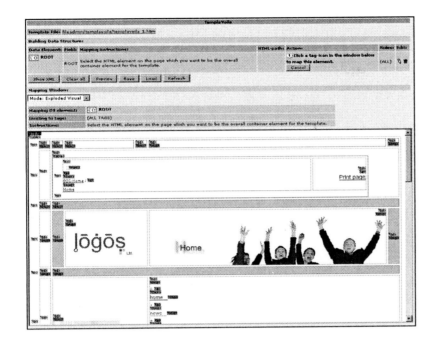

Figure 5.100:

Areas in HTML templates are selected with TemplaVoila by mouse click and configured

Data Structures (DS) and Template Objects (TO)

After the mapping of TemplaVoila, the configuration of the HTML template is saved in two XML data structures (DS and TO) and apart from the information on the areas selected, also contains information on what type of objects or data these areas can take in.

Data structures (DS) and template objects (TO) are separate definitions, but make use of each other. Data structures contain an abstract definition of areas, fields, and field types, comparable to the definition of the fields in a database—just with a few additional "gimmicks".

Template objects refer to a DS and define the output of an element of the DS. A TO, for example, contains information concerning which HTML files are to be used for rendering and which fields from the data structure are to be used at which points in the HTML structure. Multiple TOs can be defined for a DS; the basis for the different output variations.

There are still more areas where DS and TO can be used. A DS is used both for the definition of base layouts and of content types. It is also possible to integrate TypoScript into TOs and providing dynamic options for content types that in themselves are rather inflexible.

The following DS (abbreviated) defines a field for selecting image files
(`<TCEforms>`) and at the same time includes a TypoScript setup for rendering images (`<TypoScript>`).

```
<T3DataStructure>
  <ROOT type="array">
    <tx_templavoila type="array">
      <title>ROOT</title>
      <description></description>
      <eType>input</eType>
      <tags></tags>
    </tx_templavoila>
    <type>array</type>
    <el type="array">
      <field_image type="array">
        <tx_templavoila type="array">
          <title>An image</title>
          <eType>image</eType>
          <TypoScript>
10 = IMAGE
10.file.import = uploads/tx_templavoila/
10.file.import.current = 1
10.file.import.listNum = 0
10.file.maxW = 150
10.params = align=&quot;right&quot;
          </TypoScript>
        </tx_templavoila>
        <TCEforms type="array">
        <config type="array">
          <type>group</type>
          <internal_type>file</internal_type>
          <allowed>gif,png,jpg,jpeg</allowed>
          <max_size>1000</max_size>
          <uploadfolder>uploads/
                        tx_templavoila</uploadfolder>
          <show_thumbs>1</show_thumbs>
          <size>1</size>
          <maxitems>1</maxitems>
          <minitems>0</minitems>
        </config>
        <label>Bild</label>
      </TCEforms>
    </field_image>
  </el>
  <section>0</section>
</ROOT>
</T3DataStructure>
```

Template Selection and Rendering

The simplest TypoScript setup for displaying the content of the Normal column looks like this:

```
page = PAGE
page.typeNum = 0
page.10 < styles.content.get
```

A base layout is completely missing here, and only the data records of the normal column are displayed by means of the default configuration for the included standard template (e.g. content (default)).

TemplaVoila takes a different approach, taking over the rendering of a page completely. A corresponding TypoScript setup appears as follows:

```
page = PAGE
page.typeNum = 0
page.10 = USER
page.10.userFunc = tx_templavoila_pi1->main_page
```

No inclusion of columns is necessary here, because the definition of the content areas (columns or similar) is defined in the DS. This is selected in the page header for the page or for a partial page tree. A TO is chosen that matches a DS, so that the layout of the page is defined.

The rendering process with TemplaVoila looks something like this:

- Search for a DS and TO in the Rootline.

- Output the template.

- For the individual areas of the DS that can accept content elements, read information on matching data records from the current page record.

- Render the content elements and display them in the areas.

- Because content elements can also contain areas, which in turn can take in content elements, render these as well.

You can define in the page header for each page which DS and which matching TO should be used. In this way you can specify which areas are available for content, and how these areas will then be displayed.

Assigning Content to Pages

Surprisingly, content that is entered in a conventional way is not automatically displayed with TemplaVoila. In the page module of TemplaVoila such content appears as "unused records".

Normally the association of content to a page is defined simply by its records being located on the page (table field `pid`). TemplaVoila, on the other hand, saves information on the affiliation of a content element to a page in the page record itself. This means that content elements in the page can originate from any other pages, and can be used many times without the need to create a copy of the element or integrate this into the page, with **Insert record**. But for reasons of clarity, content is saved, as before, in the pages in which it is displayed.

Flexforms

Flexforms are another way of entering and saving data in TYPO3. They are already implemented in the core, but are used extensively by TemplaVoila.

Apart from the typical CMS use of TYPO3, the system is primarily a web-based database management system. In principle, all kinds of records can be processed with the help of TYPO3. But this is always limited by the structure of the corresponding database table. The `tt_content` table, which serves to save various content types such as **Text** , **Image**, **Table**, or **Form** can be used flexibly—different content types show forms of varying sizes—but this is really just a trick, since each record saved contains all the fields of the other content types, even if these are not used. If you want to store additional data in a record, the database table must be extended.

Flexforms provide a solution with which you can use practically as many fields as you wish in a record. In addition to this, each record can use other fields. Because TYPO3 is built on a relational database system (e.g. MySQL) that cannot handle such data, a trick is needed here. The trick consists of using a sufficiently large database field in which data can be saved in its own format.

Figure 5.101:

Content element with Flexform and RTE

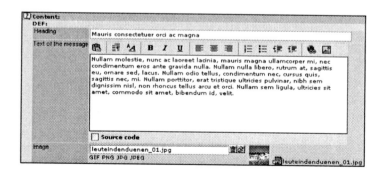

Consequently Flexform data can also be saved in normal records. In extreme cases, the table used could only have one field for content, which is used to save data. However, corresponding fields can also be used several times and mixed with conventional fields.

The already familiar data structures (DS) are also used for Flexforms, and they define what field types can be used in a Flexform. The same options as for TCEForms are therefore available in the data structure. The following XML code, for example, shows a corresponding extract from the DS for the definition of a text field with RTE integration.

```
<field_newstext type="array">
  <tx_templavoila type="array">
    <title>Newstext</title>
    <eType>text</eType>
    <proc type="array">
      <HSC>1</HSC>
    </proc>
  </tx_templavoila>
  <TCEforms type="array">
    <config type="array">
      <type>text</type>
      <cols>48</cols>
      <rows>5</rows>
    </config>
    <label>Text of message</label>
   <defaultExtras>richtext[paste|bold|italic|underline|

    formatblock|class|left|center|right|orderedlist|
    unorderedlist|outdent|indent|link|image]
    :rte_transform[flag=rte_enabled|mode=ts]
    </defaultExtras>
  </TCEforms>
</field_newstext>
```

The Flexform data itself is also saved in an XML format. As you can see, the basic components for XML processing already exist in TYPO3.

A question that one may ask is whether only Flexforms should be used for data processing. The answer is that the data in the database cannot be easily browsed or selected. The database cannot handle the stored XML data, and cannot distinguish content from the surrounding XML code. So Flexforms are not really suitable for data that needs to be selected on the basis of its content.

Flexforms are also available independently of TemplaVoila.

Flexible Content

Possibilities of visually mapping HTML templates, the use of DS, and the possibilities of Flexforms are used by TemplaVoila to introduce new and flexible content types, in addition to the static types, **Text** , **Text w/image**, etc. Here the developer can define a new content type quite easily from an HTML template that is immediately available for processing, and is also displayed correctly in the front end. In addition to this it is possible to define areas so that they can occur multiple times, such as for content elements, in which up to three links with descriptions can be created.

Flexible content types can also be used without an output template and even without TemplaVoila—in this case just the Flexforms are used. Only a data structure (DS) is necessary for this; a template object (TO) is not needed. Because TemplaVoila is dependent on an HTML template to create data structures, it is a good idea to make a simple template, even if this will not be required later.

Restrictive Content

Although the new content type is called **Flexible content**, the same concept can be used for very restrictive content types. Together with TemplaVoila's new **Web | Page** module, a content area of the template can be defined in such a way that only two specific content types should be created there, for example. If these two content types are defined specifically for this area, you have a solution that will show up defective content input, thus guaranteeing a universal layout for the entire website. This is the opposite concept to what TYPO3 has used so far, in which editors had much freedom. Both methods can be combined in any way you like, of course.

Content Areas Instead of Columns

Even if the concept of columns continues to seem practical and satisfactory, with TemplaVoila you are no longer restricted to this division. Even without TemplaVoila you are certainly in a position to edit and include content for specific areas, since any number of columns can be added and used. But it becomes more and more difficult for editors to retain an overview, the less the layout is based on columns.

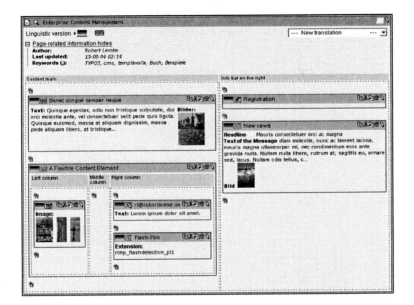

Figure 5.102:

Editing content with the page module

For this reason, TemplaVoila contains a new page module, which, in its last extension stage, is intended to display the layout of the page schematically, so that individual areas can easily be chosen for editing. In addition, rules can be set up to control the use of certain content types in individual areas.

Using TemplaVoila

If you look at these capabilities as a whole, it can easily be seen that TemplaVoila is especially well suited for websites that frequently have changing layouts or whose layouts are divided more into areas and columns, and which use many different content types. TemplaVoila in fact originated in the context of just such a project. The project contained a workflow in which a web designer had to produce precisely defined custom content elements in a WYSIWYG procedure, on the basis of HTML templates. A case study was made of this project, which can be reached through the softlink shown here.

Softlink **673845**

As you can see in Figure 5.103, a fixed column is not used in the website. The possibility of using various templates, each with different content areas, is used extensively in the website.

Figure 5.103:

TemplaVoila in productive use

TemplaVoila is a powerful tool for content and template design, and for an alpha version, is not bad at all. It will certainly be developed further, so that missing functions will be included and new functions added, but even now its development has created several basic innovations that can be used purposefully, even without TemplaVoila.

6

Extensions

6.1 Overview

An essential feature of the TYPO3 framework is its extendibility using so-called extensions. These are easy-to-install packages that can contain modules, plugins, TypoScript, and much more. Extensions are installed online, by means of the Extension Manager, from a central directory, the Extension Repository.

Extensions were introduced in TYPO3 version 3.5. Even before this version, it was possible to expand the system via interfaces. Those extensions whose database tables begin with tt_ originate from this period. Although these extensions were available, installing them was a costly business, involving different configurations in various system files. There was also a danger that extensions might clash with one another.

With the introduction of the extension system, a clear interface for installing extensions was created. In addition, the already existing interfaces were bundled, allowing decentralized further development of TYPO3 for the first time, giving this a shot in the arm. Since the extension architecture and the Extension Repository have been available, the number of such extensions has increased rapidly.

Extensions are published both by ambitious hobby developers and by professional web service providers, and are freely available. In part, these are small functions and improvements, but in many cases, there are also entire applications such as a press archive, library administration, event calendar, or hotel booking system.

The extension system provides not only the convenience of being able to install extensions easily via an administration interface—the already mentioned Extension Manager—but also security and a clear structure for developers, one which also guarantees the update capability of the core. Extensions play a central role for users and developers in TYPO3.

6.2 The Extension System

The Extension system consists of several interlinking components:

Extension API

> Interface to the TYPO3 core, enabling integration of extensions into the TYPO3 system

Extension Manager

> Back-end module for the administration and installation of extensions

Extension Repository

> Central online directory allowing extensions to be uploaded and downloaded

These components form the basis for extensions—but what do they look like in concrete terms?

6.2.1 The Structure of Extensions

An extension consists of several files within a directory. The name of the directory is simultaneously the *extension key* for this extension. Subdirectories are used for components (plugins, modules etc.) of this extension. Here is the directory tree for the `mininews` extension.

```
mininews/
  doc/
    manual.sxw
    wizard_form.dat
    wizard_form.html
  ext_emconf.php
  ext_icon.gif
  ext_localconf.php
  ext_tables.php
  ext_tables.sql
  ext_typoscript_setup.txt
  icon_tx_mininews_news.gif
  locallang.php
  locallang_db.php
  pi1/
    ce_wiz.gif
    class.tx_mininews_pi1.php
    class.tx_mininews_pi1_wizicon.php
    clear.gif
    locallang.php
  tca.php
```

Only the developer is confronted with the individual files, however, if he or she needs to make direct modifications to the extension. An administrator or website developer does not even get to see these files, or does not need to worry about them, since extensions are installed as packages, as we are about to see.

6.2.2 Extension Key

The directory name of an extension defines its extension key, and this key in turn forms the basis when naming files and program code within the extension; this means that renaming the directory (or the key) would also entail renaming files, as well as modifications to the program code.

Because extensions also share an installation directory, an extension key must have a unique name. At the same time, a unique namespace is defined by the key, helping to avoid conflicts in the system.

To guarantee extensions their unique namespace, the extension keys have to be registered in the TYPO3 Extension Repository (TER). This will be explained later on.

6.2.3 Extension Components

An extension may contain the following components and expand the system accordingly:

- New database tables * [1]
- Extension of existing database tables *
- Database tables with static data
- Front-end functions
- TypoScript *
- Content elements *
- Front-end menu *
- TypoTags *
- Front-end plugins of various types *
- Back-end functions

[1] Components marked with * can be created with the Extension Kickstarter, simplifying the development of such extensions to a large extent. The Kickstarter is described in detail in Chapter 7.2

- Back-end modules *
- Context menu entries *
- PAGE and USER TSConfig *
- Services *
- Libraries
- System configuration
- Back-end skins (colors and icons)
- Extension/modification of each PHP class in the system

6.2.4 Extension Categories

Extensions are arranged in certain basic categories, according to their place in the TYPO3 architecture. These categories are shown in the Extension Manager and basically correspond to how they are divided up technically. A further categorization is applied in the Extension Repository, describing the usage of the extension. These are categories such as communication, eCommerce, skins, administration, and others.

Back end

Extensions listed in this category expand the functionality of the back end, but do not appear as separate modules.

Back-end Modules

Back-end modules are listed here; these are new main modules (e.g. **Web**, **Tools**), modules (e.g. **Web | List**) or submodule functions (e.g. **Web | functions | Import**).

Front end

Extensions from this category contains small front-end functionalities or configurations (meta-tags, new TypoTags).

Front-end Plugins

This category contains all extensions that expand the display and functionality of the front end, for example content elements, menus, text borders, or complete front-end applications (guestbook, news, etc.).

Miscellaneous

Here you will find everything that doesn't fit into other categories, such as static database tables, functions for creating PDF files, or programming libraries.

Services

> This category contains functions that can be used by other extensions or by the system and represents a further extension interface that can be categorized beneath extensions in terms of complexity.

Templates

> Complete TypoScript site templates as extensions are grouped together in this category. These correspond to the site templates included in TYPO3, which can be found in template records under Static templates.

Examples

> Category for examples of all types; usually extensions that are constructed in tutorials or which illustrate the use of an API.

Documentation

> This category contains pure documentation extensions based on OpenOffice documents.

6.2.5 Installation: System, Global, and Local

Extensions can be installed in three different directories in the system:

typo3/sysext/ (type: System)

> System extensions such as cms and lang can be found here. No extensions can be installed here with the Extension Manager.

typo3/ext/ (type: Global)

> This is where global extensions are kept. These are normally ones that are supplied by TYPO3. These extensions contain mostly back-end modules and provide basic or extended functionality that is required or useful for most TYPO3 applications.

> It is possible to set the option allowGlobalInstall with the Installation Tool to allow extensions to be installed in this directory. This is not possible with the default settings, because version conflicts could arise in an environment where several TYPO3 websites share a TYPO3 installation.

typo3conf/ext/ (type: Local)

> All extensions are normally installed in this directory. These are referred to as local extensions, since they are only valid for the

local TYPO3 instance. In fact they even have precedence over global extensions. This means that where an extension is installed both globally and locally, the local one is always included in the system, even if it has a lower version number than the global extension.

Multiple TYPO3 instances (websites) can share a TYPO3 installation by using symbolic links, through which they also share global extensions. But local extensions are always only visible for that particular website.

6.2.6 Extension Repository

Softlink 617220

In the *TYPO3 Extension Repository* (TER), extensions are stored centrally and can be downloaded to your own TYPO3 installation and installed.

The Repository can be found at TYPO3.org. Developers can transfer an extension to the Repository with just a few mouse clicks in the Extension Manager. The extension is then available for download to specific users, or to the public, depending on its configuration. Downloading an extension is just as simple, and can also be done with just a few mouse clicks.

Figure 6.1:

Overview of extension categories in the TER on TYPO3.org.

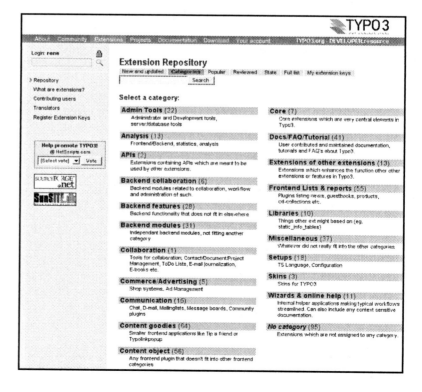

When an extension is downloaded and installed, the list of available extensions in the Extension Repository of TYPO3.org is obtained and displayed, using the Extension Manager module in your own TYPO3 installation. When an extension is selected and downloaded, the Repository sends a single file (file extension .t3x), containing the complete extension directory with all the necessary files, to the Extension Manager in the local installation. This unpacks the package into the extension directory. It is now ready to be installed by the Extension Manager. During installation, certain files within the extension directory are detected, read, and included in the system. The Extension Manager also provides installation functions for setting up the required database tables or offering the user a selection of configuration options.

The reverse path, that is, uploading an extension to the Repository, functions in a similar way and is explained in Chapter 7, in section 7.3.3.

The installation process is very simple and convenient for the user: if an extension is installed he or she can find information on the files contained, but this is not necessary. You can see that an extension is installed from the green icon in the Extension Manager in the **Loaded Extensions** view or **Extensions available to install**.

At the time of going to press, over 900 extensions are freely available. A large number of registered extensions in the Repository are not public, however. This may be because they were never completed properly, because developers are still improving the code, or because no documentation exists. We would like to point out, however, that Open Source projects live from the active contributions of users, and that it is a shame about some of these *unpolished diamonds*, which, if they were published, could indeed be given a sparkle by many different hands! It is also much easier to find help and sponsors if you already have a corresponding beta version or a project description. [2]

6.2.7 Documentation

In the TER you will also find the entire documentation of TYPO3, kept in the form of OpenOffice documents. These are extensions that only contain documentation, and which belong to the Documentation category. The documents are available on TYPO3.org as HTML pages in the "Documentation" area, and you can also add comments there.

Softlink 280413

---

[2] Project descriptions can be found in the *Projects* area on the TYPO3.org website along with present projects that are still looking for help and sponsors. Project descriptions can be written by anyone and are an effective way of introducing ideas and concepts and getting them moving on TYPO3.org.

Apart from these documentation-only extensions, which usually contain references and tutorials, there may, and should, be specific documentation for every extension. The same system is applied here as for the documentation extensions, except that these extensions also contain a plugin, module or other data. The extension-specific documentation can, if required, be downloaded from the Repository, together with the extension. This can then be found in the OpenOffice file `manual.sxw` in the `doc/` subdirectory of the extension.

Using OpenOffice documents has some advantages over other options, such as HTML, PDF, or DocBook:

- It is easy to write, using a powerful and freely available word processor.

- Printout of OpenOffice .SXW files in the desired format is possible

- PDF files can be created directly from OpenOffice.

- The open, XML-based file format of OpenOffice is simple to read and convert (to HTML, for example).

- Documentation can be displayed directly as HTML within TYPO3.org, using the *Document Suite.*

6.3 Extension Manager

The Extension Manager (EM) is a back-end module for the administration of extensions. The module is located in the **Tools** main module, which means it is normally only accessible for administrators. The functionality of the Extension Manager includes:

- Listing the installed extensions

- Listing available extensions

- Installing and removing extensions

- Transferring extensions via a T3X file to your own installation

- Transferring extensions from the online repository (TER) to your own installation (download)

- Uploading your own extensions to the TYPO3 Extension Repository

- Developing your own extensions (Kickstarter)

In the following section we will introduce individual views and their functions.

6.3.1 Listing of Available Extensions

This view displays all the available extensions in the TYPO3 installation. They are listed in the table with additional information. The **+/-** icon at the beginning of each line shows whether an extension is installed (green). Clicking on this icon will install or uninstall the corresponding extension.

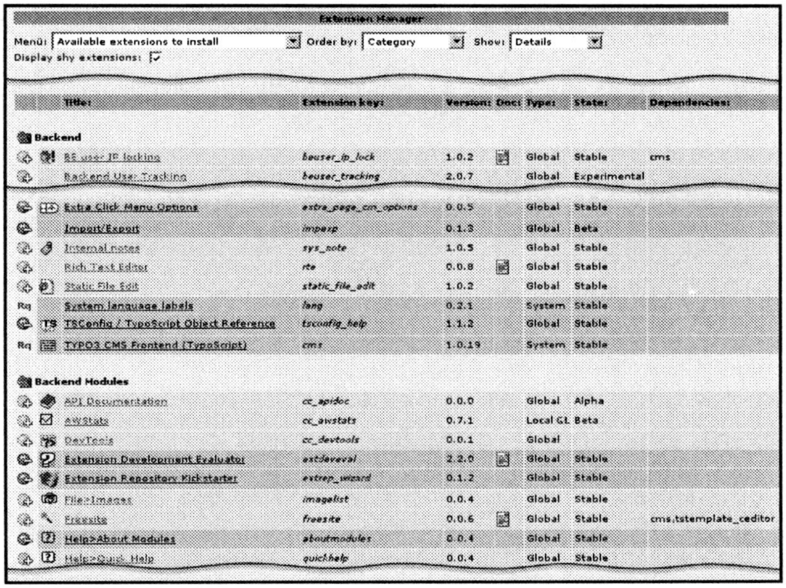

Figure 6.2:

The extension manager shows the available extensions

Each extension is displayed with its name and its own icon. Some of these have a question mark as an icon if the developer of that extension has not yet made its own icon.

The next details displayed are the extension key and version number. In the next column a document icon may appear. This means that an OpenOffice `manual.sxw` file exists in the `doc/` subdirectory of the extension. The documentation can also be obtained from TYPO3.org in the list of extensions.

It is possible for an extension to be installed both globally and locally. Such a double installation is marked in the EM as **Local GL.** In this way, the locally installed extension can be modified to your own requirements, and you can be sure that this will be included in the system, and not the original version.

6.3.2 Importing Extensions from the Repository

Extensions can be imported simply from the Online Repository into your installation. To do this, select the **Import extensions from Online Repository** option in the EM main menu.

Before we look further at transferring extensions from the Repository, we will briefly discuss how an extension package file (*.t3x) under **Upload extension file directly** is transferred to your server. This is done by selecting the T3X file and installation directory, and then transferring the file to the server by clicking on **Upload extension file**. The installation itself corresponds to accepting data from the Repository, and is described below.

You can access the Repository by clicking on **Connect to Online Repository**. A connection is made to the Repository and a list of available extensions is obtained. Also, in the lookup input field, you can specify a key with which you can access special versions of an extension. Such a protected extension version is not public, and is only accessible by specifying the key. This is useful if you want to make an extension available to testers in a development team.

The list obtained from the Repository contains other information apart from the data already mentioned. The first column shows download icons if this extension is not yet available on the local server or if a newer version is available. In the middle column you can compare version numbers. The **Access** column shows if you are the **Owner** of the extension or a **Member**. Members of an extension can download it, even if it is not freely available in the Repository. The various states (locally available or not available, Owner/Member) [3] are also highlighted by table lines in different colors.

[3] Member functions are only present if you have a user account on TYPO3.org and you have entered access data under Settings in the EM.

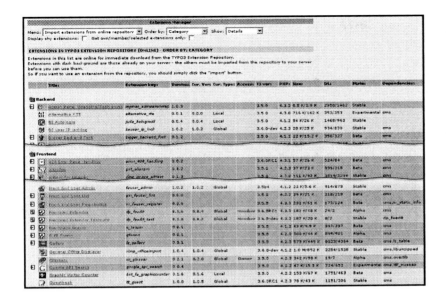

Figure 6.4:

Listing the available extensions in the Repository

In all List Views, you can have so-called "shy extensions" made visible, that is, those that make up the basic package and which are available in most installations. Different List Views can be accessed through the menus **Order by** and **Show**.

If you have decided to download an extension, it is first transferred to your server, but not yet installed. To do this, click on the **+** icon, which is shown in the view after a successful download. Alternatively you can install the extension in the **Available extensions to install** view using the **+** icon.

Details View and Options

If you want to take a closer look at the extension before you download it, click on its title. You will now see a precise overview giving details such as title, author, version, but also the files and database tables it contains.

In the Details View you can select the version to be downloaded. If the option allowGlobalInstall in the $TYPO3_CONF_VARS (Installation Tool) is enabled, you can also select the path to the global extensions in typo3/ext/ for installation. If the option em_alwaysGetOOManual is also enabled, the documentation for the extension is automatically downloaded as well, which would otherwise have to be enabled separately in this view. With the **Include most recent translation** option, you can include all available translations in the extension. This is useful if the developer has not yet included the desired translations, which are made available via the TER, in the current version.

Depending on the extension type and the modules and plugins contained, one or more steps are necessary for the installation. Some extensions can be installed with a single click. For others, you are asked if you want to perform the necessary installation steps, when setting up additional database tables or deleting caches, for example. It is sometimes necessary to make and change settings during the installation. Parameters that can be set are explained either then and there or in the documentation for the extension.

Figure 6.5:

Details View of the extension with the example of the **General Office Displayer**

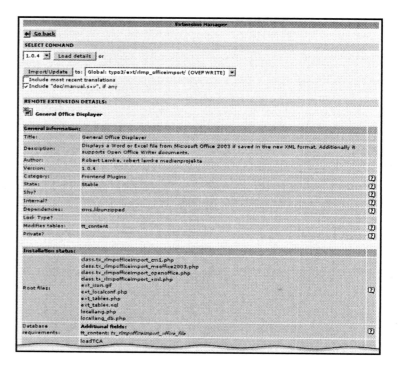

After modules have been installed, however, they are not immediately visible in the back end. For this to happen, the back end must be reloaded, by clicking in your browser on the reload button.

Uninstalling extensions is done in a similar way, by clicking on the green "–" icon. Ensure that database tables required only by this extension are not automatically removed. This is an advantage if you want to keep the data. Over time, however, many unused tables could collect in the database. These can be removed with the installation tool, which has already been introduced.

6.3.3 Extension Kickstarter

The Extension Kickstarter is *the* tool for extension development, enabling the base framework for an extension to be created quickly and simply.

The Kickstarter is stored in a separate extension (Extension Repository Kickstarter:kickstarter); if it is not available in your installation, then first load the extension. If it is installed, the Kickstarter appears as the **Make new extension** menu item in the Extension Manager.

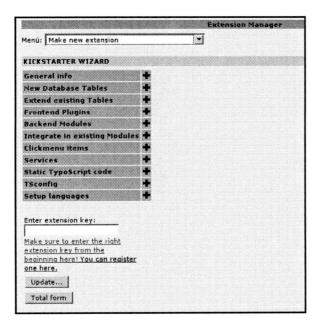

Figure 6.6:

Extension Kickstarter is ready to start a new extension

How to use the Kickstarter and functions of the Extension Manager relevant to developers are described in the next chapter.

7

Extension Development

TYPO3 is a framework for web applications. This framework can be expanded, adjusted, or even completely changed, on the basis of extensions. At its core, TYPO3 is a web-based database management system. This can be seen, for example, by the fact that the CMS is implemented as an extension, that is, it is an application of TYPO3. This separation between core and application reduces complexity and makes it easier to continue developing the system. This is made possible by a defined and structured Extension API. In addition, each extension has its own namespace. Taken together, this prevents conflicts and makes it possible to extend TYPO3 in almost every direction.

The Extension Manager has already been introduced in Chapter 6. We showed what type of extensions exist and how these can be installed online.

In this chapter we want to look at how you can program the various types of extensions (plugins, modules, ...) yourself. To do this you require a solid grounding in PHP, object-oriented programming, and SQL. Even if your knowledge in these areas is not so extensive, you should not be afraid of reading further, because TYPO3 is very well suited as a basis for delving deeper into PHP and SQL. In this case it is recommended, however, that you have documentation to hand that goes into more detail.

We should point out here that this is an introduction to the subject of TYPO3 development, and it can merely provide an overview. Even though the Extension Kickstarter takes over a large part of the work from the developer, it will still be necessary to get to grips occasionally with the documentation. Most sections contain a soft link at the beginning, referring to further literature.

7.1 A Visitor Counter in 20 Minutes

To explain how quickly and easily TYPO3 can be expanded, we are going to program a simple plugin below. Since this is merely to give a general overview, more detailed explanation will not be given in the example.

The example is of a visitor counter, the invention of which probably brought joy to millions of homepage owners, out there in the Web holosphere. The plugin uses a database table to save the status of the counter. The counter should count each visitor exactly once; this is done with the help of the user session, created and managed automatically by TYPO3. This means that a visitor is only counted once, even if he or she calls the same page several times within a session.

Normally a plugin is inserted into a page via an **Insert Plugin** content element and enabled; but we will see that there are other ways of using a plugin.

The plugin should be ready in 20 minutes. So let's get started!

We have called the back end and now select the Extension Kickstarter, which can be reached in the Extension Manager via the **make new extension** entry.

First an extension key must be specified. We will use `user_visitcounter`. The form is then updated, with **Update**.

An extension can contain several elements: plugins, modules, database tables etc. First the **General Info** element is added, which contains general information about the extension under General Info. The form is completed, and a click on **Update** accepts the entry.

The counter needs a database table to be able to count; we create this with **New Database Tables**.

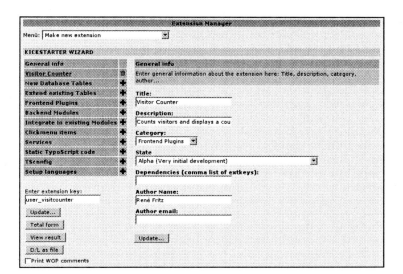

Figure 7.1:

General information on the extension under **General Info**

The table must be given a descriptive name, which is later displayed in the back end. We will call it Visitor Counter. Behind the entry field, the word **[English]** appears. This reminds us that we want to have descriptions in other languages as well. We add the German language to this extension by clicking on **Setup Languages** and selecting **German**.

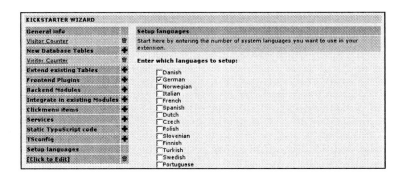

Figure 7.2:

Editing additional languages with the Extension Kickstarter

But the table is not yet finished, and needs further processing. We select the Visitor Counter table from the **New Database Tables** menu item, which is already listed now as a component of this extension. We can also specify a German title now.

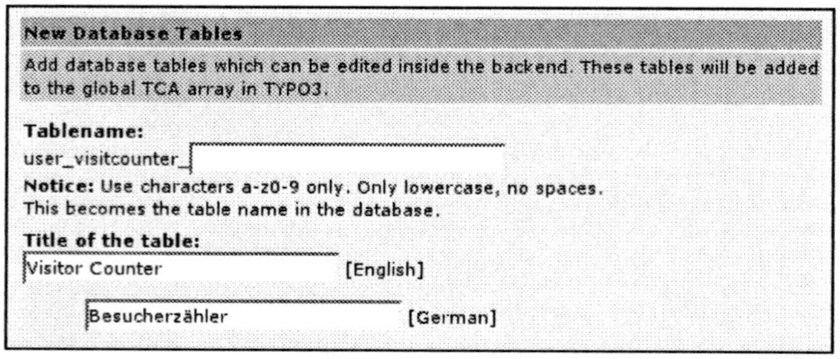

Figure 7.3:

New database table with English and German titles for display in the back end

In addition we add another field to the table, where the counter status will be stored.

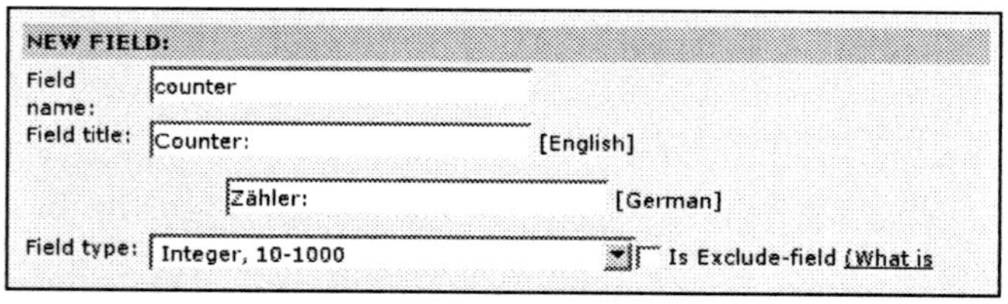

Figure 7.4:

Adding a field to the table

A few options still need to be set, as can be seen from the following figure, and then the table is finished.

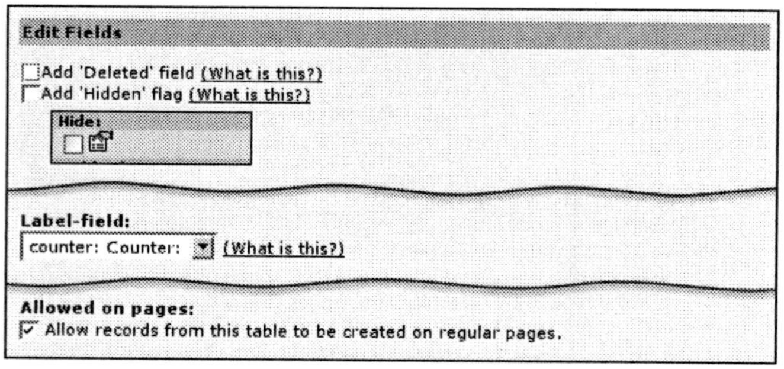

Figure 7.5:

Options in the table differing from default values

Now we insert a plugin to the extension, specify the titles in English and German, and set a few more options.

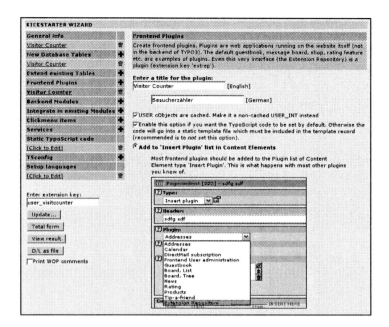

Figure 7.6:

The plugin and other components are added to the extension

Finally we add **Static TypoScript code** and have a look at the result with **View Result**. The extension can then be created in the `typo3conf/ext/user_visitorcounter/` directory, with **WRITE**.

Filename:	Size:	
ext_icon.gif	124	
ext_localconf.php	392	**View**
ext_tables.php	895	**View**
ext_tables.sql	413	**View**
ext_typoscript_editorcfg.txt	1.0 K	**View**
icon_user_visitcounter.gif	135	
locallang_db.php	515	**View**
tca.php	797	**View**
doc/wizard_form.dat	2.1 K	
doc/wizard_form.html	56 K	
pi1/class.user_visitcounter_pi1.php	2.6 K	**View**
pi1/locallang.php	1.1 K	**View**

Author name:
Author email:

Write to location:
Local: typo3conf/ext/user_visitor/ (empty)   ▾   WRITE

Figure 7.7:

The extension is finished and can be generated

Kickstarter creates the entire code for a plugin and the database table. We can install this extension immediately with the Extension Manager, edit the new table in the back end and select the front-end plugin (which will only display example contents, however).

3.39 That's it, for starters, at least. In less than four minutes, the basic framework for the visitor counter can be up and running. But the plugin does not count any visitors yet, of course.

We now move to a PHP development environment and remove the code and files that are not needed for this simple plugin.

The following files should be deleted:

`pi1/locallang.php` and `ext_typoscript_editorcfg.txt`

In the file `ext_localconf.php` the code lines integrating the file `ext_typoscript_editorcfg.txt` are deleted. A file named `ext_typoscript_setup.txt` is created. This will later contain standard TypoScript code for the plugin.

The file `tca.php` contains definitions that are necessary to be able to edit the table in the back end. In Kickstarter we selected the `integer`, `10=1000` type for the `counter` field. This does not quite match what we need, so we will change the field definition as follows:

```
'counter' => Array (
...
  'config' => Array (
    'type' => 'input',
    'size' => '5',
    'max' => '10',
    'eval' => 'int',
    'default' => 0
  )
),
```

5.20 Then we edit the file `pi1/class.user_visitcounter_pi1.php`, which contains the PHP code for the plugin, and remove the example code from Kickstarter. We can now start to implement the counter.

```
require_once(PATH_tslib.'class.tslib_pibase.php');

class user_visitcounter_pi1 extends tslib_pibase {
    var $prefixId = 'user_visitcounter_pi1';
                        // Same as class name
    var $extKey = 'user_visitcounter';
                        // The extension key.

/**
 * Main plugin function
 **/
function main($content,$conf) {
    // We do this, because it's a USER_INT object!
$this->pi_USER_INT_obj=1;
```

The function `main` is later called by the front-end system to create the content for the plugin.

First the variable $table is set; this is needed quite frequently and makes the code reusable.

```
$table = 'user_visitcounter';
```

The counter should create a record on the current page; we leave it to TypoScript to find out the ID of the page through the pid parameter. $pid is set to the current page ID, which is also available via $GLOBALS['TSFE']=>id if this does not work.

```
        // any page id configured?

$pid = intval($this->cObj->stdWrap($conf['pid'],
$conf['pid.']));
        // if not use current page

$pid = $pid ? $pid : $GLOBALS['TSFE']->id;
```

We know the page ID and search for a counter record. If none is found, we create a new array and set the counter to 0.

```
        // search for counter record

$res = $GLOBALS['TYPO3_DB']->exec_SELECTquery('*',
                                                $table,
'pid='.$pid, '', '', 1);
if ($res) {
  $row = $GLOBALS['TYPO3_DB']->sql_fetch_assoc($res);
  } else {
    // initialize a new counter

  $row = array();
  $row['counter'] = 0;
}
```

We now look to see if the user is already known, and if not, the counter is increased by 1. A check is made to see if the extension key exists in the user session, if not, it is set, and the session data is rewritten. This means that the counter counts visitors per session.

```
        // check if this user should be counted

$knownUser = $GLOBALS['TSFE']->fe_user->
                      getKey('ses', $this->extKey);
if (!$knownUser) {
  $GLOBALS['TSFE']->fe_user->setKey('ses',$this->
                                          extKey,1);
  $GLOBALS['TSFE']->fe_user->storeSessionData();

  $row['counter'] += 1;
  }
```

Now the counter record must be updated, or created if it does not exist.

```
// update the counter record

if ($row['uid']) {
    $this->cObj->DBgetUpdate($table, $row['uid'], $row,
                                        'counter', true);
} else {
    $this->cObj->DBgetInsert($table, $pid, $row,
                                        'counter', true);
}
```

To display the counter, we create an instance of `tslib_cObj` [1], which is the main rendering class of the front-end system and will be explained later in more detail. The method `cObjGetSingle()` is used to render the content, causing the TypoScript setup `renderObj` to be passed on. Afterwards the created contents are returned.

```
// render the counter with the TypoScript renderObj

$lCObj = t3lib_div::makeInstance('tslib_cObj');
$lCObj->setParent($this->cObj->data,
                    $this->cObj->currentRecord);
$lCObj->start($row, $table);
$content = $lCObj->cObjGetSingle($conf['renderObj'],
                                    $conf['renderObj.']);

return $this->pi_wrapInBaseClass($content);
    }
}
```

17.04   The following TypoScript setup is inserted into the file `ext_typoscript_setup.txt`, which identifies the page ID and defines the rendering for the counter with `renderObj`:

```
plugin.user_visitcounter_pi1 {
    pid.data = page:uid

    renderObj = COA
    renderObj {
        10 = TEXT
        10.field = counter
        10.noTrimWrap = || |
        20 = TEXT
        20.value = visitors on this page
    }
}
```

19.46 - Finished   Of course, we cut a few corners, since the time for debugging was not

---

[1] Section 7.5.5 explains why an instance is created, instead of $this->cObj being used.

included here. But the example still shows how, with Kickstarter and a bit of experience, you can quickly achieve results.

The special feature of this counter is that it can be configured by TypoScript. This is a general concept in TYPO3, which ensures as high a level of flexibility as possible. With the TypoScript set up, the plugin is both configured and its rendering defined. Both can be changed, without having to make adjustments to the PHP code.

The plugin is configured by defining the page ID on which the counter record should be located, with `pid`. You could just set the current page ID in the PHP code:

```
$pid = $GLOBALS['TSFE']->id;
```

Instead of this, an attempt is made to get an ID via TypoScript:

```
$pid = intval($this->cObj->stdWrap($conf['pid'],
                                   $conf['pid.']));
```

The TS setup of `pid` is passed on to the `stdWrap` method of the `cObj` object. This is the very method that the TypoScript `stdWrap` object provides. If you take a look at the TypoScript reference, you will see what a wide range of options this object has. We will put this to good use.

The following two bits of code are equal in their end result:

```
// PHP:
$pid = $GLOBALS['TSFE']->id;
// TypoScript:
pid.data = page:uid
```

By using TypoScript for the configuration, the plugin can be used in different ways. You can, for example write:

```
pid = 12
```

Here the plugin does not count visitors per page, but visitors for the entire website, by saving the counter status only on the page with the ID=12. Then you should also change the text that the plugin will display. The TS setup necessary for this adjustment would be as follows:

```
plugin.user_visitcounter_pi1 {
  pid = 12
  renderObj.20.value = visitors on this website
}
```

So it is possible, with the help of TypoScript, to change the functionality of plugins to a certain extent (as long as you use this in the PHP code).

You can still make other changes: the counter should display a German text, for example. This can be done by redefining `renderObj.20.value`, or adding the German text as an option.

```
plugin.user_visitcounter_pi1 {
  pid = 12
  renderObj.20.value = visitors on this website
  renderObj.20.lang.de = Besucher auf dieser Website
}
```

If the website is correctly configured for the German language, then the German text is displayed automatically.

```
config.language = de
```

It is somewhat impractical, of course, that although the counter counts visitors for the entire website, the plugin has to be activated on each page with the **Insert Plugin** content element. This can be avoided by inserting the plugin at a suitable point in the site template.

```
page.80 =< plugin.user_visitcounter_pi1
```

The plugin will now be performed on every page.

Because the plugin itself does not actually perform the rendering of the counter, but only passes on the TypoScript setup from `renderObj` to `cObjGetSingle()`, you can use everything that TypoScript has to offer for the output. So, the visitor counter is automatically graphics-capable.

To allow the visitor counter to display the output as shown in the following figure, no change in the PHP code is necessary, just a little TypoScript.

Figure 7.8:

Example counter

```
plugin.user_visitcounter_pi1.renderObj >

plugin.user_visitcounter_pi1.renderObj = IMAGE
plugin.user_visitcounter_pi1.renderObj {
  alttext.field = counter
  file = GIFBUILDER
  file {
    XY = [10.w]+20,27
    backColor = #000000
    10 = TEXT
    10 {
      text.field = counter
      fontSize = 21
      fontFile = fileadmin/Facelift.ttf
      fontColor = #00EE00
      offset = 6,22
    }

    20 = BOX
    20.dimensions = 0,0,200,1
```

```
    20.color = #00EE00
    21 < .20
    21.align = , b
    22 < .20
    22.dimensions = 0,0,1,40
    23 < .22
    23.align = r
  }
}
```

Note that the visitor counter is used here in principle just as an example. There are certainly better visitor counters than this one. Creating the counter with a graphic output was also demonstrated only to make clear the connection between PHP and TypoScript. If the counter had really been used in this way, the server would have generated a total of 135,487 graphics, which would need to be deleted at some point.

7.2 Extension Wizard: Kickstarter

As the example of the visitor counter has already illustrated, the Extension Kickstarter creates a complete framework, to which the actual functionality has to be added. All extensions created by Kickstarter can be installed immediately, and you already have a "Hello World" output. A saved extension can be reloaded and edited by Kickstarter, but code already entered manually will be lost when saving, since Kickstarter is not an editor for existing extensions, but is only meant to help you get started. Before we can start creating an extension, an extension key must be created.

7.2.1 Defining an Extension Key

Every extension has its own unique namespace, defined by the extension key. This key is a short string and can contain the characters a-z, 0-9, _. There are two types of extensions, which are differentiated by the key: on the one hand, normal extensions, which can also be published to the TYPO3 Extension Repository (TER), and on the other, project-specific extensions, which cannot be uploaded to the Repository. These are defined by the prefix user_ in the extension key. Normal extensions can have any key they want, but may not start with tx or u.

Softlink 104717

While project-specific extension keys with the prefix user_ can be named in any way you want, this is not the case for normal extensions. These must be registered for them to be unique (see soft link). After registration you have ten days in which to write the extension to the TER, otherwise the key is deleted. If you have not managed to complete your extension in this time, you can still upload it to the Repository, so that the key is not lost. After registration, the extension is initially marked as **Members only**, which means: after uploading, this extension cannot be seen by others unless they are registered as members.

It is a good idea to choose a descriptive name for the extension key, one which is as short as possible. It should be descriptive, so that you (and others) can recognize from the name of the extension directory what type of extension is involved, and short, because the program code uses this key as a namespace. A long key name would mean long designators in the PHP, HTML, and CSS code. Underscores may be used, but are removed by Kickstarter from certain designators, which can cause confusion. So the simplest way is to avoid using underscores in key names. Once you have defined an extension key, it is entered in Kickstarter in the entry field at the bottom left.

7.2.2 Kickstarter Components

An extension is shown opposite containing all the components that can be generated with Kickstarter. You can also see which files were created in doing so.

Figure 7.9:

Example extension using all possible components that Kickstarter can create

Individual components can be added with the **+** icons, and removed with the trashcan icon. If an extension contains several components of the same sort, the directories are numbered accordingly: mod1/, mod2/.

The individual components are:

General info

> Basically each extension must contain the **General info** component. This defines general information on the extension, which will be displayed in the TER and in the Extension Manager (EM).

New Database Tables

New database tables are created with this. With the help of a wizard, fields can be created and field types (string/entry field, integer/checkbox etc.) be defined.

Extend existing Tables

Existing database tables can be extended with this component, and the same wizard functions are available for field definitions.

Frontend Plugins

This adds a front-end plugin to the extension. Plugins can extend the front end in different ways. Examples of this are new content elements, menu functions or FE applications. Kickstarter provides a selection of the most common plugins.

Backend Modules

This option adds a back-end module to the extension. This can be inserted into various main modules such as **Web**, **File**, or **Tools**.

Integrate in existing Modules

Some modules can be extended by submodule functions. Kickstarter supports this for a series of **Web** modules as well as for the **User | Tasks** module.

Clickmenu items

Entries can be generated in the context menu with this.

Services

Creates a service component.

Static TypoScript code

TypoScript can be added to the extension with this component. After the extension has been installed, the TS code is active systemwide.

TSConfig

PAGE and **USER TSConfig** can be added to the extension with this.

Setup languages

Both plugins and modules contain support for multiple languages. In Kickstarter, texts (field identifiers, titles, etc.) can be defined in many different languages if the languages are added with this component.

7.2.3 Extension Structure

As already described, extensions consist of a number of files and possibly, directories. These have specific functions determined by their filename, or they are included by the Extension API.

Softlink **099886**

Since an extension is normally created with Kickstarter, and will therefore already contain all the files and directories in the correct form, we shall only give an overview below of their contents and functions. Where necessary, details are explained in the examples. In addition we would like to point out the soft link to the documentation.

ext_emconf.php

All general information and metadata on the extension is saved here, generally data from the **General info** Kickstarter component.

ext_localconf.php

For each request, this file is included both in the front end and in the back end, and can contain all configurations (`$TYPO3_CONF_VARS`), as well as `typo3conf/localconf.php`. In addition, TypoScript can be included through the Extension API.

ext_tables.php

Database tables for use in the back end are configured here, and plugins and modules are included through the Extension API. The relevant code is generated by Kickstarter and only rarely needs to be modified.

ext_tables.sql

This file contains SQL data for the table definition. The definition is recognized and evaluated by the EM and the Installation Tool. In this way the EM and the Installation Tool can recognize if a table needs to be created or updated.

ext_tables_static+adt.sql

Contains SQL table definitions, including data; this is intended for static data, as can be found in the `Static Info Tables` extension, for example. This contains data on countries, languages, and currencies. The abbreviation "adt" stands for "add drop table" and refers to the `-add-drop-table` option, which is used when the table is dumped with the `mysqldump` tool so that corresponding SQL statements can be placed in front of the dump.

```
DROP TABLE IF EXISTS static_countries;
```

The table definition itself must also exist in `ext_tables.sql` for it to be correctly recognized.

ext_typoscript_*.txt

Contains TypoScript code that is globally integrated, so that it is not just available through template records (see `static/`).

ext_conf_template.txt

This file holds definitions of extension configuration options if needed. Based on these definitions, these options are displayed for the user in the EM.

icon.gif

Icon files for the extension, database tables, plugins, modules, etc.

locallang*.php

These files contain texts in different languages for localising plugins, modules, and TCA definitions.

class.*.php

Contains PHP classes, for plugins or submodule functions.

class.ext_update.php

Makes functions available for an update of the extension in the EM; an example can be found in the `newloginbox` extension.

conf.php

With this file a module is configured and inserted into the back end.

index.php

The file `index.php` is generally the main script of a module.

pi1/

The directory containing scripts and data for a plugin.

cm1/

This directory contains context menu scripts and data.

mod1/

This is a directory for a module. It includes `conf.php` and `index.php`.

modfunc1/

> Contains scripts and data for submodule functions.

static/

> This directory contains TypoScript template files that are inserted through the Extension API, and then they are available in template records, in a similar way to static templates.

sv1/

> Directory containing services.

res/

> Directory for any kind of data ("resources")

doc/

> Directory for the documentation; also contains the file `wizard_form.dat`, in which the entire Kickstarter definition is located. With this information a new extension can be created by Kickstarter, using this extension as a basis.

7.2.4 Basic Rules of Extension Development

Components

As already described, an extension may contain several components. But not all combinations make sense, for example an extension should only contain the components of one application. An example of an extension with several components could be a hotel-booking extension, with database tables, a plugin to display data in the front end and to allow bookings, as well as a back-end module for the display and administration of reservations. It makes little sense to add a plugin to this extension showing the current news from your local tourist office. This is a separate functionality, and should also be a separate extension. The following rule of thumb applies: unless it really makes sense to have all components installed together in one extension, then they should be split up over several extensions.

Documentation

Even though it is certainly not always possible to include complete documentation with an extension, it should at least contain a manual (`doc/manual.sxw`) with the section "Introduction". This section should consist of a description of the function, and if possible a screenshot. There should also be a short description of the type of extension and how it is called or integrated. For a module, this would be a note about where the module can be found after its installation. For a plugin, it should be made clear if this is a new content element, for example, or if it must be integrated into a page using **Insert Plugin**.

In general this description does not need to be particularly long and should only provide an overview. Since the "Introduction" section is displayed in the Details View for the extension in the TER on TYPO3.org, you can already get an idea of the extension from there. Using this information, you may decide that the extension is suitable for the purpose you have in mind. For someone who is interested in a particular extension, this may save a great deal of time spent trying things out.

Please note that a manual that is uploaded to the Repository for the first time, as described in section 7.3.5, *Publishing Documentation*, first has to be initialized. Otherwise the "Introduction" section will not be recognized.

Categories

It should be pointed out that extensions have to be sorted into the correct categories. These are the basic categories on the one hand (back end, back-end modules, front end, etc.), which are used for sorting in the EM, and on the other the application-related ones in the TER, which have to be assigned to the extension on TYPO3.org (see section 7.3.4, *TER Extension Management*).

While the basic categories help more to keep a clear picture in the EM, categories in the TER help to find suitable extensions for a specific purpose.

Publishing

At this point it should be mentioned once again that all code used in the TYPO3 framework (which is what an extension you have written yourself is) is automatically subject to the GPL license. This does not mean that you have to publish your extension. But bear in mind that several years of work have been invested in this project, and that every contribution that helps TYPO3's progress is in your own interests as well.

7.3 Extension Management for Developers

7.3.1 Functions of the Extension Manager

The Extension Manager provides a number of interesting functions that are very useful in the administration of your own extensions. These functions are available in the Details View of an extension. You can reach the Details View by clicking on the title of an extension in the List View of the EM. A menu is available there containing various functions.

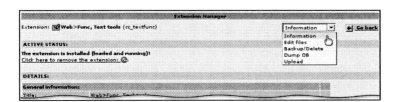

Figure 7.10:

Functions in the extended Details View of the EM

Information

Detailed information on the extension is listed here. Apart from general details such as title, description, and version number, information is also listed on the files and database tables contained. Where appropriate, any errors within this extension are also shown. These could be violations to the extension namespace, for example, or missing XCLASS definitions (see section 7.10, *Modifying and Extending XCLASS Classes*). Relevant comments are marked in red.

Edit files

Here you can edit files of the extension online; this can sometimes be useful to correct small errors on the web server.

Backup/Delete

A number of functions are gathered together under this menu item, as shown in the following figure. The following sections belong to this item.

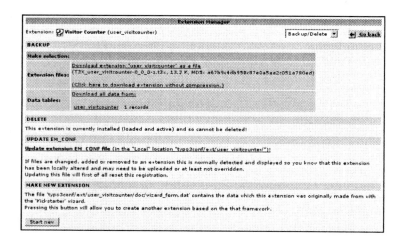

Figure 7.11:

Functions of
Backup/Delete *in*
the EM

Backup | Extension files:

It is certainly very useful to be able to download the extension as a T3X file. This package contains the entire extension, and can be installed again with the EM. In this way, extensions can be sent simply via e-mail, without having to pack all the necessary files by hand into a zip archive. Especially on Windows servers, the PHP extension for (de-)compressing data is frequently not available. For this reason, some extension packages may remain unpacked. You can distinguish the packages from the `-z` at the end of the filename (`*-z.t3x`), which identifies a compressed package.

Backup Data tables

With this function you can download the database table of the extension, if it exists.

Delete

This function deletes the complete extension from the server, but only if it is not currently activated.

Update EM_CONF

With this you can update the `ext_emconf.php` file of an extension. Bookkeeping, so to speak, is carried out in this file on the versions of the files in the extension. This helps to check if files have been changed, thus making it necessary to update the version in the TER. This is shown accordingly in the overview under **Information**. Before you transfer an extension to the TER you should call this function.

Make new extension

This function allows you to use the extension as a template, and to start a new extension in Kickstarter. There the extension key can be changed and a new extension be assembled as required. But this does not mean that the functionality of this extension is taken over, because Kickstarter creates a new framework where there is no manually written code for the extension currently selected. This function is useful, for example, for creating a new extension with an identical or similar database table to an existing one.

Dump DB

You can use this to update the database definition in `ext_tables.sql`. This is useful if you have made changes in the table definition with `phpMyAdmin`, for example, and want to include these in the extension. Bear in mind that the TCA definitions of the table may need to be adjusted.

Upload

With this function the extension can be uploaded to the TER. This is described in the following sections.

7.3.2 TER Account

Before you can upload extensions to the TER on TYPO3.org, you need to set up an account on TYPO3.org (see soft link). Enter your user name and password in the EM now under **Settings**. By the way, the EM, with only this access data, can display extensions for which you are a member (**Members only**).

Softlink **900162**

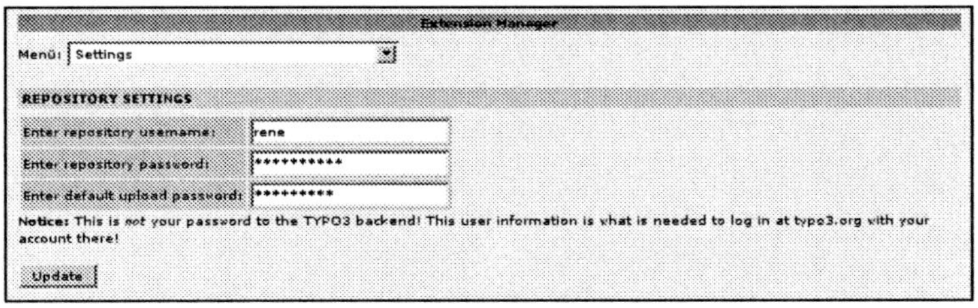

Figure 7.12:

Setting access data for the Repository in the EM

To upload extensions, a password is required, which may be different for each extension. If you frequently use the same password, you can enter a standard password in **default upload password**. The password is defined in the extension key registration, but can be changed again later on.

7.3.3 Transferring an Extension to the TER

To transfer an extension to the TER, you must click on the title of the required extension, in a List View in the Extension Manager, to reach the Details View. Then select the **Upload** menu and you will see the display as shown in the following figure.

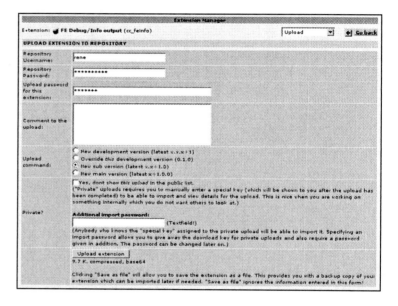

Figure 7.13:

Preparing an extension for upload to the online Repository

Normally you only have to select what procedure is to be used with the version number of the extension. This can be incremented automatically by the upload. But increasing the last number of the version number does not lead to it being displayed as a new version in the TER or the EM. This can be useful if only slight modifications need to be made in the documentation, for example, and a new download would not be worthwhile for most users. If an error has been corrected, however, you should select the middle number to increase the version number.

If you have chosen a special upload password for the selected extension, you must enter this now. Otherwise the **default upload password** from **Settings** will be used.

If an extension is transferred for the first time to the TER, it is marked as **Members only**, and is thus only accessible for registered members. The **Private** option offers a way of providing the current version of your extension with a password. This is very practical if you want to have a new version of an already accessible extension tested by selected people, without making it publicly available.

Clicking on **Upload extension** transfers the extension. When the procedure is complete, a corresponding message appears. Since the version number in the Repository may have increased, this should also be done in the local version, of course. The update must still be confirmed after the version number has been changed. The transfer to the TER is then finished.

7.3.4 TER Extension Management

On TYPO3.org you can manage your extensions in the TER. To do this, you must first log in. If you now select the **Extensions** main menu item, you can access your own extensions via the additional menu item, **My extension keys**.

Softlink **156502**

An overview will appear, as shown in the following figure. This can be sorted according to various criteria, and contains some statistical data. If you click on an entry in the list, a form appears with some details on the extension and some options for settings.

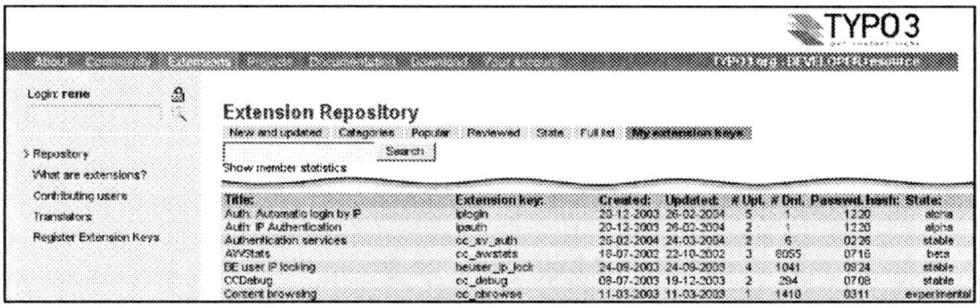

Figure 7.14:

Overview of your own extensions on TYPO3.org

Here you can change the name and description of the extension. The extension can also be sorted into a number of additional categories, which can then be found in the **Categories** view of the TER. The versions uploaded until now are listed. You can delete old versions; this should be done regularly, to free memory space in the Repository.

If the extension contains `locallang` language files, then there is an overview of translations into other languages. After this the contents directory of the documentation can be configured. More information on this is given in the next section.

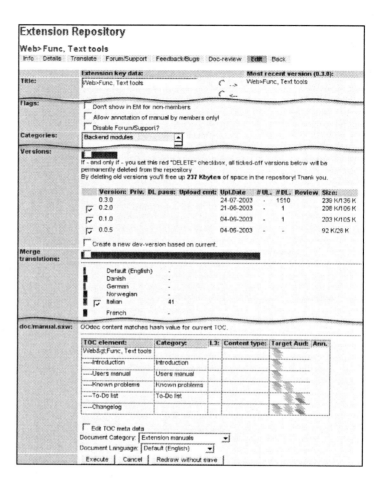

Figure 7.15:

Detailed information and settings for an Extension

Members Only

An important function consists of restricting access to extensions only to members. This is very useful during the development phase, to allow selected testers to obtain beta versions. As mentioned above, every extension is initially marked as Members only. To add members to an extension, enter their names, or alternatively the TYPO3.org user names, in the entry field under **Lookup users**. If you send off the form, all the relevant users are listed, from whom you can then choose.

To make an extension generally available, that is, to publish it in the TER, the **Members only** option must be deactivated. This cannot be undone, however. Once an extension is published, it remains so. Individual versions of an already published extension can be hidden if they are uploaded with the **Private** option, which makes them accessible only to those with the appropriate password.

7.3.5 Publishing Documentation

Documentation should be available for every extension in the specified format. But this does not mean that extensions without documentation should not be published at all. Where there is doubt, it is more in the spirit of the project to publish an undocumented but substantial work, rather than to let too much time pass by trying to reach the required standard.

The documentation can be found in the extension in the file `manual.sxw` of the `doc/` subdirectory. This file contains the manual in the OpenOffice format and is uploaded with the extension to the TER. This system of documentation is used not only for extensions with modules and plugins, but also for general documentation. Pure documentation extensions only contain the files `ext_emconf.php` and `ext_icon.gif`, apart from the file `doc/manual.sxw`.

If you do not yet have OpenOffice, you should install it now (download from `http://www.openoffice.org`). it is a very powerful Office package and is freely available for the Unix/Linux, OS X, and Windows platforms. The advantage of the OpenOffice format lies in its openness. The format is documented and is available as XML. This makes it easy for other software to read and convert it. It is also the reason that documentation is displayed within the website on TYPO3.org automatically after the extension has been uploaded.

In order for this to function smoothly, several requirements must be fulfilled. First the manual template is downloaded from TYPO3.org (see soft link) and saved in the `doc/` directory as `manual.sxw`. The template already contains sections with explanations.

Softlink **167050**

If you think it will be useful, you can add new sections to the documentation. Since not every section makes sense for every extension, a manual does not have to take over every section of the template. At the end of the template there is another section containing general hints on creating documentation with OpenOffice, which should be deleted entirely. This is a short version of the "Writing documentation for TYPO3" guide (see soft link).

Softlink **600297**

If your documentation is finished, you can also transfer it, by uploading the extension to the TER. It is advisable to at least include the "Introduction" section as an overview of the functionality of the extension. After the first upload of the documentation—or if you have added new sections, you should initialize or update the table of contents on TYPO3.org. This is done by calling the Details View for the extension in the Repository and selecting the **Edit TOC metadata** option in the **doc/manual.sxw** section. After you have sent off the form, the table of contents can be arranged. The sections from the template are recognized automatically. The language in which the documentation is written must be assigned accordingly. Even though the standard language for documentation in the TYPO3 project is English, documentation can also be written in other languages.

For each section you can also define the target group to which this will be of interest: editors, administrators, or developers. This is done by selecting the icons with variously highlighted layers. You have probably noticed that this is the TYPO3 logo. These levels symbolize the three user roles; the first level (closest to the surface) represents the editor, the middle one, the administrator, and the lowest level (closest to the core), the developer.

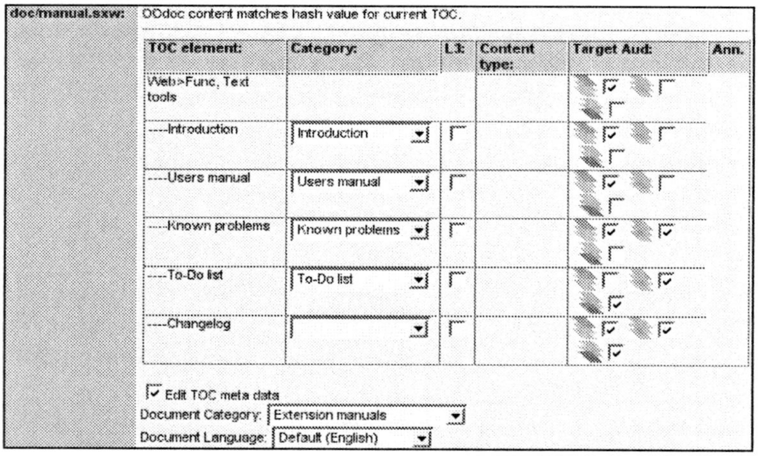

Figure 7.17:

Editing the content structure of an extension manual

7.4 The TYPO3 Framework

With its architecture, TYPO3 represents a framework that can be expanded very efficiently via extensions through its own developments. The modularity of the framework allows the principles of the architecture to be maintained, despite the high level of functionality. This capacity for expansion, which can be used quickly with the help of the *Extension*

Kickstarter, has already found many supporters, as can be seen from the large number of publicly available extensions. The synergy effect caused through the mutual use of functions that are made available by the core of the system and other extensions, helps new developments to achieve a significantly higher level of implementation compared to stand-alone solutions.

We will provide an overview of the TYPO3 framework below. This includes concepts, data models, core functions, and general notes on programming in the framework. Special observations on the framework, from the perspective of front-end and back-end programming, are made in further sections.

To give an overview does not mean to replace the existing documentation and reference—which wouldn't make sense anyway. You still need to look in the reference material to examine detailed functionality and options, but we believe that the overview will guide you to the right entry points into the system.

7.4.1 Framework Structure

TYPO3 is not monolithic, but has a modular structure. So much so, that both the front end and back end can be replaced or removed. Even though more than 99 percent of TYPO3 installations are used as a CMS, the system is primarily a database management system, based on Web technologies.

The core of TYPO3 is essentially defined by a database model and corresponding access functions in `class.t3lib_tcemain.php` (TCE). In this model, any database tables whatsoever can be organized in a type of directory structure—similar to a file system. The administration of users and user permissions is already part of the basic system.

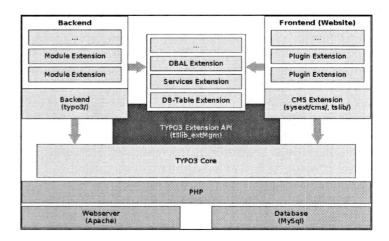

The CMS uses this data model for the administration of page structures with contents. This means that the front end and the accompanying database tables (tt_content, ...) and page types (**Extended, Not in the menu,** ...) represent an application (extension) of the TYPO3 framework. It is quite possible not even to install the CMS front end, and to implement an Intranet bookkeeping software, for example, on the basis of the TYPO3 back end.

Another scenario is a specialized high-performance front end, which is not structured on the TypoScript technique, but creates output (HTML, XML, ...) directly.

But even the back end is replaceable, as has been proven in practice. If you have not been using TYPO3 for very long, you will probably not yet know the *Classic Backend*. This back end was quite an impressive JavaScript application, but was admittedly a little bit slow and difficult to maintain.

As you already know, TYPO3 can be expanded simply with the help of extensions. Even the CMS itself is an extension. Seen from the framework extensions can basically be divided into five categories:

- Based only on the core
- Based on the standard back end (typo3/)
- Based on the CMS front end (sysext/cms/)
- Based on a different back end
- Based on a different front end

The first three categories are also frequently mixed with each other, for example an extension with a database table (core) and a suitable plugin (CMS) for display.

The last two categories are much more seldom, since TYPO3 is normally used as a CMS with standard front end and back end.

7.4.2 Coding Guidelines

Before we take a closer look at the framework, the *Coding Guidelines* for the TYPO3 project should be briefly introduced. They will be particularly helpful to you if you are used to embedding PHP in HTML documents, because this concept is hardly ever used in TYPO3.

Softlink **485098**

So code in the following form is *not* used in TYPO3:

```
<?php for ($a=1;$a<=$count;$a++) { ?>
  <input type="file" name="upload_<?php echo $a ?>"
                     size="50" /><br />';
<?php } ?>
```

Instead of embedding PHP code in HTML, this is done exactly the other way round in the TYPO3 project:

```
for ($a=1;$a<=$count;$a++) {
  $code.= '<input type="file" name="upload_'.$a.'"
                     size="50" /><br />';
}
...
echo $code
```

This procedure is perhaps nothing new to you: especially in smaller projects, the first variation is still frequently used, although the second is much more clearly written, and even runs faster.

In general, emphasis is placed in the TYPO3 project on meeting the following criteria for PHP and HTML code:

- XHTML (transitional) and CSS compatibility

- Use of simple quotation marks for strings

- Use of `htmlspecialchars()`, `$GLOBALS['TYPO3_DB']->quoteStr()` and `intval()` to prevent cross-site scripting attacks

- Full documentation of classes and functions with Javadoc/PHPDoc comments

Almost the entire TYPO3 code is encapsulated in classes. There are hardly any global functions and only a very limited number of global variables. This convention must also be followed in extensions, because only in this way can it be guaranteed that the system will still be secure and stable when several dozen extensions are installed on it. Most classes are also instantiated as objects, but there are exceptions, such as `class.t3lib_div.php`. Here the `t3lib_div` class only serves as a container or namespace for the functions contained in it.

More detailed information on the coding guidelines can be obtained under the soft link for this section. Please keep in mind that the code formating in this book does not stick to the guidelines strictly due to limited printing space. All examples can be downloaded and are well formated.

7.4.3 Directory Structure

Below is an overview of the TYPO3 directory structure, because a quick look at the source code can often quickly clarify unanswered questions in extension development.

The overview refers only to directories that contain code or which are interesting in other ways, and has been shortened accordingly.

```
t3lib/
t3lib/gfx/
t3lib/stddb/
tslib -> typo3/sysext/cms/tslib
typo3/
typo3/t3lib -> ../t3lib
typo3/install/
typo3/ext/
typo3/mod/
typo3/sysext/
typo3/sysext/cms/
typo3/sysext/cms/tslib/
typo3/sysext/lang/
```

Tthere are three basic directories: `t3lib/`, `tslib/`, and `typo3/`.

t3lib

The t3lib/ directory basically contains `class.t3lib_*.php` files, containing PHP classes. Some of these are core functionalities, but there are also base classes for modules or services. Other classes in turn contain useful functions that can be used by both front-end and back-end applications. The next section, *Libraries*, provides an overview.

```
t3lib/
   class.gzip_encode.php
   class.t3lib_befunc.php
   class.t3lib_div.php
   class.t3lib_extmgm.php
```

```
class.t3lib_extobjbase.php
class.t3lib_iconworks.php
class.t3lib_scbase.php
class.t3lib_svbase.php
...
class.t3lib_xml.php
config_default.php
```

The file `config_default.php` contains the default configuration, which can be adjusted in the file `typo3conf/localconf.php` with the `$TYPO3_CONF_VARS` configuration array variable.

```
jsfunc.evalfield.js
jsfunc.menu.js
jsfunc.updateform.js
jsfunc.validateform.js
```

The JavaScript files, for example, contain functions for checking the entries of `TCEForms` (back-end forms).

```
thumbs.php
```

To generate thumbnails, `thumb.php` is used in the `src` attribute of `<img>` tags.

```
gfx/
```

This directory contains all the icons and graphics used by TYPO3. These can be adjusted with the help of skins.

```
stddb/
    load_ext_tables.php
    tables.php
    tables.sql
    tbl_be.php
```

A number of fundamental database tables are defined here, but not the tables of the CMS.

tslib

This directory is a symbolic link to the CMS extension and is described later in this section in more detail.

```
tslib -> typo3/sysext/cms/tslib
```


typo3

The back end is located in this directory, as well as the Installation Tool and the extension directories `ext/` and `sysext/`.

```
typo3/
  alt_clickmenu.php
  alt_db_navframe.php
  alt_doc.php
  ...
  init.php
  md5.js
  stylesheet.css
  tce_db.php
  tce_file.php
  template.php
  wizard_rte.php
  wizard_table.php
  wizard_tsconfig.php
```

The files in this directory contain a number of scripts and classes, as well as JavaScript and CSS files representing the basic functions of the back end.

```
install/
```

This is where the Installation Tool can be found, which is normally called via the URL, with the amendment .../typo3/install/.

```
mod/
  doc/
  file/
  help/
  tools/
    em/
  user/
  web/
```

A number of back-end modules and their conf.php files are located in the mod/ directory. The module scripts themselves are frequently in the typo3/ directory. Normally these should be found as an extension in the ext/ directory; this is not the case here, for historical reasons. New modules are implemented as extensions in all cases.

```
ext/
  aboutmodules/
  ...
  wizard_sortpages/
```

Global extensions are installed in the ext/ directory. In general these are the ones which are supplied with TYPO3 and which to a large extent contain back-end modules.

```
sysext/
```

The sysext/ directory contains system extensions. These cannot normally be uninstalled with the EM. An update with the EM is possible if the `em_systemInstall` option is set in the `$TYPO3_CONF_VARS` (Installation Tool).

```
cms/
    ext_tables.php
    ext_tables.sql
    locallang_tca.php
    locallang_ttc.php
    tbl_cms.php
    tbl_tt_content.php
```

The CMS extension defines additional tables with the above files, as well as new fields and page types in the `pages` table.

```
tslib/
    class.tslib_content.php
    class.tslib_fe.php
    class.tslib_fetce.php
    class.tslib_feuserauth.php
    class.tslib_gifbuilder.php
    class.tslib_menu.php
    class.tslib_pagegen.php
    class.tslib_pibase.php
    class.tslib_search.php
    index_ts.php
    pagegen.php
    publish.php
    showpic.php
```

The `tslib/` directory contains the front end and the code for generating HTML pages for the website. Classes from `t3lib/` are also used here.

```
lang/
    lang.php
    locallang_core.ar.php
    locallang_core.bg.php
    locallang_core.br.php
    locallang_core.ch.php
    locallang_core.cz.php
    locallang_core.de.php
```

The `lang` system extension implements multi-language capability for the back end in the file `lang.php`. Individual `locallang` files each contain translations for various core functions and standard modules.

7.4.4 Libraries

Typo3 provides a series of PHP classes that can be used in your own projects. Apart from the front-end libraries, located in `tslib/`, and some back-end classes in the `typo3/` directory, all other libraries are to be found in `t3lib/`.

Softlink **569519**

441

While the special front-end and back-end libraries are explained in the following sections, we will first present an overview of the classes in t3lib/.

You should remember here that not all classes in t3lib/ are intended to be used in your own projects. This lies on the one hand in the fact that core classes that should not be accessed directly are also located in this directory; and on the other hand, classes can be found here that have been moved here from standard modules. Although these classes are available for your own use, they are not really a part of the API, and may change in the future. A rule of thumb is that classes whose API documentation is provided by the ExtDevEval extension are part of the official API.

The Basic API

t3lib_extMgm

ExtensionAPI

Example: t3lib_extMgm::extPath('myextkey')

t3lib_DB

Database abstraction that is available as an object via $GLOBALS['TYPO3_DB']

t3lib_pageSelect

Page functions that are available in the front end in the object $GLOBALS['TSFE']->sys_page

Backend

t3lib_BEfunc

A collection of useful back end functions.

Example: t3lib_BEfunc::deleteClause('pages')

t3lib_iconWorks

Generates icons for use in back end modules and in the page tree

t3lib_clipboard

Implements the clipboard for back end modules

Base Classes

TYPO3 provides the following base classes for modules, submodule functions, services, and RTE implementations:

t3lib_SCbase

> Back-end module base class

t3lib_extobjbase

> Submodule function base class

t3lib_rteapi

> RTE base class

t3lib_svbase

> Services base class

Miscellaneous

t3lib_div

> General function collection for BE and FE

t3lib_exec

> Generates platform-independent calls for external applications, which can then be run with `exec()`

t3lib_cs

> Converts texts to different character encodings

Tree View, Page Tree, Directory Tree

t3lib_treeView

t3lib_pageTree extends t3lib_treeView

t3lib_browseTree extends t3lib_treeView

t3lib_folderTree extends t3lib_treeView

These classes generate the page tree in the navigation area of the back end, for example. At the same time they can also be used to represent a tree of any database tables, or to collect their data, as is shown in the example **Tools | Last Changes**.

TCEForms

t3lib_TCEmain

t3lib_transferData

t3lib_loadDBGroup

t3lib_TCEforms

t3lib_TCEforms_FE extends t3lib_TCEforms

The TCE (TYPO3 Core Engine) and TCEForms, which form the core of data manipulation in the database (TCE) and their data processing in forms (TCEForms), are implemented by the above classes.

Authentication

t3lib_userAuth:

t3lib_userAuthGroup extends t3lib_userAuth

t3lib_beUserAuth extends t3lib_userAuthGroup

t3lib_tsfeBeUserAuth extends t3lib_beUserAuth

In the *Auth classes, user authentication takes place for the front end and back end (beUserAuth).

TypoScript

t3lib_TStemplate

t3lib_tsparser_ext extends t3lib_TStemplate

t3lib_tsStyleConfig extends t3lib_tsparser_ext

t3lib_TSparser

t3lib_matchCondition

The above classes implement the TypoScript parser and accompanying functions.

E-mail

t3lib_htmlmail.

t3lib_formmail extends t3lib_htmlmail

t3lib_dmailer extends t3lib_htmlmail

t3lib_readmail

These classes contain functions for sending, reading, and processing e-mail (text and HTML). The **Direct Mail** module is based on the above classes.

HTML

t3lib_parsehtml

t3lib_parsehtml_proc extends t3lib_parsehtml

These are classes for processing HTML code, and are also used in connection with the RTE.

Others

t3lib_xml

> Generates XML from records

t3lib_diff

> Makes visible the differences between two texts

t3lib_syntaxhl

> Generates source code highlighting, e.g. Flexform XML and possibly other formats

t3lib_div

At this point the `t3lib_div` class will again be introduced separately, since it has an extensive collection of functions and is used very frequently by extensions. For this reason we recommend that you study the API documentation for the class. The following function groups are contained in the `t3lib_div` class:

- Processing of GET and POST data
- String functions
- Array functions
- HTML and XML processing
- File functions
- Debug output functions
- System information
- Special TYPO3 functions

7.4.5 Extension API

All important interfaces for expanding TYPO3 are gathered together via *Softlink* **915540** the Extension API. The API is available after system initialization via the `t3lib_extMgm` class, both in the front end and back end.

The Extension API provides functions for the following tasks:

- Determination of absolute and relative files paths of extensions
- Extension of the TCA (*Table Configuration Array*)
- Registration of modules
- Registration of TSConfig
- Registration and administration of services
- Registration of plugins
- Registration of TypoScript

At this point we will choose not to introduce the API in great detail, as corresponding extension API calls for integrating an extension into the system are automatically generated by the Extension Kickstarter. You can obtain the API documentation, for example, using the **Tools | ExtDevEval** module.

As an example, we will briefly introduce the following functions, as they frequently occur in plugins and modules. All the functions have the `$key` parameter in common, in which the extension key is passed whose data is to be determined. In addition you should note that the `t3lib_extMgm` class is not instantiated, so that its functions can be called directly.

Example:

```
$extPath = t3lib_extMgm::extPath('myextkey');
```

function isLoaded($key, $exitOnError=0)

Checks whether an extension is installed; this is useful, since the functions which follow it will terminate with an error if the extension specified is not installed. This function will also terminate with an error if the `$exitOnError` parameter is set to `true`.

function extPath($key, $script='')

This function returns the absolute path to the extension. If required, a file name can be passed on and appended to the path in `$script`.

function extRelPath($key)

Determines the relative path from the extension to the back-end directory (`TYPO3_mainDir`, `typo3/`) and returns this

function siteRelPath($key)

> Supplies the relative path for the website directory, relative to the extension

Please remember that determining extension paths requires more time than simply accessing variables. For this reason we recommend that you save a path in a variable, once it has been determined, and use this variable if the path is frequently used.

7.4.6 Database Structure

The database design of TYPO3 is kept relatively simple. As a database professional and SQL guru you would probably have several suggestions for improvement. There are two reasons that explain the structure of the TYPO3 database: on the one hand, it is based on a pragmatic approach, as is the rest of TYPO3; on the other hand this database was developed at a time when MySQL could not handle *subselects* or *unions*, for example. This means that TYPO3 uses a concept in which logic is implemented as little as possible in the database, and this is done instead in PHP.

Softlink **641730**

Even though TYPO3 supports MM relations, text fields are used now and again with comma-separated ID lists. People may argue about this procedure, but frequently no great advantage is gained, from the perspective of programming logic, in using MM relations here. You can of course use any relations you want in your own applications. but for these to be supported when processing records in the back end, additional work may be necessary.

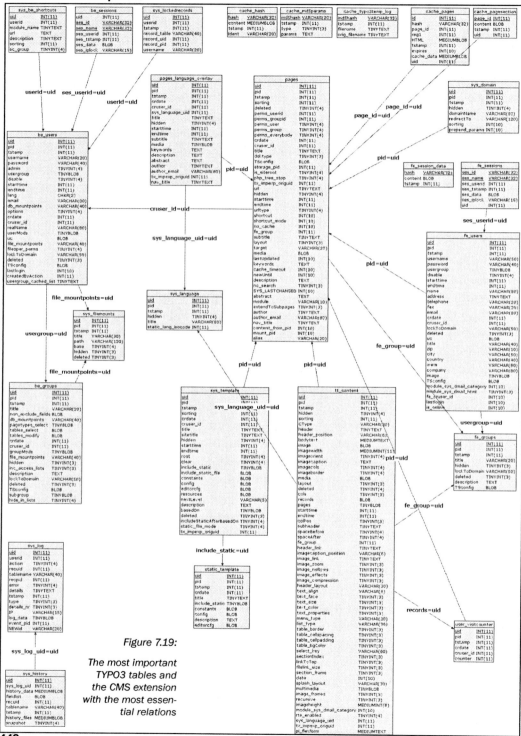

Figure 7.19:

The most important TYPO3 tables and the CMS extension with the most essential relations

Page Tree and Contents

The central point of focus in the database structure is the page, which is provided with a unique ID, so that it can be linked and referenced by other pages. Pages automatically receive an ID when they are created, which is stored in the uid (unique id) field of the database table pages. The page is displayed in the front end by calling the URL with the respective ID, for example `http://www.your-domain.com/index.php?id=18`. This example would call the page "B2C Home" in the application shown. Using this principle, every page can be uniquely called via the front end. The page assigned by the system is shown if you move the mouse over the page icon next to the page title [1].

All contents and records are saved in TYPO3 in a tree structure, comparable to the directory tree in a file system. This tree structure is formed with the help of pages; assigning a page to the one above it is implemented using the pid (parent id) field in which the uid for the parent page (the page lying above) is entered.

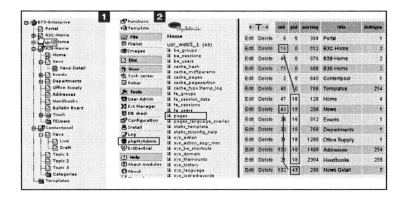

Figure 7.20:

Hierarchy of the Page Tree [1], displayed with phpMyAdmin, and selected fields of the table pages [2]

At the same time the tree structure represents the site structure as well as being a means to organize any data at all. Menus and submenus for a website can be generated automatically from this structure.

In the example page tree shown, "B2C Home" is located as the start page for the website on the so-called Root level; it is not assigned to a parent page. Its pid therefore has the value 0. All its subpages in the first level contain the corresponding value 18 in pid as a reference to "B2C Home". In the same way, the "News Detail" page in the second level is assigned via the pid 43 to the "News" page with uid 43. The order of the output in the page tree and in the menus is determined via the sorting field.

The same thing applies to the contents of the page, which, as long as they are not extensions, are stored in the database table tt_content. When they are created they are also given a unique `uid`; at the same time they are linked—depending on the place where they were created—via the `pid` to the corresponding page. The order of display is also organized here via the `sorting` field. Assigning the record to one of the content types available (e.g. text, image, former, table, ...) is done in the `CType` field.

In the following figure you can see how content elements of the `tt_content` table are assigned to individual pages via the `pid` field [1]—in this case, a page with the title "Home" and `uid` 56. In the list field in the back end you can also see the change in the `sorting` field when moving contents ([2] and [3]).

Figure 7.21:

Connections between the uid, pid, and the sorting fields in the tt_content table in phpMyAdmin [1] and in the List View in the back end [2] / [3]

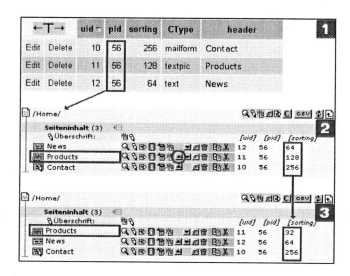

As with pages, the editor does not come into contact with the technical background when editing contents. He or she defines which contents are assigned to which pages with the user interface, and also assigns the kind of content via the type, and determines the order of output by positioning or changing the order of content.

Tables and Fields

Even though Kickstarter already provides the necessary standard fields when creating a table, the basic structure of a database table under TYPO3 will be briefly explained here. This is particularly of interest when porting applications to TYPO3.

To be able to edit tables in the back end, a few conventions must be observed and defined by the TCA (see next section). Each table must contain the two obligatory fields, `uid` and `pid`. The `uid` (unique ID) field is an auto-increment field with a unique ID for the records of this table. The `pid` (page ID) field contains the ID of the page to which the record belongs, that is, the `uid` from the `pages` table.

Furthermore there are several standard fields that are not obligatory, and which may vary in how they are named. For the sake of clarity, though, it is a good idea to keep the standard names. Some typical standard fields:

Field	Meaning
title	Is shown as the title in the back end
nav_title	Alternative title for use in menus
crdate	Time when record was created (Unix timestamp)
cruser_id	ID of the user who created the record
tstamp	Time of last modification (Unix timestamp)
sorting	For manual sorting
deleted	Marks record as deleted
hidden	Identifies record as hidden (front end)
starttime	Time when record becomes active in the FE (Unix timestamp)
endtime	Time from which record becomes inactive in the FE (Unix timestamp)

Table 7.1:

Standard fields in tables

7.4.7 Database, TCA, and TCEForms

As in every database management system involving more than the capabilities of simple tools, meta information is necessary on the database structure and its fields. Input forms for records, as used by TYPO3 in the back end, would not otherwise be possible.

Softlink **392081**

phpMyAdmin also provides a way, just like TYPO3, of editing individual data sets in a database table with a web interface. So what is the difference between them? phpMyAdmin generates entry forms for records from the database definition itself. phpMyAdmin therefore knows that a field can only accept integer values, because the field is defined as such in the database. But phpMyAdmin does not known if only a certain value range is permissible as input, and is accordingly not in a position to display a selection field with predefined values. Additional settings are necessary to carry out such tasks, which are not implied in the database definition. TYPO3 uses such additional information to correctly process database tables, records, and fields, and also to make additional functionality available that phpMyAdmin cannot provide.

With the help of this meta-information (TCA) and the TCEforms, editing forms are made available in the back end. The data entered is then checked by the TYPO3 Core Engine (TCE) (where the TCA definitions are used) and written to the database.

Figure 7.22:

Data processng in phpMyAdmin and TYPO3 (TCEForms)

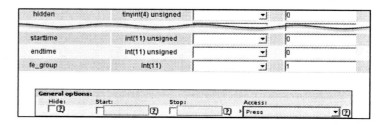

The meta-information necessary for TYPO3 is available in the TCA (Table Configuration Array) in the global variable $TCA. The TCA data is defined in the following files, which can be used as an information source for extension programming:

```
t3lib/stddb/tables.php
t3lib/stddb/tbl_be.php
typo3/sysext/cms/ext_tables.php
typo3/sysext/cms/tbl_cms.php
typo3/sysext/cms/tbl_tt_content.php
.../extension/ext_tables.php
```

The current definition of the TCA array can, by the way, be shown as a tree that can be searched through, which can be very useful if you happen to be searching for an error.

Below we shall present an overview of TCA options. A complete list of options would go beyond the boundaries of this book. You can find the reference via the soft link for this section. In many cases the options of Kickstarter for defining fields are sufficient, so that you only rarely need to consult the reference.

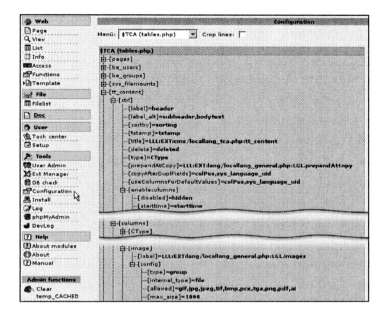

Figure 7.23:

TCA browser with extracts from the tt_content definition

As an example of the TCA array, here is an extract, which defines the tt_content table. As we know, this table is used to save content elements (text, image, ...).

The TCA definition starts with the ctrl array, which contains some metadata details for using the table. The field contents to be displayed as an extract in lists are first defined.

```
$TCA['tt_content'] = Array (
  'ctrl' => Array (
    'label' => 'header',
    'label_alt' => 'subheader,bodytext',
```

The next three lines define which field is to be used for sorting (sortby), which one contains the timestamp (tstamp), and how the table is named in the back end (title). For this purpose, a reference is specified to an external locallang language file.

```
'sortby' => 'sorting',
'tstamp' => 'tstamp',
'title' => 'LLL:EXT:cms/locallang_tca.php:tt_content',

'delete' => 'deleted',
'type' => 'CType',
'prependAtCopy' => 'LLL:EXT:lang/locallang_general.php:
                            LGL.prependAtCopy',
'copyAfterDuplFields' => 'colPos,sys_language_uid',
'useColumnsForDefaultValues' =>
                'colPos,sys_language_uid',
```

The following array `enablecolumns` defines the fields that decide whether the record is visible or not in the front end. The `enableFields()` function generates SQL code from this, which filters out invisible records.

```
'enablecolumns' => Array (
  'disabled' => 'hidden',
  'starttime' => 'starttime',
  'endtime' => 'endtime',
  'fe_group' => 'fe_group',
),
...
  'mainpalette' => '1',
  'thumbnail' => 'image',
)
'interface' => Array (
  'always_description' => 0,
  'showRecordFieldList' =>
        'CType,header,header_link,bodytext,image,...
),
```

In the `columns` array, the individual fields of the database tables are defined. These essentially contain information on what type of form field is used (selection field, checkbox, ...) to edit the fields, and of what type (text, integer, ...) they are. In addition value ranges can be defined or standard values can be preset.

TCEForms uses this information to generate the corresponding form fields. With these, TCA forms the basis for handling records (sorting, hiding, ...) on the one hand and for editing with TCEForms on the other.

```
'columns' => Array (
```

The `CType` field is defined here as a selection field. It is used to specify the content type (text, image, ...).

```
'CType' => Array (
  'label' =>
'LLL:EXT:lang/locallang_general.php:LGL.type',
  'config' => Array (
    'type' => 'select',
    'items' => Array (
        Array('LLL:EXT:cms/locallang_ttc.php:CType.I.0',
                                    'header'),
        Array('LLL:EXT:cms/locallang_ttc.php:CType.I.1',
                                    'text'),
        Array('LLL:EXT:cms/locallang_ttc.php:CType.I.2',
                                    'textpic'),
        Array('LLL:EXT:cms/locallang_ttc.php:CType.I.3',
                                    'image'),
        Array('LLL:EXT:cms/locallang_ttc.php:CType.I.4',
                                    'bullets'),
        ...
```

```
        ),
        'default' => 'text'
    )
),
```

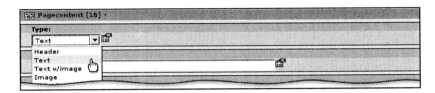

Figure 7.24:

TCEForms shows a
selection field for the
CType field

The `hidden` field is defined as a checkbox; it is used to deactivate the record for the front end (hide).

```
'hidden' => Array (
    'exclude' => 1,
    'label' => 'LLL:EXT:lang/locallang_general.php:
                                    LGL.hidden',
    'config' => Array (
        'type' => 'check'
    )
),
...
```

`bodytext` is the entry field that takes the text for the **Text** and **Text with image** content elements, for example.

```
'bodytext' => Array (
    'label' => 'LLL:EXT:lang/locallang_general.php:
                                    LGL.text',
    'config' => Array (
        'type' => 'text',
        'cols' => '48',
        'rows' => '5',
    )
),
...
```

The `image` is somewhat more complex in its definition. It is a selection field of the `group` type and contains a number of additional details. The maximum number of entries, for example, is restricted to 200, with `maxitems`.

```
'image' => Array (
    'label' => 'LLL:EXT:lang/locallang_general.php:
                                    LGL.images',
    'config' => Array (
        'type' => 'group',
        'internal_type' => 'file',
```

455

```
                         'allowed' => $GLOBALS['TYPO3_CONF_VARS']['GFX']
                                                        ['imagefile_ext'],
                         'max_size' => '1000',
                         'uploadfolder' => 'uploads/pics',
                         'show_thumbs' => '1',
                         'size' => '3',
                         'maxitems' => '200',
                         'minitems' => '0',
                         'autoSizeMax' => 40,
                         )
                    ),
            ...
            ),
```

Figure 7.25:

*Group selection field
for the image field*

In the `types` array the various content types are defined (text, image, ...),
for example which fields can be seen for each type. Which type a record
belongs to is decided by the value of the `Ctype` field, because it was set in
the `ctrl` array, via the `type` key, as the field which defines the record type.
If the value is `text`, that is, a **text** content type, `CType` fields are displayed
with palette 4, `header` fields with palette 3, `bodytext` fields with palette 9,
and so on.

```
'types' => Array (
    '1' => Array('showitem' => 'CType'),
  'header' => Array('showitem' =>
              'CType;;4;button;1-1-1, header;;3;;2-2
                     -2, subheader;;8'),
     'text' => Array('showitem' =>
              'CType;;4;button;1-1-1,header;;3;;2-2-2,
                     bodytext;;9;...
    ...

    ),
```

Palettes are defined in the `palettes` array. The above definition,
`header;;3;;,` inserts the palette 3 option into the `header` field, which
contains options such as layout and date for the header, as seen here.

```
'palettes' => Array (
   '1' => Array('showitem' => 'hidden, starttime,
                                endtime, fe_group'),
    '2' => Array('showitem' => 'imagecols, image_noRows,
                                imageborder'),
      '3' => Array('showitem' =>
```

```
'header_position, header_layout,
                 header_link, date'),
...
   )
);
```

The fields themselves are already defined in the top `columns` array and are presented as a palette in one row, instead of separate rows.

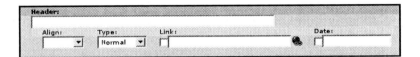

Figure 7.26:

Palette 3 under the header field

7.4.8 Flexforms

Database fields can only be used in one way in each case in the TCA definition. This means that an entry field for numbers cannot be used to save a date, although an integer value is stored in both fields. Moreover, a database table is a fixed structure. A more flexible method of saving data, as is possible with an XML format, is offered by Flexforms.

Softlink **353987**

Flexforms can be used for many types of tasks, and are already known to us through **Templa Voila**. At the time of going to press, however, no support of Flexform fields was available in Kickstarter, so some manual work is needed before they can be used. You will find the corresponding reference via the soft link for this section.

Because no direct query options currently exist for the Flexform data, its use is restricted to tasks in which SQL queries are not required to search through data stored in Flexforms. Typically, plugin options can be considered to configure the plugin, which might be provided by the **Insert Plugin** content element.

One possibility for making specific plugin options available is to add one or more fields to the `tt_content` table, for the purpose of saving the settings. The corresponding TCA definition then displays the options with the **Insert Plugin** content element. The disadvantage in this method is that every plugin adds its own fields to `tt_content`, which slows down database queries unnecessarily.

A more elegant possibility is to use Flexforms, which only require one field. In fact `tt_content` already contains the `pi_flexform` field, which, as its name suggests, is intended for this very purpose. [2]

Below we will show you how Flexforms can be used with the `pi_flexform` field, using the `Newloginbox` extension.

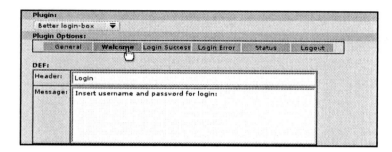

Figure 7.27:

Saving the settings for newloginbox *with Flexforms*

In order for a plugin such as `newloginbox` to be configured via Flexforms, the following requirements must be met:

- TCA definition of the `tt_content.pi_flexform` field as `flex` type

- Activation of the `pi_flexform` field for the plugin in the TCA

- Creation of a data structure definition

- Activation of the data structure for the plugin

- Reading in the configuration from the Flexform data in the plugin

The `pi_flexform` field is already predefined as a `flex` type. The TCA definition is as follows:

```
'pi_flexform' => array(
  'label' =>
'LLL:EXT:cms/locallang_ttc.php:pi_flexform',
  'config' => Array (
    'type' => 'flex',
    'ds_pointerField' => 'list_type',
    'ds' => array(
      'default' => '
```

[2] Robert Lemke, co-developer of Templa Voila and Flexforms, urgently points out that the use of Flexforms to configure plugins is preferable: "Anyone who still inserts their own configuration fields into tt_content will be tarred and feathered." The authors approve of this from a technical point of view, but distance themselves from the type of punishment advocated. Instead of this, we threaten to use public scorn and other methods of being put to shame, when taking part in the TYPO3 Snowboard Tour.

```
              <T3DataStructure>
                <ROOT>
                <type>array</type>
                <el>
                  <xmlTitle>
                  <TCEforms>
                    <label>The Title:</label>
                    <config>
                      <type>input</type>
                      <size>48</size>
                    </config>
                  </TCEforms>
                  </xmlTitle>
                </el>
                </ROOT>
              </T3DataStructure>
            ',
          )
        )
      ),
```

As you can see, the config array contains the two keys ds (Data Structure) and ds_pointerField. ds in turn contains an array whose elements contain the Flexform data structures. The data structures are defined in XML and contain information on the desired fields and their data types.

In the file ext_tables.php of the newloginbox extension, the pi_flexform field is added to the plugin for display:

```
$TCA['tt_content']['types']['list']['subtypes_addlist']
         [$_EXTKEY.'_pi1'] ='pi_flexform';
```

Still no Flexform element can be seen with this configuration in the **Insert Plugin** content element. The reason for this is that no data structure has yet been registered with the newloginbox_pi1 key in the ds array. The list_type field (in the BE as a selection field with available plugins) in the tt_content table in this example contains the value newloginbox_pi1, because this plugin was selected in the **Insert Plugin** content element. list_type is defined with the config parameter ds_pointerField, as the field whose content is used as the key for the ds array, and which therefore selects the file structure.

Explaining details of the newloginbox data structure is too complex to go into it here, so we shall just point out the reference. The data structure is set up in the same way as the above-listed example structure, which is defined via the default key. The part enclosed in the <TCEForms> tag is of interest. The same definitions can be found here as in the TCA array—only in the form of an XML structure.

The structure for the plugin can be found in the file `flexform_ds.xml` inside the extension, and is registered via the Extension API in the file `ext_tables.php` in the TCA definition.

```
t3lib_extMgm::addPiFlexFormValue($_EXTKEY.'_pi1',
    'FILE:EXT:newloginbox/flexform_ds.xml');
```

Now the Flexform element is displayed in the plugin form in which entries can be made. The data entered is transferred via the TCE to XML and saved in the `pi_flexform` field. The plugin base class `tslib_pibase` has methods available for the use of data in the plugin.

The Flexform field `pi_flexform` must first be initialized, and this should be done at the beginning of the plugin code:

```
// Init FlexForm configuration for plugin:
$this->pi_initPIflexForm();
```

The `pi_flexform` field can be accessed with `$this->cObj->data['pi_flexform']` within the plugin. Since the field contains an array in a specific format after initialization, access is made to it with the `pi_getFFvalue()` method, which returns the data of the pseudo-fields contained in it.

```
$this->pi_getFFvalue($this->cObj->
    data['pi_flexform'], 'show_forgot_password','sDEF')
```

The `newloginbox` plugin contains several options, arranged by index tabs (**General, Welcome, ...**). The data contained is organized in so-called sheets. The above line supplies the value of the `show_forgot_password` pseudo-field from the `sDEF` sheet.

There are many areas where Flexforms can be used. You can use them in your own database tables, of course, to save product variations of an Online Shop, for example. In addition Flexforms have a framework for editing XML data, which is certainly of great interest for many applications.

7.4.9 TYPO3 Core Engine (TCE)

Softlink **119361**

The TYPO3 Core Engine (TCE) is located in the `t3lib_TCEmain` class and is responsible for manipulating data in TCA-defined database tables. The TCE guarantees a consistent processing of records, and is used by back-end modules. In addition, access to the TCE is possible via the `typo3/tce_db.php` and `typo3/tce_file.php` scripts, and is achieved by passing on commands to the scripts. This will be demonstrated later in an example.

The TCE uses the metadata from the TCA definition to check data that has been passed on for its validity. Access permissions are also taken into account, and accesses logged. The TCE is designed to work together with TCEForms. This means that the TCE knows the data formats of the TCEForms and takes account of these accordingly. If the field is defined as an MM relation in the TCA, for example, the records of the relation must be searched for before the editing form is displayed, so that they are available for selection in the form. In precisely the same way, the TCE must set up the selected records as MM relations in the database.

If the TCE is used directly via the `t3lib_TCEmain` class, it will appear as follows:

```
require_once (PATH_t3lib.'class.t3lib_tcemain.php');
$tce = t3lib_div::makeInstance('t3lib_TCEmain');
$tce->start($data,$cmd);
$tce->process_datamap();
$tce->process_cmdmap();
```

The TCE is controlled through two arrays, of which `datamap` can contain data and `cmdmap`, commands. These two arrays are passed to the TCE with `$tce->start($data,$cmd)`. The respective arrays are processed with `process_datamap()` and `process_cmdmap()`.

Commands (cmdmap)

The following commands can be applied to records (or pages) via the cmdmap:

delete

> Delete record

copy

> Copy record

move

> Move record

The `cmdmap` array has the following format:

`$cmd[table name][uid][command] = value`

table name

> Name of the database tables to be processed, which must be defined in the TCA.

uid

> `uid` of the record

command

> The command to be performed: delete, copy or move

value

> For the delete command, value is simply set to TRUE. For the copy and move commands, a page id is expected in value. This can accept negative values, however, which then means that a record is inserted after this page id (as an absolute value), instead of inserting the record into the page, as would happen for a positive value.

The individual commands are therefore created as follows:

```
$cmd[table name][[uid]['delete'] = TRUE
```

```
$cmd[table name][uid][copy] = +/- pid
```

```
$cmd[table name][uid]['move'] = +/- pid
```

The following example deletes the record with uid=54 from the tt_content table:

```
$cmd = array();
$cmd['tt_content'][54]['delete'] = 1;
$tce->start(array(),$cmd);
$tce->process_cmdmap();
```

This command moves the page with uid=1203 to the first position within the page with uid=303.

```
$cmd = array();
$cmd['pages'][1203]['move]' = 303;
$tce->start(array(),$cmd);
$tce->process_cmdmap();
```

In the next example, page 1203 is not copied to page 303, but to the page directly after it, on the same level 303.

```
$cmd = array();
$cmd['pages'][1203]['copy'] = -303;
$tce->start(array(),$cmd);
$tce->process_cmdmap();
```

Various options can be set for the commands. The copyTree option sets the depth for copying pages, for example.

```
$cmd = array();
$cmd['pages'][1203]['copy'] = 303;
$tce->copyTree = 3;
$tce->start(array(),$cmd);
$tce->process_cmdmap();
```

The copying level is set to three levels in this example, so that page 1203 is copied, but also its subpages, down to three levels. For individual options, look up the documentation, which can be found via the soft link for this section.

Data (datamap)

The datamap array serves to manipulate or create records, and has the following format:

```
$cmd[table name][uid][Field name] = Value
```

table name

> Name of the database table to be processed; this must be defined in the TCA.

uid

> The uid of the record that is to be changed; if a record is newly created, uid must contain a chosen value with the prefix NEW.

field name

> Name of the database field that is to be changed; the field must be defined in the TCA.

value

> New value of the field

The following example illustrates that multiple records can be edited or created at the same time:

```
$data['pages']['NEW9823be87'] = array(
    'title' => 'Page 1',
    'pid' => '45'
)
```

First a new page should be created with the title "Page 1", within the page with uid=45.

```
$data['pages']['NEWbe68s587'] = array(
    'title' => 'Page 2',
    'pid' => '-NEW9823be87'
)
```

A second page will now be created after the new page, on the same level, with the pseudo uid NEW9823be87. The same concept of negative uid is used here as in cmdmap.

```
$data['pages'][9834] = array(
    'title' => 'New title for this page',
    'subtitle' => 'New sub title'
```

```
)
$tce->start($data,array());
$tce->process_datamap();
```

Finally the title of the page with `uid=9834` is changed.

Clear Cache

The TCE also provides functions for manipulating the cache.

```
$tce->clear_cacheCmd($cacheCmd);
```

The following commands can be passed on in $cacheCmd

page id

> deletes the cache for the specified page

'pages'

> deletes all page caches

'all'

> deletes all caches

tce_db.php

The functions made available by the TCE can also be addressed by the script `typo3/tce_db.php`. For this, the datamap and cmdmap are passed on as parameters via GET or POST with `data[]` and `cmd[]`. A typical example of using tce_db.php can be found in the section 7.4.4, *Web | Functions | Wizards Submodule Function*.

7.4.10 SQL and TCA-Defined Tables

While data manipulation in the database is carried out via the TCE to guarantee data consistency, database queries are performed directly with SQL. But a number of things must be considered here. On the one hand, access permissions must be taken into account, on the other, you must ensure that records are active (hidden, deleted, ...).

In back-end modules, the variable `$this->perms_clause` is preset with an SQL-WHERE statement that applied to the `pages` table, only selects pages for which the current back-end user has the necessary access permissions.

It must also be taken into account whether or not a record is active. In the back end this usually means the same as whether the record is deleted or not. If a field is defined that marks the record as deleted, as in the case of the `tt_content` table, then this field must be queried so that such records are not displayed in the back end.

```
$TCA['tt_content']['ctrl']['delete'] => 'deleted'
```

A WHERE statement is created for the back end with the following function:

```
$deleteClause =
t3lib_BEfunc::deleteClause('table_name');
```

There is a corresponding method for the front end in the TSFE object:

```
$deleteClause = $TSFE->sys_page->
          deleteClause('table_name');
```

In addition to this there is a series of fields defining the validity of the record for the front end. These fields are used to hide the record, to let it appear just for a certain time or to define access permissions for front-end user groups. All these fields are named **enable fields**. A matching WHERE statement can be created in the following methods, in which case the query of deleted records is already included in this, so that the above deleteClause() calls can be omitted.

```
$enableFields = $TSFE->sys_page->
          enableFields('table_name');

$enableFields = $this->cObj->
          enableFields('table_name');
```

Within plugins, the last method is used, so that a query looks something like this:

```
$res = $GLOBALS['TYPO3_DB']->exec_SELECTquery(
              '*',
              $table,
              'pid IN ('.$pidList.')'.
              $this->cObj->enableFields($table),
              '',
              'crdate DESC');
while($row = $GLOBALS['TYPO3_DB']->
                    sql_fetch_assoc($res)) {
...
```

The database query is performed with the methods of the $GLOBALS['TYPO3_DB'] object. TYPO3 implements a database abstraction layer (DAL) via this interface. The API can be found in the t3lib_DB class. You can find a description of the DAL via the soft link shown here.

Softlink **215109**

If enableFields() or deleteClause() are used correctly in SQL queries, you do not need to worry about which fields and functions are defined for the table in the TCA. If a plugin uses enableFields() correctly for database queries, the starttime and endtime fields can be added to the table queried later on (with TCA entries), without the PHP code of the plugin having to be changed.

7.4.11 Users, Sessions, and Authentication

Softlink **358205**

TYPO3 takes account of access permissions, records and files on the basis of users. It is necessary that a user who requests a resource is known, of course. This involves two essential aspects: on the one hand, being able to authenticate a user when logging in, that is, recognising the identity of a specific user. This is usually done with the help of a login form and by checking user name and password. On the other hand it is necessary to identify a user continuously: since HTTP is a protocol without status, for each page called it must be determined whether the user is already known, and if specific data is reserved for the user. This monitoring of the user is called a *session*.

A typical example that illustrates the differences between these two functions is an Online Shop. While the shopping basket is a function of the session, the user must register during the order process at the very latest (depending on the shop), and is authenticated by this.

In the context of web applications, three user states can be defined:

- Unknown users

- Identified users (user session without authentication)

- Authenticated users (login)

While an authenticated user is essential for the back end, all three states can be applied in the front end. Most websites allow access without registration, and also are not dependent on users sessions. This means that they are fully functional for unknown users.

If data is collected during the visit to the website (such as a shopping basket) that is relevant to the user, however, a session must be set up. In a session, a user is tracked during his or her visit to the website. This status is not the same as authentication, since the identity of the user does not have to be known for this purpose.

If access to specific resources (pages, content elements) is to be controlled, this is done through user groups for which the user must be authenticated. Without a user session, authentication cannot be meaningfully applied.

A user session is recognized by means of a cookie compiled automatically by TYPO3, containing only an ID, but no user data. These are stored in the database and are read after the cookie has been identified, and also contain data for the session. They are also used to save the status of authentication, which is why a user need log in only once per session.

Here is a summary of front-end user identification:

- An existing user ID is detected by means of a cookie

- If it does not exist, authentication is attempted by checking the username and password supplied.

- A cookie with the user ID is created.

- If the user has been successfully authenticated, the user data is read in.

- User settings are read in.

- Session data is read in; it could contain entries for a shopping basket, for example, from a shop application.

The use of cookies in the front end can be stopped with the following configuration:

```
$TYPO3_CONF_VARS['FE']['dontSetCookie'] = 1;
```

In order that users can still be authenticated and sessions used, the option `config.ftu` (*Frontend Track User*) can be set in the TypoScript setup, identifying a user by means of the parameters supplied. But you must bear in mind that plugins that do not generate links using the system functions correctly can terminate the session; this is why the use of cookies is recommended.

Session administration, authentication, and providing user data are handled by the `t3lib_*userAuth` and `tslib_feUserAuth` classes. An object is available via an instance of these classes after identification, and authentication where necessary, that holds user data in the `->user[]` array, and which also contains a number of methods for accessing session data or for checking user permissions.

The user objects in the front end and back end are very similar in their basic structure, as the same base class is used for both. But there is a difference between them, particularly in the methods. In the back end, the method `->isAdmin()` is available for example, but it is not in the front end, since there is no "administrator" user role there.

The user objects are available in the following global variables:

$GLOBALS['TSFE']->fe_user

> Front-end user object

$GLOBALS['BE_USER']

> Back-end user object

Here are some code examples involving user objects.

Front End

```
global $TSFE;
$mySessionData = $TSFE->fe_user->getKey('ses',
                                        $mySessionKey);
$mySessionData = ...
$TSFE->fe_user->setKey('ses',$mySessionKey,
                                        $mySessionData);
$TSFE->fe_user->storeSessionData();
```

The example shows how session data is saved in plugins. The data can be in any format at all, since it is serialized (serialize()) stored, and accordingly restored by the system. The data is identified via a key. It is a good idea to use $this->$prefixId for this, that is, the extension name of the plugin.

```
$userID = $TSFE->fe_user->user['uid'];
$username = $TSFE->fe_user->user['username'];
```

If a user is authenticated in the front end, then his user data is available in the user[] array.

```
$userTSconf = $TSFE->fe_user->getUserTSconf();
```

The TSConfig data can be determined with getUserTSconf().

Back End

```
global $BE_USER;
$userID = $BE_USER->user['uid'];
```

The user[] array is available in the user object containing the user data.

```
$userIsAdmin = $BE_USER->isAdmin();
```

You can check if the user has administrator status with isAdmin().

```
$uc_titleLen = $BE_USER->uc['titleLen'];
```

Settings for the user are stored in the uc[] (*User Config*) array. Here you can find data from **User | Settings**, for example, but also other settings such as module settings, which are automatically stored in this array by the `t3lib_SCbase` base class, and restored the next time this module is called (see section *Module Framework*). The examples shown present only a part of the User API. You can obtain further information on the implementation of user objects via the soft link for this section.

7.4.12 Platform-Independent Programming

In theory, TYPO3 will run on every platform on which PHP also runs. There are a number of differences, however, depending on the platform, PHP version, and server configuration. Especially under Windows, several PHP functions are missing, or behave differently to some extent.

Softlink **219501**

TYPO3 provides functions in its API that iron out most of these differences. If you also stick to a number of conventions, your extensions should run without problem in different environments.

Server and Environment Variables

If you want to access server variables, never use `getenv()` or even `$HTTP_SERVER_VARS`, but use the `t3lib_div::getIndpEnv()` function instead. This function unites known server variables and provides some additional information.

A number of these variables deal with the URL with which the current page is requested. The URL has the following scheme:

```
[scheme]://[host][:[port]][path][?[query]]
```

The following URL serves as an example:

```
http://www.example.net:80/t3book/index.php?id=26&tx_myext[my
param]=1234
```

The TYPO3 installation can be found in the `/var/www/t3book/` directory, while the base directory for the web server is `/var/www/`.

General Information

REMOTE_ADDR

> IP address of the client computer (browser)

REMOTE_HOST

> Hostname of the client computer (browser)

HTTP_USER_AGENT

Contains the type and name of the requesting client (browser)

Example:

Mozilla/5.0 (X11; U; Linux i686; de-AT; rv:1.6) Gecko/20040413 Debian/1.6-5

HTTP_ACCEPT_LANGUAGE

The languages accepted or requested by the calling client (browser)

Example: de-de,en-gb

HTTP_HOST

[host][:[port]]—the host requested by the client

Example: www.example.net:80

TYPO3_HOST_ONLY

[host]

Example: www.example.net

TYPO3_PORT

[port]

Example: 80

HTTP_REFERER

[scheme]://[host][:[port]][path][?[query]]

The URL from which the current page was called

URL Information
SCRIPT_NAME

[path+file]—the script name with the URL path

Example: /t3book/index.php

QUERY_STRING

[query]—the query string

Example: id=26&tx_myext[myparam]=1234

TYPO3_SITE_SCRIPT

[file][?[query]]—the script file called with the query string

Example: `index.php?id=26&tx_myext[myparam]=1234`

TYPO3_REQUEST_URL

`[scheme]://[host][:[port]][path][?[query]]`—the complete URL being called

TYPO3_REQUEST_HOST

`[scheme]://[host][:[port]]`

Example: `http://www.example.net:80`

TYPO3_REQUEST_SCRIPT

`[scheme]://[host][:[port]][path+file]`

Example: `http://www.example.net:80/t3book/index.php`

TYPO3_REQUEST_DIR

`[scheme]://[host][:[port]][path]`

Example Backend module

```
http://www.example.net:80/t3book/typo3/ext/
                                cc_beinfo/mod1/
```

TYPO3_SITE_URL

`[scheme]://[host][:[port]][path]`—URL path to the TYPO3 Website

Example: `http://www.example.net:80/t3book/`

Files and Directories

`TYPO3_DOCUMENT_ROOT`
`[path]`

Absolute path to the root directory of the web server

Example: `/var/www`

`SCRIPT_FILENAME`
`[path+file]`

Example: `/var/www/t3book/index.php`

You can make visible the environment variables shown, for example, with the extensions `FE Debug/Info output` (`cc_feinfo`)/`Backend Environment Information` (`cc_beinfo`).

GET and POST

`GET` and `POST` data are available through the variables

471

$GLOBALS['HTTP_POST_VARS'] and $GLOBALS['HTTP_GET_VARS']. Nevertheless you should use the following functions:

```
t3lib_div::_GET($var)

t3lib_div::_POST($var)

t3lib_div::_GP($var)
```

With _GET() and _POST(), data that has been sent by GET or POST is returned. In most cases it does not matter how the data was sent. That's why you can use the _GP() function. In most cases it does not matter how the data was sent. That's why you can use the _GP() function. This searches first in POST data and then in GET data for the key passed on. Bear in mind that these functions return data without slashes: the function $GLOBALS['TYPO3_B']->quoteStr() must be applied to the data before it can be written to the database.

Within plugins, parameters are accessed via $this->piVars[], so that you normally do not have to worry about the above functions.

Files

When handling files you should note that on Windows systems, text and binary files are treated differently. But in most cases this is not desired and can lead to malfunctions as a result. To avoid this, you should always open these files in binary mode to have read and write access to files. Binary mode is activated by adding the letter b to the mode parameter in fopen().

```
$fp = fopen ($filename, 'rb');
```

PHP provides the tempnam() function for creating temporary files, but this can lead to problems if *Safe Mode* for PHP is activated. For this reason TYPO3 offers the t3lib_div:tempnam() function, which stores temporary files in typo3temp/.

Running external programs also has hidden problems: the path of the program must be known or configured; executable files under Windows have the suffix .exe, and the function is_executable() does not work on Windows systems. If you want to call Perl, for example, there are a number of ways of doing this: C:/perl/bin/perl.exe, /usr/bin/perl or /usr/local/bin/perl. The t3lib_exec class tries to resolve the matter here. The following call provides the complete path to the Perl interpreter:

```
$cmd = t3lib_exec::getCommand ('perl');
```

So in this way program paths can be queried without having to be configured statically.

7.4.13 Multi-Language Capability

TYPO3 provides support for multiple languages, both in the back end and front end. So much so, that the extensions that you have published in the Repository could be translated by a registered translator into Swahili, for example, without you having arranged this. When did you last publish something in six different languages?

Softlink **104717**

The texts of modules and plugins in different languages are contained in files corresponding to the sample file `locallang*.php`. The Kickstarter provides corresponding support and generates these files. As can be seen in the following example, a `locallang` file contains an array `$LOCAL_LANG`, which in turn contains arrays with the different languages.

```
$LOCAL_LANG = Array (
    'default' => Array (
        'todos_new' => 'Create new To-Do',
        'todos_update' => 'Update To-Do',
        'todos_target' => 'Target user',
        'todos_type' => 'Workflow',
    ),

    'dk' => Array (
        'todos_new' => 'Opret ny opgave',
        'todos_update' => 'Opdater opgave',
        'todos_target' => 'Mål-bruger',
        'todos_type' => 'Arbejdsgang',
    ),
    'de' => Array (
        'todos_new' => 'Neue To-Do Liste anlegen',
        'todos_update' => 'To-Do-Liste aktualisieren',
        'todos_target' => 'Zielbenutzer',
        'todos_type' => 'Workflow',
    ),
);
```

At run time, texts are then created in the correct language, via keys (`'todos_new'`, `'todos_update'`). This is implemented in plugins with the method `$this->pi_getLL()`, and in modules with the method `$LANG->getLL()`. With `$LANG->getLL('todos_update')`, for example, the text "Update To-Do" is specified if the current back-end user has set English as the language, or if no translation is available for the set language.

It is admittedly somewhat tiresome to use key texts in program code, and to enter the actual text in `locallang` files. The extension `ExtDevEval` (see section *Tools for the Developer*) can be of use here, by extracting text from the code and replacing it with key texts.

As already mentioned, TYPO3 also offers support for multi-language websites within a page tree, via the table `pages_language_overlay`.

Contents are assigned to the different languages stored in the `sys_language` table, with the `sys_language_uid` field in the `tt_content` table.

There is no special support for this concept for data inside plugins. but experience has shown that multi-language capability is rarely necessary, or even sensible, for plugin data. The simplest way is usually to use a separate SysFolder for each language for the records of the plugin. It is also possible, of course, to create the fields for the required languages in the table. This procedure is normally only of interest for special applications.

Another possibility is to use the concept of `tt_content` in your own table. To do this, a corresponding `sys_language_uid` field is created. It makes sense to take the TCA definition from `tt_content`, and then you will have a language selection field in the records. The matching records with the language of the current page can then be selected as follows:

```
SELECT ... WHERE sys_language_uid='.$GLOBALS['TSFE']
    ->sys_language_uid ...
```

If the extension `Static Info Tables` is installed, you will also have access to the ISO-639 code [3] of the language with `$GLOBALS['TSFE']->sys_language_isocode`.

7.4.14 Character Encoding

Before we start on the special features of TYPO3 in connection with various character encodings, we will first explain some basics. If you are familiar with these principles, you can skip the next section.

Principles of Character Encoding

Softlink **996712**

Normally people lose little sleep over character encoding, and often it is not even clear what is meant by it. After all it's all very simple—you press the "ö" (o umlaut) character on the keyboard and the same letter appears on the monitor. What more do you need to know? Well, perhaps years ago you were tempted to throw a matrix or daisy wheel printer out the window, because it simply wouldn't print umlauts, and printed graphic characters instead?—a problem of character encoding.

It is generally assumed that when a letter such as "ö" is saved, the character itself is saved. But this is not true. The "ö" character, for example,

---

[3] (http://en.wikipedia.org/wiki/ISO_639)

comes from a TrueType character set and is drawn on the monitor by the operating system. In fact the "ö" is encoded and saved as a number, the "ö" character in the character set is also addressed by the operating system as a number. The interesting thing is that these two numbers can be different, and yet you still see an "ö" on the screen when you press the "ö" key (which in turn can have another number).

So it's no good just knowing the value (number) of a character, you can only know which character is involved once you know which coding has been used, i.e. which system is used for the numbering of characters. The first standardized coding was ASCII, which only uses seven bits (0–127) for coding, and which does not even contain German umlauts. Because the smallest unit for saving data is the byte, with 8 bits [4], you could use an additional bit and thus define a further 128 characters. This ultimately led to the ISO-8859 coding, which defines the following character sets:

- ISO 8859-1 (Latin-1)—West European

- ISO 8859-2 (Latin-2)—East European

- ISO 8859-3 (Latin-3)—South European and Esperanto

- ISO 8859-4 (Latin-4)—Baltic

- ISO 8859-5 (Cyrillic)

- ISO 8859-6 (Arabic)

- SO 8859-7 (Greek)

- SO 8859-8 (Hebrew)

- ISO 8859-9 (Latin-5)—Turkish instead of Icelandic, otherwise same as Latin-1

- ISO 8859-10 (Latin-6)—Nordic

- ISO 8859-11 (Thai)

- SO 8859-12 (Celtic) (never adopted)

- ISO 8859-13 (Latin-7)—Baltic (replaces Latin-4 and Latin-6)

- ISO 8859-14 (Latin-8)—Celtic

- ISO 8859-15 (Latin-9)—WestEuropean, with Euro character

- ISO 8859-16 (Latin-10)—South European, with Euro character

---

[4] It is quite possible to use any bit lengths you want. In fact other bit lengths than 8-bit are used in various specialized applications and processors.

All these character sets have the US-ASCII in common as coding for the first 128 characters. The second 128 characters differ, depending on the coding used. In Western Europe the ISO 8859-1 coding is normally used. This is also called Latin-1 and contains the German umlauts, for example. But the Greek alphabet is not included in this character set. This alphabet is defined in ISO 8859-7, which does not contain any umlauts. This means that it is not possible to use umlauts and Greek letters in the same text.

The following table should illustrate this; it shows four characters and how they are defined in the various codings.

Character	HTML	Unicode in HTML	ISO 8859-1	ISO 8859-7	DOS CP850	Unicode	Unicode UTF-8
ö	&ouml;	&#x00F6;	0xF6	-	0x93	U+00F6	0xC3B6
φ	&phi;	&#x03C6;	-	0xF6	-	U+0278	0xC9B8
÷	&divide;	&#x00F7;	0xF7	-	0xF6	U+00F7	0xC3B7
„	&bdquo;	&#x201E;	-	-	-	U+201E	0xE2809

The table may be a little confusing at first glance, but should be a little clearer after this example: [5]

> Nach der Erfindung der Telegrafie benötigte man auch hier eine Zeichenkodierung. Aus den ursprünglichen Ideen des Engländers Alfred Brain entstand 1837 der Morsecode.

For those who don't know German, here's the translation:

> After the invention of telegraphy, character encoding was also required. Morse code was created in 1837, based on original ideas by the Englishman Alfred Brain.

Apart from the characters defined in US-ASCII, this text also contains the ö, ü, and ä umlauts. Let's assume that this text was written with a text editor on a system using the ISO 8859-1 coding, and saved to a file. If that file is now transferred to a computer on which the German version of the DOS operating system is run, and opened there in an editor, you will see:

> Nach der Erfindung der Telegrafie ben÷tigte man auch hier eine Zeichenkodierung. Aus den ursprönglichen Ideen des

[5] Source: http://de.wikipedia.org/wiki/character encoding

Englanõers Alfred Brain entstand 1837 der Morsecode.

What has happened? The data has not changed, it is only assumed that the text is encoded with DOS codepage 850 and is displayed with the coresponding characters. The "ö" was saved in the ISO 8859-1 coding, that is, with the value $0xF6$ (hexadecimal). In the DOS codepage 850, though, the value $0xF6$ is reserved for another character, the ÷, as can be seen from the above table.

If the text is wrongly displayed with the ISO-8859-7 coding, you will get the following result:

Nach der Erfindung der Telegrafie benφtigte man auch hier eine Zeichenkodierung. Aus den ursprônglichen Ideen des Englônders Alfred Brain entstand 1837 der Morsecode.

Here the value $0xF6$ produces the Greek letter phi, which is why the text here also does not contain the desired character. So you always need to know which coding has been used for data. For this reason the coding is specified in the headers of HTML pages.

```
<head>
<meta http-equiv="content-type" content="text/html;
                               charset=ISO-8859-1">
```

As you can see from the table, it is not possible with the ISO-8859 coding to use the characters "ö", "÷" and "φ" simultaneously in a text. To resolve this problem, the Unicode system was introduced, which was intended to include all characters.

The advantage is that there is only *one* character system containing all the characters in the world (assuming they have already been defined in Unicode). But since there are more than 256 (corresponds to 1 byte) different characters, two or even four bytes are required to identify a character. This means that when saving data, up to four times as much space is required, however, and since this is incompatible with other codings, which are usually based on US-ASCII, UTF-8 was introduced. UTF-8 is Unicode as a 1-byte (8-bit) coding, so to speak. In this coding, US-ASCII is stored with one byte. All other Unicode characters are stored with several bytes. This means that UTF-8 uses a variable number of bytes for storing data, but usually only one byte, if the data consists of texts largely composed of the letters a to z or A to Z. Even if some applications do not yet support Unicode, it is foreseeable that this coding will become the standard, and sooner or later all other codings will disappear. Practice shows, however, that mainly the UTF-8 version of Unicode coding is used in storing and transmitting data, while the UCS-2 (2-byte) coding is frequently used for internal processing.

Different Character Enodings with TYPO3

If not configured differently, TYPO3 uses ISO-8859-1 coding, which seems to manage for most users in the Western world. But even the typographic quotation marks used in Germany („") cannot be displayed with this coding. Microsoft Windows uses Windows-1252 coding, which in the main is identical to ISO 8859-1, but contains German quotation marks. So there is no problem using these characters when writing content.

This problem can be avoided in the display in the front end by falling back on the HTML coding of special characters, and using `bdquo;`. But when saving, this coding would also have to be used, since data in the database is also encoded with ISO 8859-1. As soon as you want to use the data for a different output than HTML, problems will arise from this.

By the way, TYPO3 uses a different coding than ISO 8859-1 for a number of languages in the back end, so that it can display the relevant characters. If you use Greek as the back-end language, the ISO 8859-7 coding will be used for input and saving to the database. To ensure that the contents entered are also reproduced correctly in the front end, sites must be configured accordingly via TypoScript.

```
config.metaCharset = iso-8859-7
```

For the purposes of standardization and simplification, the aim should be to use UTF-8 for character encoding in TYPO3. All modern browsers support this coding, so that no conversion is necessary for the output. If older browsers such as Netscape 4 or Internet Explorer 4 are supported in the front-end, pages must be offered separately for these browsers, or you have to do without UTF-8, as this could also lead to problems here.

UTF-8 can be used from TYPO3 version 3.6. We cannot give a general recommendation to use UTF-8 with this version, however, as some minor problems still have to be cleared up. This section should therefore be treated as a look at future prospects.

To activate UTF-8 for TYPO3, the `forceCharset` option must be set via the Installation Tool, or directly in `typo3conf/localconf.php`:

```
$TYPO3_CONF_VARS['BE']['forceCharset'] = 'utf-8';
```

The back end, and thus the data storage in the database, are now running with UTF-8 coding. The UTF-8 coding still needs to be made known to the database. The Installation Tool in TYPO3 cannot do this automatically yet, so you have to carry out the configuration yourself, with the corresponding SQL commands. For MySQL 4.0 [6], coding for a table is changed as follows:

---

[6] Database support for UTF-8 is available in MySQL from version 4.

```
ALTER TABLE table_name CHARACTER SET utf8;
```

The following TypoScript option should be set in the setup for UTF-8 encoded output in the front end:

```
config.metaCharset = utf-8
```

In this way UTF-8 is used universally for character encoding in TYPO3, and the texts from the `locallang` language files are automatically transformed to the correct coding via the corresponding `getLL()` (BE) and `pi_getLL()` (FE) methods. HTML templates must also use the matching coding, of course; especially if they contain text, incorrect encoding in the front end would otherwise lead to the wrong output.

The question still remains as to how the data, that is, the texts, will be processed and what must be taken into account. Problems really can occur here, for the following reasons: since UTF-8-encoded texts may consist of more bytes than the letters that they symbolize, peculiarities must be expected during processing. The PHP function `strlen()`, for example, supplies the length of text by means of the bytes that are required for saving it. With UTF-8-encoded texts, this can cause a discrepancy between the actual length of the text and the result given by `strlen()`. For this reason the coding used must be made known to the database. If a search is carried out, for example, in which no distinction is to be made between upper and lower case, this may go wrong if UTF-8 coding is used.

TYPO3 itself provides the `t3lib_cs` class for the conversion of different character encodings, since PHP does not have the necessary functions available in every installation. An API for plugins that is used transparently, e.g. a `strlen()` function in `tslib_pibase`, has not yet been introduced, however. This API is necessary to begin developing plugins that can handle texts however they are encoded. It is quite probable that corresponding solutions will already exist by the time you are holding this book in your hands. Up-to-date information can be obtained via the soft link for this section.

7.5 Front-End Programming: Principles

By front end (FE), we generally mean the CMS extension, which can be found as a system extension in the directory `typo3/sysext/cms/`, and which is prominent in the main directory of a TYPO3 website through a symbolic link to the directory `tslib/`. Even if other front ends for TYPO3 are possible in theory, this is the common application for the system.

Just like the back end, the front end can also be expanded using extensions. A large range of possible front-end extensions (plugins) is already supported by Kickstarter so that the framework for an extension of your own can be quickly put together. Extensions for the front end may contain just a few lines of TypoScript, or they could involve an entire PHP application with several database tables.

7.5.1 Front-End Rendering Process

Here we will give you an overview about the rendering process of a page, which is in principle the working of the script `tslib/index_ts.php`.

- During the initialization phase, constants are set, a database connection is established and front-end libraries are integrated.

- The globally available object `$TSFE` from the class `tslib_fe`, which controls the rendering process, is created.

- The object for the front-end user authentication and session administration is created.

- If a back-end user is active, additional functions such as FE editing and the Admin Panel are initialized.

- The requested page ID and page type are determined. Access permissions are checked at the same time.

- The TypoScript Template Engine (TSFE) is initialized.

- If available, the finished page is read from the database cache.

- The `config` array (`config.*`) is read from the TypoScript setup.

- TCA basis data is read in.

- The language is determined (see section 7.4.14).

- Transmitted data, such as that in an e-mail form, is processed.

- If the page cannot be read from the cache, it is rendered by the TypoScript setup and written to the database cache.

- Non-cached content objects (`cobject`) are rendered and inserted into the output: `PHP_SCRIPT_INT`, `USER_INT`, `PHP_SCRIPT_EXT`.

- The rendered page (`$TSFE->content`) is displayed with `echo()`.

- Session data for front-end users is saved.

- Log data is written.

- If a `jumpurl` was specified, a redirect to the URL is activated.

- If required, a preview box is inserted if a back-end user has initiated a preview of the page.

- A static HTML is written if this has been activated in the Admin Panel.

- The Admin Panel is inserted, if it has been configured.

- If a debug extension is installed, it is called so it can deal with your output.

7.5.2 Front-End API

As well as the t3lib libraries, additional libraries and objects are available in the front end. The rendering process produces the object structure:

```
$TSFE (tslib_fe)
        |
        ---> fe_user (tslib_feUserAuth)
        |
        ---> sys_page (t3lib_pageSelect)
        |
        ---> cObj (tslib_cObj)
                |
                ---> myPluginObj (extends tslib_pibase)
                                |
                                ---> cObj (tslib_cObj)
```

In most cases a front-end extension is a plugin representing an extension of the `tslib_pibase` class. From the plugin you therefore have direct access to the following classes and objects:

tslib_fe

> The TypoScript Front end (TSFE) is available as a global object for plugins in `$GLOBALS['TSFE']`.

481

tslib_cObj

Is available as an object for plugins via `$this->cObj` and contains methods for rendering TypoScript objects such as TEXT and IMAGE; in addition, TypoScript functions such as `stdWrap` or `parseFunc` can be found in this class.

tslib_pibase

Plugins are an extension of this class, which provides a number of useful functions for plugins.

t3lib_pageSelect

Pages function; can be addressed in the FE via the `$GLOBALS['TSFE']->sys_page` object.

t3lib_div

The `t3lib_div` function collection is also automatically available in the front end.

The individual libraries will now be introduced in more detail.

7.5.3 TypoScript Front End (TSFE)

The TypoScript Front end (TSFE) is available as an object for plugins in the global variable `$TSFE` and contains information, methods, and objects. As has already been mentioned, the TSFE is the central object controlling the entire front-end rendering process. For most plugins it is sufficient to use the functions of `tslib_pibase` and the `cObj` object.

Here is an extract from the data and objects available in the `$TSFE` object.

$TSFE->id

`uid` of the current page

$TSFE->page[]

Array containing the record for the current page

$TSFE->sys_page

Object with several page-relevant methods

$TSFE->additionalHeaderData[]

Array for additional HTML header data

$TSFE->sys_language_uid

ID of the current language

$TSFE->tmpl

TypoScript template object

$TSFE->tmpl->setup[]

Array for the entire TypoScript setup

$TSFE->pSetup[]

Array of the TypoScript setup for the page object

$TSFE->config[]

Configuration array (TS config array)

$TSFE->register[]

TypoScript register

$TSFE->cObj

Central `cObjet` object; a cObject is available in plugins via `$this->cObj`.

$TSFE->fe_user

Current front-end user (object)

The `$TSFE` provides a number of interesting methods specifically for plugins:

getStorageSiterootPids()

Returns an array with `_SITEROOT` and `_STORAGE_PID` containing the page IDs of the root page of the website and the page in which the records are to be stored

getPagesTSconfig()

Based on the current Rootline, this method returns the pages TSconfig array.

setJS()

Sets JavaScript code which is integrated in the HTML header

setCSS()

Sets CSS data that is integrated in the HTML header

uniqueHash()

TypoScript template object

set_no_cache()

Sets current page to non-cachable

483

set_cache_timeout_default()

Sets the cache timeout for the current page

The extension FE Debug/Info output (cc_feinfo) provides a plugin that you can use to have the current values of the TSFE object and other relevant data displayed in the front end. This can be very useful when debugging, or just to obtain an overview of the data available.

7.5.4 cObject, tslib_cObj

A cObject (Content Object) is a TypoScript object, such as TEXT, IMAGE, or HMENU. The objects are implemented in PHP in the class tslib_cObj (class.tslib_content.php). In addition you can find TypoScript functions such as stdWrap or parseFunc in this class.

In plugins there is an instance of tslib_cObj available via $this->cObj. This object reference is set automatically during the initialization of the plugin.

Here is an extract from the tslib_cObj API:

data[]

This also makes the current record available (normally from the tt_content table).

cObjGetSingle()

Renders a cObject by means of the name passed on (TEXT, IMAGE, ...) and with a TypoScript setup; this is described in more detail in the following section.

stdWrap()

Standard wrap function; applied to your own TypoScript parameters, this can create a wide range of options, as could be seen from the visitor counter example (see section 7.1, *A Visitor Counter in 20 Minutes*).

enableFields()

Creates an SQL WHERE clause that only selects valid records in FE queries; it takes into account access permissions and the starttime and endtime fields.

DBgetUpdate()

Creates an Update SQL statement for a table that takes account of the table configuration in the TCA array

DBgetInsert()

Similar to `DbgetUpdate`, but for inserting records

Parameters

In PHP implementation, content objects and many methods in `tslib_cObj` share the same parameter concept:

```
function cImage($file,$conf)

function stdWrap($content,$conf)

function typoLink($linktxt, $conf)
```

The first parameter contains a value (such as a string), which is to be processed. The second parameter `$conf` parameter contains a TypoScript setup array, which configures the behavior of the method.

Plugins also follow this concept, since they are called via USER or USER_INT, and a method with the `$content` and `$conf` parameters is expected. In normal plugins `$content` is unused, however, and can be ignored.

The $conf Array

The `$conf` array represents the connection between TypoScript and PHP. On the one hand it serves to configure the PHP code, on the other, by using cObjects within the PHP code, the functionality can be changed or expanded, as was already seen in the graphic output of the visitor counter (see section 7.1, *A Visitor Counter in 20 Minutes*).

Using the example of the visitor counter, we shall now demonstrate how the `$conf` array works. In the figure below, the TypoScript setup for the visitor counter can be seen in the *TypoScript Object Browser*.

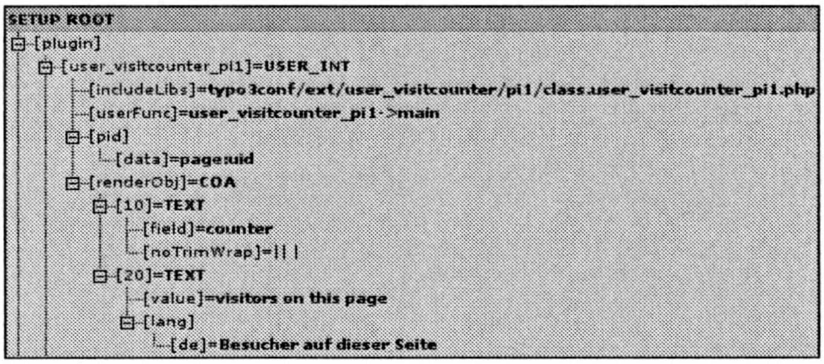

Figure 7.28:

TS setup in the TypoScript Object Browser

As you can see, TypoScript has been converted into a hierarchial list. This has already been described in detail.

The entire TS setup is passed on to the cObject USER_INT within plugin.user_visitcounter_pi1. Output with the debug(), this appears as follows:

USER_INT only knows the two parameters includeLibs and userFunc, which define the methods that are to be called. The USER_INT object therefore calls the method user_visitcounter_pi1->main and hands over the TS setup or the $conf array that it has itself received.

As can be seen in the above figure, it gives it the keys renderObj and renderObj. (with a final dot). Keys without a dot are set with = in TS and usually define the object type. The same key with a dot contains the setup for this object.

```
renderObj = COA
renderObj {
// here we are in renderObj. (with dot)
```

The second possibility is that a = sets a value instead of an object type. This concept is illustrated by the pid parameter from the above example. In the TS setup array, only pid. (with a dot) is available. Obviously pid is not defined with = as an object type. Let's take a look at the TypoScript line:

```
pid.data = page:uid
```

Omitting the definition of pid works because the pid parameter is, by definition, of the stdWrap type, and is treated accordingly in the PHP code for the plugin.

```
$pid = intval($this->cObj->
                stdWrap($conf['pid'],$conf['pid.']));
```

So the stdWrap() function is used to obtain the value of pid. If you look at the parameters you can recognize the concept of $content and $conf. In the above setup, $content or $conf['pid'] would be empty. The setup will be passed on with $conf['pid.'] and then contains data = page:uid. This means that the stdWrap() function is passed an empty value for processing, but with the configuration of `data`, it generates a value to be returned.

This would be quite different with the following TypoScript:

```
pid = 21
```

Here `stdWrap()` would be given the value 21 (`$content`), but not a configuration (`$conf`). In this case `stdWrap()` simply returns 21.

Here is an example where, although a value is passed on, it is overwritten with `override`:

```
pid = 21
pid.override.data = register: user_visitcounter_pid
```

As you can see, the combination of TypoScript and PHP provides a number of ways of making the PHP code flexible, by being able to configure parameters.

7.5.5 Rendering cObjects with PHP

As the example of the visitor counter has shown, the output of a plugin can also be produced via a `cObject`. Even if a plugin creates a large part of its output itself, and its appearance is adjusted with CSS, it can be useful to control certain parts with TypoScript. One example of this would be the display of images.

```
$outputHTML = $this->cObj->cImage($file,
                                  $conf['image.']);
```

The `cImage()` (`IMAGE`) method renders an image for the front end whose file name is passed on in `$file` using the TS setup, `$conf['image.']`. With this you can alter the image size from TS, for example. In addition the image is scaled, of course, and the `<img>` tag is generated.

In the visitor counter, the entire output is left to a cObject. This is done by the setup of `renderObj` being passed on to the `cObjGetSingle()` method, which renders the output by means of this configuration, or calls the appropriate rendering function for the defined cObject. This means that the rendering can be defined absolutely freely. It is even possible to define `renderObj` as a `USER` object and to generate the output with an external script.

The method is informed through `$conf['renderObj']` of what kind of object type is involved, which means that `renderObj` can be any type of cObject (`TEXT`, `IMAGE`, `COA`, ...).

```
// render the counter with the TypoScript renderObj
$lCObj = t3lib_div::makeInstance('tslib_cObj');
```

```
$lCObj->setParent($this->cObj->data, $this->cObj->
                                    currentRecord);
$lCObj->start($row, $table);
$content = $lCObj->cObjGetSingle($conf['renderObj'],
            $conf['renderObj.']);
```

As you can see, `$this->cObj`, which is automatically available within plugins, is not used. The reason for this is that data always belongs to a cObject with which the object works. In general these are the fields of the current record, which is normally the record of the `tt_content` table.

The following example shows an extract from a TypoScript from the setup of the `Heading` content element type. With `field = subheader` you can, from TS, directly access the `subheader` field of the current `tt_content` record.

```
tt_content.header = COA
tt_content.header {
  ...
  20.1 = TEXT
  20.1.field = subheader
```

So in the visitor counter, `$this->cObj->cObjGetSingle()` would not function with the following TS setup, since the current data does not come from `user_visitcounter` table, but from `tt_content`—the record that inserts the plugin into the page.

```
10 = TEXT
10.field = counter
```

For this reason, a local instance of `tslib_cObj` is created and then the previously read in visitor counter record is set as the current record with `$lCObj->start($row, $table)`, and then the above TS setup will function as required.

7.5.6 tslib_pibase

TYPO3 makes the base class `tslib_pibase` available for front-end plugins. Plugins created by Kickstarter are based on `tslib_pibase`. A plugin is not forced to use this class, but it does provide methods that are helpful for most plugins. Several methods are provided, in particular for the correct generation of links and for processing parameters.

The following range of functions are provided by `tslib_pibase`:

Parameter Recognition

`tslib_pibase` recognizes parameters passed on to the plugin. Exactly how it functions is described in the next section.

Link methods

Methods for generating links with and without parameters; this is also discussed in more detail in the next section.

Methods for Listing Records

The Kickstarter can create plugins that can already list records and show them in the Details Views. `tslib_pibase` provides the basic methods for this.

Stylesheet and CSS

A number of methods for using CSS classes are made available, which take into account the namespace of the plugin.

Frontend Editing

Methods to generate FE editing elements (icons) for records

Localization, Languages

Support of multi-language plugins on the basis of `locallang` language files

Database Accesses

Methods for accessing databases

Cache

Cache support for plugins with parameters

Flexforms

Support for processing Flexform data

Character Encoding

An upcoming TYPO3 version will probably have a number of methods in this class for processing strings, taking account of character encoding.

7.5.7 Links and Parameters in Plugins

When generating links within plugins, two things must be observed: on the one hand the link must have a correct format, that is, for links to a TYPO3 page the page ID and the `type` parameter must be taken into account. On the other hand the `GET` parameters passed on must correspond with the namespace of the extension, to avoid conflicts with other plugins.

Added to this is the fact that there are many ways of displaying URLs in

TYPO3. The first one worthy of mention is the normal, uncoded form:

```
index.php?id=123&tx_example_pi1[showUid]=456
```

In addition to this, the `simulateStaticDocuments` option or the `SpeakingURIs` extension enable you, when writing code, to considerably increase readability and make the website accessible to search engines.

The plugin base class `tslib_pibase` offers a corresponding framework for creating URLs and for the administration of plugin parameters. So you don't need to worry about the correct format.

The following example code shows the typical elements of a plugin that has been generated by Kickstarter, and which are relevant for parameter administration.

```
require_once(PATH_tslib.'class.tslib_pibase.php');
class tx_example_pi1 extends tslib_pibase {
  var $prefixId = 'tx_example_pi1';
  . . .
    function main($content,$conf)     {
      $this->conf = $conf;
      $this->pi_setPiVarDefaults();
  . . .
```

First of all, parameters in the `$this->piVars[]` array are managed. During the initialization phase, this array is filled by the constructor of the base class called `tslib_pibase` (which is run automatically), with passed GET and POST parameters that match `$this->prefixId`.

```
function tslib_pibase() {
    if ($this->prefixId) {
        $this->piVars = t3lib_div::
                        GParrayMerged($this->prefixId);
    }
```

If the plugin is called with the `main()` method, defined default values for parameters are set by TypoScript (with `_DEFAULT_PI_VARS`) with the help of the `pi_setPiVarDefaults()` method. But these are overwritten by the values (passed) that already exist in `$this->piVars[]`.

```
function pi_setPiVarDefaults() {
    if (is_array($this->conf['_DEFAULT_PI_VARS.'])) {
        $this->piVars =
            t3lib_div::array_merge_recursive_overrule(
                $this->conf['_DEFAULT_PI_VARS.'],
                $this->piVars);
    }
```

The following possibilities exist when generating URLs or links:

- URL only with page ID and `type` parameter

- URL with specific parameters

- URL with selected parameters from `$this->piVars[]`

- URL with all `$this->piVars[]` parameters

- URL with all `$this->piVars[]` parameters and additional or overwriting parameters

The base class `tslib_pibase` makes methods available for all these cases. These fall back on the link methods of `tslib_cObj`, which are mentioned here just for the sake of completeness.

```
$this->cObj->getTypoLink($label, $params,
                $urlParameters=array(), $target='')
$this->cObj->getTypoLink_URL($params,
                $urlParameters=array(), $target='')
$this->cObj->typoLink($linktxt, $conf)
```

Normally you should manage with the existing methods of `tslib_pibase`.

pi_getPageLink()

This method creates URLs for a specific page ID. You can specify an array with parameters for the URL.

pi_linkToPage()

Same as `pi_getPageLink()`, but a link is created (`<a>` tag) around the string passed to the method.

In contrast to the above methods, the following ones also take caching into account, which is explained in the next section.

pi_linkTP()

As `pi_linkToPage()`, with the difference that details on caching are taken into account

pi_linkTP_keepPIvars_url()

Generates an URL, in which all current `piVars` are attached as parameters; parameters can be overwritten or appended.

pi_linkTP_keepPIvars()

As above, but creates a link

pi_list_linkSingle()

Creates a link with the parameter `showUid` to show an individual record

A simple URL for the current page, to be used in forms, for example, can be generated as follows:

```
$url = $this->pi_getPageLink($GLOBALS['TSFE']->id);
```

The following code creates a link for browsing through a list. `pi_linkTP_keepPIvars()` is used for this, since the current parameters should be kept. The `pointer` parameter is passed and thus overwrites the existing value, if there is one, in `$this->piVars[]`.

```
$browseNext = $this->pi_linkTP_keepPIvars(
    $this->pi_getLL('pi_list_browseresults_next','Next
        >',TRUE), array('pointer'=>$pointer+1));
```

Using the `piVars` and `tslib_pibase` link methods requires a certain amount of discipline. But once you are familiar with it, you will learn to appreciate this clear-cut concept. In addition to this, it is imperative that you use this framework if your own plugin has to conform to the API, otherwise it would collide with other applications. The main use it has is its compatibility with the `simulateStaticDocuments` option, the `SpeakingURIs` extension, and similar solutions. In addition you have the possibility, described below, of caching parametrized plugins.

7.5.8 USER, USER_INT, Caching, and Parameters

The front end uses a temporary memory (cache) for rendered pages to be able to deliver these directly the next time they are requested, and not have to render them again. TYPO3 has a wide range of options to influence caching.

First the cache behavior can be defined with the following options in the TS setup:

config.no_cache = 1

> Deactivates caching

config.cache_period = 3600

> Sets the default time period (in seconds), after which a cache entry expires

config.cache_clearAtMidnight = 1

> Clears the cache at midnight

In addition you can specify in the page record individual pages that should normally not be cached (**Do not cache** field). Alternatively you can define how long the cache is valid, that is how soon the page should be completely reconstructed (**Cache expires** field, corresponds with `cache_period`).

The cache behavior can also be specified through PHP code from plugins. If your plugin is integrated as a USER object, for example, which is normally cached, you can force the page to be reconstructed in 15 minutes, using the following line:

```
$GLOBALS['TSFE']->set_cache_timeout_default(60*15);
```

You can also stop caching of the current page during rendering, by running the following script:

```
$GLOBALS['TSFE']->set_no_cache();
```

But this method of preventing caching is rarely necessary, or even sensible. Much more frequent is the need for a plugin to react to form input. A cached USER object cannot do this, however, since it is not even called if the page exists in the cache. A remedy is provided by the parameter no_cache=1, which causes the front end not to use the page from the cache, but to render it completely from scratch. In forms you can simply include this parameter as a hidden field.

```
<input type="hidden" name="no_cache" value="1">
```

Caching is not always sensible or possible, for example if a plugin needs to react to data passed on, or to parameters. For this reason, plugins can be integrated into a cached page as an uncached object with USER_INT, which has advantages in terms of speed, as only the variable parts of a page need to be rendered.

TYPO3 still offers the possibility of caching the output from plugins with changeable parameters. But this functionality must be taken into account during programming, and should be well thought out, since a separate page is cached for every parameter combination requested.

Let's assume we have a plugin that shows the List View of a data table that is only updated every few days, so that it is very well suited for caching. The records displayed are selected by means of three variable options, each with two states. This results in eight (2^3) different lists. In addition, the sorting order for four fields can be selected, giving us a total of 128 ($2^{7)}$) different views.

The list has an average length of some 100 entries which are browsed through, with 20 entries per page. This means that there are some 640 (128 X 5) page variations to be expected in the cache.

If two more options are added to this, one with five options and one with eight, that already makes 25,600 possible variations, which will presumably not all be called or created.

As you can see, a handful of plugins can quite easily generate millions of cached pages, putting a heavy strain on the database server. It is difficult to make a recommendation here. A resource-hungry application, with few options, can profit considerably from caching, while a plugin to display current data is not cached, of course.

Here is an example plugin to demonstrate caching. The following output is generated by the plugin:

The plugin has a form with three options; it shows the time when rendering was performed, and two links. Finally the `cc_feinfo` plugin is integrated to make passed parameters visible.

The page has just been called via the link **Link with Parameter**. Under **GET Variables** you can see the parameters that have been transferred with the following link:

```
http://www.example.org/index.php?id=28&tx_linkexample_pi
1[opt1]=1&tx_linkexample_pi1[opt2]=1&cHash=4901bb2eda
```

First the page ID, then the two parameters `opt1` and `opt2` for the plugin, which were automatically registered via `tslib_pibase`, and which are now available in `$this->piVars[]`. In the final parameter `cHash` lies the secret of caching plugins with parameters.

A page cache entry is basically set up by TYPO3 by means of the page ID and the `type` parameter. If `cHash` is set, the passed parameters are included and a check is made to see if the value of `cHash` matches the current parameters.

In this way the page cache can be prevented from being flooded deliberately with forged hashes. [7]

But now back to the example plugin. The plugin is registered in the `ext_localconf.php` file of the extension.

```
t3lib_extMgm::addPItoST43($_EXTKEY,

'pi1/class.tx_linkexample_pi1.php',
                            '_pi1',
                            'list_type',
                            1 /*cached*/);
```

The last parameter of `t3lib_extMgm::addPItoST43()` determines whether the plugin should be integrated as USER_INT (0) or as USER object (1). Because USER_INT objects are normally not cached, 1 should be specified here as the parameter. But this configuration does not mean that different variations of the page are cached—for this, the `cHash` parameter is required, which is generated by the link functions of the `tslib_pibase` class (ultimately by `cObj->typoLink()`). If, for example, the parameter `$cache` is set to TRUE when calling the `pi_linkTP_keepPIvars()` method, the URL generated is appended by the `cHash` parameter.

```
function pi_linkTP_keepPIvars($str,
                            $overrulePIvars=array(),
                            $cache=0,
                            $clearAnyway=0,
                            $altPageId=0)
```

So you must decide in the plugin whether the parameters currently set should create a cached page or not, and set `$cache` accordingly. If all output created by the plugin is to be cached, you must always set `$cache` to TRUE. But remember that this can bring your database server to its knees, depending on the range of parameters involved.

The base class `tslib_pibase` provides a way of specifying the parameters that set `$cache` to TRUE in advance with the `pi_autoCacheFields[]` array. This function will be used in the following example plugin. We will limit this to showing the `main()` method, omitting the header and footer of the plugin file.

---

[7] The function for generating the hash involves $TYPO3_CONF_VARS['SYS']['encryptionKey']. This value is also used by other functions and should not be empty, to increase security (see Installation Tool).

```
function main($content,$conf) {

$this->conf=$conf;
$this->pi_setPiVarDefaults();

    // If set caching is disabled
$this->pi_USER_INT_obj=0;
```

The variable `pi_USER_INT_obj` must be set to FALSE so that `tslib_pibase` allows caching, or generates the cHash.

```
    // enable auto caching
$this->pi_autoCacheEn = 1;

$this->pi_autoCacheFields = array(
        'opt1' => array('list' => array(0,1)),
        'opt2' => array('list' => array(0,1)),
);
```

The auto-cache function is activated. The `pi_autoCacheFields[]` array specifies for which parameter caching is to be allowed. If all the parameters used to create a URL are available in this array (`opt1`, `opt2`), and if their values are defined, the cHash is generated. Otherwise the `no_cache=1` parameter is appended, so that the page is re-rendered completely, and the plugin can react to the parameters.

The valid values can be defined either with `list` or `range`. While `list` contains an array with a list of values, `range` defines an integer value range through an array, with beginning and end values.

```
$params = array('opt1','opt2','opt3');

// build options form
$options = '';
foreach ($params as $opt) {
$options.= '<input type="checkbox" '.
'name="'.$this->prefixId.'['.$opt.']" '.
    'value="1" '.
($this->piVars[$opt]?'checked="checked":'').
                                    '> '.$opt.'<br />';
}

$content = '
<h3>Options:</h3>
<form action=".
htmlspecialchars($this->
            pi_getPageLink($GLOBALS['TSFE']->id)).
'" method="post">
'.$options.'
<input type="hidden" name="no_cache" value="1">
```

```
<input type="submit" name=".$this->
                prefixId.'_submit_button"
value="Submit">
</form>
<br />
';
```

In the example plugin, the three parameters `opt1`, `opt2`, and `opt3` are used. In the above code a form is generated with which these values can be set. The form is sent to the current page. The `no_cache` parameter is included as a hidden form field.

```
// show the current time - will not change with
// cached pages
$content.= 'Rendering time: '.date('H:m:s',time());
$content.= '<br /><br />';
```

The current time is displayed so that the effect of caching can be clearly seen. If the time changes each time the page is reloaded, then it has been freshly constructed and does not come from the cache. Please bear in mind that caching may be deactivated, for various reasons, if you are logged in to the back end.

```
// link with current piVars set by options form
$content.= $this->pi_linkTP_keepPIvars('Link with
                                    Parameter');
$content.= '<br />';
```

A link is created that sends the current `piVars` as a parameter to the current page. It would be possible here to set the `$cache` parameter of the function, but the activated auto-cache function does this itself automatically. If the `opt1` and/or `opt2` parameters are set, a link to a `cHash` parameter is created. If the `opt3` parameter is also set, then `cache=1` is appended to the URL instead, because `opt3` is not entered in the `pi_autoCacheFields[]` array.

```
// overrule opt3=1 which will force no_cache=1
// (opt3 is not set in pi_autoCacheFields)
$overrule = array('opt3' => 1);
$content.= $this->pi_linkTP_keepPIvars('Link with
                                    Parameter opt3=1',
$overrule);
$content.= '<br />';
```

The above call of the `pi_linkTP_keepPIvars()` method is passed to the `$overrule` array, which contains the parameter `opt3`. This parameter is thus added to the link, irrespective of whether this is contained in `piVars[]` or not. As a result, this link never creates a `cHash`.

```
// insert feinfo
$info = t3lib_div::makeInstance('tx_ccfeinfo');
```

```
        $info->init($this);
        $content.= $info->pi_getInfoOutput();

        return $this->pi_wrapInBaseClass($content);
    }
```

Finally the `tx_ccfeinfo` is integrated, which is used for the output of the GET and POST variables.

This plugin is great for trying things out and viewing current data with the integrated `tx_ccfeinfo` function.

7.6 Front-End Programming: Examples

TYPO3 Version 3.7 was used for programming the examples. Some code fragments have been left out for the sake of clarity in the following example, such as the PHP tag `<?php~?>` and the following line, which can be found in files such as `ext_tables.php` and `ext_localconf.php`:

```
    if (!defined ('TYPO3_MODE')) die ('Access denied.');
```

But all these elements are generated by Kickstarter, so that the examples can be reconstructed without problem. Furthermore all examples are available for download.

The prefix `user_`, which is reserved for local extensions, is always used for the extension keys.

The examples were developed on the basis of the CSS Styled Content extension, which renders content in such a way that it is marked exclusively with CSS classes. This concept is also used in the example extensions. It has the advantage that content and layout can be more easily separated. Most examples also function without being adjusted to the static template content (default); but it is possible that the results will differ somewhat in their appearance. But this is of no significance as far as the programming of a plugin is concerned.

7.6.1 Content Borders

This example is a small extension that inserts new borders for content elements.

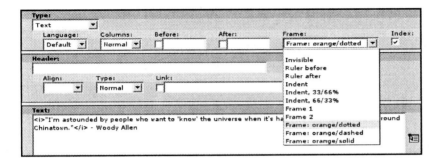

Figure 7.31:

Output of the linkexample *plugin*

In order to create new borders, you must of course know how the existing ones function. Since these are not encapsulated in a small extension where they can be quickly found, you have to do a little searching. As you know, content elements are stored in the `tt_content` database table, and in turn these are rendered via the TypoScript setup `tt_content`. So there are a number of places where you can start searching for the border.

The file `typo3/sysext/cms/tbl_tt_content.php` contains the TCA definition of the fields in the table `tt_content`. Unfortunately this definition at first glance doesn't seem to contain much that would be of help to us. As described in section 7.4.7, *Database, TCA, and TCEForms*, the appearance of the back-end form for content elements is defined in this file. Therefore the entries from the selection field for borders should also appear here. These entries, however, have been moved to a separate file containing the various languages. A look at the file `tbl_tt_content.php` shows that the labels can be found in the file `locallang_ttc.php`.

```
Array('LLL:EXT:cms/locallang_ttc.php:CType.I.0',
                                        'header'),
Array('LLL:EXT:cms/locallang_ttc.php:CType.I.1',
                                        'text'),
```

The entries from the selection field are quickly found. The keys for the labels are now known.

```
'section_frame' => 'Rahmen:', 'Frame:'
'section_frame.I.1' => 'Invisible',
'section_frame.I.2' => 'Line in front',
'section_frame.I.3' => 'Ruler after',
'section_frame.I.4' => 'Indent',
'section_frame.I.5' => 'Indent, 33/66%',
```

```
'section_frame.I.6' => 'Indent, 66/33%',
'section_frame.I.7' => ' Frame 1',
'section_frame.I.8' => ' Frame 2',
```

Using the (section_frame) key in the TCA definition, you can now search for the field for the borders (this is also possible via **Tools | Configuration | $TCA**). The following section can be found in the file tbl_tt_content.php:

```
'section_frame' => Array (
'exclude' => 1,
'label' => 'LLL:EXT:cms/locallang_ttc.php:
                                  section_frame',
'config' => Array (
'type' => 'select',
'items' => Array (
  Array('', '0'),
  Array('LLL:EXT:cms/locallang_ttc.php:
                   section_frame.I.1','1'),
  Array('LLL:EXT:cms/locallang_ttc.php:
                   section_frame.I.2', '5'),
```

Here the section_frame field in the tt_content table defines the border for content elements. Now search through the TypoScript setup for the place that renders the border; to do this, use the *TypoScript Object Browser* in the **Web | Template** module. You can look through the setup for section_frame in the search form.

Now the position in the TypoScript setup where the new borders must be inserted is also known.

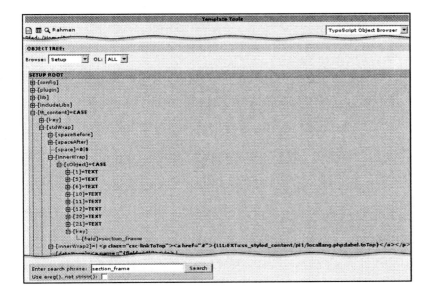

Figure 7.32:

Searching through the TypoScript setup

So for new borders, the new entry in the TypoScript object is necessary to render borders:

```
tt_content.stdWrap.innerWrap.cObject
```

as well as entries in

```
$TCA['tt_content']['columns']['section_frame']
            ['config']['items']
```

so that these borders are available for the user in the back end.

Unfortunately the Extension Kickstarter does not make provisions for creating such an extension. You could copy the required files from other extensions and adjust them, or you can create an extension with Kickstarter that contains roughly what you need, and then modify this, deleting unnecessary components.

It is a good idea to create an **Add as a Textbox type** plugin with Kickstarter for this extension. Since a PHP plugin is not required here, the `pi1/` directory can be deleted again, and the extension contains the following files:

```
ext_emconf.php
ext_icon.gif
ext_localconf.php
ext_tables.php
locallang_db.php
```

Extending the TCA definition is done in `ext_tables.php` and looks like this:

```
// add new frames to select box
t3lib_div::loadTCA('tt_content');

for ($key = 75; $key <= 77; $key++) {
  $TCA['tt_content']['columns']['section_frame']
          ['config']['items'][] =
                        Array('LLL:EXT:'.$_EXTKEY.
 '/locallang_db.php:
          tt_content.section_frames_'.$key,   $key);
}
```

First the TCA definition must be loaded from tt_content with
t3lib_div::loadTCA(), so that it can be extended. The extension takes
place here using a for() loop. This is not absolutely essential, but does
make the code more easily re-usable, since only the start value (75) and
end value (77), which are used as keys, need to be changed.

The matching definition of the labels can be found in locallang_db.php.

```
$LOCAL_LANG = Array (
'default' => Array (
  'tt_content.section_frames_75' => 'Frame:
                              orange/dotted',
  'tt_content.section_frames_76' => 'Frame:
                              orange/dashed',
  'tt_content.section_frames_77' => 'Frame:
                              orange/solid',
  ),
'de' => Array (
  'tt_content.section_frames_75' => 'Rahmen:
                              Orange/gepunktet',
  'tt_content.section_frames_76' => 'Rahmen:
                              Orange/gestrichelt',
  'tt_content.section_frames_77' => 'Rahmen:
                              Orange/durchgezogen',
  ),
);
```

A wrap is necessary to create the border. **Border 1** can serve here as a
template:

```
tt_content.stdWrap.innerWrap.cObject.20 = TEXT
tt_content.stdWrap.innerWrap.cObject.20.value =
    <div class="csc-frame csc-frame-frame1">|</div>
```

The necessary TypoScript is inserted in ext_localconf.php. A for loop is
again used here to generate the required TypoScript via
t3lib_extMgm::addTypoScript().

```
// generate frames with key 75 - 77
for ($key = 75; $key <= 77; $key++) {
```

502

```
t3lib_extMgm::addTypoScript($_EXTKEY,'setup','
tt_content.stdWrap.innerWrap.cObject.'.$key.' = TEXT
tt_content.stdWrap.innerWrap.cObject.'.$key.
'.value = <div class="csc-frame-frame'.$key.'">|</div>
',43);

}
```

What is still missing is a little CSS to make the border visible. This should be done in the stylesheet of the website. But you can include CSS code in the extension, which can be inserted into the template as required. To do this, create a new file:

```
static/
    setup.txt
```

This file should then contain something like the following code (abbreviated):

```
# Example of default set CSS styles (these go into
# the document header):
plugin.tx_userframes._CSS_DEFAULT_STYLE (
DIV.csc-frame-frame75 {
background-color: #FAAC27; border: 3px dotted #000; }
DIV.csc-frame-frame76 {
background-color: #FAAC27; border: 3px dashed #000; }
DIV.csc-frame-frame77 {
background-color: #FAAC27; border: 3px solid #000; }
)
```

The extension is now finished and can be installed with the Extension Manager. To make the border visible, the supplied CSS code can be integrated by adding the static template to the template record.

Figure 7.33:

Adding the static template

One disadvantage in this procedure is that CSS code in the header of the HTML page is used, making the pages somewhat larger. On the other hand this process may be intended, because then the CSS code is available together with the page, and does not have to be loaded afterwards with an external stylesheet.

In the following figure you can see the result of this small extension.

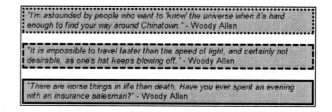

The HTML code generated appears as follows:

```
<style type="text/css">
   /*<![CDATA[*/
<!--
/* default styles for extension "tx_userframes" */
DIV.csc-frame-frame75 {
   background-color: #FAAC27; border:
                              3px dotted #000; }
DIV.csc-frame-frame76 {
   background-color: #FAAC27; border:
                              3px dashed #000; }
DIV.csc-frame-frame77 {
   background-color: #FAAC27; border: 3px solid #000; }
-->
   /*]]>*/
</style>
...
</head>
<body>
...
<!-- CONTENT ELEMENT, uid:15/text [begin] -->
  <a name="15"></a><div class="csc-frame-frame75">
  <!-- Text: [begin] -->
    <p class="bodytext"></p>
  <!-- Text: [end] -->
    </div>
<!-- CONTENT ELEMENT, uid:15/text [end] -->
```

7.6.2 The Countdown TypoTag

Although a CMS is supposed to separate layout and content, it is often necessary to mark the contents first. TYPO3 provides its own tags for marking. These tags are not to be confused with HTML tags, because so-called *TypoTags* are transformed during the rendering process into HTML (or something else).

The following example introduces the `<countdown>` tag. Its purpose is to count down the days until a certain day is reached. In a **Text** content element, the following contents:

```
There are still <countdown>23 June 2004</countdown>
days till the Linux
Days 2004.
```

should lead to the following output:

```
There are still 104 days till the Linux Days 2004.
```

The date enclosed in the tag should therefore be converted to the number of days until this date.

A new tag can be easily created in Kickstarter with the corresponding option. The Kickstarter provides the following files:

```
ext_emconf.php
ext_icon.gif
ext_localconf.php
pi1/
class.user_tagcountdown_pi1.php
```

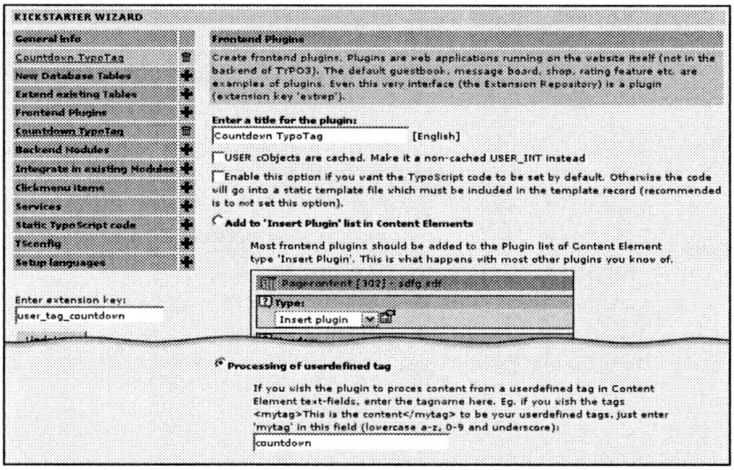

Figure 7.35:

*The <countdown>
tag is created as a
plugin in Kickstarter*

In the file `ext_localconf.php`, `class.user_tagcountdown_pi1.php` (the PHP script) and the plugin are integrated into the TypoScript template.

```
t3lib_extMgm::addPItoST43($_EXTKEY,
                'pi1/class.user_tagcountdown_pi1.php',
                    '_pi1',
                    '',
                    1);

t3lib_extMgm::addTypoScript($_EXTKEY,'setup','
```

```
lib.parseFunc_RTE.tags.countdown = < plugin.'.
t3lib_extMgm::getCN($_EXTKEY).
'_pi1',43);
```

You should note here that this does not function with the `content` (`default`) template, because `parseFunc` is in a different location there. So if the plugin is to function with this template, it must be inserted in a different way. Generally the TypoScript Object Browser in the **Web | Template** module can be of help to find such locations.

```
t3lib_extMgm::addTypoScript($_EXTKEY,'setup','
tt_content.text.20.parseFunc.tags.countdown =
                                    < plugin.'.
t3lib_extMgm::getCN($_EXTKEY).
'_pi1',43);
```

But let's go back to the first variation. The resulting TypoScript integration, summarized, appears as follows:

```
plugin.user_tagcountdown_pi1 = USER
plugin.user_tagcountdown_pi1.userFunc =
                            user_tagcountdown_pi1->main

includeLibs.user_tagcountdown_pi1 =
                typo3conf/ext/user_tag_countdown/pi1/
                class.user_tagcountdown_pi1.php
lib.parseFunc_RTE.tags.countdown =
                        <plugin.user_tagcountdown_pi1
```

You could also specify this directly as a TypoScript template in the file `ext_setup.txt`. But the correct variation, which is also more portable, is to integrate the plugin via `t3lib_extMgm`, since no fixed file paths are used.

The finished `class.user_tagcountdown_pi1.php` script will then appear as follows:

```
require_once(PATH_tslib.'class.tslib_pibase.php');

class user_tagcountdown_pi1 extends tslib_pibase {
    var $prefixId = 'user_tagcountdown_pi1';
    var $scriptRelPath =
'pi1/class.user_tagcountdown_pi1.php';
    var $extKey = 'user_tag_countdown';

/**
* processes the <countdown> tag
*/
function main($content, $conf) {
    $date = $this->cObj->getCurrentVal();
    $timestamp = strtotime($date);
    $delta = $timestamp - time();
    $days = intval($delta / (60 * 60 * 24)) + 1;
```

```
        return $days;
    }
}
```

The `$this->cObj->getCurrentVal()` function returns the contents of the `<countdown>` tag (the date), which is converted to days in the following lines. It should be pointed out that the PHP function `strtotime()` cannot handle some national date conventions, but this plays no role in this example.

Parameters can be passed to the `main()` function in two different ways. In the first, the handover occurs directly in the Typo tag, just as with HTML tags.

```
There are still <countdown unit=hour>23 Jun
2004</countdown> hours till the
Linux Days 2004.
```

All parameters in the tag are accessible to the plugin object via the `$this->cObj->parameters` array. In this case `$this->cObj->parameters['unit']` will contain the value `hour`. This also functions with multiple parameters. In addition, `$this->cObj->parameters['allParams']` contains all parameters as a string, in the form in which they were passed on. To have the hours displayed, the plugin must be modified as follows:

```
function main($content,$conf) {
    // get parameter from tag
    $unit = $this->cObj->parameters['unit'];
    // get parameter from TypoScript
    $unit = $unit ? $unit : $this->cObj->
                            stdWrap($conf['unit'],

$conf['unit.']);

    if ($unit=='min') {
        $divider = 60;
    } elseif ($unit=='hour') {
    $divider = 60 * 60;
    } else {
            // day - default
            $divider = 60 * 60 * 24;
    }

    $date = $this->cObj->getCurrentVal();
    $timestamp = strtotime($date);
    $delta = $timestamp - time();
    $days = intval($delta / $divider) + 1;

    return $days;
}
```

Now the `<countdown>` tag can handle minutes, hours and days.

The second way of passing on parameters is, as with all plugins, through TypoScript. The code that fetches the `unit` parameter via TypoScript is already contained in the above variation.

```
$unit = $unit ? $unit : $this->cObj->
                                stdWrap($conf['unit'],

$conf['unit.']);
```

If `unit` has not already been passed as a parameter in the tag, `stdWrap()` is called to fetch this value from the TypoScript setup. The `stdWrap()` method is a component of the `cObj` content object. The `cObj` object is set externally while a plugin is initialized, and is available to the plugin. `cObj` is an instance of `tslib/class.tslib_content.php`, and renders all known TypoScript objects such as TEXT or IMAGE.

```
plugin.user_tagcountdown_pi1.unit = min
```

This TypoScript setup defines the value `min` for `unit`; this means that the default value is no longer `day`. So now minutes are counted, as long as `unit` is not set in the `<countdown>` tag.

Because `plugin.user_tagcountdown_pi1.unit` is an object of the `stdWrap` type, it also has the same properties. This makes the following TypoScript setup possible:

```
plugin.user_tagcountdown_pi1.unit = min
plugin.user_tagcountdown_pi1.unit.override.data =
                         register: user_tagcountdown_unit
```

Here `unit` is filled with the value `min`, but if `user_tagcountdown_unit` contains a value there, then this is overwritten with the TS register.

TYPO3 reads TypoScript into a PHP array. you can make this array visible by inserting the `debug($conf);` function at the beginning. If you now reload the page in the front end you will obtain the output as shown in the following figure:

Figure 7.36:

Output of the debug() function

This is the entire TypoScript for this plugin. The tables reproduce the embedding found in the arrays. In standard text form, this appears as follows:

```
plugin.user_tagcountdown_pi1 = USER
```

```
plugin.user_tagcountdown_pi1 {
  userFunc = user_tagcountdown_pi1->main
  unit = min
  unit.override.data = register:
                           user_tagcountdown_unit
}
```

If `stdWrap()` is called up, the first parameter to be passed is the value of `$conf['unit']`, in this case, `min`.

```
$this->cObj->stdWrap($conf['unit'], $conf['unit.']);
```

This first parameter of `stdWrap()` is the value or content that the method is intended to process. The second parameter `$conf['unit.']` defines the behavior of `stdWrap` by means of a parameter array. You should take a look at the `stdWrap()` function in `tslib/class.tslib_content.php` and try to understand how it works. You will find this principle over and again in TYPO3. And if you have another look at the PHP code for this plugin, you will realize that even `main()` follows this principle.

7.6.3 Countdown Tag with JavaScript

The countdown tag will now be extended so that the counter in the front end continues running via JavaScript. It is a good idea here to extend the plugin so that it is able to display seconds, because otherwise there will be nothing much to see in the front end. In addition the new `animate` parameter is introduced.

```
There are still <countdown unit=sec animate>23 Jun
2004</countdown> seconds to go until the Linux Days
2004.
```

JavaScript should only be inserted into the page if this is set.

Even if this goes slightly beyond the limits of this book, we want to briefly mention JavaScript programming here. Because a number of extensions can insert JavaScript into HTML pages, the JavaScript code must also adhere to the namespace made available by the extension. The simplest way to obtain this is to encapsulate the entire script in an object, thus avoiding global variables.

Objects work in JavaScript similarly to classes in PHP. One function serves here as a container. This container can be expanded via the `prototype` property.

```
function myClass() {
  this.myInstanceVar = 0;
}

myClass.prototype.myFirstMethod = function (param1,
```

```
param2) {
    this.myInstanceVar = (param1 + param2)/2;
}

myClass.prototype.mySecondMethod = function () {
    return this.myInstanceVar;
}
```

In this way, only `myClass()` is present in the global namespace. All other functions and variables are encapsulated. It makes sense to use `$this->extKey` or `$this->prefixId` as the namespace for JavaScript code. This results in the following structure for the JavaScript code for this extension:

```
function user_tagcountdown_pi1(id,countdown,unit) {
...
}

user_tagcountdown_pi1.prototype.showcount = function ()
{
...
}
```

The `additionalHeaderData` array in the global object `TSFE` is available so that you can insert something into the HTML header. The following example shows how you insert JavaScript into the header.

```
// check if JavaScript is already set
if (!$GLOBALS['TSFE']->additionalHeaderData[$this->
                                            prefixId]) {

    $jsCode = '
      alert("This is JavaScript");';

    // wrap JavaScript in script tags and add to page
    // header
    $GLOBALS['TSFE']->additionalHeaderData[$this->prefixId]
                    = t3lib_div::wrapJS($jsCode);
}
```

First a check is made to see if the JavaScript code has already been inserted. This should only happen once of course, no matter how many times the plugin is called up. Through the function `t3lib_div::wrapJS()`, the JavaScript code is provided with `<script>` tags and then added to the HTML header.

If you want to use the JavaScript `onload()` event handler in the body tag, you have to share this with other extensions. You do this by entering your JavaScript `onload` code into an array in the `TSFE` object.

```
$GLOBALS['TSFE']->JSeventFuncCalls['onload'][$this->
    prefixId] =

'alert("JS executed on load");';
```

In the modified code of the plugin, first the counter is introduced, so that the elements can later be given a unique ID. A global variable is used for this:

```
function main($content,$conf) {
    // count items for JavaScript usage
    $GLOBALS['T3_VAR']['ext'][$this->
                        prefixId]['count']++;
```

With `$GLOBALS['T3_VAR']['ext'][$this->prefixId]`, only the namespace of the plugin is used.

```
    // get parameter from tag
    $unit = $this->cObj->parameters['unit'];
    // get parameter from TypoScript
    $unit = $unit ? $unit : $this->cObj->
                        stdWrap($conf['unit'],

$conf['unit.']);
```

Seconds are then added to the calculation:

```
    if ($unit=='sec') {
        $divider = 1;
    } elseif ($unit=='min') {
...
    $days = intval($delta / $divider) + 1;
```

The new `animate` parameter is introduced. Note that the check is made with `isset()`, since `animate` does not have a value unless you write the following: `<countdown animate=1 ...>`.

```
    // check if "animate" parameter is set in tag
    $animate = isset($this->cObj->parameters['animate']);
    // get parameter from TypoScript
    $animate = $animate ? $animate :
        $this->cObj->stdWrap($conf['animate'],
                                $conf['animate.']);
```

Finally, there is the code that integrates the animation. This only happens for seconds or minutes, because nobody would notice an animation that only changed hourly or daily.

```
// do animation for seconds or minutes only
if ($animate AND ($unit=='sec' OR $unit=='min')) {
```

An ID for the HTML element is created:

```
// unique id for every element (HTML DOM doesn't
accept '_')
$domId = str_replace('_','-',$this->prefixId).'-'.
                      $GLOBALS[$this->
                              prefixId]['count'];
```

The function to integrate the JavaScript code, which follows later, is called:

```
// include JS code
$this->addJsCounter($domId, $days, $unit);
```

Finally the text is provided with a `<span>` tag, including an ID.

```
// add an id to the content
$days = '<span id=".$domId.'">'.$days.'</span>';
}

return $days;
}
```

Now comes the function that integrates the JavaScript code. The locations containing Java-Script are marked in bold. Please note that it contains PHP variables such as `$this->prefixId`, which make the code portable.

```
/**
 * Add JavaScript counter code to the page
 *
 * @param string dom id
 * @param integer start value for the counter
 * @param string unit: 'sec' or 'min'
 * @return void
 */
   function addJsCounter($id, $countdown, $unit) {
     // include JS code once
     if (!$GLOBALS['TSFE']->additionalHeaderData[$this->
            prefixId]) {

       $jsCode = <<<EOD
         {$this->prefixId}ObjArr = new Array();

           function {$this->prefixId}(id,countdown,unit)
   {
               this.id = id;
               this.countdown = countdown;
               setInterval(
                 "{$this->
                 prefixId}ObjArr['"+id+"'].showcount()",
                 unit);
           }
```

```
    {$this->prefixId}.prototype.showcount = function ()
{
        this.countdown = this.countdown-1;
        element = document.getElementById(this.id);
        element.innerHTML = this.countdown;
    }
EOD;
    // wrap JavaScript in script tags and add to page
    // header
$GLOBALS['TSFE']->additionalHeaderData[$this->
    prefixId] =
        t3lib_div::wrapJS($jsCode);
    }

$unit = ($unit=="min") ? 60000 : 1000;

    // add JS onload handler
$GLOBALS['TSFE']->JSeventFuncCalls['onload'][$id] =
    "{$this->prefixId}ObjArr['{$id}'] =
    new {$this->prefixId}('{$id}', {$countdown},
                                    '{$unit}');";
}
```

Since the principle applied here has already been explained, we will not be going into any more detail regarding the example code.

As you can see, it's not that difficult to integrate JavaScript so that several JavaScript plugins can be used on the same page, without coming into conflict with one another.

7.6.4 Integrating External PHP Scripts

The simpler and more clearly structured external scripts are, the easier it is to use them in TYPO3. If scripts already exist as classes, writing a wrapper seems like the obvious thing to do. This will then insert the class and call it correspondingly. More work is involved if parameters are sent. As a rule, the URL, and possibly the parameters themselves, must be adjusted. If the script is less structured or if it is an old script, using now obsolete PHP variables, for example, adjustments will be necessary.

Softlink **680352**

External PHP scripts can be integrated in the TYPO3 front end in many different ways, via the following TypoScript objects:

USER, USER_INT

These objects represent the standard method. All plugins created by the Kickstarter are integrated as USER or USER_INT. The difference between the two methods is that the output is cached when integrated with USER, while this is not the case with

USER_INT. The latter method is used if the script is intended to react to parameters (GET, POST) in order to generate different outputs, and where it is not worthwhile to use the cHash functionality. Integrating scripts with USER objects is certainly preferable to doing this with PHP_SCRIPT. Integration with PHP_SCRIPT is only necessary if a script is not available as a class, and if porting is not an option.

PHP_SCRIPT

Integrating a script looks something like this in TypoScript:

```
page.90 = PHP_SCRIPT
page.90.file = fileadmin/scripts/myscript.php
```

The script is then included in tslib_cObj. This means that you have access to all the methods of this object, via $this. The output of the script must be contained in the variable $content.

PHP_SCRIPT_INT

This method functions like PHP_SCRIPT. The output of the script is not cached, however.

PHP_SCRIPT_EXT

In this method, the output is also not cached. But integration functions here differently to the two methods above, since the script can produce its output with echo/print.

Converting PHP Script

If you want to insert scripts into TYPO3 that have not been developed specially for it, this is usually possible with relatively little work. Using the example of the following small script, which fetches a few pieces of information on a web server, we will show you what possibilities are available.

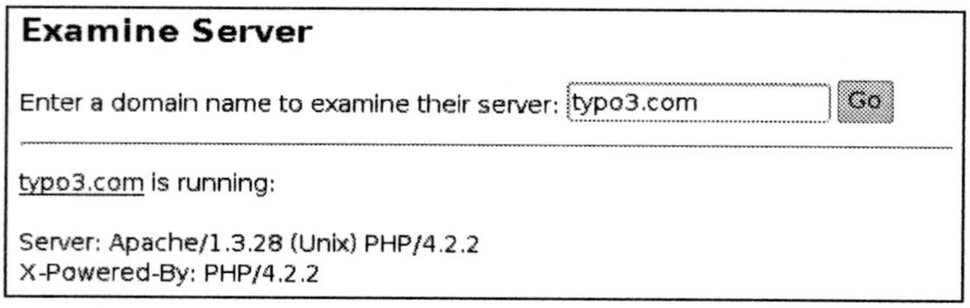

Figure 7.37:

Output of the **Examine Server** *script*

This is the original script:

```php
<?php
# based on a script from http://px.sklar.com by Matt
DeLong

   // examine server information with GET request
 function examine($domain){
   $result = '';

   if($domain){
 if($fp = @fsockopen($domain, 80, &$errno, &$errstr,
30)){
     fputs($fp, "GET /
     $data = array();
     while(!feof($fp)) {
        $data[] = fgets($fp, 128);
   }
   fclose ($fp);
 }

 for($x=0; $x<7; $x++) {
  $result = (strstr(strtolower($data[$x]), 'server:'))?
                                  $data[$x] : $result;
 }
 $result.= (strstr($data[3], 'X-Powered-By')) ?
                             '<br>.$data[3] : '';
 }

   $result = ($domain && !$result) ?
     '<b>ERROR:</b> connection could not be estab-
lished with '. htmlspecialchars($domain) : $result;
   return $result;
 }
 $domain = stripslashes($HTTP_POST_VARS['domain']);

 ?>
 <html>
 <body>
 <h2>Examine Server</h2>
 <form action="<?php echo $_SERVER['PHP_SELF']; ?>"
                                 method="POST">
   <p>Enter a domain name to examine their server:
   <input type="text" name="domain" value="<?php
                        echo
htmlspecialchars($domain); ?>">
   <input type="submit" value="Go"></p>
 </form>
 <hr>
 <p>
 <?php
   $result = examine($domain);
     if($result && !strstr($result, 'ERROR'))
         echo htmlspecialchars($domain).'
                         is running:<br><br>';
```

```
        echo $result;
?>
</p>
</body>
</html>
```

It is possible to have a complete front-end page created by a script. The following TypoScript setup only calls the above script, and does not create any further output:

```
page >
page = PAGE
page.typeNum = 0
page.config.disableAllHeaderCode = 1

page.50 = PHP_SCRIPT_EXT
page.50.file = fileadmin/scripts/examine-server-ext.php
```

But if you integrate the script, as in the last two lines, into your own page (with your own `page` setup), it is necessary to remove everything from the script that has already been created by TYPO3. Normally this will be the HTML header and the `<body>` tags (in bold). In addition—and in contrast to `PHP_SCRIPT_EXT`—output with `echo/print` is not possible for `PHP_SCRIPT` and `PHP_SCRIPT_INT`. Here the script must return its content in the `$content` variable. But this is easily achieved via the PHP output buffer.

```
...
ob_start();

?>
<h2>Examine Server</h2>
...

<?php

$content = ob_get_contents();
ob_end_clean();

?>
```

One problem that frequently occurs with external scripts is with the handling of parameters and URLs. This script does not work either, because the destination URL of the form is not correct. The corrected version of the script appears as follows in the `PHP_SCRIPT_INT` variation:

```
<?php
# based on a script from http://px.sklar.com by Matt
# DeLong

function examine($domain){
...
    return $result;
```

```
}

$domain = t3lib_div::_GP('domain');

ob_start();
?>
<h2>Examine Server</h2>
<form action="<?php
  echo htmlspecialchars(t3lib_div::getIndpEnv
                                ('REQUEST_URI'));
  ?>" method="POST">
  <p>Enter a domain name to examine their server:
  <input type="text" name="domain" value="<?php
              echo htmlspecialchars($domain);?>">

  <input type="submit" value="Go"></p>
</form>
<hr>
<p>

<?php
  $result = examine($domain);
  if($result && !strstr($result, 'ERROR'))
       htmlspecialchars($domain).'
                   is running:<br><br>';
            echo $result;?>
</p>
<?php

$content = ob_get_contents();

ob_end_clean();
?>
```

The question may well be asked as to whether it might not be better to do this via an extension, and create a plugin—hardly any more work is involved, a better framework is retained for extensions, and the script is integrated correctly. Moreover, integration via PHP_SCRIPT can lead to instability in TYPO3 if the script manipulates global variables.

The implemenation as a plugin appears as follows:

```
class user_exmsv_pi1 extends tslib_pibase {

var $prefixId = 'user_exmsv_pi1';
var $scriptRelPath = 'pi1/class.user_exmsv_pi1.php';
var $extKey = 'user_exm_sv';

/**
* Examine Server main function
*/
function main($content,$conf) {
  $this->conf=$conf;
```

517

```
            $this->pi_setPiVarDefaults();
            $this->pi_USER_INT_obj=1;

            $domain = $this->piVars['domain'];

            $result = $this->examine($domain);

            if($result && !strstr($result, 'ERROR')) {
                $result = '
                    <hr>
                    <p>'.htmlspecialchars($domain).'
                            is running:<br />
                    <br />
                    '.$result.'</p>';
        }

            $content = '
              <h2>Examine Server</h2>
              <form action="'.

        htmlspecialchars(t3lib_div::getIndpEnv('REQUEST_URI')).
                '" method="post">

                <p>Enter a domain name to examine their server:
                <input type="text" name="'.$this->prefixId.
                    '[domain]"
        value="'.htmlspecialchars($domain).'">
                <input type="hidden" name="no_cache" value="1"
        />
                <input type="submit" value="Go"></p>
                </form>'.$result;

            return $this->pi_wrapInBaseClass($content);
        }

        /**
        * Examine server information with GET request
        *
        * @param string domain name
        * @return string
        */
        function examine($domain){
        ...
           return $result;
        }
        }
```

The main difference lies in the use of the parameter system by tslib_pibase. This means that all parameters that are passed with $this->prefixId as an array element are automatically available in $this->piVars[].

```
            $domain = $this->piVars['domain'];
```

```
<input type="text" name=".$this->prefixId.'[domain]"
value=". htmlspecialchars($domain).'">
```

For smaller scripts such as this, it is usually worth the trouble to convert the script into a plugin. The functionality of the script is quickly understood, which also makes it easy to use again.

7.6.5 Porting PHP Scripts

Using the example of the *dataMiner* [8] PHP application, we want to demonstrate how scripts are ported to TYPO3. dataMiner is used to display database tables in list and Details Views. Individual records can also be edited.

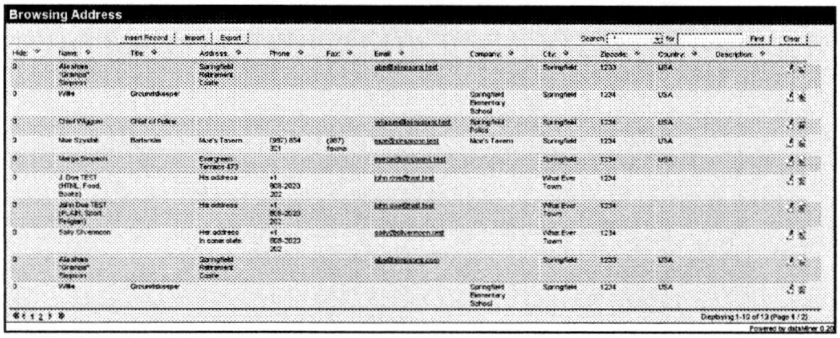

Figure 7.38:

Output of dataMiner *in list form*

The aim of porting is to integrate dataMiner as well as possible into the TYPO3 system, whereby work should be kept to a minimum.

The dataMiner directory contains the following files:

```
dataMiner-0.20.0/
   LICENSE
   NOTES
   README
   img/
      asc.gif
      cal.gif
      delete.gif
      ...
index.html
index.php
lib/
   dM.js
   dataBrowser.php
   dataDBI.php
```

[8] http://greenhell.com/dataMiner

```
        dataDetailer.php
        dataEditor.php
        dataMiner.php
    metabase/
        ...
    sample.sql
```

A look at the source code shows that dataMiner is programmed in a very structured way. The files in the lib/ directory contain the actual application. The code is encapsulated in classes, which should make porting easier.

The application is to be embedded in a page later on, as a plugin. A non-cached plugin (USER_INT) is therefore created in Kickstarter. The dataMiner directory is then copied to the new extension. Files not required are deleted, but the files LICENSE, NOTES and README should be left where they are.

First it is a good idea to "tune" the source code with the module **Tools | ExtDevEval** and convert double quotes to single ones (see section 7.4.2., *Encoding Guidelines*).

The scripts contain various Include commands. These must be modified in form so that the path to the extension can be determined with t3lib_extMgm::extPath().

```php
include_once('lib/dataMiner.php');
```

```php
require_once(t3lib_extMgm::extPath('dataminer').'dataMin
er/lib/dataMiner.
php');
```

The file index.php in the dataMiner directory is only one example of how the dataMiner classes are used. The structure looks something like this (abbreviated):

```php
$foo = new dataBrowser();
$foo->type    =   "mysql";      // database server type

$foo->name    =   "MYDB";       // name of the database
$foo->user    =   "root";       // database user name
$foo->pass    =   "";           // database password
$foo->host    =   "localhost";  // database server
                                // hostname

// The browser needs a table name and its primary key
(required)
$foo->table  =   "city_directory";   // database   table
$foo->key  = "Rid";   // table primary key field name

// Assigning a table title will display the title
```

```
// instead of the actual database table name.
// title = "string";
$foo->title = "Businesses";

// print results (required)
$foo->Main();
```

The code from `index.php` is taken over by the `main()` method of the plugin, into the file `pi1/tx_dataminer_pi1.php`. The main class of dataMiner still needs to be integrated into the header of the file.

```
require_once(t3lib_extMgm::extPath('dataminer').'dataMi
ner/lib/dataMiner.
 php');
```

It turns out that the complete output of dataMiner is generated with the `Main()` method. However, all content is output with `print`. This does not fit in at all with the concept of a plugin, of course, which has to return its output through `return`. Luckily PHP provides functions for buffering output. The following code fragment shows how output buffering is initially activated. Then the `Main()` method of dataMiner is called up. All `print` output is now buffered by PHP. This buffer is read out in the following line and passed on to the `$content` variable. Finally the output buffer is deactivated and its contents returned to the system.

```
ob_start();

$dm->Main();
$content = ob_get_contents();

ob_end_clean();

return $this->pi_wrapInBaseClass($content);
```

dataMiner uses *Metabase* for accessing databases. To be able to test the plugin, the necessary configurations must be made for the database, where the constants used by TYPO3 are used.

```
$dm->type  =   'mysql';       // database server type

$dm->name  =   TYPO3_db;      // name of the database
$dm->user  =   TYPO3_db_username; // database username
$dm->pass  =   TYPO3_db_password;   // database
                                    // password
$dm->host  =   TYPO3_db_host;   // database server
                                // hostname
```

This is a perfectly usable solution, although you do not need to use Metabase. But we will return to that later.

The concept of dataMiner is designed so that it can work with any kind of database tables, after a little configuration. For testing purposes, the `tt_address` table is chosen and configured.

```
// The browser needs a table name and it's primary
// key (required)
$dm->table = 'tt_address'; // database table
$dm->key = 'uid'; // table primary key field name
```

At this point in time the plugin can already be installed and tested. The `tt_address` table is correctly displayed as a list. The icons cannot be seen, though, since the paths are no longer correct. In addition, links or forms will no longer work, because the URLs do not conform to TYPO3.

The paths for the icons can be adjusted very simply using text replacement. First, at a central point in the dataMiner code, the relative path to the extension is initialized.

```
function _var_setup() {
   $this->iconPath =
t3lib_extMgm::siteRelPath('dataminer').

'/dataMiner/';
```

Then `$this->iconPath` is inserted into the path details for all images.

(Hello?! textbackslash is from Latex)

```
"<img src="img/details.gif" ...
```

```
"<img src="".$this->
           iconPath."img/details.gif" ...
```

A further problem comes to light if you look at the HTML code of the plugin in the front-end output. dataMiner issues its own HTML header, which of course has to be removed. The `_head()` method can be found in the code, containing the corresponding HTML code.

```
function _head($title) {
   $this->_load_skin();
   ?>
<!-- $Id: dataMiner.php,v 1.11 2003/06/02 17:55:18
rlineweaver Exp $ -->
<!DOCTYPE HTML PUBLIC "-//W3C//DTD HTML 3.2
                                    Final//EN">
<html>
<head>
<title><?php echo $title; ?></title>
<meta name="robots" content="noindex">
<style>
   BODY,TD,P,H1,H2,H3,H4,FORM {
        font-family:Helvetica,Arial,sans-serif;
          font-size:95; }
```

```
    .NEW {
          color:<?php echo $this->newFileColor; ?>; }
    .HDR {
          color:<?php echo $this->bodyTextColor; ?>;
                        font-size:10pt;
          font-weight: bold; }
    .TIT {
          color:<?php echo $this->siteNameColor; ?>;
          background-color:<?php echo $this->
                                        menubarColor; ?>;
          font-size:14pt; font-weight: bold; }
...
</style>
</head>
<body bgcolor="#<?php echo $this->bodyBgColor; ?>"
  link="#<?php echo $this->rowLinkColor; ?>"
...
  marginwidth="<?php echo $this->bodyMarginSize; ?>">
<?php echo $this->_colorbars($this->headDiv); ?>

<table border=0 cellspacing=0 cellpadding=2
        width="<?php echo $this->siteWidth; ?>">
<tr><td class="TIT"><?php echo $title; ?></td></tr>
...
```

In principle, the entire header, including the <body> tag, can be deleted. The appearance is controlled via CSS, however, which in turn can be defined by so-called skins, as can be seen when the _load_skin() function is called up, and in the variables in the CSS code. The functionality of the skins is to be removed, but the control via CSS should remain. It is a good idea to save the newly created CSS code from the front-end HTML, because the variables there have been replaced by the corresponding colors of the default skin. This means that the HTML header code in _head(), as well as the _load_skin() method can be deleted. In the _foot() method, </body></html> is also deleted accordingly, in which case the plugin is restricted to the output of the actual dataMiner.

Now the page created does not contain any CSS at all, and dataMiner no longer looks quite right. You could include the saved CSS code in the CSS file for the site, but it would be more sensible if the extension already included CSS. This is possible if you use TypoScript to integrate style details.

```
plugin.tx_dataminer._CSS_DEFAULT_STYLE (
.tx-dataminer-pi1 .NEW {
color:ffff00; }
.tx-dataminer-pi1 .HDR {
color:000000;
font-size:10pt; font-weight: bold; }
.tx-dataminer-pi1 .TIT {
color:ffffff; background-color:111111;
```

```
font-size:14pt; font-weight: bold; }
...
```

Because such a TypoScript setup integrates the CSS code into the page header, this cannot be overwritten by an external stylesheet file. This is why the TypoScript setup in the file `static/setup.txt` is saved in the extension. The file is integrated into `ext_tables.php`, making it available as a static template.

```
// add TS/CSS to static templates

t3lib_extMgm::addStaticFile($_EXTKEY,'static/','dataMine
r: CSS');
```

This only integrates the CSS code if the static template was inserted into a template record.

The front-end HTML code generated already looks very good. The `_load_javascript()` method, which integrates a JavaScript file with the help of a `<script>` tag, can be found in the `dataMiner` class. This is modified so that on the one hand the path to the file is set directly, and on the other, so that the tag appears in the HTML header.

```
_load_javascript() {
print "<script language=/"javascripttextbackslash/"
src=textbackslash/"lib/dM.jstextbackslash/"></script>";
```

```
_load_javascript() {
$GLOBALS['TSFE']->additionalHeaderData[$this->pObj->
    prefixId] =
'<script type="text/javascript" src=".
$GLOBALS['TSFE']->
    absRefPrefix.t3lib_extMgm::siteRelPath('dataminer').
'dataMiner/lib/dM.js"></script>';
```

In order for this to work, the plugin object in `tx_dataminer_pi1` must be made available to the dataMiner object.

```
$dm->pObj = & $this;
```

In order for links to also be capable of functioning with this plugin, unfortunately a little manual work is necessary. Simple text replacement does not work here. The `_=b` parameter is simply omitted, because `b` activates the "List View" mode, which is the default anyway. At other places the underscore is replaced by `mode`, which makes a bit more sense.

In addition, `page` is renamed `pointer` for the sake of uniformity, since the same function in `tslib_pibase` is controlled with the `pointer` parameter.

```
$string.= "<a href="".$_SERVER['PHP_SELF'].
"?_=b&page={$this->num_pages}">".
```

```
    "<img src="img/last.gif" border="0" alt="Last"></a>";

$icon = '<img src=".$this->iconPath.
'img/last.gif" border="0" alt="Last">';

$string.= $this->pObj->pi_linkTP_keepPIvars($icon,
array('pointer'=>$this->num_pages), 0);
```

The destination URL of forms must also be changed, of course.

```
print '<form action=".$_SERVER['PHP_SELF'] ...

print '<form action=".$this->pObj->
                pi_linkTP_keepPIvars_url() ...
```

At this point in time the links function correctly, but the parameters passed on are not recognized. But this is relatively simple to resolve, since these parameters are evaluated in dataMiner in the `_get_value()` method. If you introduce the use of `$this->pObj->piVars[]` here, most parameters will be correctly recognized. A few adjustments for POST data still need to be made in the `_var_setup()` method.

Because parameter handling is now dealt with completely by `t3lib_pibase`, the remaining code based on PHP sessions can be removed.

Although the database access functions, it would be desirable to do without the metabase layer. Because dataMiner encapsulates database accesses in a separate class, this must also be done, through MySQL wrapper functions of the TYPO3 database layer. The wrapper functions do not guarantee any database abstraction, like the `exec_*` functions from `t3lib_DB`, but can be implemented into this application with little effort.

```
$result = $this->query($query);
$row = $this->fetch_array($result);

$result = $GLOBALS['TYPO3_DB']->sql_query($query);
$row = $GLOBALS['TYPO3_DB']->sql_fetch_assoc($result);
```

dataMiner is widely configurable in terms of which fields can be displayed and edited, and how these fields are named. You will see very quickly that there are parallels with the TCA definition. It seems appropriate to configure dataMiner automatically via the TCA. To do this, the System language labels (lang) extension is inserted, as it is not available by default in the front end. It is required to determine the appropriate label for the fields.

```
require_once(t3lib_extMgm::extPath('lang').'lang.php');
. . .
$LANG = t3lib_div::makeInstance('language');
. . .
$dm->fields = array_keys($TCA[$dm->table]['columns']);
$dm->title = $LANG->sL($TCA
                [$dm->table]['ctrl']['title']);
$dm->orderby = $TCA[$dm->table]['ctrl']['sorting'];

foreach ($TCA[$dm->table]['columns'] as $column =>
    $def) {
  $dm->humanize($column,$LANG->sL($def['label']));
  if($def['config']['default']) {
  $dm->defvalue($column,$def['config']['default']);
  }
}
. . .
```

What still needs to be done? Configurability via TypoScript is still desirable, as well as a way of being able to select the tables to be shown in the plugin content element.

Whether the efforts in porting have been worthwhile or not is difficult to answer. It would have been possible to insert the script with far less effort—but also much less correctly. Even rewriting it from scratch is possible, or using an existing template and modifying it. With dataMiner you have an application that is already capable of running, allowing tests *during* the porting process, which is a great advantage.

In a final step you could remove redundant code and achieve a TCA-like functionality with dataMiner, which in its results would match a pure TYPO3 application.

7.7 Back-End Programming: Principles

Back-end programming means programming components that provide functionality in the back end. In general these are modules, submodule functions or entries in the context menu.

As you can see from the URL when logging in, the back end is to be found in the `typo3/` directory. It is quite possible, by the way, to delete the back end from the TYPO3 installation, and just keep the front-end functioning.

Modules are normally located in their own extensions; with standard modules, this is not always the case, for historical and practical reasons. Nevertheless they are correctly integrated into the system, of course, and some of them could certainly find their way into extensions. Some more modules are located in the `typo3/mod/` directory, and others directly in `typo3/`. The **Web | List** module for example has its `conf.php` file in the `typo3/mod/web/list/` directory; but the actual module script is located in `typo3/db_list.php`. It is correctly configured through the file `conf.php`, which is why it is available in the system. Apart from these exceptions, all new modules are programmed as extensions.

7.7.1 Module Structure

While in the front end all queries are dealt with via a file—namely `index.php`, a symbolic link to `tslib/index_ts.php`—in the back end each module has its own PHP file providing complete module functionality. For the **Web | List** module, this is the file `db_list.php`. The module file name in extensions, sensibly, is `index.php`, since each module there lies in its own directory.

In general a module consists of the following files:

```
conf.php
index.php
locallang.php
locallang_mod.php
moduleicon.gif
```

conf.php

The module is integrated into the system with this file. It is generated by Kickstarter and normally does not need to be changed.

```
define('TYPO3_MOD_PATH',
'../typo3conf/ext/user_recentchanges/mod1/');
$BACK_PATH='../../../../typo3/';
```

```
$MCONF['name'] = 'tools_urecentchangesM1';
$MCONF['access'] = 'admin';
$MCONF['script'] = 'index.php';
$MLANG['default']['tabs_images']['tab'] =
'moduleicon.gif';
$MLANG['default']['ll_ref'] =
'LLL:EXT:user_recentchanges/mod1/locallang_mod.php';
```

First the constant TYPO3_MOD_PATH is defined. This is the path to the module from the typo3/ directory.

The $BACK_PATH variable contains the relative path to the typo3/ directory. With this variable it is possible to make modules independently of their position in the directory tree. The Extension Manager adjusts these paths in the first two lines during installation, which is the reason why extensions containing modules cannot simply be shifted manually to another extension directory.

The $MCONF[] array defines a unique name for the module with the name key. The access key defines the access permissions for the module. While the value admin allows access exclusively to administrators, the module is typically made available to normal users with user,group. But actual access is obtained by users only via the configuration in the records for users and user groups.

The icon which can be seen in the module menu bar is inserted with the $MLANG[] array. The reference to an external language file is specified.

locallang_mod.php

This file is also generated by Kickstarter and contains the title and description of the module in different languages. The following keys are used for this:

mlang_tabs_tab

A short title for navigation

mlang_labels_tablabel

A somewhat longer title as a description of the short title or as a heading in **Help | About Modules**

mlang_labels_tabdescr

Description of the module in several sentences; is also shown in **Help | About Modules**

index.php

The actual module script can be found here

locallang.php

The language file belonging to the module script; the only absolutely essential file for the module is `conf.php`. All the other files can have other names and be in different locations, as long as they are correctly defined in `conf.php`. But since Kickstarter set up these files in this form, and any deviations from this scheme do not provide more clarity, you should try to retain the structure as much as possible.

ext_tables.php

The module must be made known to the system. This is done in extensions in the file `ext_tables.php`, with the following line:

```
t3lib_extMgm::addModule('web',
'ushopinfoM1',
'',
t3lib_extMgm::extPath($_EXTKEY).'mod1/');
```

In the above example the `ushopinfoM1` module is entered in the `web` main module.

7.7.2 Module Framework

The following files or classes are normally inserted by modules:

init.php

This file must be integrated by every module. A number of libraries are inserted, the user is authenticated, the system configuration is loaded, and paths are initialized.

Defined path constants after `init.php` is called:

PATH_thisScript

Absolute path to the module script

PATH_typo3

Absolute path to the TYPO3 back end

PATH_typo3_mod

Relative path to the module from the `typo3/` path

PATH_site

> Absolute path to the website

PATH_t3lib

> Absolute path to `t3lib/`

The following global objects are available after `init.php` has been called:

$BE_USER

> Back-end user

$LANG

> Language administration

$TYPO3_DB

> Database access

t3lib_SCbase

This is the base class for module scripts. In particular it provides a complete framework for the support of submodule functions. In addition to this it automatically copes with the administration of module settings, menus and parameters passed on. Its functionality is described in more detail in the following examples.

The following variables are available in module scripts:

$this->id

> Contains the ID of the current page, as long as the module is located in the **Web** main module; modules in the **file** area find the current path here.

$this->cmd

> Is set with `t3lib_div::_GP('CMD')` and is available for your own use

$this->perms_clause

> Contains an SQL WHERE clause for the `pages` table, which excludes pages for which the current user has no permissions

$this->MOD_MENU

> Menu array; its use is explained in the following examples

$this->MOD_SETTINGS

> The matching array for the menu with current settings

$this->modTSconfig

The modules TSConfig, based on pages and User TSConfig

template, smallDoc, mediumDoc, bigDoc

The file `typo3/template.php` contains several classes for rendering modules. The various classes are only variations of `template`, however, and define various output widths, since modules in the **Web** have to be somewhat narrower than modules under **Tools**, because of the navigation frame. By convention, `$this->doc` in modules contains an instance of `template`, or one of its variations. The Kickstarter already uses `$this->doc` in generated code:

```
        // Ouput page header
$this->content.=$this->doc->startPage($LANG->
                                 getLL('title'));
$this->content.=$this->doc->header($LANG->
                                 getLL('title'));
$this->content.=$this->doc->spacer(5);
```

t3lib_BEfunc

This class contains various helpful functions for back-end programming, namely for database access, caching, TSConfig, page tree and for output in modules. The menu functions in particular are frequently used. This class, as with the two following ones, is not instantiated, but functions are called from it directly, instead:

```
t3lib_BEfunc::getFuncMenu($this->id,
                    'SET[function]', $this->
                        MOD_SETTINGS['function'],
                        $this->MOD_MENU['function']);
```

t3lib_div

The already familiar `t3lib_div` collection of functions is also available for back-end programming, of course.

t3lib_iconworks

A collection of functions for creating and providing icons; examples:

```
t3lib_iconWorks::getIconImage('tt_content_search',array(
),
 $BACK_PATH)

t3lib_iconworks::getIconImage($table, $row, $BACK_PATH,
'class="c-recicon" title=".$iconAltText.'")
```

The function `t3lib_iconWorks::skinImg()` finds out the file name for an icon and supports skinning. You should use this function for your own icons as well, to make your application skinnable.

For the exact API of the classes, please consult the API documentation, available to you with the `ExtDevEval` extension, for example.

7.7.3 Module Scripts

The basic structure of a module script usually looks like this:

```
unset($MCONF);
require ('conf.php');
require ($BACK_PATH.'init.php');
require ($BACK_PATH.'template.php');

$LANG->includeLLFile('EXT:user_example/mod1
                                /locallang.php');

require_once (PATH_t3lib.'class.t3lib_scbase.php');

$BE_USER->modAccess($MCONF,1);

class user_example_module1 extends t3lib_SCbase {

function menuConfig() {
}

function main() {
}

function printContent() {
}
}
$SOBE =
   t3lib_div::makeInstance('user_example_module1');
$SOBE->init();
$SOBE->main();
$SOBE->printContent();
```

`conf.php` is the first to be integrated. As already mentioned, `conf.php` not only contains some information that is important for the back end, but also the variable `$BACK_PATH`, which contains the relative path to the `typo3/` directory, and which is frequently used within the script.

Then `init.php` from the `typo3/` directory is integrated. `init.php` initializes the environment of a module, and is absolutely essential. The next file to be integrated, `template.php`, contains a library for rendering the module output.

By now the object for the administration of multiple languages is available in `$LANG`. The language definition for the module is loaded and initialized.

The module base class `t3lib_SCbase` is then integrated. The module is an expanded class of `t3lib_SCbase`. The `menuConfig()` method defines menus and options for the module. It is called by the base class.

Finally at the end of the script, an instance of the module class is created and called. This is also the reason why modules are called "SC" (`t3lib_SCbase`), that is, *script classes* : they contain the module class, but this class is also called. The name `$SOBE` is obligatory for the module object, as it is possible that external libraries may refer to it.

7.7.4 Main Modules

It is also possible to create new main modules such as **Web**, **User**, and **Tools**. This is is also supported by Kickstarter. Creating a main module with a navigation frame (like **Web** and **File**) is not yet supported by Kickstarter, but is possible. Here is an example of the **Media** main module and the **Media | List** module.

mod1/conf.php

```
define('TYPO3_MOD_PATH',
              '../typo3conf/ext/dam/mod1/');
$BACK_PATH='../../../../typo3/';

$MCONF['name']='txdamM1';
$MCONF['access']='user,group';
$MCONF['navFrameScript']='alt_dam_navframe.php';
$MCONF['defaultMod']='list';
```

The `navFrameScript` key defines the script to be called in the navigation frame. The frameset itself is created by the back end.

```
mod1/list/conf.php

define('TYPO3_MOD_PATH',
                '../typo3conf/ext/dam/mod1/list/');
$BACK_PATH='../../../../../typo3/';

$MCONF['name']='txdamM1_list';
$MCONF['access']='group,user';
```

```
$MCONF['script']='index.php';
```

ext_tables.php

```
t3lib_extMgm::addModule('txdamM1', '', '',
t3lib_extMgm::extPath('dam').'mod1/');
t3lib_extMgm::addModule('txdamM1', 'list', '',
t3lib_extMgm::extPath('dam').'mod1/list/');
```

Here the modules are made known to the system: first the new `txdamM1` main module, then the `list` module as a submodule.

7.7.5 Submodule Functions

Several modules such as **Web | Functions** or **User | Taskcenter** provide a way of embedding functions. Such submodule functions can be separate extensions; after installation, they appear in the corresponding module menu. Some module functions are discussed in more detail in the example **Web | Functions | Wizard submodule function.**

7.8 Backend Programming: Examples

The following examples provide an overview of options for extending the back end with new functions.

For your own projects Kickstarter already offers a suitable border. If you can't find certain functions, have a look at other modules to see if you can find similar functions there. If you hold the right mouse button over the module frame, most browsers will give you information on the URL called, which should tell you in which directory the module script is located, so that you can study its source code.

TYPO3 version 3.7 was used for the back-end examples, as it was for the earlier front-end examples.

7.8.1 Tools | Recent Changes

The first example of back-end programming will be a module to display the most recently edited pages. The module will only be accessible to administrators under **Tools,** and will have a few display options in the form of a selection field menu and a checkbox. In addition the listed pages and records are provided with links to the page module where they can be edited, or to call the records directly.

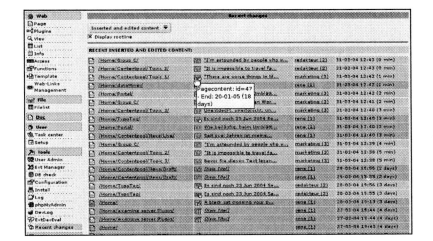

Figure 7.39:

The module Recent Changes

In Kickstarter an extension with a module is first created. The module is saved under **Tools** and the **Admin-only access!** option is activated.

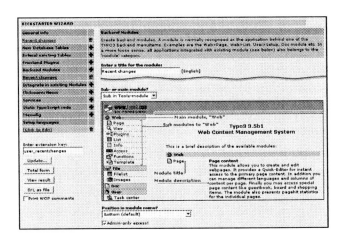

Figure 7.40:

Creating a module in the Extension Kickstarter

The module is quickly configured, as there are only a few options to be set. The Kickstarter creates the following files:

```
ext_emconf.php
ext_icon.gif
ext_tables.php
mod1/
    clear.gif
    conf.php
    index.php
    locallang.php
    locallang_mod.php
```

```
moduleicon.gif
```

In the file `ext_tables.php` the module is made known to the system.

```
t3lib_extMgm::addModule('tools',
                           'urecentchangesM1', '',
t3lib_extMgm::extPath($_EXTKEY).'mod1/');
```

The file `mod1/index.php` contains the actual module. If the newly created extension is installed, the module will already produce the output as shown in the following figure.

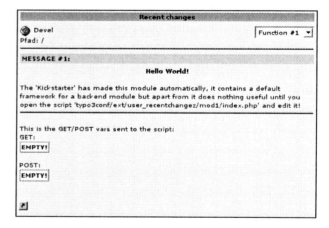

Figure 7.41:

Output of the module created by Kickstarter

In `index.php` it seems that the basic structure for the module already exists. A menu and some example output have also been generated.

Below you will see the code for the finished module. It is a good idea to create the module using Kickstarter, so that you can see the differences. The concept of the module consists of selecting the information from the `sys_log` table that provides details of the most recently edited pages and records, and arranging these in a table. This includes additional information such as icons, title, Rootline, and Tooltips with IDs.

First the module in `index.php` is initialized. In contrast to the code generated by Kickstarter, no changes are needed here.

```
    // DEFAULT initialization of a module [BEGIN]
unset($MCONF);
require ('conf.php');
require ($BACK_PATH.'init.php');
require ($BACK_PATH.'template.php');

    // Include locallang file for module
$LANG->includeLLFile('EXT:user_recentchanges/mod1/
                                    locallang.php');
```

```
      // Include module base class
require_once (PATH_t3lib.'class.t3lib_scbase.php');

      // This checks permissions and exits if the users
      // has no permission for entry.

$BE_USER->modAccess($MCONF,1);

      // DEFAULT initialization of a module [END]


class user_recentchanges_module1 extends t3lib_SCbase {
```

The first method of the module class overwrites `menuConfig()` from `t3lib_SCbase`. The definitions of all menus and options for the module are located in `$this->MOD_MENU[]`. Typically, `'function'` contains the definition of the main menu, which is usually rendered as a selection field. This is already created by Kickstarter as an example. The option to display only newly added contents, edited contents, or both should be included in the main menu of the module. The menu array is filled with keys, accordingly.

```
/**
 * Adds items to the ->MOD_MENU array.
 * Used for the function menu selector.
 *
 * @return void
 */
function menuConfig() {
  global $LANG;

  $this->MOD_MENU = Array (
    'function' => Array (
      'newAndUpdated' => $LANG>getLL('newAndUpdated'),
      'updated' => $LANG->getLL('updated'),
      'new' => $LANG->getLL('new'),
    ),

    'showRootline' => true,
  );

  parent::menuConfig();
}
```

The texts of the individual menu items are converted into the language of the user via `$LANG->getLL()`, if this exists. The language definitions are to be found in `mod1/locallang.php`:

```
$LOCAL_LANG = Array (
   'default' => Array (
'title' => 'Recent changes',
```

```
'showRootline' => 'Display rootline',
'new' => 'Inserted content',
'updated' => 'Edited content',
'newAndUpdated' => 'Inserted and edited content',
'new_header' => 'Recent inserted content:',
'updated_header' => 'Recent edited content:',
'newAndUpdated_header' => 'Recent inserted and edited
                         content:',
'admins_only' => 'Only admins have access to this
                 module!',

  'de' => Array (
    'title' => 'Letzte Änderungen',
...
),
```

For the sake of simplicity, we have used the same key for the menu and for the language definition. This is not necessary, however, and is used here only because it is easier to handle.

Back to the module code. Apart from `'function'`, `$this->MOD_MENU` contains the entry `'showRootline'`, which is defined as a Boolean value and is used for the checkbox. Finally `parent::menuConfig()` is called to complete the menu configuration.

The next method is `main()`, the main method of the module script. The name follows a convention, but is not obligatory. A number of initializations of the module are performed here and the output of the module is generated, where, for the sake of clarity, its functionality is called via `moduleContent()`, and is not located within this method.

```
/**
 * Main function of the module. Write the content to
$this->content
 *
 * @return void
 */
function main() {
        global $BE_USER,$LANG,$BACK_PATH;
```

First a check is made to see if the user really does have administrator status.

```
if ($BE_USER->user['admin']) {
```

In the code created by Kickstarter, this line was a bit different. In addition, `$this->pageinfo` was set, which refers to the currently selected page. The Kickstarter code is is set up to be used in the **Web** module. But since this module works under the **Tools** main module, so that there is no currently selected page, this code was left out here.

Then a `template` or `bigDoc` object is created in `$this->doc` (see section 7.7.2).

```
    // Init the module doc
$this->doc = t3lib_div::makeInstance('bigDoc');
$this->doc->backPath = $BACK_PATH;
$this->doc->form = '<form action="" method="POST">';
```

The following JavaScript code was generated by Kickstarter, and is necessary for the functionality of the following menu functions:

```
    // JavaScript, used for menus
$this->doc->JScode = '
<script language="javascript" type="text/javascript">
    function jumpToUrl(URL) {
                document.location = URL;
    }
</script>
';
```

The HTML page to be displayed is initialized via the `template` object, the title of the modules displayed and stored in the `$this->content` variable.

```
    // Ouput page header
$this->content.= $this->doc->startPage($LANG->
                                    getLL('title'));
$this->content.= $this->doc->header($LANG->
                                    getLL('title'));
$this->content.= $this->doc->spacer(5);
```

Then the menu is created. To do this, functions from `t3lib_BEfunc` are used. `$this->id` is passed to the functions. For modules in the **Web** area, this variable contains the currently selected page ID. This is sent to the current script by the menu function with the `id` parameter and recognized by `t3lib_SCbase`. This makes no sense for a module in the **Tools** area, of course, because no page navigation is available here, and the module is supposed to display all changed pages anyway. But it is also not in the way, so we can leave the code in this form, so that it can be easily modified if the module is to be later rewritten for the Web area.

```
    // Output menu
$menu = array();
$menu[] = t3lib_BEfunc::getFuncMenu($this->id,

'SET[function]',
                        $this->MOD_SETTINGS['function'],
                        $this->MOD_MENU['function']);
```

`SET[function]` defines the parameter with which the value of the menu is to be sent to the module script. `$this->MOD_SETTINGS['function']` contains the current value and `$this->MOD_MENU['function']` is the definition of the menu array containing the values and texts that the user gets to see. The whole thing functions as follows: a selection field menu is created that, with the help of the JavaScript function `jumpToUrl()` added above, sends the value of the menu entry selected by the user to the module script with the `SET[function]` parameter. The `SET` parameter is evaluated by the module base class `t3lib_SCbase`, compared with `$this->MOD_MENU[]`, and saved in `$this->MOD_SETTINGS[]`. Finally these module settings for the current user are written to the database and reconstructed the next time the module is called up.

The checkbox also functions in the same way.

```
$menu[] = t3lib_BEfunc::getFuncCheck($this->id,
                        'SET[showRootline]',
        $this->MOD_SETTINGS['showRootline']).' '.
        $LANG->getLL('showRootline');
$this->content.=$this->doc->section('',
                        implode('<br />',$menu));
$this->content.=$this->doc->divider(5);
```

The contents of the module created by calling the `moduleContent()` method.

```
// Render content:
$this->moduleContent();
```

Finally the shortcut icon is displayed.

```
// ShortCut
if ($BE_USER->mayMakeShortcut()) {
  $this->content.=$this->doc->spacer(20).
    $this->doc->section('',
      $this->doc->makeShortcutIcon('id',
        implode(',',array_keys($this->MOD_MENU)),
        $this->MCONF['name'])
    );
}

$this->content.=$this->doc->spacer(10);
```

If the user is not an administrator, he or she is warned of this with the following output:

```
} else {
  // If no access: output message

  $this->doc = t3lib_div::makeInstance('bigDoc');
  $this->doc->backPath = $BACK_PATH;

  $this->content.=$this->doc->startPage($LANG->
                        getLL('title'));
  $this->content.=$this->doc->header($LANG->
                        getLL('title'));
  $this->content.=$this->doc->spacer(5);
```

```
    $this->content.=$this->doc->section('',
    $LANG->getLL('admins_only'));
    $this->content.=$this->doc->spacer(10);
    }
}
```

The next method, `printContent()`, was created by Kickstarter in this way. When it is called up, the HTML page generated is finally displayed, which happens at the end of the file.

```
/**
 * Prints out the module's HTML code
 *
 * @return void
 */
function printContent() {
    $this->content.=$this->doc->endPage();
    echo $this->content;
}
```

`moduleContent()` was also set up by Kickstarter. In many modules it contains a `switch()` construction to call the various functions of the module by means of `$this->MOD_SETTINGS['function']` or other options. In this case the value of `MOD_SETTINGS['function']` is only determined in the `$this->getRecentChangesTable()` method. The `_header` value is also attached, so the text for the header is determined, which in turn can be found in `locallang.php`.

```
/**
 * Generates the module content
 *
 * @return void
 */
function moduleContent() {
  global $LANG;

  $mode = $this->MOD_SETTINGS['function'];
  $content = $this->getRecentChangesTable($mode);
  $this->content.=$this->doc->section($LANG->
                            getLL($mode.'_header'),
  $content,0,1);
}


/**
 * Render the table with recently changed records
 *
 * @param string Mode from $this->
                            MOD_SETTINGS['function']
 * @return string Rendered Table
 */
function getRecentChangesTable($mode) {
```

541

```
global $BACK_PATH, $BE_USER, $LANG, $TCA;
```

Using this method, the actual table with the most recently edited pages
is created, by means of the passed $mode parameter, the variable $action
is set, which filters out the corresponding entries from the sys_log table
in the following database query.

```
// Set sys_log actions depending on selected mode
if ($mode=='new') {
    $action = '1';
} elseif ($mode=='updated') {
    $action = '2';
} else {
    $action = '1,2';
}

  // Query sys_log for non-deleted pages only
$res = $GLOBALS['TYPO3_DB']->exec_SELECTquery(
            'sys_log.*',
            'sys_log,pages',
            'pages.uid=sys_log.event_pid'.
              ' AND sys_log.event_pid>0'.
              ' AND sys_log.type=1'.
              ' AND sys_log.action IN ('.$action.')'.
              ' AND sys_log.error=0'.
              t3lib_BEfunc::deleteClause('pages'),
          '',
          'tstamp DESC',
          40);
```

For output using a table, the $this->doc->table() method is used,
which displays a table using the following definition. The $table array is
used to store the data of the table.

```
    // init table layout
$tableLayout = array (
  'table' => array ('<table border="0" cellpadding="1"
        cellspacing="1" class="typo3-recent-edited">',
  '</table>'),
  'defRow' => array (
    'tr' => array('<tr class="bgColor4">','</tr>'),
    'defCol' => Array('<td valign="top">','</td>')
  )
);

$table=array();
$tr=0;
```

In the following loop the selected `sys_log` entries are processed for output in the table.

```
while($logRow = $GLOBALS['TYPO3_DB']->
                        sql_fetch_assoc($res)) {

    $page_id = $logRow['event_pid'];
    $pageRow = t3lib_BEfunc::getRecord('pages',
                                    $page_id);
```

First the page record is fetched using the page ID from the `sys_log` table. For the first column of the table output, a link is generated with an icon for the `getItemFromRecord()` method to follow for editing the page (`$contentPageLink`). For the final column, the time of the last change is generated (`$contentAge`).

```
    if (is_array($pageRow)) {

        // Create output item for page record
    $contentPageLink = $this->getItemFromRecord('pages',
    $pageRow);

        // Create output text describing the age
    $contentAge =
        t3lib_BEfunc::dateTimeAge($logRow['tstamp'],1);
```

After this the details of the changed page element are created.

```
    $contentElementLink = '';
    $contentUser = '';

        // Fetch record if table is not "pages"
    if(!($logRow['tablename']=='pages')) {
            $elementRow = t3lib_BEfunc::getRecord(
                            $logRow['tablename'],
                            $logRow['recuid']);
```

The `sys_log` entry contains information on the table and the `uid` of the modified record. This `uid` is fetched; if it exists, a link for editing the record is created for the second column (`$contentElementLink`).

```
        // If record is deleted continue with next log
        // entry
    if (!is_array($elementRow)) {
        continue;
    }
        // Create output item for non-page record
    $contentElementLink = $this->getItemFromRecord(
            $logRow['tablename'], $elementRow);

    }
```

The table also has information on which user has processed the page. First the record is taken from the be_users table and then an editing link is created ($contentUser).

```
// Create user item
$userRow = t3lib_BEfunc::getRecord('be_users',
$logRow['userid']);
 if(is_array($userRow)) {
      $contentUser =
htmlspecialchars($userRow['username'].
                          '('.$userRow['uid'].')');
      $contentUser = $this->wrapEditLink($contentUser,
 'be_users', $userRow['uid']);
```

If the user is the current user, a different background color is used in the $tableLayout array for the current table line, to make it clear that this page was changed by the user.

```
// Use different row color
// if record was edited by current user
if ($userRow['uid']==$BE_USER->user['uid']) {
  $tableLayout[$tr]['tr'] = array(
                            '<tr class="bgColor5">',
                            '</tr>');

  }
}
```

Finally the data is written to the $table array. After the loop, that is, after all log entries have been processed, the table is rendered with $this->doc->table(). You could of course simply build up the HTML table using strings—this is just a matter of taste.

```
// Add row to table
$td=0;
$table[$tr][$td++] = $contentPageLink;
$table[$tr][$td++] = $contentElementLink;
$table[$tr][$td++] = $contentUser;
$table[$tr][$td++] = $contentAge;
$tr++;
  }
}

  // Return rendered table
 return $this->doc->table($table, $tableLayout);
  }
```

The following method creates a record element for the table output, based on the table name passed, and on a record array.

```
/**
 * Returns a linked icon with title from a record
 *
 * @param     string     Table name (tt_content,...)
 * @param     array      Record array
 * @return    string     Rendered icon
 */
function getItemFromRecord($table, $row) {
global $BACK_PATH, $LANG, $TCA, $BE_USER;
```

First the text for the `title` attribute (Tooltip) of the icon is created. The Tooltip can be seen if you move the mouse over an icon.

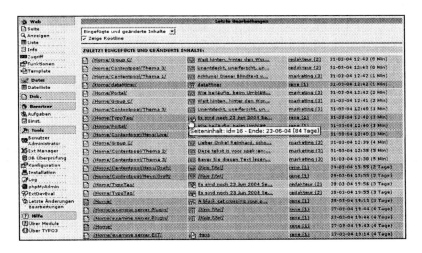

Figure 7.42:

The finished recent changes module

```
$iconAltText =
t3lib_BEfunc::getRecordIconAltText($row, $table);

    // Prepend table description for non-pages tables
if(!($table=='pages')) {
    $iconAltText = $LANG->
            sl($TCA[$table]['ctrl']['title']).': '.
    $iconAltText;
}
```

To make it clear what type of record is involved, that is, to which table it belongs, the title of the table is placed in front of the text, as long as it is not the `pages` table.

The title of the record is then determined. The TCA definition contains information on which database fields should be displayed as titles. On the basis of this information, the `t3lib_BEfunc::getRecordTitle()` function determines the title. As long as the `showRootline` option has been set with the checkbox, the Rootline path for the page is determined, and if necessary, shortened to the length that the user has set under **User | Settings**.

```
        // Create record title or Rootline for pages
        // if option is selected
    if($table=='pages' AND $this->
        MOD_SETTINGS['showRootline']) {
        $elementTitle = t3lib_BEfunc::getRecordPath($row
                        ['uid'],'1=1', 0);
        $elementTitle = t3lib_div::fixed_lgd_cs
            ($elementTitle, ($BE_USER->uc['titleLen']));
    } else {
        $elementTitle =
            t3lib_BEfunc::getRecordTitle($table, $row, 1);
    }
```

Finally the icon generated with the title is provided with a link for editing and returned.

```
    // Create icon for record
    $elementIcon = t3lib_iconworks::getIconImage
                                      ($table, $row,
    $BACK_PATH,
    'class="c-recicon" title=".$iconAltText.'");

    // Return item with edit link
    return $this->wrapEditLink($elementIcon.$elementTitle,
    $table,
    $row['uid']);
    }
```

The final method of the module creates a link that either calls the page module (for pages) with JavaScript, or displays a record directly for editing (for records from other tables).

```
    /**
    * Wraps an edit link around a string.
    * Creates a page module link for pages, edit link for
    * other tables.
    *
    * @param string The string to be wrapped
    * @param string Table name (tt_content,...)
    * @param integer uid of the record
    * @return string Rendered link
    */
    function wrapEditLink($str, $table, $id) {
    global $BACK_PATH;

    if($table=='pages') {
```

```
    $editOnClick =
            "top.fsMod.recentIds['web']=".$id.";";
    $editOnClick.= "top.goToModule('web_layout',1);";
} else {
    $params = '&edit['.$table.']['.$id.']=edit';
    $editOnClick = t3lib_BEfunc::editOnClick
                            ($params,$BACK_PATH);
}

    return '<a href="#"
        onclick="'.htmlspecialchars($editOnClick).'">'.
    $str.'</a>';
}
}
```

As you can see, the page module is called via a JavaScript function of the main frame, after the ID of the page has been set previously, which in turn is then passed to the module when it is called up.

The link for editing a record is created with the corresponding parameters with the `t3lib_BEfunc::editOnClick()` function.

Finally at the end of the file, an instance of the class of the module is made and called.

```
    // Make instance:
$SOBE = t3lib_div::makeInstance
                ('user_recentchanges_module1');
$SOBE->init();

    // Include files?
foreach($SOBE->include_once as $INC_FILE)
                            include_once($INC_FILE);

$SOBE->main();
$SOBE->printContent();
```

The structure of the module makes extensions quite easy. It is simple to add menu items or new options. For example, a Details View could easily be added with a seperate method and called from `moduleContent()`.

7.8.2 The Web | Functions | Wizards Submodule Function

As a basis for submodule functions, TYPO3 provides the `t3lib_extobjbase` class. The `t3lib_SCbase` module bases class contains an interface to `t3lib_extobjbase`. With this combination it is relatively easy to build modules that can take in submodule functions as well as the submodule functions themselves.

In the example below, a submodule function will be embedded into **Web | Functions | Wizards**. The function will mark pages recursively as enabled or disabled for searching. This option is normally available when editing the page header, and there it is called **No search**. but now, via a wizard, you should be able to modify the **No search** option so that it applies for an entire page tree. The finished module looks like this.

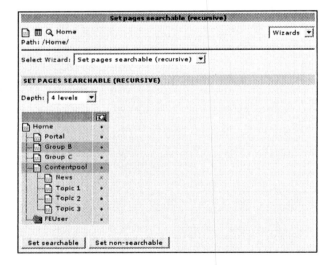

Figure 7.43:

New Wizard as a submodule function of **Web | functions**

The output of the submodule function only starts with the header **SET PAGES SEARCHABLE**, since it is embedded in the **Functions | Wizards** module. Every module that allows submodule functions provides, where necessary, a border or basic functions, which can be of various kinds, depending on the functionality of the module. In this case the module shows menus for selecting the submodule functions, as well as a header with the current page that the user has selected via the page tree of the navigation frame in the **Web** module. This page defines the start page for the wizards.

The new submodule function uses the current page as the starting point from which it will walk through the page tree. How deep this move is made into the tree can be specified by the user with a selection field. The pages for editing are also shown as a tree where the current status for **No search** is identified for each page. Pages are also highlighted for which the user has no editing permissions to change their status. Finally he or she can change the status of all pages displayed, with just two buttons.

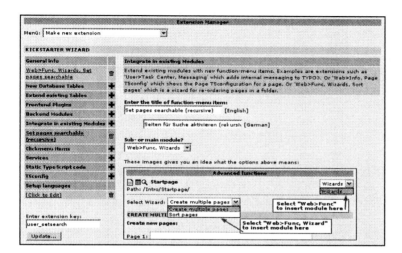

Figure 7.44:

Creating a **Web | Functions | Wizards** submodule function via Kickstarter

As Kickstarter directly supports submodule functions in **Web | Functions | Wizards,** a basic framework is quickly assembled.

Apart from the **General info** and the additional **German** language components, the extension only contains the submodule function, which is created with the **Include in existing modules** option.

The Kickstarter creates the following files:

```
ext_emconf.php
ext_icon.gif
ext_tables.php
locallang_db.php
modfunc1/
    class.user_setsearch_modfunc1.php
    locallang.php
```

The locallang files contain the various languages, as always. In the file ext_tables.php the submodule function is registered:

```
t3lib_extMgm::insertModuleFunction(
  'web_func',
  'user_setsearch_modfunc1',
        t3lib_extMgm::extPath($_EXTKEY) .
  'modfunc1/class.user_setsearch_modfunc1.php',
```

```
'LLL:EXT:user_setsearch/locallang_db.php:moduleFunction.
user_setsearc
 h_modfunc1','wiz'
 );
```

In `class.user_setsearch_modfunc1.php` Kickstarter has created a little example code in which a menu option is introduced and displayed as a checkbox.

```
require_once(PATH_t3lib.'class.t3lib_extobjbase.php');

class user_setsearch_modfunc1 extends t3lib_extobjbase
{
   function modMenu() {
     global $LANG;

     return Array (
        'user_setsearch_modfunc1_check' => '',
     );
   }

   function main() {
     global $BE_USER, $LANG, $BACK_PATH;

     $out.=$this->pObj->doc->spacer(5);
     $out.=$this->pObj->doc->section($LANG->
               getLL('title'),
                     'Dummy content here...', 0, 1);

     $menu=array();
     $menu[]=t3lib_BEfunc::getFuncCheck($this->pObj>id,
       'SET[user_setsearch_modfunc1_check]',
       $this->pObj->MOD_SETTINGS
            ['user_setsearch_modfunc1_check']).
       $LANG->getLL('checklabel');
     $out.=$this->pObj->doc->spacer(5);
     $out.=$this->pObj->doc->section('Menu',implode
                                  (' - ',$menu),0,1);

     return $out;
   }
}
```

A submodule function is an extended class of `t3lib_extobjbase`. Submodule functions are instantiated and initialized by the module or by the `t3lib_SCbase` class. This means that submodule functions may normally contain only the `modMenu()` and `main()` methods. If the submodule function does not have its own menus options that need to be stored in the module setting, then the `modMenu()` method is not necessary.

The `main()` method is called by the parent module and must return the HTML code for the submodule function. HTML is normally generated in back-end modules via the instance of the `template` (`typo3/template.php`) class, available in modules via `$this->doc`. Because the object of the parent module is available in submodule functions via `$this->pObj`, the `template` object can be accessed via `$this->pObj->doc`. This is also the main difference between submodule functions and modules or submodules.

The function should display the page tree to be edited. The already available `t3lib_pageTree` class is used for this. But it needs to be slightly adjusted and expanded. Because this extension, through the extension key, has the namespace `user_setsearch`, the class derived from this is named `user_setsearch_pageTree`.

```
/**
 * local version of the page tree
 * which points the title link to the current script
 *
 * @author René Fritz <r.fritz@colorcube.de>
 */
class user_setsearch_pageTree extends t3lib_pageTree {
    function wrapTitle($title,$v) {
        $aOnClick = 'returnjumpToUrl(textbackslash''.
          $this->thisScript.'?id='.$v['uid'].
          'textbackslash',this);';
        return '<a href="#" onclick=".htmlspecialchars
          ($aOnClick).'">'.$title.'</a>';
    }
}
```

Only the `wrapTitle()` method is changed to create a suitable link for the page title. By clicking on the page title, the user can also determine the start page when the page tree is displayed. To do this, the current script (the parent module) is called again with the `id` parameter and the page `uid` as the value. The `id` parameter is standard for **web** modules, and is also passed by the page tree of the navigation frame. The module base class `t3lib_SCbase` recognizes this parameter and saves it in the variable `$this->id`. Consequently the ID is also available in the submodule function via `$this->pObj->id`.

The class of the submodule function, as already mentioned, is an extension of `t3lib_extobjbase`. Required variables are defined in the header of the class.

```
require_once(PATH_t3lib.'class.t3lib_extobjbase.php');

/**
 * Creates the "set searchable" wizard
 *
```

```
 * @author René Fritz <r.fritz@colorcube.de>
 */
class user_setsearch_modfunc1 extends t3lib_extobjbase
{

/**
 * Page tree object
 * @see t3lib_pageTree
 */
var $tree;

/**
 * The current target script (index.php)
 */
var $thisScript;
```

The selection box for the depth of the page tree is defined in the modMenu() method and returned as an array. This is attached to the $MOD_MENU array of the module, and its values are saved automatically with the settings of the module. There is already a translation of "levels", which is accessed here.

```
/**
 * Adds menu items: Levels menu
 *
 * @return array
 * @ignore
 */
function modMenu() {
  global $LANG;

  $levelsLabel = $LANG->sL(
'LLL:EXT:lang/locallang_mod_web_perm.php:levels');
  return array(
    'user_setsearch_modfunc1_depth' => array(
      1 => '1 '.$levelsLabel,
      2 => '2 '.$levelsLabel,
      3 => '3 '.$levelsLabel,
      4 => '4 '.$levelsLabel,
      10 => '10 '.$levelsLabel
    )
  );
}
```

The main() method is called by the parent module and returns HTML.

```
/**
 * Main function creating the content for the module.
 *
 * @return string HTML content for the module, actually
 * a "section"
 * made through the parent object in $this->pObj
 */
```

```
function main() {
  global $BE_USER,$LANG,$BACK_PATH;

      $this->thisScript = basename(PATH_thisScript);
```

The name of the current script (the parent module) is assigned to $this->thisScript, as it will be used many times.

Then $this->getPageTree() is called up. This method follows later and is intended to initialize the page tree.

```
$this->getPageTree();

$out = '';

    // title
$out.= $this->pObj->doc->spacer(5);
$out.= $this->pObj->doc->section($LANG->
                        getLL('title'),'',0,1);
```

The $out variable collects the HTML output. First the title of this submodule function is displayed. The title is defined in the file locallang.php, and read in automatically when the submodule function was initialized.

The selection menu for the depth of the page tree is printed below. The t3lib_BEfunc::getFuncMenu() function creates a menu based on the parameters, using the SET[] parameter. The t3lib_SCbase module base class recognizes all parameters passed with SET[] and compares them with the module settings, which are available in MOD_SETTINGS. In this way, the module itself does not have to worry about saving module options. The correct prefix (user_setsearch_modfunc1) must be used, however, so that the parameters do not collide with other extensions.

```
    // depth menu
$menu = $LANG->
        sL('LLL:EXT:lang/locallang_mod_web_perm.php
                        :Depth').': '.
t3lib_BEfunc::getFuncMenu($this->pObj->id,
'SET[user_setsearch_modfunc1_depth]',
$this->pObj->MOD_SETTINGS
            ['user_setsearch_modfunc1_depth'],
$this->pObj->MOD_MENU
            ['user_setsearch_modfunc1_depth']);

$out.= $this->pObj->doc->spacer(5);
$out.= $this->pObj->doc->section('',$menu,0,1);
```

After this, the page tree created in the following showPageTree() method is displayed.

```
    // output page tree
$out.= $this->pObj->doc->spacer(10);
```

```
$out.= $this->pObj->doc->section('',$this->
                                showPageTree(),0,1);
```

Since the parent module has already displayed a `<form>` tag, this must first be closed, because another URL is required as the `action` for this submodule function.

```
// new form (close old)
$out.= '</form>';
$out.= $this->pObj->doc->spacer(10);
```

The submodule functions such that IDs are collected only for the pages whose search flag is to be modified. The modification to the flag is carried out via the TCE (TYPO3 Core Engine), which is available for modules in the `typo3/tce_db.php` script. A new `<form>` tag is set up with `tce_db.php` as the target.

```
// call tce_db.php script with the commands
$out.= '<form action=".
$BACK_PATH.'tce_db.php" method="POST"
                        name="editform">';
$out.= '<input type="hidden" name="id" value=".
$this->pObj->id.'">';
```

The `tce_db.php` script understands a range of commands, which are passed in the following lines as `hidden` form elements. First the URL to where redirection should take place is passed on, with `redirect`. This is the parent module, whose name is already known with `$this->thisScript`. The constant `TYPO3_MOD_PATH` defines the relative path to the script from the `typo3/` directory in which `tce_db.php` is located.

```
$out.= '<input type="hidden" name="redirect" value=".
TYPO3_MOD_PATH.$this->thisScript.'?id='.$this->pObj->
                                            id.'">';
```

In this way, a return is made via a redirect to the calling script, without the user noticing the call of `tce_db.php` at all.

Now come the commands for changing the search flag. The first line instructs `tce_db.php` to set the `no_search` field in the `pages` table of the record with the ID `$this->pObj->id` to 1. In theory this now has to be repeated for every page in the selected page tree; but there is a more elegant way of doing this.

```
$out.= '<input type="hidden" name="data[pages]
            ['.this->pObj->id.'][no_search]" value="1">';
```

With the command `mirror`, you can instruct `tce_db.php` to carry out the same changes to a series of records. The method that then follows, `$this->getEditablePagesIDList()`, provides the page IDs of the selected page tree for this.

```
$out.= '<input type="hidden" name="mirror[pages][' .
$this->pObj->id.']" value=".$this->
                        getEditablePagesIDList().'">';
```

The submit buttons are labeled according to their function and send the form off. A button previously sets the value for the search flag in the above `<input>` tag from 1 to 0, via JavaScript.

```
    // submit buttons
$out.= '<input type="submit" name="setSearchable"
        value=".$LANG->getLL('setSearchable').'"
        onclick="document.editform[textbackslash'data
        [pages]['.$this->pObj->id.'][no_search]
        [textbackslash'].value=0;"> ';
$out.= '<input type="submit" name="setNonSearchable"
        value=".$LANG->getLL('setNonSearchable').'">';

return $out;
}
```

Finally the HTML code is returned to the calling module. The `<form>` tag is not closed, by the way, since the module will display one more matching tag to close its own form. The following `getPageTree()` method uses the `user_setsearch_pageTree` class to create the page tree. With `$this->pObj->perms_clause` there is an SQL expression available which excludes pages for which users have no permissions.

```
/**
 * Reads the page tree
 *
 * @return void
 */
function getPageTree() {
global $BE_USER,$LANG,$BACK_PATH;

$this->tree = t3lib_div::makeInstance
                    ('user_setsearch_pageTree');
$this->tree->init(' AND '.$this->pObj->perms_clause);
```

With `setRecs=true`, the records of the pages are collected by the object, and are later available. `makeHTML=true` switches on the generation of the page tree as HTML code. `$this->thisScript` is passed, since `wrapTitle()` has to build a matching link.

```
$this->tree->setRecs = true;
$this->tree->makeHTML = true;
$this->tree->thisScript = $this->thisScript;
```

Then the set of database fields are that will later be made available are added.

```
$this->tree->addField('no_search');
$this->tree->addField('perms_userid',1);
$this->tree->addField('perms_groupid',1);
$this->tree->addField('perms_user',1);
$this->tree->addField('perms_group',1);
$this->tree->addField('perms_everybody',1);

   // Creating top icon; the current page
$HTML = t3lib_iconWorks::getIconImage('pages', $this->
                                      pObj->pageinfo,
$BACK_PATH, 'align="top"');
$this->tree->tree[] =
array('row'=>$this->pObj->pageinfo, 'HTML'=>$HTML);

   // read the page data and create the tree
$this->tree->getTree($this->pObj->id,
$this->pObj->
   MOD_SETTINGS['user_setsearch_modfunc1_depth']);
}
```

Before the page tree is finally read in with getTree(), the root, that is the current page, must be set for the tree.

The showPageTree() method creates the table with a page tree and status display. Although the t3lib_pageTree class contains the method to display a complete page tree as HTML, this cannot be used here, because the search flag should be displayed in the table next to the page.

It is quite normal to construct HTML code in modules manually, so to speak. But there are a number of functions in t3lib_BEfunc or in the template object (->doc) that can help you. t3lib_BEfunc::getFuncMenu() and ->doc->section() have already been shown as examples. In this method the page tree table is created with ->doc->table(). As already mentioned, you could also put the table together directly in the code.

First the layout of the table is defined with the $tableLayout array. The <table> tag is defined, with defRow as the standard tag for rows and columns 0 and 1. A different background color is also set for row 0 in the <tr> tag.

```
/**
* Creates the page tree table
*
* @return string rendered HTML table
*/
function showPageTree() {
global $BE_USER,$LANG,$BACK_PATH;

// init table layout
$tableLayout = array (
'table' => array ('<table border="0" cellspacing="0"
cellpadding="0" id="typo3-tree"
                  style="width:auto;">',  '</table>'),
'defRow' => array (
'tr' => array('<tr class="bgColor-20">','</tr>'),
'0' => array('<td nowrap="nowrap">','</td>'),
'1' => array('<td align="center"
  style="border-left: solid 1px '.$this->pObj->
                        doc->bgColor.'">','</td>'),
),
'0' => array (
'tr' => array('<tr class="bgColor2">','</tr>'),
)
);
```

The two-dimensional `$table` array takes up the contents of the table in rows and columns. The `tt_content_search` icon is inserted into the first row. The icon is normally used for the **Search** content type and is intended as an explanation for the column with the search flags.

```
$table=array();
$tr=0;

// add header row
$table[$tr][0] =' ';

$table[$tr++][1]=' '.t3lib_iconWorks::getIconImage
(
'tt_content_search',
array(),
$BACK_PATH).' ';

// walk through the tree list
// proceed through the page tree
foreach($this->tree->tree as $pageItem) {
```

Now each item of the already assembled page tree is processed in turn, with a `foreach` loop. The following lines set a different background color for the table line if the user has no editing permissions (2) for the page.

```
// if user has no access use a darker row background
if (!($this->admin ||
$BE_USER->doesUserHaveAccess($pageItem['row'],2))) {
```

```
$tableLayout[$tr]['tr'] =
array('<tr class="bgColor4">','</tr>');
}

// get one page tree item
$title = t3lib_div::fixed_lgd(
$this->tree->getTitleStr($pageItem['row']),
$BE_USER->uc['titleLen']);
$treeItem = $pageItem['HTML'].
$this->tree->wrapTitle($title,$pageItem['row']);
```

When the page title has been created and the existing icon added, the status of the search flag is determined: appropriate red and green characters are set for the display.

```
// get current no_search flag
if ($pageItem['row']['no_search']) {
$searchFlag = '<span style="color:red">&times;</span>';
} else {
$searchFlag =
    '<span style="color:green">&bull;</span>';
}
// add row to table
$table[$tr][0] = $treeItem.'  ';
$table[$tr++][1] = $searchFlag;
}
// return rendered table
return $this->pObj->doc->table($table, $tableLayout);
}
```

Then the table line is added, and when the loop is finished the table is created with ->doc->table() and returned.

By using the t3lib_pageTree class (cf. t3lib_browseTree) you can save yourself some work if you are handling page trees in your own modules. On the one hand the class supplies all the records, and on the other, if required, it supplies a tree for display.

The getEditablePagesIDList() method is still missing, which returns a comma list of page IDs for which the user has editing permission. These are built into the form in the main() method and passed on to tce_db.php.

```
/**
 * Returns a comma separated list of page id's
 * which are accessible to the user
 *
 * @return string pages uid list
 */
function getEditablePagesIDList() {
global $BE_USER, $LANG, $BACK_PATH;
```

```
$idListArr=array();

foreach ($this->tree->tree as $pageItem) {
  if ($this->admin ||
  $BE_USER->doesUserHaveAccess($pageItem['row'],2)) {
      $idListArr[] = $pageItem['row']['uid'];
      }
    }
return implode(',', $idListArr);
  }

}
```

7.8.3 Context Menu Entry

In this example a context menu should provide the same functionality as the previous submodule function, that is, mark pages as browsable or non-browsable. But this time the function is applied exclusively to the selected page.

An extension is quickly created with Kickstarter, which inserts a new element into the context menu. As always, the extension consists of the **General info** component, the additional language, and the components for the context menu, which is created with **Clickmenu items**.

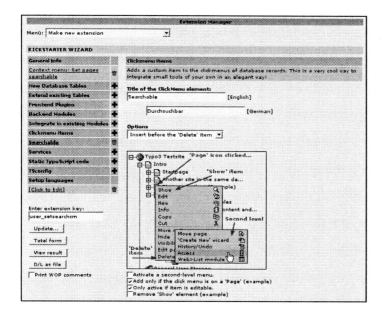

Figure 7.45:

Creating the context menu entry with Kickstarter

The Kickstarter creates the following files:

```
ext_emconf.php
ext_icon.gif
ext_tables.php
class.user_setsearchcm_cm1.php
locallang.php
cm1/
    clear.gif
    cm_icon.gif
    conf.php
    index.php
    locallang.php
```

If you install and test this extension, the new entry will appear in the context menu, as expected. But clicking on it will not yet produce the desired effect. An example module created by Kickstarter is called up, which is located in the cm1/ directory.

Figure 7.46:

New entry with example module called

The Extra Click Menu Options extension (extra_page_cm_options) contains roughly the design functionality of being able to show or hide a page. If you look at how this function is implemented, you will arrive at the DB_changeFlag() method, which can be found in typo3/alt_clickmenu.php.

```
/**
 * Adding CM element for a flag field of the input
record
 *
 * @param    string    Table name
 * @param    array     Record array
 * @param    string    Name of the flag field
 * @param    string    Menu item Title
 * @param    string    Name of the item used for icons
 *                     and labels
 * @param    string    Icon path relative to typo3/
 *                     folder
 * @return array Item array, element in $menuItems
 */
function DB_changeFlag($table, $rec, $flagField,
                       $title, $name,
```

```
            $iconRelPath='gfx/') {
            $uid=$rec['uid'];
            $editOnClick='';
    $loc='top.content'.($this->listFrame && !$this->
                                    alwaysContentFrame ?
                        '.list_frame':'');
    $editOnClick='if('.$loc.')
{'.$loc.".document.location=top.TS.
            PATH_typo3+'tce_db.p hp?redirect='+top.
            rawurlencode(".$this>frameLocation
            ($loc.'.document').".") +'".
            "&data[".$table.'] ['.$uid.']
            ['.$flagField.']='.($rec[$flagField]?
            0:1).'&prErr=1&vC='.$GLOBALS['BE_USER']->
            veriCode().";hideCM();}";
        return $this->linkItem(
            $title,$this>excludeIcon
            ('<img'.t3lib_iconWorks::
            skinImg($this ->PH_backPath,$iconRelPath.
            'button_'.($rec[$flagField]?'un':'').
            $name.'.gif','width="11" height="10").
            'alt="" />'), $editOnClick.'return false;',1);
    }
```

This method already provides the desired functionality of switching the value of a database field between 0 and 1. The method is relatively compact, and you do not have to understand it completely at this point. But it is interesting here that the same concept is again used, of calling the TCE, via the `tce_db.php` script, to perform the changes to the record of the page. This means that your own module, in cm1/, is not needed and can be deleted.

The icons representing the buttons in the context menu are added to the extension, so that now the following files exist in the extension:

```
button_no_search.gif
button_unno_search.gif
ext_emconf.php
ext_icon.gif
ext_tables.php
class.user_setsearchcm_cm1.php
locallang.php
```

The file `class.user_setsearchcm_cm1.php` contains the class that generates the new menu entry. Essentially the code was created by the Kickstarter, which is why we will only mention the special features here.

```
class user_setsearchcm_cm1 {

/**
* Adding options to the context menu.
*
```

```
*  @param      object     The click menu object
*  @param      array      Menu items array
*  @param      string     Name of the table of the
*                         clicked record item
*  @param      integer    uid of the record
*  @return     array      Menu items array, processed.
*/
function main(&$cmObj, $menuItems, $table, $uid) {
  global $LANG;

  if (!$cmObj->cmLevel) {
  if ($cmObj->editOK) {

    // Returns directly, because the clicked item was
    // not from the pages table

    if ($table != 'pages') return $menuItems;

    // load the language array
    $LL = $this->includeLL();

    // array for new menu items
    $localItems = array();

    // create new menu item if not disabled
    if (!in_array('user_setsearchcm_cm1',
        $cmObj->disabledItems)) {
```

A check is made here to see if the menu entry was deactivated, which is possible via TSConfig, for example.

```
$flagField = 'no_search';
$title = ($cmObj->rec[$flagField]) ?
  $LANG->getLLL('searchable',$LL) :
  $LANG->getLLL('non_searchable',$LL);

$localItems['user_setsearchcm_cm1'] =
  $cmObj->DB_changeFlag(
          'pages',
          $cmObj->rec,
          $flagField,
          $title,
          'no_search',

  t3lib_extMgm::extRelPath('user_setsearchcm'));
```

Via the DB_changeFlag() method of the context menu object, a menu entry is generated for the no_search field of the pages table which, depending on the status, shows one of the button_* icons and contains a link to the tce_db.php script, to set the field to 0 or 1.

```
      // add menu item
  $menuItems = $cmObj->addMenuItems(
```

```
                            $menuItems,
                            $localItems,
                'after:hide,before-spacer:delete');
```

The menu entry created is inserted with the `addMenuItems()` method into the relevant point in the existing menu, which is after the `hide` entry (if available) or before the `delete` entry (including the spacer/line).

```
            }
          }
        }
    return $menuItems;
    }
```

Finally the changed menu array is returned.

```
    /**
    * Includes the [extDir]/locallang.php and
    * returns the $LOCAL_LANG array found in that file.
    *
    * @return array $LOCAL_LANG array
    */
        function includeLL() {
          include(t3lib_extMgm::extPath
                ('user_setsearchcm').'locallang.php');
          return $LOCAL_LANG;
        }

        }
```

In addition to this, the class now only contains one method for reading in the language file.

Of course, multiple entries can be inserted with the method shown. Menus in the second layer are also possible. The Extra Click Menu Options extension (extra_page_cm_options) can serve as an example here.

7.8.4 Skins—Changing the Backend Appearance

Softlink **840654**

The appearance of the TYPO3 back end can be modified to a large extent. This is easy to do because there is a defined interface with which the back end can be provided both with new colors, logos and icons. But there are limits. The copyright sign and GPL license in the login may not be changed, as well as all scripts.

Apart from these restrictions, you can certainly use your own logo or that of your customer instead of the default graphics, as this example shows.

Figure 7.47:

Skin for the book

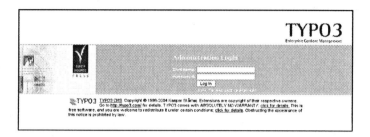

The adjustments are made, as always, via extensions. Here is a list of the files for this example skin. Files in which changes are made to the login are highlighted in bold.

```
ext_tables.php
stylesheet_post.css
backgrounds/
   csm_back.png
   login_back.jpg
   logoframe_back.png
   mainmenu_back.png
   menu_back.jpg
   topframe_back.png
icons/
   gfx/
      alt_backend_logo.png
      altmenuline.png
      typo3logo.png
      fileicons/
         ai.png
         au.png
         avi.png
         ...
      i/
         _icon_folders.png
         ...
         tt_content.png
```

```
...
loginimages/
   01.png
   02.png
```

As you can see, there is only one known extension file here:
`ext_tables.php`. The skin is made known to the system here. All the
other files are stylesheets, graphics, or icons.

ext_tables.php

First the extension path relative to the back-end directory (`typo3/`) is
determined and saved in a temporary variable. This saves several
function calls from `t3lib_extMgm::extRelPath()` in the example below.

```
// Setting the relative path to the extension in
// temp.
variable:$temp_eP = t3lib_extMgm::extRelPath($_EXTKEY);
```

All modifications are made known to TYPO3 via the `$TBE_STYLES` global
array. The path is specified for the login page from which the decorative
images on the left of the page are fetched. If several images are available,
they will change randomly.

```
// Setting login box image rotation folder:
$TBE_STYLES['loginBoxImage_rotationFolder'] =
                         $temp_eP.'loginimages/';
```

All graphics files from TYPO3 are located in the `t3lib/gfx/` directory. To
replace images and icons, you must inform TYPO3 of the directory where
the new images are located. If you set up the directory structure of `gfx/`
in the new image folder, files there will replace the original files of the
same name from `t3lib/gfx/`. This also applies for `gfx/typo3logo.gif`,
which is shown as the logo on the top right of the login page.

```
// Setting up auto detection of alternative icons:
$TBE_STYLES['skinImgAutoCfg']=array(
   'absDir' =>
        t3lib_extMgm::extPath($_EXTKEY).'icons/',
         'relDir' => $temp_eP.'icons/',
   // Force to look for PNG alternatives...
   'forceFileExtension' => 'png',
);
```

The other adjustments are made via a stylesheet.

```
// Additional stylesheet. Set AFTER any styles in
// the document
$TBE_STYLES['styleSheetFile_post'] =
$temp_eP.'stylesheet_post.css';
```

stylesheet_post.css

```
/* Login Screen */
 BODY#typo3-index-php { background-color: #fff; }
 BODY#typo3-index-php TABLE#loginwrapper
                      { background- color: #C2C9CD; }
 BODY#typo3-index-php DIV#copyrightnotice { font-size:
11px;}
   TABLE#logintable INPUT { border: #7B8295 solid 1px; }
```

As already mentioned, these possibilities are not restricted to the login. You can give the entire back end a new appearance as the following figure shows. An example of a full back-end skin is the `skin360` extension (see the soft link for this section).

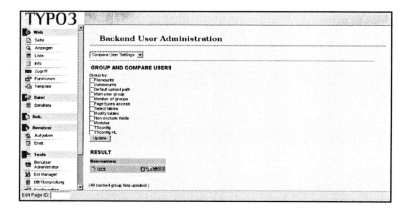

Figure 7.48:

TYPO3 book skin in the back end

7.9 Services

Softlink **052294**

Services provide a way of implementing functionalities in TYPO3 that can be extended or replaced.

The DAM uses services, for example, to read metadata from files. Each file format saves metadata differently (if this is even allowed). It is therefore necessary to write a special function or class for each file type to read this data, process it, and convert it to a uniform format. The DAM would then have to call the appropriate function, depending on the file type. This procedure is not very flexible, of course. New functions or file types would then only be available after an update of the DAM. In addition, third parties would have few possibilities of adding extensions. Services offer a layer of abstraction, which circumnavigates these disadvantages.

With services you are in a position to use PHP classes without knowing their names. Normally the instancing of a class within TYPO3 looks like this:

```
require_once(t3lib_extMgm::extPath('some_extension').

'class.tx_some_extension_class.php');
$obj = t3lib_div::makeInstance
                ('tx_some_extension_class');
```

To be able to create an object, you must know the PHP file in which the class is located, as well as the name of the class. This is not necessary when using services. An object is created as follows:

```
$serviceObj =
t3lib_div::makeInstanceService('my_service_type');
```

The difference is that a class is automatically searched for and an object created on the basis of the service type specified. Services must therefore have a type. The DAM uses services of the metaExtract type, for example, to read metadata.

Two reasons for services:

1. Freedom of implementation: A service can be implemented in different ways, many times, and is therefore replaceable. This is an advantage if functionality is only available on specific platforms, or through external tools. The service that is available and active is used automatically.

2. Expanding functionality through extensions: Services are familiar with subtypes. This means that it is possible to implement a metaExtract service for the mp3 subtype. Once the extension is installed, the DAM automatically reads metadata from MP3 files without changes having to be made in the DAM.

Each service is of a type defined by a string, and comparable to an extension key. metaExtract is such a type. Each service type has its own API, that is, a service that reads out metadata ought to have different methods than a service that writes log data.

7.9.1 Applying Services

To be able to use a service, you must of course know the service type and its API. A simple example looks like this:

```
if (is_object($serviceObj =
t3lib_div::makeInstanceService('textLang'))) {
    $language = $serviceObj->guessLanguage($text);
}
```

567

An object of the `textLang` service type is requested and at the same time is checked, with `is_object()`, to see if an object was returned. This check is necessary, because there are several reasons why a service may not be available:

- A service of the desired type is not installed.

- The service has deactivated itself during system registration, because it cannot run on your system, for example.

- The service was deactivated by the system as a result of checks.

- During the initialization of the service, the service itself may have checked again to see if it can run, and then deactivated itself.

Of course, it is possible that no `textLang` service is installed on the system. It depends on your application whether it is dependent on the service, or if it can function without it. If necessary, you can display an error message, pointing out to the user the need to install the corresponding service.

Subtypes

Service objects can be selected not only via types, but also via subtypes.

```
$absFile = '/tmp/testfile.pdf';
$fileType = 'pdf';

$meta = array();
if (is_object($serviceObj =
t3lib_div::makeInstanceService('metaExtract',

$fileType))) {
    $serviceObj->setInputFile($absFile, $fileType);
    if ($serviceObj->process('', '', $meta) > 0
            AND (is_array($svmeta = $serviceObj->
                    getOutput()))) {
                $meta = $svmeta;
    }
}
```

Here a service of the `metaExtract` type is requested, which can handle the `pdf` subtype. In this way you can set up a library of services that all have the same functionality and API (e.g. for reading out metadata), but which are implemented for different subtypes. Subtypes are not restricted to the file types shown in this example. They can, and must, be defined for each service type that contains them. There are services without subtypes, of course.

Services as a Chain

Until now, only one service type was created in each instance to edit data. But it can be useful to apply all the available services of a type to your data, or simply to try out all the services until you get a result.

```
$subType = 'getUserFE';
$serviceChain = array();
while (is_object($serviceObj =
t3lib_div::makeInstanceService('auth',
                                    $subType,
$serviceChain))) {

    // add service key ti list of tried services
    $serviceChain[] = $serviceObj->getServiceKey();

    // initialize service
    $serviceObj->initAuth($subType,
                        $loginData, $info, $this);

    // call the service to get a login user
    if ($tempuser = $serviceObj->getUser()) {
    // user found, just stop to search
    break;
    }
}
```

The code is an extract from an implementation to use services for user authentication.

In the third parameter of `makeInstanceService()`, a list (comma-delimited list or array) of service keys can be passed. The services in this list are then ignored. In this way you can call each service of a type in turn. In the above example the `while` loop is stopped when a user has been found.

Calling Specific Services

It can sometimes be useful to do without the abstraction, and not have to automatically select a service from `makeInstanceService()`, but call just one specific service. This is possible, because the service is registered not only with its service type, but also with a service key, similar to the extension key.

```
$serviceObj = t3lib_div::makeInstanceService
                                    ('textExtract')

$serviceObj =  t3lib_div::makeInstanceService
                            ('tx_cctxtextphp_sv1')
```

While a service type is specified with `textExtract` to have a search made for a corresponding service, in the second example a specific service is created via its `tx_cctxtextphp_sv1` service key.

7.9.2 Implementing Services

Implementing a service is done as an extension. As with all extensions, we start in the Extension Kickstarter. It is quite possible to add a plugin or module to an extension instead of a service. But this does not make much sense, because to use this service, the plugin contained would always have to be installed, which might not be such a good idea.

Select **Services** as the category for the extension. The service type should be prefixed to the title of the extension. In this way you can see straight away which service type is included. In addition the extensions are automatically sorted in the Extension Manager, and you retain a clear overview. A new service is added to the extension with the **Services** menu item.

Figure 7.49:

Form for defining the service in Kickstarter

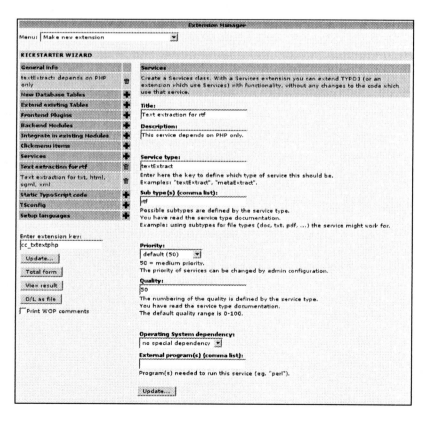

The following details must be entered in the form:

Title

>   A short descriptive title

Description

>   A short description of the function

Service type

>   Service type, defined by a short string; examples: `metaExtract`, `textLang`

Sub type

>   Comma-delimited list of possible subtypes; these are defined by the service type. Some types do not have any subtypes. The `metaExtract` service defines file formats (`jpg`, `sxw`, `pdf`, ...) as possible subtypes.

Priority

>   Here the priority is determined. Because services are selected automatically, a mechanism must exist to select one when several are available. This is done using this value. The normal value is 50 and ranges from 0-100. Values over 100 can be defined later by the administrator, to give priority to specific services. If you want to use services as a chain, this value controls the order in which this is done. In most cases it is not necessary to change the value.

Quality

>   Another value to specify which service is preferred; for the `texLang` service, which determines the language of text, **Quality** defines the number of languages that are recognized by `textLang`. If two `textLang` services are installed with **Priority**=50, the one is chosen that recognizes the most languages. This value is therefore dependent on the definition of the service type.

Operating system dependency

>   Defines whether this service can basically run only under Windows or UNIX systems

External programs

>   Names of external programs used by this service; these should normally be given without a path, as the system tries to find the necessary programs itself.

The following files are created by Kickstarter from the above example:

```
doc/
   wizard_form.dat
   wizard_form.html
sv1/
   class.tx_cctxtextphp_sv1.php
sv2/
   class.tx_cctxtextphp_sv2.php
ext_emconf.php
ext_icon.gif
ext_tables.php
```

As you can see, this extension contains two services in the directories sv1/ and sv2/. But it is sensible to only have extensions containing services of the same type.

The service is registered in the system with the function called t3lib_extMgm::addService().

```
t3lib_extMgm::addService($_EXTKEY,
                    'textExtract' /* sv  type */,
'tx_cctxtextphp_sv1' /* sv key */,
   array(

      'title' => 'Text extraction for rtf',
      'description' => 'This service depends on PHP
                         only.',

      'subtype' => 'rtf',

      'available' => true,
      'priority' => 50,
      'quality' => 50,

      'os' => '',
      'exec' => '',

      'classFile' => t3lib_extMgm::extPath($_EXTKEY).
'sv1/class.tx_cctxtextphp_sv1.php',
      'className' => 'tx_cctxtextphp_sv1',
   )
);
```

This corresponds fundamentally to the details from the Kickstarter form.

By default, a service is registered as available by setting available to true. You could also specify a Boolean expression here, of course. If a service is dependent on the PHP function exif_read_data() for example, available only from PHP version 4.2.0, this can be checked with the following line:

```
'available' => function_exists('exif_read_data'),
```

The service is then automatically deactivated if this function is not available.

Service classes generated by Kickstarter extend the `t3lib_svbase` base class and by default contain the `init()` and `process()` methods. The `init()` method is called by the system. In this method you can initialize the object and also test if the service really is available. If this is the case, `true` is returned. if no other tests are necessary, the method can be left out, as it is included in the base class.

An example of a `textExtract` service is shown below, which extracts text from Word and Excel documents. This service type helps merely to obtain pure text from different documents. All formatting is ignored.

Two services are registered in `ext_tables.php`.

```php
t3lib_extMgm::addService($_EXTKEY, 'textExtract' /* sv
type */,
 'tx_cctxtextexec_sv2a' /* sv key */,
   array(

      'title' => 'Text extraction for Word documents
                  (doc)',
      'description' => 'This service depends on
                        catdoc',

      'subtype' => 'doc,dot',

      'available' => TRUE,
      'priority' => 50,
      'quality' => 50,

      'os' => '',
      'exec' => 'catdoc',

      'classFile' => t3lib_extMgm::extPath($_EXTKEY).
                     'sv2/class.tx_cctxtextexec_sv2.php',
      'className' => 'tx_cctxtextexec_sv2',
   )
);

t3lib_extMgm::addService($_EXTKEY, 'textExtract' /* sv
type */,
 'tx_cctxtextexec_sv2b' /* sv key */,
   array(
      'title' => 'Text extraction for Excel documents
                  (xls)',
      'description' => 'This service depends on
                        xls2csv',
      'subtype' => 'xls,xlt,xlw',
```

```
                    'available' => TRUE,
                    'priority' => 50,
                    'quality' => 50,

                    'os' => '',
                    'exec' => 'xls2csv',

                    'classFile' => t3lib_extMgm::extPath($_EXTKEY).
            'sv2/class.tx_cctxtextexec_sv2.php',
                    'className' => 'tx_cctxtextexec_sv2',
                )
            );
```

If you take a look at the definition of the (tx_cctxtextexec_sv2x) service keys and the class specified, you will see that two services are registered with the same class. This is quite permissible. Since the implementation is almost the same for the two services, and since they are also for similar file types, they were implemented in one class. As subtypes, the file types doc and dot for Word documents and xls, xlt, and xlw for Excel documents were specified—as intended for this service type. The exec variable contains the file names (catdoc, xls2csv) for the external tools that are required by these services. In the init() method of the base class a check is made to see if this program is available.

As you can see, the tx_cctxtextexec_sv2 class only implements the process() method. The process() method is reserved by convention. A service containing this method works like a filter, and can handle data passed in the $content variable, as well as files. The calling application can retain data in the same way as a variable or as a file. The process() method is specified to be able to uniformly test such "filter" services. If you introduce a new service type, you can use your own API and do not have to implement the process() method.

```
        require_once(PATH_t3lib.'class.t3lib_svbase.php');

        class tx_cctxtextexec_sv2 extends t3lib_svbase {
          var $prefixId = 'tx_cctxtextexec_sv2';
          var $scriptRelPath =  'sv2/
                        class.tx_cctxtextexec_sv2.php';
          var $extKey = 'cc_txtextexec';

          /**
           * performs the text extraction
           *
           * @param string Content which should be processed to
           * extract text.
           * @param string Content type 'doc', 'dot', ...
           * @param array Configuration array
           * @return boolean
           */
```

```
    function process($content='', $type='',
$conf=array()) {

        $this->out = '';

        if ($content) {

            $this->setInput ($content, $type);
        }

        if($inputFile = $this->getInputFile()) {
            switch ($this->inputType) {

                case 'doc':
                case 'dot':
                    $cmd = t3lib_exec::getCommand('catdoc').'
                            d8859-1".$inputFile.'";
                    $this->out = shell_exec($cmd);
                    break;
                    case 'xls':
                    case 'xlt':
                    case 'xlw':
                        $cmd =  t3lib_exec::getCommand
                                    ('xls2csv').' -d8859-1
                                ".$inputFile.'";
                        $this->out = shell_exec($cmd);
                    break;

                    // if that is reached the caller made
                    // a mistake
                default:
                    $this->errorPush(T3_ERR_SV_WRONG_SUBTYPE,
                        'Subtype ".$this->inputType.'" is not
                                        supported.');
                    break;
            }
        } else {
            $this->errorPush(T3_ERR_SV_NO_INPUT,
                                'No or empty input.');
        }

        if ($this->out AND intval($conf['limitOutput'])) {
            $this->out = substr($this->out, 0,
intval($conf['limitOutput']));
        }

        return $this->getLastError();
    }
}
```

A number of functions are available in the base class that simplify setting up a filter. Temporary files are created automatically, for example, or files read into a variable, depending on what the service or calling application requires.

In this example, data passed on is registered, where required:

```
if ($content) {
    $this->setInput ($content, $type);
}
```

But because the external programs `catdoc` and `xls2csv` require a file for processing, a file is requested with the data in the next line. This would be created automatically if it doesn't exist, because the data was registered with `setInput()`. If the calling application has previously registered a file with `setInputFile()`, then this is used directly. The calling application can request a variable with `getOutput()` or a file with `getOutputFile()` in the same way. The call for the `textExtract` service looks like this:

```
if (is_object($serviceObj =
t3lib_div::makeInstanceService('textExtract',

$file_type))) {

    $serviceObj->setInputFile($absFile, $file_type);
    $serviceObj->process('', '', $conf);
    $output = $serviceObj->getOutput();

    $serviceObj->unlinkTempFiles();
}
```

Calling the `unlinkTempFiles()` method is important in order that temporary files stored within the service can be deleted. Alternatively you can, with

```
... = &t3lib_div::makeInstanceService( ...
```

request a reference to the object, which will independently remove the temporary files.

7.9.3 Configuration

Configuration data for services is stored in the array `$TYPO3_CONF_VARS['SVCONF'][serviceType]`.

```
$TYPO3_CONF_VARS['SVCONF'][serviceType]['setup']
```

This array may contain configuration data for the calling scripts, and is not taken into account by the services themselves.

```
$TYPO3_CONF_VARS['SVCONF'][serviceType]['default']
```

Default values for the service type are set in this array. These are used as long as no special values are defined via the service key.

```
$TYPO3_CONF_VARS['SVCONF'][serviceType][serviceKey]
```

The `t3lib_svbase` services base class provides the method `getServiceConfig()` to read out configuration values from the above arrays, whereby the configuration with the service key has priority over the `default` configuration.

7.9.4 Introducing a New Service Type

The different service types are not fixed. Anyone can introduce a new service type. If you want to do this, the API for the new type should be discussed with other developers, because a service used only once does not make much sense. You should introduce the new service in the TYPO3 developers mailing list, and possibly include an example implementation for download. A documentation on the API and subtypes should later be made generally available.

7.10 Modifying and Extending XCLASS Class

As has been seen, TYPO3 can be expanded in a simple way through extensions. Functionality is encapsulated in plugins or modules, and these are easily installed. But for more sophisticated applications it may still be necessary to make changes to TYPO3 itself. This is no problem, of course, since the source code of TYPO3 is available. But it does make an update to renew a version of TYPO3 more difficult. The changes made must be documented so that they can later be added to the new version.

Softlink **745255**

TYPO3 provides an elegant solution to this problem in the form of XCLASSes. The concept of XCLASSes enables almost every TYPO3 class to be extended or modified.

Let's assume that you need a function in the `stdWrap` TypoScript object to convert an integer into written words. This function will then be available systemwide, and you will be able to use it wherever there is a TypoScript object of the `stdWrap` type.

A suitable script for converting numbers is quickly found on the Internet; it is now just a question of how best to build it into an `stdWrap` function. There are various possibilities here:

- Build the functionality directly into the `stdWrap()` function in class.tslib_content.php. Here we have the disadvantage, just mentioned, that TYPO3 updates are made more difficult.

- stdWrap provides a way of integrating user functions. This is basically a good and useful variation. But in our example we would like to address the new function directly with the userNumToWord identifier.

- Extending the stdWrap method in the tslib_content class as an XCLASS. This is the method best suited to our purposes.

If we look at the file end of class.tslib_content.php, we will see the following lines:

```
if (defined('TYPO3_MODE') &&
        $TYPO3_CONF_VARS[TYPO3_MODE]['XCLASS'][
'tslib/class.tslib_content.php']) {
    include_once($TYPO3_CONF_VARS[TYPO3_MODE]['XCLASS'][
    'tslib/class.tslib_content.php']);
}
```

So if the variable

```
$TYPO3_CONF_VARS[TYPO3_MODE]['XCLASS']['tslib/class.tsl
        ib_content.php']
```

contains a file name, this file will be inserted with include_once(). This means that we can have a file inserted that can then extend the tslib_content class. Nearly every file in TYPO3 containing a class, even those of extensions, has these XCLASS lines at the end of the file.

Now you only have to set the above variable accordingly, and your own script will be integrated. This is done in the ext_localconf.php file of your own extension. You must remember that TYPO3_MODE is a constant, defined either as 'FE' or 'BE', depending on whether we are in the front end or back end. In our front-end example, we must therefore enter 'FE' instead of TYPO3_MODE.

The example extension with the user_NumToWord extension key now looks like this:

```
doc/
    ext_emconf.php
    ext_icon.gif
    ext_localconf.php
    class.ux_tslib_content.php
```

ext_localconf.php

```
if (!defined ('TYPO3_MODE')) die ('Access denied.');
 $TYPO3_CONF_VARS['FE']['XCLASS']
               ['tslib/class.tslib_content.php']

=t3lib_extMgm::extPath('user_NumToWord').'class.ux_tsli
b_content.php';
```

class.ux_tslib_content.php

```
class ux_tslib_cObj extends tslib_cObj {

    function stdWrap($content,$conf) {
        // Call the real stdWrap function in the
        // parent class:

    $content = parent::stdWrap($content,$conf);

        // Process according to my user-defined
        // property:
    if ($conf['userNumToWord']) {
        $content = $this->ux_numToWord($content,
$conf['userNumToWord .']);
    }
    return $content;
    }

    function ux_numToWord($content,$conf) {
        ...
      return $content;
    }
}

if (defined('TYPO3_MODE') &&  $TYPO3_CONF_VARS
                     [TYPO3_MODE]['XCLASS']
['ext/user_NumToWord/class.ux_tslib_content.php'])
{include_once($TYPO3_CONF_VARS[TYPO3_MODE]['XCLASS']
['ext/user_NumToWord/class.ux_tslib_content.php']);
}
```

The XCLASS extension is finished. But if you have been paying attention, you might be wondering how the system knows that the ux_tslib_cObj instead of tslib_cObj class is now to be instantiated. This is done by t3lib_div::makeInstance(), which is used instead of new() inside TYPO3. The t3lib_div::makeInstance() function tests whether a class with the passed on name and with the ux_ prefix exists, and then creates an object from this class.

The last lines of the class.ux_tslib_content.php file again contain the familiar XCLASS code. So it is also possible to extend the `ux_tslib_cObj` class.

The XCLASS method also has disadvantages: on the one hand, only one XCLASS is possible per file, on the other, you are not really safe from problems with a TYPO3 upgrade, since the API of the extended class may have changed. But it is still a useful way of making changes to the core.

7.11 TYPO3 and Other Programming Languages

Other programming languages than PHP can currently only be used to a limited extent with TYPO3. While for compiler languages it is possible, and even quite normal, to mix various programming languages within a project, this is still at a very early stage for script languages. Experimental PHP extensions currently exist to call Java and .NET from PHP. It is also possible to access PHP objects from Java, and vice-versa. This means that extensions in Java are certainly possible. But they would have to include all the PHP files needed for an extension. This means that a PHP wrapper would be necessary, from which the Java code is called.

In the meantime it is possible, of course, to call external programs with `exec()` (see `t3lib_exec`) or to address external resources as web services. But this is nothing like a complete integration.

Overall, integration is becoming ever more important in the IT world, not least because it has only been made possible at all through the interoperable standards of recent years. PHP is also moving in this direction. So it is fairly certain that the possibilities of integration will improve even more in future.

7.12 Tools for the Developer

7.12.1 ExtDevEval

The back-end module **Tools | ExtDevEval** provides a number of helpful functions for the extension developer.

It is noticeable that through the `ExtDevEval` extension in the back end, a series of links appears at the top. These open a window containing the API documentation or point to documentation on TYPO3.org.

In addition to this, the module contains the following functions:

getLL() converter

> Converts embedded texts into source code for use in `locallang` files

PHP script documentation help

> Inserts missing JavaDoc comments into functions

Create/Update Extensions PHP API data

> Reads in JavaDoc comments and creates a `ext_php_api.dat` file from these, which helps to create the API documentation

Display API from "ext.php.api.dat" file

> Displays the API documentation from a `ext_php_api.dat` file

temp_CACHED files confirmed removal

> Deletes the `temp_CACHED_*` files from `typo3conf/`

PHP source code tuning

> Reformatting of PHP source code and adjustment to the coding guidelines

Code highlighting

> Displays PHP, TypoScript and XML in color; helpful when used within documentation

CSS analyzer

> Represents the CSS selectors for the elements of the specified HTML codes

Table Icon Listing

> Shows variations of record icons (hidden, restricted access, …)

7.12.2 Debugging with debug()

TYPO3 provides a little support for PHP debugging in the form of the global `debug()` function. This function outputs variables directly in a readable form, which also includes nested arrays.

Softlink **705356**

The `debug()` function forwards the variables to be displayed, if available, to the `$GLOBALS['error']->debug()` method. This object is not created by TYPO3 itself, and can therefore be made available by an extension. One such example of this is the `CCDebug` extension (`cc_debug`), which collects the debug output and displays it in its own window, which can be activated via a stylish bomb icon.

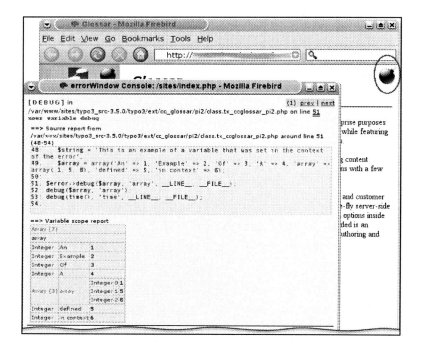

Figure 7.50:

Debug output in a separate window with CCDebug

The debug() function is defined as follows:

```
function debug($variable, $name =
                '*variable*', $line = '*line*',
$file = '*file*', $level = E_DEBUG)
```

The built-in debug function only returns the variable itself, as well as the description in $name. All other parameters are ignored. These are taken into account by CCDebug, though, and output the line number and filename, as long as the PHP constants __LINE__ and __FILE__ were also passed on.

```
debug(time(), 'current time', __LINE__, __FILE__);
```

If you want to use the built-in debug function, by the way, although a debug extension is installed, this can always be called with xdebug().

Debug Extension

It is quite simple to build your own debug extension. In ext_localconf.php you must create an object in $GLOBALS['error'] that contains the debug() function with the above parameters. If this extension is intended to collect output and only display it with the page, in a similar way to CCDebug, then it must also include the debugOutput() method.

7.12.3 Debugging with t3lib_div::devLog()

Apart from the possibility of creating appropriate output for error searches with the debug() function, TYPO3 offers a second interface via the t3lib_div::devLog() function. In contrast to debug(), TYPO3 does not implement a standard function for t3lib_div::devLog(), which means that the function has only one uniform interface available, in which case calling t3lib_div::devLog() without an additional extension has not the slightest effect.

Softlink **544345**

One implementation for the interface is the CCDevLog (cc_devlog) extension. This places the log entries in a database table. A back-end module helps to display data, and the module can also be opened in a separate window, making it available parallel to the back end.

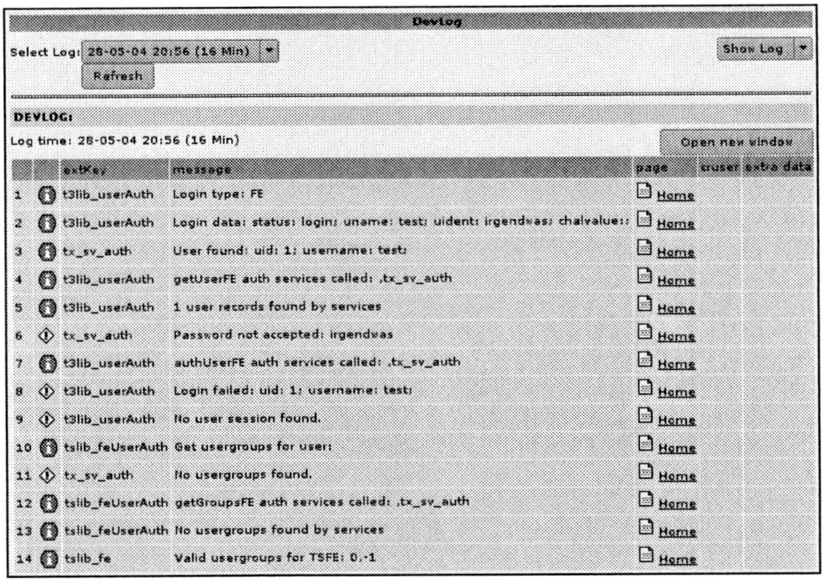

Figure 7.51:

The CCDevLog module for evaluating log entries

The devLog() in t3lib_div function is defined as follows:

```
 *  @param      string         Message (in english).
 *  @param      string         Extension key (from which
 *                             extension you are
 *                             calling the log)
 *  @param      integer        Severity: 0 is info, 1 is
 *                             notice, 2 is warning,
 *                             3 is fatal error, -1 is "OK"

 *  @param      array          Additional data you want to
 *                             pass to the logger.
 *  @return     void
 */
function devLog($msg, $extKey,
                    $severity=0, $dataVar=FALSE)
```

Here is an extract from t3lib_userAuth, intended to illustrate the use of t3lib_div::devLog().

```
if ($TYPO3_CONF_VARS['SC_OPTIONS']['t3lib/
                            class.t3lib_userauth.php']
['writeDevLog']) $this->writeDevLog = TRUE;
if (TYPO3_DLOG) $this->writeDevLog = TRUE;

...

if ($this->writeDevLog) t3lib_div::devLog('No user
                            session found.',
    't3lib_userAuth', 2);
```

First a check is made to see if writeDevLog is set in $TYPO3_CONF_VARS for the current script. If this is the case, $this->writeDevLog is set to TRUE. The constant TYPO3_DLOG is handled in exactly the same way. It is thus possible to activate logging just for this script or for the object, or to activate it systemwide with the constant TYPO3_DLOG. The actual devLog() call is always preceded by a test on the $this->writeDevLog variable.

DevLog Extension

A devLog extension must basically register a function, which is then called by t3lib_div::devLog() with the log data. This is shown below using extracts from the CCDevLog extension.

localconf.php

First the devLog() function of the tx_ccdevlog class is registered in the localconf.php file of the CCDevLog extension, which is located in class.tx_ccdevlog.php.

```
$TYPO3_CONF_VARS['SC_OPTIONS']
['t3lib/class.t3lib_div.php']['devLog']
 [$_EXTKEY] =
    'EXT:'.$_EXTKEY.'/class.tx_ccdevlog.php:tx_ccdevlog
              ->devLog';
```

As you can see, your own devLog function is entered in the `'devLog'` array with your own extension key: `...['devLog'][$_EXTKEY]`. This means that several devLog extensions can be installed at the same time. They are then called, one after another, with the log data.

class.tx_ccdevlog.php

The above registered `devLog()` function is located in this file. In your own extension, this file must be named to match the extension key, of course. In the case of the CCDevLog extension, the passed on log data is processed and written to a database table.

```
    class tx_ccdevlog {

  /**
   * DevLog function - writes log to db
   *
   * @param array log data array
   * @return void
   */

  function devLog($logArr) {
    $insertFields = array();
    $insertFields['msg'] = $logArr['msg'];
    $insertFields['extkey'] = $logArr['extKey'];
    $insertFields['severity'] = $logArr['severity'];
    if (!empty($logArr['dataVar']))
      {
        $insertFields['data_var'] =
        $GLOBALS['TYPO3_DB']->
          quoteStr(serialize($logArr['dataVar'],
        'tx_ccdevlog');
      }
    $GLOBALS['TYPO3_DB']->
      exec_INSERTquery('tx_ccdevlog', $insertFields);
  }
}
```

A further option of debugging is completely independent of TYPO3, and takes place inside development environments such as the Zend IDE or PHPeclipse. To describe this would go beyond the remit of this book. Instead, we will briefly introduce a few IDEs.

7.12.4 FE Debug/Info output and BE Env Info

It is sometimes helpful to display data of typical objects such as $TSFE and $BE_USER or the environment variables of the t3lib_div::getIndpEnv() function.

These can be made visible, for example, with the FE Debug/Info output (cc_feinfo) and Backend Environment Information (cc_beinfo) extensions, without the need to create output via the debug() function.

The first extension is a plugin, which you can embed in a page, the second is a module. The module cannot display the data that is currently valid in your own module. But you can use the module as a template and easily build the output into your own module for test purposes, since this output is encapsulated in a separate class.

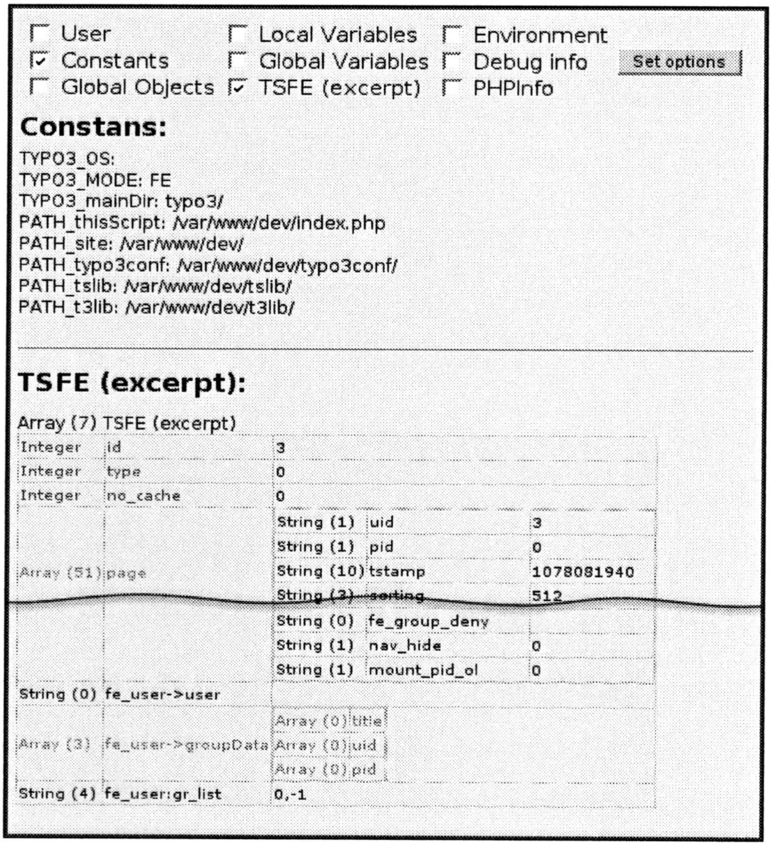

Figure 7.52:

Example output of the FE Debug/ Info output plugin

586

If you want to build the output into your own plugin for test purposes, this can be done very easily with the following code lines:

```
require_once(t3lib_extMgm::extPath('cc_feinfo').
'class.tx_ccfeinfo.php');

$info = t3lib_div::makeInstance('tx_ccfeinfo');
$info->init($this);
$content.= $info->pi_getInfoOutput();
```

7.12.5 PHP Development Environments

If you program a lot, and in complex projects, a simple text editor is not usually the most suitable tool. But even an occasional programmer can profit from an IDE (*Integrated Development Environment*). IDEs usually provide syntax checking in the editor, include a project management system, and integrate CVS, FTP, and WebDAV. A good IDE also provides support for debugging.

Finding the most suitable IDE is a matter of taste, which is why we can only recommend here that you try out a few of them. Test versions from manufacturers are generally available, or even freely available anyway, as Open Source software.

Here is a shortlist of PHP development environments:

Zend Development Environment

> IDE directly from the PHP developer, Zend.
>
> Platforms: Unix/Linux, Mac OS X, Windows
>
> `http://www.zend.com`

PHPeclipse

> Open Source project which implements a PHP plugin based on Eclipse (`http://www.eclipse.org`); one advantage is the large number of plugins for the Eclipse IDE: CVS, SQL, XML, HTML, JavaScript, Regex, Team support, ...
>
> Platforms: Unix/Linux, Mac OS X, Windows
>
> `http:// www.phpeclipse.de`

Index

Thank you for buying TYPO3: Enterprise Content Management

Packt Open Source Project Royalties

When we sell a book written on an Open Source project, we pay a royalty directly to that project. Therefore by purchasing *TYPO3: Enterprise Content Management*, Packt will have given some of the money received to the TYPO3 Association.

In the long term, we see ourselves and you—customers and readers of our books—as part of the Open Source ecosystem, providing sustainable revenue for the projects we publish on. Our aim at Packt is to establish publishing royalties as an essential part of the service and support a business model that sustains Open Source.

If you're working with an Open Source project that you would like us to publish on, and subsequently pay royalties to, please get in touch with us.

Writing for Packt

We welcome all inquiries from people who are interested in authoring. Book proposals should be sent to authors@packtpub.com. If your book idea is still at an early stage and you would like to discuss it first before writing a formal book proposal, contact us; one of our development editors will get in touch with you.

We're not just looking for published authors; if you have strong technical skills but no writing experience, our experienced editors can help you develop a writing career, or simply get some additional reward for your expertise.

About Packt Publishing

Packt, pronounced "packed", published its first book "*Mastering phpMyAdmin for Effective MySQL Management*" in April 2004 and subsequently continued to specialize in publishing highly focused books on specific technologies and solutions.

Our books and publications share the experiences of your fellow IT professionals in adapting and customizing today's systems, applications, and frameworks. Our solution-based books give you the knowledge and power to customize the software and technologies you're using to get the job done. Packt books are more specific and less general than the IT books you have seen in the past. Our unique business model allows us to bring you more focused information, giving you more of what you need to know, and less of what you don't.

Packt is a modern, yet unique publishing company, which focuses on producing quality, cutting-edge books for communities of developers, administrators, and newbies alike. For more information, please visit our website: www.PacktPub.com.

Printed in the United Kingdom
by Lightning Source UK Ltd.
113099UKS00001B/1-6